Persia: *through writers' eyes*

Persia

through writers' eyes

DAVID BLOW

ELAND

London

First published by Eland Publishing Ltd
61 Exmouth Market, London EC1R 4QL in 2007

Editorial content © David Blow
All extracts © of the authors, as attributed in the
text and acknowledgements

ISBN 978 0955010 55 2

Cover design by Nick Randall
Editor: Georgina Matthews
Cover image: *Pass between Imamzadeh Davud and
Shahristanak 1926/9* by Lawrence Lockhart © The Faculty of
Oriental Studies,University of Cambridge
Maps © Reginald Piggott
Printed in Spain by GraphyCems, Navarra

Contents

Acknowledgements

My thanks to my publishers Rose Baring and Barnaby Rogerson
for their encouragement and enthusiasm, to Georgina Matthews for
her painstaking editing, to the staff of the London Library, the
British Library, and the Library of the School of Oriental and African
Studies, and last but not least to my wife Laurence, who has been a
demanding and valuable reader.

The author and publishers gratefully acknowledge permission to
reprint copyright material as follows:

Walter de Gruyter GmbH & Co. for the extracts from *Agathias: The
Histories* by Joseph D. Frendo (Trans); Macmillan for the extracts from
Mirrors of the Unseen by Jason Elliot, and *Strange Places, Questionable
People* by John Simpson; Bantam and Random House for the extract
from *Daughter of Persia* by Sattereh Farman Farmaian; John Murray
for the extract from *The Valley of the Assassins & Other Persian Travels*
by Freya Stark; Random House for the extract from *The Pride and the
Fall* by Anthony Parsons; W. W. Norton & Co. for the extract from
Persian Pilgrimages: Journeys Across Iran by Afshin Molavi; Simon &
Schuster for the extract from *Persian Mirrors: The Elusive Face of Iran*
by Elaine Sciolino; Carcanet for the extract from *The Complete Poems
in One Volume* by Robert Graves; Peters Fraser & Dunlop for the
extract from *The Road to Oxiana* by Robert Byron; Penguin and
Harcourt for the extract from *Shah of Shahs* by Ryszard Kapuscinski;
HarperCollins for the extract from *In the Rose Garden* of the Martyrs
by Christopher de Bellaigue; HarperCollins and I.B Tauris for the
extract from *Reading Lolita in Tehran* by Azar Nafisi; The University of
California Press for the extract from *Holy Women of the Syrian Orient*
by Sebastian Brock and Susan Ashbrook; Anthony Smith for the
extract from his book *Blind White Fish in Persia*; Shusha Guppy for the
extract from her book *The Blindfold Horse;* and Juliet Nicolson for
permission to publish two letter from *Letters of Harold Nicolson* by
Harold Nicolson, and for the extract from Vita Sackville-West's
Passage to Tehran.

EDITORIAL NOTE
No attempt has been made to regularise the spellings in the extracts, which vary from author to author and century to century. Translations and explanations have been given where necessary.

Dedication
To Peter Avery, who first introduced me to Persia.

Introduction

WHEN I WAS FIRST IN Persia many years ago I often took the bus between Tehran and Isfahan, where I was living. The buses were notoriously accident-prone, so as we set off the passengers would invoke divine protection by crying out three times, '*Bismillah ar-Rahman ar-Rahim*' ('In the name of God, the Merciful, the Compassionate'). I remember on one occasion as we left the modern capital behind, a smartly dressed Tehrani looked out of the window and exclaimed with feigned astonishment '*Voy, Voy, een biyaban-e khushk!*' ('Oh dear, Oh dear, this dry desert!'). But for me it was not an alien, arid wasteland that we were passing through. It was filled with the footsoldiers and horsemen of countless Persian and foreign armies that had crossed this land – the armies of Darius and Xerxes, of Shah Abbas and Nader Shah, and of foreign conquerors like Alexander the Great and Tamerlane. More peaceful visions also came to mind, like the entire, richly apparelled Persian court on the move as the king set off for the summer hunting grounds, and the merchant caravans moving slowly along the road with their long lines of camels and mules, perhaps bearing bales of raw Persian silk to be shipped to Europe.

As a student who had just graduated in history, I started learning Persian in order to get away from an excessively Eurocentric view of the world. I was also attracted to Persia for its long and colourful history and its high culture. When I later went out to Persia I was further captivated by its people, by their friendliness, humour and quick intelligence. I divided my time between left-wing intellectuals, who taxed me with questions about Jean-Paul Sartre, and the decadent remnants of the old Qajar aristocracy with whom

1

I could relax over an occasional pipe of opium while listening to the plaintive notes of the Persian flute. I was also soon made aware of the almost universal conviction that all Britons in Persia were spies – a belief rooted in attempts by Britain during the nineteenth and much of the twentieth centuries to pull the strings in Persia in order to protect its interests, first in the defence of India and later of Persian oil.

I hope that this book will make Persia's past as vivid for its readers as it has become for me. There is no better way of doing this than by reading the first-hand accounts of people who spent time there. Most were Europeans who did not go out to Persia in the first instance to write about it. They went there to do a job, often as diplomats or merchants. The professional travel writer only emerged on the scene during the nineteenth century. But, whatever the reason for their presence, the picture they paint of Persia is a colourful and lively one, informative and often entertaining, perceptive and discerning, sympathetic but not uncritical.

The European accounts of Persia provide a great deal of information about the country which would not otherwise be available, as Persian sources are often seriously deficient. This is most true of the ancient period, but it also applies to later periods, particularly the seventeenth and nineteenth centuries, when European accounts are very numerous. They cover almost every aspect of Persian life, whereas the Persian sources, many of them court chronicles, are much more restricted in their scope. In addition, much of the official documentary evidence has been lost or destroyed in the course of Persia's turbulent history. When the Afghans captured the Safavid capital of Isfahan in 1722, they are said to have thrown the entire state archive into the river.

One difficult question for which it is impossible to lay down a simple rule is when to speak of Persia and when of Iran. Until as late as the 1930s Europeans invariably spoke of Persia and things Persian, which were terms they inherited from the ancient Greeks. The Greeks used them because the empire of Cyrus, Darius, and Xerxes was founded by a federation of tribes called the Persians whose homeland in the present-day south-western province of Fars was called Parsa (in Greek Persis). These Persians belonged to the wider family of Iranian peoples, but it is clear from the inscriptions of Darius that they attached more importance to their Persian identity. The emphasis on an Iranian identity and the use of the term Iran to denote the country we know today, though within more extensive borders, was first introduced by the Sasanids, the rulers of the last empire before the Arab conquest in the mid-seventh century AD. Iran as a political term then fell out of use until revived by the Mongol rulers of the country in the thirteenth century, after which it became firmly established. The language, however, has always been called Farsi or Persian.

However, in Europe that first empire, and the Greek authors who wrote about it, made such a strong impression that the country continued to be known as Persia. This was reinforced by an educational system that gave pride of place to the study of Greek and Latin as well as by familiarity with the Old Testament of the Bible and its many references to the Persians.

As a result of this long usage, the term Persia has a richer resonance for Europeans, though this may change in time. For the present, it remains the preferred term for products of the country's culture with a long historical tradition, so that we speak of Persian cuisine, Persian gardens and Persian carpets, but of the Iranian cinema. It also remains the more common term when speaking about the country up until the 1930s. I too have used it for this period, not least because the European writers represented in this anthology do so. In the end, there is no reason to get too exercised about the alternative usages, which an Iranian historian writing in English has likened to the difference between America and the United States. It is a matter of what feels right in a given context.

The hardest thing about putting this book together has been having to leave out, for lack of space, so much that I would like to have included. I have tried to provide as varied a subject matter as possible, as well as choosing pieces for their intrinsic quality. And like the greatest of all the seventeenth century writers on Persia, Sir John Chardin, I have borne in mind 'what would merit the curiosity of us Europeans'.

David Blow

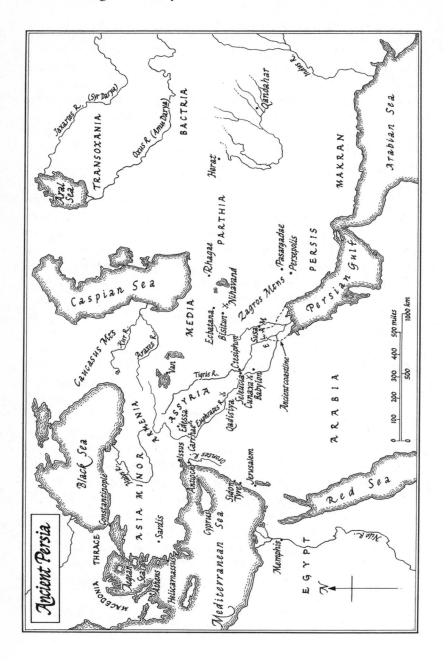

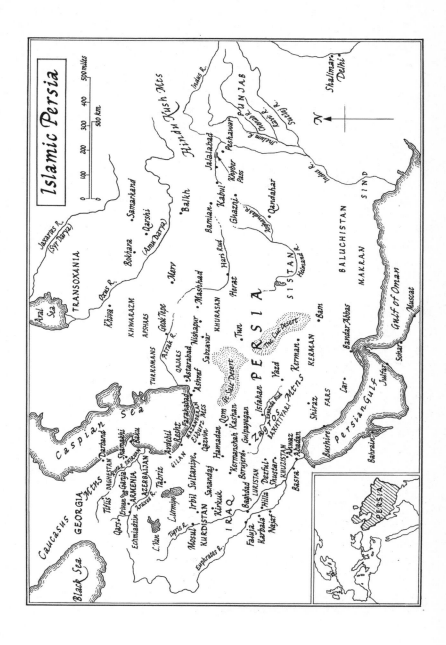

Islamic Persia

1
Ancient Persia

*D*URING THIS PERIOD *Persia was one of the great powers of the ancient world – the most formidable rival of Greece, Rome and the early Byzantine Empire. It begins with the establishment of the first Persian Empire in the sixth century BC and ends some twelve hundred years later with the conquest of Persia by the Arabs, bringing their new religion of Islam. For most of this time the dominant religion of Persia was Zoroastrianism, which means that Persia has been a Zoroastrian country for almost as long as it has been a Muslim one. Zoroastrianism has only small pockets of adherents today, mainly in India, but it has been the source of some of the key doctrines of Judaism, Christianity and Islam, such as the resurrection of the body and the Last Judgement. Ancient Persia saw the rise and fall of three great indigenous empires – those of the Achaemenids, the Parthians and the Sasanids – and of one Hellenistic Empire, that of the Seleucids, following the conquest of Persia by Alexander the Great. Of these, the Achaemenid Empire is the best known through its great kings – Cyrus, Darius and Xerxes – and the impressive ruins of the Achaemenid palace of Persepolis. But the Parthian and Sasanid empires were scarcely less magnificent and lasted considerably longer. All contributed to the development of a rich culture that proved strong enough to survive the destruction by the conquering Arabs of the political and religious institutions of Ancient Persia.*

The Persians first enter history as a confederation of Iranian tribes. Around the beginning of the first millennium BC, they migrated from the steppes of southern Russia into the country we know

7

today as Iran. Another Iranian tribal group which followed the same migration route at this time was that of the Medes. Both were part of a much larger migration of Iranian tribes, which eventually killed off, displaced or absorbed the pre-existing population of Iran.

While other Iranian tribes entered Iran from the north-east, the Medes and the Persians crossed the Caucasus, and moved down through the valleys of the Zagros Mountains in western Iran. The Medes settled in the northern Zagros, where their kings built themselves a new capital, Ecbatana, on the site of the modern city of Hamadan. The Persians finally settled further to the south-west in the territory that still bears their name – the province of Fars, the capital of which today is Shiraz. They called their new home Parsa, after themselves, which became Persis to the Greeks. As they moved south, the Medes and the Persians came into contact with ancient powers and civilizations. There was Urartu in the north around Lake Van (in present-day Turkey), Assyria and Babylonia (in present-day Iraq), and Elam in the far south-west corner of Iran, in today's oil-producing province of Khuzistan. But in the seventh and sixth centuries BC these old powers were destroyed one after another and finally supplanted by the newcomers. The Medes were the first to establish an Iranian empire when they overthrew the Assyrians in 612BC. But their empire was short-lived. In 553BC the Medes were overthrown by their southern neighbours and vassals, the Persians, under their king, Cyrus II, known as Cyrus the Great. Already in his late forties, Cyrus went on to establish a vast Persian empire stretching from the shores of the Mediterranean to the Jaxartes River in Central Asia. He fell in battle in 530BC, at the age of seventy, defending the Jaxartes frontier from marauding Iranian nomads. At his death, his empire embraced the whole of Iran, Asia Minor (modern Turkey), Mesopotamia (modern Iraq), the Levant, Afghanistan and Transoxania – the land between the Oxus and Jaxartes Rivers. It was further enlarged by his son and successor, Cambyses, who conquered Egypt, and reached its zenith under Cambyses's successor, Darius I (522–486BC), who added north-west India as far as the Indus River, Thrace (modern Bulgaria) and Macedonia in the Balkans.

This first Persian Empire is known as the Achaemenid Empire after the clan or family to which its kings belonged. The eastern half of the Empire was largely made up of Iranian peoples, speaking a variety of Iranian languages and dialects. The western half was much more ethnically mixed, with Babylonians, Assyrians, Greeks, Phoenicians, Egyptians, and others. The Achaemenid system of government had a strong element of decentralisation, with the Empire being divided into about twenty large governorships, called satrapies. Within these were many pre-existing indigenous political structures, like the Greek city-states on the coast of Asia Minor, which were able to retain their autonomy. The satraps, along with the senior military commanders and other high-ranking officials, were drawn almost exclusively from the Achaemenid family and the Persian nobility, while the indigenous peoples filled the lower ranks. The king kept a watch on his satraps through officials known as 'the King's Eye.' The administration employed an army of scribes and financial officials who used Aramaic as their lingua franca alongside local languages, such as Elamite, Akkadian, Egyptian or Greek. The Persian language of this period, known as Old Persian, is thought to have been written down for the first time in the great cuneiform inscription which Darius I had engraved on the rock face at Bisitun in north-west Iran in about 519BC. Persian, too, was a purely local language at this stage, the language of Persis. This multi-ethnic, multilingual empire was held together by the imperial administration, by Persian garrisons, Persian colonies and a network of royal roads, mainly reserved for official or military business.

The Achaemenid kings claimed to rule by divine right. At least from the reign of Darius I, they adopted the religion of the Iranian prophet, Zoroaster, who probably lived and taught among the Iranians several centuries earlier, before their migration into Iran. The Achaemenids asserted that kingship had been bestowed on them by the supreme deity of Zoroastrianism, Ahura Mazda, the creator of the world. They portrayed themselves as playing a crucial role in the cosmic conflict of Zoroastrianism, between Ahura Mazda, the Wise Lord, and Ahriman, the Evil Spirit. They upheld the Goodness, Order and Truth, for which Ahura Mazda stood, against the Evil and the Lie of Ahriman. Naturally, they identified their own enemies as followers of the Lie.

The Achaemenid king was a universal ruler who bore the title of 'King of Kings'. This title is thought to be of ancient Mesopotamian origin and implied that the Achaemenid king stood above the kings of all the preceding empires. The greatness of the Achaemenid king was symbolised by the huge scale and magnificence of his palaces at Pasargadae and Persepolis. It was further displayed to his subjects in the splendour of his camp and entourage when he was travelling or on hunting expeditions. His skill in hunting, in riding a horse and in using a bow and spear, were considered necessary attributes of kingship. He was surrounded by an elaborate court ceremonial and had a harem of wives and concubines, overseen by eunuchs. Much of this remained characteristic of Persian monarchs until well into the nineteenth century. Although the Achaemenid kings adopted Zoroastrianism, they never made it a state religion and continued to patronise other cults and religions, so long as the followers of these cults were loyal and obedient. They also worshipped several other deities besides Ahura Mazda, 'the greatest of the gods', and made frequent sacrifices to the forces of nature. The later Achaemenids promoted the worship of two other gods in particular: Mithra, an ancient Iranian god of oaths and contracts, associated with fire, and Anahita, a fertility goddess. The annual festival of Mithra was a major event when large numbers of horses were sacrificed and the king led worshippers in the Persian national dance, the *Persica*, which involved crouching down and leaping up and crashing shields together. The main Zoroastrian festival, however, was the New Year or *No Ruz* (literally 'New Day') festival at the spring equinox, on or around March 21st. This was celebrated with much ceremony at Persepolis, where the friezes are generally thought to show the different peoples of the Empire bringing *No Ruz* gifts for the Great King. Despite the coming of Islam, *No Ruz* has continued to be the most popular Iranian festival.

There were no Zoroastrian temples in the early Achaemenid period. They were later built to house statues of the goddess Anahita, and then for the fire cult, which was the central ritual of Zoroastrianism. The sacred fire was tended on an altar by the priests, known as the Magi, who were in charge of all the Zoroastrian rituals. Large estates also came to be attached to the temples. We still depend to a great extent on Greek and Roman authors for our knowledge of the Achaemenid Empire. There are no Persian histories, apart from the great inscription of Darius I at Bisitun, which deals exclusively with how he became king and put down a series of rebellions in the first year of his reign. Persian culture at this time was an oral one, with bards and priests acting as the collective memory. Persian boys, according to the Greek historian, Herodotus, were taught to ride, to use the bow, and to tell the truth. They were not taught to read or write which was the occupation of professional scribes. As far as is known, all the Achaemenid kings were illiterate.

The Greeks, and later the Romans and Byzantines, had good reason to be interested in the Persian Empire, because it was the most formidable, and also the most civilised and sophisticated enemy they had to face. The Persians were 'barbarians' in Greek and Roman eyes, but they were recognised as 'barbarians' of a very superior kind. Herodotus says his purpose in writing his *Histories* was to record 'the astonishing achievements' of the Greeks and the Persians, as well as to show how they came into conflict. His work is a testimony to the enormous Persian achievement in conquering and administering a vast multi-ethnic empire. Many conservative Greeks, such as the Athenian writer and soldier, Xenophon, were attracted to the monarchical and aristocratic world of the Persians. Xenophon made Cyrus the Great, also known as Cyrus the Elder, his model of the ideal ruler, and sang the praises of Cyrus the Younger, whose failed attempt to overthrow his elder brother, the Persian King, Artaxerxes II, he supported as a Greek mercenary.

Herodotus and Xenophon are the principal Greek writers on Persia whose works have survived. But there are a number of others who are known to have written histories of Persia which have since been lost, or at best have survived in part at second hand, quoted by later authors. Not all tried to be as truthful and accurate as Herodotus and Xenophon; some preferred to make up colourful and sensational stories which their readers would enjoy. What is clear is that there was a ready market in the Greek world for books on Persia, a country which many Greeks got to know personally. There were Greek doctors at the Persian Court, Greek craftsmen helped to build the Persian palaces, and tens of thousands of Greek soldiers served in mercenary units attached to the Persian army. As has been noted, the Greek cities on the west coast of what is now Turkey were also intermittently part of the Persian Empire and provided it with part of its fleet. To a large extent, the ancient Greek authors fixed an image of Persia which endured in Europe until very recent times – until, in fact, Europeans ceased to have a Classical education. When European visitors to Persia in the seventeenth century wanted to convey an idea of the magnificence of the Safavid court in Isfahan, they would often compare it with the Achaemenid court, which they knew from the Classical Greek authors they had grown up with to have been the epitome of regal splendour. Because of the Greeks, the best-known episodes in the history of the Achaemenid Empire are the successive invasions of Greece under Darius I and Xerxes – the latter led by the Great King in person – which were defeated at the battles of Marathon (490BC), Salamis (480BC) and Platea (479BC). After this the Greeks went on the offensive until the conclusion of a peace in 449BC. The Persians agreed to leave the Greek cities on the coast of Asia Minor alone and to stay out of the Aegean, while the Greeks, who had lent support to a rebellion in Egypt, undertook to refrain from military interventions on the territory of the Empire.

The Greek victories were obviously of supreme importance to the Greeks, but perhaps less so to the Persians. They were certainly damaging to the prestige of the Great King, but they only affected a small part of his vast empire and did not seriously weaken it. The disunity of the Greeks, highlighted by the outbreak of the Peloponnesian War between Athens and Sparta in 431BC, ultimately enabled the Persians to recover control of the Aegean coast of Asia Minor and even to become the arbiter of Greek internal quarrels. This, however, aroused a fear of Persia among the Greeks, many of whom began to look to the strong man from the north, Philip of Macedon, to lead them in a crusade against Persia, and at the same time to ease Greece's problem of over-population by establishing new Greek colonies in Asia Minor.

In the end it was not Philip but his son, Alexander, who overthrew the Achaemenid Empire. A military genius, he defeated the armies of the last of the Great Kings, Darius III, in three successive battles between May 334 and October 331BC. In the course of this, he burnt a part of the palace of Persepolis in retribution for the Persian invasions of Greece under Darius I and Xerxes. But he had a vision of a new empire that would be a partnership of the Greeks and Macedonians on the one hand, and the Persians and other Iranian peoples on the other. He adopted the clothing and manners of an Achaemenid king, married three Iranian princesses – two of them Achaemenids – had his officers and thousands of his soldiers take Iranian wives, and recruited Persians and other Iranians into his army. At the same time he founded a string of new towns, which he populated with Graeco-Macedonian soldiers and settlers.

But in June 323, 'the last of the Achaemenids', as Alexander has been called, died of a fever in Babylon, before he had a real chance to turn his vision into a reality. He was subsequently remembered in two very different ways by the Persians. In the Zoroastrian tradition, he was ranked with the followers of the Evil Spirit, while in Islamic times the Persian poets sang his praises and he became the embodiment of chivalry and wisdom.

One of Alexander's generals, Seleucus, eventually won control of most of his Asian empire and established a dynasty that ruled Persia for the best part of two hundred years. Seleucus, who declared himself king, created two new capitals: Seleucia-on-the-Tigris, which replaced Babylon and became the administrative capital of his eastern Empire, of which Persia was the core, and Antioch-on-the-Orontes near the Mediterranean in Syria, which had vital function of keeping the door open to new immigrants from Greece. Although Seleucus's successors were all descended from his Iranian wife, they remained essentially Macedonians and depended on Greek and Macedonian soldiers and civilians to enable them to go on ruling an alien population. They followed Alexander's example in settling these immigrants in new towns, villages, and military colonies, as well as in old towns, which they refounded and renamed.

The Seleucids retained the Achaemenid satrapies, as Alexander had done, appointing Greeks and Macedonians to run them. They also recognised many petty native rulers as their vassals, including a new local dynasty which emerged in Persis. Like Alexander, they adopted the ceremony and manners of the Achaemenid court and, like him, they went further than the Achaemenids by claiming to be divine. A cult of the Seleucid king was instituted in the Greek-style towns, where it existed alongside all the other cults and religions. Zoroastrianism, however, seems to have gone into a decline, now that it was deprived of the royal patronage it had enjoyed under the Achaemenids, which explains the Zoroastrian antipathy towards Alexander.

There was no Seleucid policy of Hellenising Persia, but Herodotus tells us that no people were so ready to adopt foreign ways as the Persians. Greek became a lingua franca alongside Aramaic, and Persians and other Iranians living in or near the new towns would have adopted Greek speech and Greek ways, especially if they were involved in commercial or administrative activities. Most of the countryside, however, and regions like Persis, where there was no significant Greek or Macedonian presence, remained untouched by Hellenism.

The Seleucids were never able to give their full attention to their eastern possessions, because they had to spend so much of their time defending their Syrian gateway to Greece, first against the Ptolemies in Egypt and later against the expanding power of Rome. Consequently they lost control either temporarily or permanently of large parts of Persia before their rule in the east was finally extinguished in 129BC by a new Iranian dynasty, the Parthian Arsacids. The Parthian Empire, which lasted until 224AD, much longer than the Achaemenid Empire, is the truly forgotten empire of ancient Iran. Its founder, Arsaces, was the chief of an Iranian tribe, the Parni, which had left its lands in Transoxania and begun to move west during the early days of the Seleucids. Arsaces was proclaimed king in about 247BC and conquered the Seleucid satrapy of Parthia some ten years later, after which he and his people came to be known as Parthians. He died in 217BC, after surviving spirited Seleucid counter-attacks, and the decisive Parthian advance into western Persia and Mesopotamia came some seventy years later under King Mithridates I (c.171–139/8BC). The Parthian kingdom was transformed into an empire with a new capital at Ctesiphon on the Tigris, opposite the former Seleucid capital of Seleucia and twenty miles south-east of the modern city of Baghdad.

The Arsacid dynasty associated itself both with the Hellenism of the Seleucids and with the Iranian traditions of the Achaemenids, with the emphasis gradually shifting from the former to the latter. Their priority in the beginning was to gain the acceptance of the Graeco-Macedonian population of the cities, who had been the principal support for the Seleucids. So they minted coins with Greek inscriptions, in which they described themselves as 'philhellenes'. But they also adopted on their coins the Achaemenid title of 'King of Kings', and the image of the bow on the reverse, which was an Achaemenid symbol of royalty. Later, they added inscriptions on the coins in Parthian, which was an Iranian language closely related to Persian, evolved a genealogy showing their descent from the Achaemenids, and laid claim to the whole territory of the former Achaemenid Empire. The Parthians were also Zoroastrians. They promoted the fire cult and ordered that the sacred texts of Zoroastrianism, which had become scattered following Alexander's invasion, be gathered together. It was during the Parthian period too that minstrel bards began popularising the legends from a heroic Iranian past that were later to provide the material for the great national epic, the *Shah-nama* or *Book of Kings*, composed by Firdausi in the eleventh century AD. This contributed to the Achaemenid period eventually fading from the Persian consciousness, since these legends were drawn from the eastern Iranian world and had nothing to say about the Achaemenids.

It is surprising that the Parthian Empire should have lasted so long, given that the central government was often weak and that it faced formidable challenges on its frontiers – from the Romans in the west and from nomadic tribes in the Caucasus and in the east. The Empire consisted of a few directly administered satrapies and a large number of kingdoms of varying size, which acknowledged the suzerainty of the Parthian Great King. Among the latter was the Persian homeland of Persis, where the local dynasty also seems to have claimed descent from the Achaemenids. The leading Parthian nobles were extremely powerful with vast estates and private armies, and frequently made and unmade Arsacid kings.

The language of the court and the administration was Parthian, which was written in a version of the Aramaic script. This script was also adopted for the Persian language and cuneiform ceased to be used. Persian, which by this stage had evolved into what is known as Middle Persian, remained largely confined to Persis. Greek and Aramaic remained important, and some of the Parthian kings and nobles were familiar with Greek literature. From 54BC, when the Roman general Crassus launched a disastrous attack on the Parthian Empire, there was repeated warfare between the Parthian and Roman empires. The Parthians often proved more than a match for the Romans, as Crassus discovered to his cost. They were expert horsemen and their main fighting force consisted of two kinds of cavalry – swift-moving mounted archers with powerful bows who could rain down a storm of arrows on the enemy, and heavily armoured knights, known as cataphracts, who carried long lances and could deliver a shattering charge. The Romans also became acquainted with the famous 'Parthian shot', which involved the rider turning around as he galloped away to shoot his arrows at a pursuing enemy. The Persians remained skilled exponents of the 'Parthian shot' until well into the nineteenth century, with guns replacing bows and arrows.

Both sides made dramatic advances at various times, the Parthians sweeping through Asia Minor, Syria and Palestine, and the Romans occupying the Parthian capital, Ctesiphon. But these advances were invariably followed by withdrawals, and in the end the frontier between the two empires remained where it had been at the start – on the Euphrates. A major cause of conflict was the buffer state of Armenia, which was ruled by kings from the Arsacid family, who were nonetheless sometimes allies of Rome. But the Parthian influence predominated, to the extent that Armenia became largely Zoroastrian until its conversion to Christianity early in the fourth century AD. Relations between Parthia and Rome were by no means always unfriendly and the Parthian King, Phraates IV (38BC–AD3/2) sent four of his sons to be brought up in Rome. But the wars with Rome contributed to a weakening of the Parthian Empire, which was suddenly and rapidly overthrown. A Parthian vassal by the name of Ardashir Sasan had been expanding his power from Persis, and in AD224 he inflicted a decisive defeat on the Parthian King, Artabanus IV. Two years later Ardashir crowned himself King of Kings and by AD230 he had brought the rest of the Parthian Empire under his control. He and his descendants, known as the Sasanids, were to rule Persia for more than four hundred years, until they in turn were overthrown and their empire conquered by the Muslim Arabs. The Sasanids based their legitimacy in part on their claim that their land had been ruled by their 'forefathers', meaning the Achaemenids, although they had the vaguest ideas about them. They established a genealogy, which mentioned only the last of the Achaemenid kings. Otherwise they traced their descent from the legendary Kayanid kings of eastern Persia, one of whom was believed to have been the patron of the prophet Zoroaster. This line of Iranian rulers was immortalised in Firdausi's national epic, which is almost wholly ignorant of the Achaemenid and Parthian dynasties. They claimed to rule by divine right, having been invested with sovereignty by the Zoroastrian creator-god, Ahura Mazda. In the coronation ceremony, it was the Zoroastrian chief priest who placed the crown on the ruler's head.

The Sasanid commitment to Zoroastrianism was symbolised by the image of the king's own sacred fire on the reverse of their coins. The Sasanid kings founded innumerable fire-temples and helped to support an army of Zoroastrian priests, who spread out into every corner of the country. Zoroastrianism became very much the national religion of Persia and Zoroastrian practices, like the exposure of the dead, were generally adopted in a way they had not been before. An official canon of Zoroastrian teachings and liturgies, known as the *Avesta*, was finally compiled and given written form in a version of Middle Persian.

The Zoroastrian clergy were hierarchically organised under the chief priest and represented a powerful political force at the highest level of the state. They were instrumental in forcing the Sasanid kings to end their support for two religious leaders the Zoroastrian clergy denounced as heretics – the prophet Mani (AD216–276), who taught that all matter was evil, and Mazdak (end of the fifth century AD), who was more of a social reformer, preaching common ownership. Both Manichaeanism and Mazdakism were savagely suppressed, but survived to exert their influence in other places and at other times.

The Zoroastrian clergy also instigated the persecution of the very large Christian community. Christian missionaries had begun to make converts in Parthian times, but the Christian community only became really significant when the Sasanid King, Shapur I (c.AD240–272) deported hundreds of thousands of Christians to Persia from Syria and Asia Minor in the course of his campaigns against the Romans. He settled them in new towns in regions he felt to be under-developed, such as Khuzistan in the south-west corner of Persia. Along with other religious minorities they suffered some persecution at the hands of the militant Zoroastrian high priest, Kirdir, during the reign of King Bahram II (AD276–293), but their situation deteriorated sharply in the middle of the fourth century AD when King Shapur II (AD309–379) was at war with a Roman Empire that had recently made Christianity its state religion. Shapur suspected the Christians of disloyalty and his suspicions were reinforced when they refused to pay a special tax to help finance the war. In 339AD, egged on by the Zoroastrian clergy, he began what came to be known as the Great Persecution, which lasted until his death forty years later. In the course of this, about 35,000 Christians are thought to have been put to death. There were intermittent persecutions thereafter, mainly at times of conflict with the Roman Empire, but steps taken in the fifth century by the Christian church in the Sasanid Empire to distance itself from Constantinople, both organisationally and doctrinally, led to a gradual improvement in relations between the Sasanid state and the Christian community. These steps took the form of a declaration of independence, followed later by the adoption of the Nestorian doctrine of the two natures of Christ, which was condemned as a heresy by the Byzantine and other western churches.

In their persecution of the Christians, the Sasanid kings were motivated by political considerations and they did not generally share the bigotry of their Zoroastrian clergy. Some of the kings were notably tolerant and open-minded. Khosrow I, in particular, became famous for his intellectual curiosity and his encouragement of learning. He welcomed Greek and Indian philosophers to his court, enjoyed taking part in discussions with them, and established an important medical school in Jundeshapur in Khuzistan, a town founded by Shapur I for the settlement of captives from Syrian Antioch.

The Sasanids were frequently involved in costly wars with Rome and later Byzantium in the west, as well as with powerful nomadic states in the east. Other nomadic peoples had to be kept at bay in the Caucasus. The control of Armenia, and also of Georgia, remained sources of conflict. For a time Armenia was partitioned, but later it fell wholly into the Sasanid sphere. It had been converted to Christianity in the meantime, but after an abortive attempt to restore Zoroastrianism, the Sasanid kings granted the Armenians full religious freedom. Georgia was eventually partitioned, with the Sasanids taking control of the eastern half, with its capital of Tiflis. Like the rest of Georgia, it had been converted to Christianity, but strong efforts were made to promote Zoroastrianism.

The fortunes of war fluctuated as they had with the Parthians and in the end the frontiers remained more or less unchanged. One of the earliest and most dramatic Sasanid successes was the capture by King Shapur I of the Roman Emperor, Valerian, in a battle near Edessa, in northern Mesopotamia, in ca.AD259. This was commemorated by Shapur in rock-carvings in Persis, which show the Sasanid king on horseback and the Roman emperor kneeling before him. Valerian's subsequent fate remains unknown, but 70,000 Roman legionaries who were taken prisoner were resettled in Khuzistan where they were employed in building bridges, dams and roads, the remains of some of which can still be seen today. The Sasanid armies were very similar to those of the Parthians, with the difference that the Sasanids made use of war elephants.

Sasanid power reached its apogee under Khosrow II (AD590–628), who succeeded in a brutal, whirlwind campaign in briefly making himself master of Asia Minor, the Levant and even Egypt, thereby restoring to Persian rule the former western territories of the

Achaemenid Empire. But a Byzantine counter-attack soon forced him to abandon these conquests and drove him back to Ctesiphon, where a revolt broke out and he was murdered. He was followed by a series of weak kings, none of whom reigned for long and all of whom were at the mercy of the great nobles and the higher Zoroastrian clergy. The failure of the Sasanids to curb the power of the great nobles and their growing inability to assert their authority over the Zoroastrian clergy contributed to their downfall as much as the war-weariness brought about by Khosrow I's campaigns in the west. The last of the Sasanid kings, Yazdgird III, was a grandson of Khosrow II who was placed on the throne by the nobles in AD632, the year of the death of the Prophet Muhammad in Arabia. The following year Arab Muslim forces began raids into Mesopotamia. But their main assault on the Sasanid Empire came four years later when they inflicted a crushing defeat on the Sasanid army at Qadisiya on the west bank of the Euphrates, near Hira, and went on to capture the Sasanid capital of Ctesiphon. The final blow came in AD642, when the army Yazdgird had managed to assemble on the Iranian plateau was defeated at Nihavand, south of Hamadan. Yazdgird became a fugitive, fleeing from one place to another, until in AD651 he reached Merv in north-eastern Persia. Finding the gates of the city closed against him he fled to the house of a miller, only to be murdered there, his body stripped and thrown into the river. His death marks the end of the Sasanid dynasty and the beginning of a new Islamic era in Persia.

It also brought to an end a long period during which Europe and Persia – or at least the Europe of Greece and Rome – had been in close proximity to one another, with frequent contacts and cultural interchange, as well as conflict. Throughout this time, the principal European writers on Persia continued to be Greeks, who were the closest, while Latin writers, living further away in the west, tended to focus more on Rome itself and its enemies on other frontiers. After the Arab conquest, Persia was for several centuries effectively cut off from Europe, separated not only by a deeper religious divide, but by other intervening Muslim powers.

Tidings from Greece...

The hopes of the Persian King, Xerxes, of conquering Greece were effectively ended by the Greek victory over the Persian fleet in the straits of Salamis in September 480BC. The Persian fleet was not, in fact, Persian at all. It was composed of ships from Phoenicia (modern Lebanon) and from the Greek cities on the coast of Asia Minor – both regions that were under Persian rule. Their crews went into the battle exhausted. They had spent the night patrolling the entrances to the straits, after Xerxes had been being deceived into believing that the Greek fleet would try to escape under cover of darkness. They were then outmanoeuvred by the Greeks, so that their many ships became entangled with one another in the narrow confines of the straits. The first of the great Athenian dramatists, Aeschylus (525/4–456BC), took part in the battle and describes what happened with poetry, drama and patriotic fervour in his play, The Persians, *which was first performed in Athens eight years later, in 472BC. The play is set in the Persian imperial capital of Susa, in the south-west corner of Iran, where a messenger breaks the news of the disaster to Xerxes's mother, Atossa.*

Atossa:
How first began the battle? Tell me all.
Was it the Greek who struck, or did the King,
My son, his great force to the hazard fling?

Messenger:
Queen, for the first beginning of these woes,
Some fiend or madman – whence he came, who knows? –
Greek-seeming, from the Athenian ranks drew near
To Xerxes' self, and whispered in his ear
That, once the veil of hiding night should fall,
The Greeks would wait no more, but one and all
Leap to their oars and, scattering left and right,
Make off to save their lives in headlong flight.
Xerxes gave ear, and reckoning not the while

Of heaven's malignity or Grecian guile,
His word to all the ship-masters sent round;
Soon as the sun should leave the parched ground
And darkness take the temples of the sky,
The main fleet in three columns should stand by,
Closing the way to Athens, while the rest
Went round the island, guarding on the west
The narrow ways and races loud with foam.
Else, if the Greeks escaped an evil doom
Finding some secret way of flight, he said,
Each master of a ship would lose his head.
Such was his word; right full of mirth was he,
So little guessed he what the end should be!
In order and obedience all the fleet
Supped and prepared; each oarsman took his seat
And nimbly to the rowlock strapped his oar.
Meantime the sunlight melted from the shore
And night drew on, and in their ships arrayed
Each man at arms, each bender of the blade,
Waited. From rank to rank the word was passed
Down the long line, and on they moved at last,
Each to his station. All the night long through
Each captain rowing, rowing, kept his crew;
And night wore on, and never sound nor sight
From the Greek fleet gave sign of secret flight;
Not till the wild white horses of the morn
Took all the earth with glory; then was bourne
A sound across the sea, a voice, a strong
Clamour exultant like a leaping song,
And each answering from the island rock
Cried battle. To our men there came a shock
Of fear and hopes undone. No note there rang
Of flight in that high paean that they sang,
Only glad courage, hot to do and dare.
Out burst their trumpets, flaming through the air.
In splashed their foaming oars, and straining stirred
The briny furrows at the helmsman's word,

And all the ships were out and clear to view.
The right wing led the van, in order due,
Behind it the whole fleet, prow after prow.
Then one great shout: 'Now, sons of Hellas, now!
Set Hellas free, set free your wives, your homes,
Your gods' high altars and your fathers' tombs.
Now all is on the stake!' At once from us
A storm of Persian voices clamorous
Made answer, but no time was left to speak.
Already ship on ship its brazen beak
Had driven. The first rammer was a Greek,
Which sheared away a great Sidonian's crest;
Then close, one on another, charged the rest.
At first the log-drawn Persian line was strong
And held; but in those narrows such a throng
Was crowded, ship to ship could bring no aid.
Nay, with their own bronze-fanged beaks they made
Destruction; a whole length of oars one beak
Would shatter; and with purposed art the Greek
Ringed us outside, and pressed, and struck; and we –
Our oarless hulls went over, till the sea
Could scarce be seen, with wrecks and corpses spread.
The reefs and beaches too were filled with dead,
And every ship in our great fleet away
Rowed in wild flight. And there, through all the bay,
As men kill tunnies (tuna) crowded on the shore,
Or some great fish, with clubs of broken oar
And spars of wreck, they beat and broke and killed
Our men. With crying all the air was filled,
Out from the narrows to the shoreless main,
Of slain men and women wailing for the slain,
Till the blind veil of night swept all away.

    Not though for ten long days, day after day,
I spoke, could I express that mass of woe.
For never yet – this ye may surely know –
Have on one day so many thousands died.

Atossa:
Ah me, a flood of suffering deep and wide
Hath broke on Persia, yea, on all the east.

From *The Persians* by Aeschylus
translated by Gilbert Murray

The Persian Version

The English poet, Robert Graves, provides a counter-balance to the triumphalist Athenian patriotism of Aeschylus. In his poem The Persian Version, *he wittily imagines how relatively unimportant the Persian defeats at the hands of the Greeks might have seemed from the perspective of the rulers of a vast empire. The poem gives the Persian version of the land battle at Marathon in 490BC, which put an end to the first invasion of Greece ordered by Xerxes' father, Darius I.*

Truth-loving Persians do not dwell upon
The trivial skirmish fought near Marathon.
As for the Greek theatrical tradition
Which represents that summer's expedition
Not as a mere reconnaissance in force
By three brigades of foot and one of horse
(Their left flank covered by some obsolete
Light craft detached from the main Persian fleet)
But as a grandiose, ill-starred attempt
To conquer Greece – they treat it with contempt;
And only incidentally refute
Major Greek claims, by stressing what repute
The Persian monarch and the Persian nation
Won by this salutary demonstration:
Despite a strong defence and adverse weather
All arms combined magnificently together.

From *The Persion Version* by Robert Graves

Persian Customs

The Greek author who did more than anyone to shape the European view of Ancient Persia was Herodotus (c.484–425BC). No other Classical author whose work has survived wrote so extensively about the history and customs of the Persians. He remains by far the most important single source for the early history of the Achaemenid Empire. Herodotus, who has been called 'the father of history', was born and grew up in Helicarnassus (now the Turkish town of Bodrum), a Greek city on the south-west coast of Asia Minor that was part of the Achaemenid Empire. One of its rulers, a princess by the name of Artemisia, fought with the Persian fleet at the battle of Salamis. The origin and course of the Persian-Greek wars are the main themes of his Histories, *and he tells us as much as he has been able to find out about the Persians and their kings – and a great deal else besides. He criticises and praises the Greeks and the Persians in fairly equal measure, which caused the later Greek historian, Plutarch, to accuse him of being 'pro-barbarian' (philo-barbaros). Herodotus obtained much of his information from what he saw and heard during his extensive travels in the western half of the Persian Empire, particularly in Asia Minor, the Levant, Egypt and Mesopotamia, where he visited Babylon. He had an immense curiosity and knew how to tell a good story. At the same time, he handled his information in a critical spirit and his account of early Persian history has received a fair degree of support from more recent archaeological and other discoveries, notably the great rock inscription of Darius I at Bisitun in north-west Iran. This passage on the religion and customs of the Persians is Herodotus at his most fascinating, although it does contain one or two errors, such as the description of Mithra as a female goddess when he was a male solar deity and the assertion that all Persian names end in 's', which he can only have derived from their Greek form.*

The customs which I know the Persians to observe are the following. They have no images of the gods, no temples nor altars, and consider the use of them a sign of folly. This comes, I think, from their not believing the gods to have the same nature with men, as the Greeks imagine. Their wont, however, is to ascend the summits of the loftiest mountains, and there to offer sacrifice to Jupiter, which is the name they give to the whole circle of the firmament. They likewise offer to the sun and moon, to the earth, to fire, to water, and to the winds. These are the only gods whose worship has come down to them from ancient times. At a later period they began the worship of Urania, which they borrowed from the Arabians and Assyrians. Mylitta is the name by which the Assyrians know this goddess, whom the Arabians call Alitta, and the Persians Mitra. To these the Persians offer sacrifice in the following manner: they raise no altar, light no fire, pour no libations; there is no sound of the flute, no putting on of chaplets, no consecrated barley-cake; but the man who wishes to sacrifice brings his victim to a spot of ground which is pure from pollution, and there calls upon the name of the god to whom he intends to offer. It is usual to have the turban encircled with a wreath, most commonly of myrtle. The sacrificer is not allowed to pray for blessings on himself alone, but he prays for the welfare of the king, and of the whole Persian people, among whom he is of necessity included. He cuts the victim in pieces, and having boiled the flesh he lays it out upon the tenderest herbage that he can find, trefoil especially. It is not lawful to offer sacrifice unless there is a Magus present. After waiting a short time, the sacrificer carries the flesh of the victim away with him, and makes whatever use of it he may please.

Of all the days in the year, the one which they celebrate most is their birthday. It is customary to have the board furnished on that day with an ampler supply than common. The richer Persians cause an ox, a horse, a camel, and an ass to be baked whole, and so served up to them; the poorer classes use instead the smaller kinds of cattle. They eat little solid food but abundance of dessert, which is set on the table a few dishes at a time; this it is which makes them say that 'the Greeks, when they eat, leave off hungry, having nothing worth mention served up to them after the meats; whereas, if they had more put before them, they would not stop eating.' They are very fond of wine, and drink it in large quantities. To vomit or obey natural calls in the presence of another is forbidden among them. Such are their customs in these matters. It is also their general practice to deliberate upon affairs of weight when they are drunk; and then on the morrow, when they are sober, the decision to which they came the night before is put before them by the master of the house in which it was made; and if it is then approved of, they act on it; if not, they set it aside. Sometimes, however, they are sober at their first deliberation, but in this case they always reconsider the matter under the influence of wine.

When they meet each other in the streets, you may know if the persons meeting are of equal rank by the following token; if they are, instead of speaking, they kiss each other on the lips. In the case where one is a little inferior to the other, the kiss is given on the cheek; where the difference of rank is great, the inferior prostrates himself upon the ground. Of nations, they honour most their nearest neighbours, whom they esteem next to themselves; those who live beyond these they honour in the second degree; and so with the remainder, the further they are removed, the less the esteem in which they hold them. The reason is, that they look upon themselves as very greatly superior in all respects to the rest of mankind, regarding others as approaching to excellence in proportion as they dwell nearer to them; whence it comes to pass that those who are the farthest off must be the most degraded of mankind. Under the dominion of the Medes, the several nations of the empire exercised authority over each other in this order. The Medes were lords over all, and governed the nations upon their borders, who in their turn governed the States beyond, who likewise bore rule over the nations which adjoined on them. And this is the order which the Persians also follow in their distribution of honour; for that people, like the Medes, has a progressive scale of administration and government. There is no nation which so readily adopts foreign ways as the Persians. Thus, they have taken the dress of the Medes, considering it superior to their own; and in war they wear the Egyptian breastplate. As soon as they hear of any luxury, they instantly make it their own: and hence, among other novelties, they have learnt unnatural lust from the Greeks. Each of them has several wives, and a still larger number of concubines.

Next to prowess in arms, it is regarded as the greatest proof of manly excellence, to be the father of many sons. Every year the king sends rich gifts to the man who can show the largest number: for they hold that number is strength. Their sons are carefully instructed from their fifth to their twentieth year, in three things alone, – to ride, to draw the bow, and to speak the truth. Until their fifth year they are not allowed to come into the sight of their father, but pass their lives with the women. This is done that, if the child die young, the father may not be afflicted by its loss. To my mind it is a wise rule, as also is the following – that the king shall not put any one to death for a single fault, and that none of the Persians shall visit a single fault in a slave with any extreme penalty; but in every case the services of the offender shall be set against his misdoings; and, if the latter be found to outweigh the former, the aggrieved party shall then proceed to punishment.

The Persians maintain that never yet did any one kill his own father or mother; but in all such cases they are quite sure that, if matters were sifted to the bottom, it would be found that the child was either a changeling or else the fruit of adultery; for it is not likely, they say, that the real father should perish by the hands of his child.

They hold it unlawful to talk of anything which it is unlawful to do. The most disgraceful thing in the world, they think, is to tell a lie; the next worst, to owe a debt: because, among other reasons, the debtor is obliged to tell lies. If a Persian has the leprosy he is not allowed to enter into a city, or to have any dealings with the other Persians; he must, they say, have sinned against the sun. Foreigners attacked by this disorder are forced to leave the country: even white pigeons are often driven away, as guilty of the same offence. They never defile a river with the secretions of their bodies, nor even wash their hands in one; nor will they allow others to do so, as they have a great reverence for rivers. There is another peculiarity, which the Persians themselves have never noticed, but which has not escaped my observation. Their names, which are expressive of some bodily or mental excellence, all end with the same letter – the letter which is called San by the Dorians and Sigma by the Ionians. Any one who examines will find that the Persian names, one and all without exception, end with this letter.

Thus much I can declare of the Persians with entire certainty, from my own actual knowledge. There is another custom which is spoken of with reserve, and not openly, concerning their dead. It is said that the body of a male Persian is never buried, until it has been torn either by a dog or a bird of prey. That the Magi have this custom is beyond a doubt, for they practice it without any concealment. The dead bodies are covered with wax, and then buried in the ground. The Magi are a very peculiar race, differing entirely from the Egyptian priests, and indeed from all other men whatsoever. The Egyptian priests make it a point of religion not to kill any live animals except those which they offer in sacrifice. The Magi, on the contrary, kill animals of all kinds with their own hands, excepting dogs and men. They even seem to take a delight in the employment, and kill, as readily as they do other animals, ants and snakes, and such like flying or creeping things. However, since this has always been their custom, let them keep to it.

From *The Histories* by Herodotus
translated by George Rawlinson

The Persians as Cultivators and Gardeners

The cultivation of the land was a religious duty in Zoroastrianism and is one reason why the Persians were famous for their gardens even in Achaemenid times. Someone who testifies to this is the Greek writer, Xenophon (431–c.350BC). An Athenian aristocrat, soldier and philosopher, Xenophon gained first-hand knowledge of the Achaemenid Empire from accompanying the Greek mercenaries recruited by the Achaemenid prince, Cyrus the Younger, in his attempt to overthrow his elder brother, King Artaxerxes II, in 401BC. When the attempt failed with the defeat and death of Cyrus at the battle of Cunaxa on the Euphrates, Xenophon led the mercenaries on an epic march from the heart of the Persian Empire back home to Greece. His vivid account of this, entitled the Anabasis Kyrou *(The Expedition of Cyrus), has always been one of the most popular works of Greek literature. However, this passage on the importance the Persians attached to farming, and to creating parks and gardens which they called 'paradises', comes from his* Oeconomicus, *a treatise on estate management. The treatise takes the form of a discussion between the Athenian philosopher, Socrates, and a group of his friends and followers, one of whom was called Critobulus. Socrates illustrates his argument with a story about Cyrus the Younger, when he was satrap at Sardis in western Asia Minor, showing the Spartan general, Lysander, around his 'paradise.' The passage begins with a question to Socrates from one of the group.*

'But what arts, pray, do you advise us to follow, Socrates? Need we be ashamed of imitating the king of the Persians? For they say that he pays close attention to husbandry and the art of war, holding that these are two of the noblest and most necessary pursuits.'

'And do you really believe, Socrates,' exclaimed Critobulus on hearing this, 'that the king of the Persians includes husbandry among his occupations?'

'Perhaps, Critobulus, the following considerations will enable us to discover whether he does so. We allow that he pays close attention to warfare, because he has given a standing order to every governor of the nations from which he receives tribute, to supply maintenance for a specified number of horsemen and archers and slingers and light infantry, that they may be strong enough to control his subjects and to protect the country in the event of an invasion; and, apart from these, he maintains garrisons in the citadels.

'As for the country, he personally examines so much of it as he sees in the course of his progress through it; and he receives reports from his trusted agents on the territories that he does not see for himself. To those governors who are able to show him that their country is densely populated and that the land is in cultivation and well stocked with the trees of the district and with the crops, he assigns more territory and gives presents, and rewards them with seats of honour. Those whose territory he finds uncultivated and thinly populated either through harsh administration or through contempt or through carelessness, he punishes and appoints others to take their office. By such action, does he seem to provide less for the cultivation of the land by the inhabitants than for its protection by the garrison?' At this point Critobulus said: 'Well, Socrates, if the Great King does this, it seems to me that he pays as much attention to husbandry as to warfare.'

'Yet further,' continued Socrates, 'in all the districts he resides in and visits he takes care that there are "paradises", as they call them, full of all the good and beautiful things that the soil will produce, and in this he himself spends most of his time, except when the season precludes it.'

'Then it is of course necessary, Socrates, to take care that these "paradises" in which the king spends his time shall contain a fine stock of trees and all other beautiful things that the soil produces.'

'And some say, Critobulus, that when the king makes gifts, he first invites those who have distinguished themselves in war, because it is useless to have broad acres under tillage unless there are men to defend them; and next to them, those who stock and cultivate the land best, saying that even stout-hearted warriors cannot live without the aid of workers. There is a story that Cyrus, lately the most illustrious of princes, once said to the company invited to receive his gifts, "I myself deserve to receive the gifts awarded in both classes; for I am the best at stocking land and the best at protecting the stock."

'Further, the story goes that when Lysander came to him bringing the gifts from the allies, this Cyrus showed him various marks of friendliness, as Lysander himself related once to a stranger at Megara, adding besides that Cyrus personally showed him round his "paradise" at Sardis. Now Lysander admired the beauty of the trees in it, the accuracy of the spacing, the straightness of the rows, the regularity of the angles and the multitude of the sweet scents that clung round them as they walked; and for wonder of these things he cried, "Cyrus, I really do admire all these lovely things, but I am far more impressed with your agent's skill in measuring and arranging everything so exactly." Cyrus was delighted to hear this and said: "Well, Lysander, the whole of the measurement and arrangement is my own work, and I did some of the planting myself." "What, Cyrus?" exclaimed Lysander, looking at him, and marking the beauty and perfume of his robes, and the splendour of the necklaces and bangles and other jewels that he was wearing; "did you really plant part of this with your own hands?" "Does that surprise you Lysander?"asked Cyrus in reply. "I swear by the Sun-god that I never yet sat down to dinner when in sound health, without first working hard at some task of war or agriculture, or exerting myself somehow."

From *Oeconomicus* by Xenophon
translated by E. C. Marchant

Persian Decadence

Xenophon was for long an admirer of the Achaemenid Empire – influenced in part, no doubt, by his dislike of the Athenian democracy which put to death his teacher, Socrates, and sent Xenophon himself into exile. Later, however, his admiration cooled. In a work on statecraft entitled the Cyropaedia, *he portrays the founder of the Empire, Cyrus the Elder, as the ideal ruler, but claims that since then the Persians have become decadent. Xenophon is the first of a long line of European writers on Persia who have accused its ruling class of an excessive love of luxury. The charge was frequently levelled against the Safavid ruling class in the seventeenth century. The decadence described by Xenophon came to be accepted as one of the reasons for the downfall of the Achaemenid Empire, though that argument is rather discounted by modern historians.*

In the first place, they are not satisfied with only having their couches upholstered with down, but they actually set the posts of their beds upon carpets, so that the floor may offer no resistance, but that the carpets may yield. Again whatever sorts of bread and pastry for the table had been discovered before, none of all those have fallen into disuse, but they keep on always inventing something new besides; and it is the same way with meats; for in both branches of cookery they actually have artists to invent new dishes.

Again, in winter they are not satisfied with having clothing on their heads and bodies and legs, but they must have also sleeves thickly lined to the very tips of their fingers, and gloves besides. In summer, on the other hand, they are not satisfied with the shade afforded by the trees and rocks, but amid these they have people stand by them to provide artificial shade.

They take great pride also in having as many cups as possible; but they are not ashamed if it transpires that they came by them by dishonest means, for dishonesty and sordid love of gain have greatly increased among them.

Furthermore, it was of old a national custom not to be seen going anywhere on foot; and that was for no other purpose than to make themselves as knightly as possible. But now they have more coverings upon their horses than upon their beds, for they do not care so much for knighthood as for a soft seat. And so is it not to be expected that in military prowess they should be wholly inferior to what they used to be? In times past it was their national custom that those who held lands should furnish cavalrymen from their possessions and that these, in case of war, should also take the field, while those who performed outpost duty in defence of the country received pay for their services. But now the rulers make knights out of their porters, bakers, cooks, cup-bearers, bath-room attendants, butlers, waiters, chamberlains who assist them in retiring at night and in rising in the morning, and beauty-doctors who pencil their eyes and rouge their cheeks for them and otherwise beautify them; these are the sort that they make into knights to serve for pay for them. From such recruits, therefore, a host is obtained, but they are of no use in war; and that is clear from actual occurrences: for enemies may range up and down their land with less hindrance than friends. For Cyrus had abolished skirmishing at a distance, had armed both horses and men with breastplates, had put a javelin into each man's hand, and had introduced the method of fighting hand-to-hand. But now they neither skirmish at a distance any longer, nor yet do they fight in a hand-to-hand engagement. The infantry still have their wicker shields and bills and sabres, just as those had who set the battle in array in the times of Cyrus; but not even they are willing to come into a hand-to-hand conflict.

Neither do they employ the scythed chariot any longer for the purpose for which Cyrus had it made. For he advanced the charioteers to honour and made them objects of admiration and so had men who were ready to hurl themselves against even a heavy-armed line. The officers of the present day, however, do not so much as know the men in the chariots, and they think that untrained drivers will be just as serviceable to them as trained charioteers. Such untrained men do indeed charge, but before they penetrate the enemy's lines some of them are unintentionally thrown out, some of them jump out on purpose, and so the teams without drivers often create more havoc on their own side than on the enemy's. However, inasmuch as even they understand what sort of material for war they have, they abandon the effort; and no one ever goes to war any more without the help of Greek mercenaries, be it when they are at war with one another or when the Greeks make war upon them; but even against Greeks they recognize that they can conduct their wars only with the assistance of Greeks.

From *Cyropaedia VIII, 16–26* by Xenophon

The King's Dinner

A Greek author by the name of Heracleides has left a rare and fascinating account of dining customs at the Achaemenid court. It is all that survives from his Persika *or* Persian History, *which he wrote in about 350BC, at the end of the Achaemenid era, and which has since been lost. Nothing is known about Heracleides, beyond the fact that he was a Greek from Cumae, a city on the west coast of Asia Minor. His account of Achaemenid dining customs was fortunately preserved by Athenaeus, a Greek from Egypt, in his work entitled* The Deipnosophists, *or* The Learned Banquet, *which is thought to have been completed in AD192. In this, a group of well-educated people at a banquet lasting several days discuss all the things that accompany a convivial occasion. As they do so, they quote from the works of more than one thousand two hundred authors, most of which, like the* Persica *of Heracleides, are now lost. The passage by Heracleides reveals features that are also found at Persian courts in Islamic times, such as the boon-companions who joined the king in drinking sessions, the music and singing that accompanied the dinner, and the practice of giving payment in food.*

Heracleides of Cumae, author of the *Persian History*, writes, in the second book of the work entitled *Equipment*: 'All who attend upon the Persian kings when they dine first bathe themselves and then serve in white clothes, and spend nearly half the day on preparations for the dinner. Of those who are invited to eat with the king, some dine outdoors, in full sight of anyone who wishes to look on; others dine indoors in the king's company. Yet even these do not eat in his presence, for there are two rooms opposite each other, in one of which the king has his meal, in the other the invited guests. The king can see them through the curtain at the door but they cannot see him. Sometimes, however, on the occasion of a public holiday, all dine in a single room with the king, in the great hall. And whenever the king commands a symposium (which he does often) he has about a dozen companions at the drinking. When they have finished dinner, that is, the king by himself, the guests in the other room, these fellow-drinkers are summoned by one of the eunuchs; and entering they drink with him, though even they do not have the same wine; moreover, they sit on the floor, while he reclines on a couch supported by feet of gold; and they depart after having drunk to excess. In most cases the king breakfasts and dines alone, but sometimes his wife and some of his sons dine with him. And throughout the dinner his concubines sing and play the lyre; one of them is the soloist, the others sing in chorus. And so, Heracleides continues, the 'king's dinner,' as it is called, will appear prodigal to one who merely hears about it, but when one examines it carefully it will be found to have been got up with economy and even with parsimony; and the same is true of the dinners among other Persians in high station. For one thousand animals are slaughtered daily for the king; these comprise horses, camels, oxen, asses, deer, and most of the smaller animals; many birds also are consumed, including Arabian ostriches – and the creature is large – geese, and cocks. And of all these only moderate portions are served to each of the king's guests and each of them may carry home whatever he leaves untouched at the meal. But the greater part of these meats and other food are taken out into the courtyard for the bodyguard and light-armed troopers maintained by the king; there they divide all the half-eaten remnants of meat and bread and share them in equal portions. Just as hired soldiers in Greece receive their wages in money, so these men receive food from the king in requital for services. Similarly among other Persians of high rank, all the food is served on the table at one and the same time; but when their guests have done eating, whatever is left from the table, consisting chiefly of meat and bread, is given by the officer in charge of the table to each of the slaves; this they take and so obtain their daily food. Hence the most highly-honoured of the king's guests go to court only for breakfast; for they beg to be excused in order that they may not be required to go twice, but may be able to entertain their own guests.'

From *The Deipnosophists* by Athenaeus
translated by Charles Burton Gulick

The Persian Army on the March

The size and splendour of the armies of Ancient Persia always impressed the Greeks and the Romans. The Roman historian, Quintus Curtius, in his History of Alexander, *has left a vivid and colourful picture of the army of the last of the Achaemenid Kings, Darius III, as it marched through Mesopotamia in the autumn of 323BC to confront the invading army of Alexander the Great. Quintus Curtius, who lived in Rome during the first century AD, based his* History of Alexander *on a popular account, which was written within thirteen years of Alexander's death in 323BC by Clitarchus, a Greek from the Aegean coastal region of Asia Minor. Clitarchus may well have talked to Greek soldiers who had fought as mercenaries in Darius's army. In the ensuing battle near the village of Issus by the Mediterranean in what is now southern Turkey, Darius was heavily defeated. He was to fight and lose one more major battle against Alexander, before he and his empire were finally overthrown.*

It was an ancestral custom of the Persians not to begin a march before sunrise. When the day was already bright, the signal was given from the King's tent with the horn; above the tent, from which it might be seen by all, there gleamed an image of the sun enclosed in crystal. In front on silver altars was carried the fire which they called sacred and eternal. Next came the Magi, chanting their traditional hymn. These were followed by three hundred and sixty-five young men clad in purple robes, equal in number to the days of the whole year; for the Persians also divided the year into that number of days. After that, white horses drew the chariot consecrated to Jupiter;[1] these were followed by a horse of extraordinary size, which they called the steed of the Sun. Golden wands and white robes adorned the drivers of the horses. Not far off there were ten chariots, embossed with much gold and silver. These were followed by the horsemen of twelve nations of varying arms and customs.

Next marched those whom the Persians call 'the Immortals' to the number of ten thousand. No others were more adorned with the splendour of barbaric wealth; theirs were golden necklets, and garments adorned with cloth of gold and long-sleeved tunics adorned even with gems. At a short interval came those whom they call the king's kindred, 15,000 men. This throng indeed, with its almost feminine elegance, was conspicuous rather for luxury than for suitable arms. The troop next to these, who were accustomed to take care of the royal robes, were called Spear-bearers. These preceded the King's chariot, in which he rode outstanding among the rest. Both sides of the chariot were adorned with images of the gods, embossed in gold and silver; the yoke was ornamented with sparkling gems, and on it rose two golden images a cubit high of the King's ancestors, one of Ninus, the other of Belus. Between these they had consecrated a golden eagle, represented with outstretched wings. The attire of the King was noteworthy beyond all else in luxury; a purple-edged tunic woven about a white centre, a cloak of cloth of gold, ornamented with golden hawks, which seemed to attack each other with their beaks; from a golden belt, with which

---

[1] The Romans identified the Zoroastrian creator-god, Ahura Mazda, with Jupiter, just as the Greeks had identified him with Zeus.

he was girt woman-fashion, he had hung a scimitar, the scabbard of which was a single gem. The Persians called the king's head-dress *cidaris*; this was bound with a blue fillet variegated with white. The chariot was followed by 10,000 lancers, carrying spears richly adorned with silver and tipped with a point of gold. About two hundred of the noblest relatives of the king attended him on the right and on the left. The rear of this part of the procession was brought up by thirty thousand foot soldiers, followed by four hundred of the king's horses.

Next, at an interval of a single stade, one chariot carried Sisigambis, Darius's mother, and in another was his wife. A throng of women of the queen's household rode on horses. Then followed fifteen of what they call *harmamaxae* (enclosed litters); in these were the King's children and their governesses, and a herd of eunuchs, who are not at all despised by these peoples. Next rode the 365 concubines of the King, these also regally dressed and adorned. After these 600 mules and 300 camels carried the King's money, preceded by a guard of bowmen. Next to this division rode the wives of his relatives and friends, and troops of sutlers and batmen. Last of all were bands of light-armed troops, to bring up the rear, each with its own officers.

From *History of Alexander* by Quintus Curtius
translated by John C. Rolfe

Zoroastrian Rites

A rare and valuable description of Zoroastrian religious practices is given by the Greek historian and geographer Strabo (64/3BC–AD21 or later), who came from a region of northern Asia Minor known as Pontus. This had been part of the Achaemenid Empire and had a largely Iranian population. Its long line of Hellenised Iranian rulers was overthrown at the time of Strabo's birth by the Roman general, Pompey. He spent much of his life in Pontus so this passage from his Geography *is based for the most part, as he says, on personal experience.*

Now the Persians do not erect statues or altars, but offer sacrifice on a high place, regarding the heavens as Zeus; and they also worship Helius (the Sun), whom they call Mithras, and Selene (the Moon) and Aphrodite, and fire and earth and winds and water; and with earnest prayer they offer sacrifice in a purified place, presenting the victim crowned; and when the Magus, who directs the sacrifice, has divided the meat the people go away with their shares, without setting apart a portion for the gods, for they say that the god requires only the soul of the victim and nothing else; but still, according to some writers, they place a small portion of the caul[2] upon the fire.

But it is especially to fire and water that they offer sacrifice. To fire they offer sacrifice by adding dry wood without the bark and by placing fat on top of it; and then they pour oil upon it and light it below, not blowing with their breath, but fanning it; and those who blow the fire with their breath or put anything dead or filthy upon it are put to death. And to water they offer sacrifice by going to a lake or river or spring, where, having dug a trench leading thereto, they slaughter a victim, being on their guard lest any of the water near by should be made bloody, believing that the blood would pollute the water; and then, placing pieces of meat on myrtle or laurel branches, the Magi touch them with slender wands and make incantations, pouring oil mixed with both milk and honey, though not into fire or water, but upon the ground; and they carry on their incantations for a long time, holding in their hands a bundle of slender myrtle wands.

In Cappadocia (for there the sect of the Magi, who are also called Pyraethi or fire-kindlers, is large, and in that country are also many temples of the Persian gods), the people do not sacrifice victims with a sword either, but with a kind of tree-trunk, beating them to death as with a cudgel. They also have Pyraetheia, noteworthy enclosures; and in the midst of these there is an altar, on which there is a large quantity of ashes and where the Magi keep the fire ever burning. And there, entering daily, they make incantations for about an hour, holding before the fire their bundle of rods and

---

[2] The membrane enclosing the paunch of the sacrificed animal.

wearing round their heads high turbans of felt, which reach down over their cheeks far enough to cover their lips. The same customs are observed in the temples of Anaitis and Omanus; and these temples also have sacred enclosures; and the people carry in procession a wooden statue of Omanus. Now I have seen this myself; but those other things, as also what follows, are recorded in the histories. For the Persians neither urinate, nor wash themselves, in a river; nor yet bathe therein or cast therein anything dead or any other thing that is considered unclean. And to whatever god they offer sacrifice, to him they first offer prayer with fire.

They are governed by hereditary kings. And he who is disobedient has his head and arms cut off and his body cast forth. The men marry many wives, and at the same time maintain several concubines, for the sake of having many children. The kings set forth prizes annually for those who have the most children; but the children are not brought into the presence of their parents until they are four years old. Marriages are consummated at the beginning of the vernal equinox; and the bridegroom passes to the bridal chamber, having first eaten an apple or a camel's marrow, but nothing else during that day.

From *The Geography of Strabo*
translated by H.L. Jones

The Fish-Eaters of Makran

Strabo's Geography *also includes this interesting account of the 'Ichthyophagi,' or fish-eaters of the arid coastal region of Makran, in the far south-east corner of Iran. They were called 'Ichthyophagi' by the soldiers of Alexander the Great's army, many of whom died from hunger and thirst as they marched through this notoriously inhospitable region on their way back from India in September 325BC.*

The country of the Ichthyophagi is on the sea-level; and most of it is without trees, except palms and a kind of thorn and the tamarisk; and there is a scarcity both of water and of foods produced by cultivation; and both the people and their cattle use fish for food and drink waters supplied by rains and wells; and the meat of their cattle smells like fish; and they build their dwellings mostly with the bones of whales and with oyster-shells using the ribs of whales as beams and supports, and the jawbones as doorposts; and they use the vertebral bones of whales as mortars, in which they pound the fish after roasting them in the sun; and then they make bread of this, mixing a small amount of flour with it, for they have grinding-mills although they have no iron. And this is indeed not so surprising, for they could import grinding-mills from other places; but how do they cut them anew when worn smooth? Why, with the same stones, they say, with which they sharpen arrows and javelins that have been hardened in fire. As for fish, they bake some in covered earthen vessels, but for the most part eat them raw; and they catch them, among other ways, with nets made of palm-bark.

From *The Geography of Strabo*
translated by H. L. Jones

The Parthians Annihilate a Roman Army

One of the worst defeats ever suffered by a Roman army was at the hands of the Parthians in 53BC at the battle of Carrhae in northern Mesopotamia. The Roman army was commanded by the politician and general, Marcus Licinius Crassus, who sought to match the military reputation of his political allies, Caesar and Pompey, by making war on the Parthians, despite strong opposition in Rome. In the event, Crassus lost half his army of forty thousand men, as well as his own life and that of his son, Publius. The Greek philosopher and biographer, Plutarch (c.AD50–120) gives a gripping account of the battle in his essay on Crassus. As Plutarch makes clear, the Roman soldiers found themselves terrifyingly vulnerable to the fire-power of the mounted Parthian archers and the long lances of the mailed Parthian knights.

It is said that on that day Crassus did not make his appearance in a purple robe, as is the custom with Roman generals, but in a black one, and that he changed it as soon as he noticed his mistake; also that some of the standard-bearers had great difficulty in raising their standards, which seemed to be imbedded, as it were, in the earth. Crassus made light of these things and hurried on the march, compelling the men-at-arms to keep up with the cavalry, until a few of those who had been sent out as scouts came riding up and announced that the rest of their number had been slain by the enemy, that they themselves had with difficulty escaped, and that their foes were coming up to fight them with a large force and great confidence. All were greatly disturbed, of course, but Crassus was altogether frightened out of his senses, and began to draw up his forces in haste and with no great consistency. At first, as Cassius recommended, he extended the line of his men-at-arms as far as possible along the plain, with little depth, to prevent the enemy from surrounding them, and divided all his cavalry between the two wings. Then he changed his mind and concentrated his men, forming them in a hollow square of four fronts, with twelve cohorts on each side. With each cohort he placed a squadron of horse, that no part of the line might lack cavalry support, but that the whole body might advance to the attack with equal protection everywhere. He gave one of the wings to Cassius, and one to the young Crassus, and took his own position in the centre.

Advancing in this formation, they came to a stream called Balissus, which was not large, to be sure, nor plentiful, but by this time the soldiers were delighted to see it in the midst of the drought and heat and after their previous toilsome march without water. Most of the officers, accordingly, thought they ought to bivouac and spend the night there, and after learning as much as they could of the number and disposition of the enemy, to advance against them at day-break. But Crassus was carried away by the eagerness of his son and the cavalry with him, who urged him to advance and give battle, and he therefore ordered that the men who needed it should eat and drink as they stood in the ranks. And before they were all done with this, he led them on, not slowly, nor halting from time to time, as is usual on the way to battle, but with a quick and sustained pace until the enemy came in sight, who, to the surprise of the Romans, appeared to be neither numerous nor formidable. For Surena (the Parthian commander) had veiled his main force behind his advance guard, and concealed the gleam of their armour by ordering them to cover themselves with robes and skins. But when they were near the Romans and the signal was raised by their commander, first of all they filled the plain with the sound of a deep and terrifying roar. For the Parthians do not incite themselves to battle with horns or trumpets, but they have hollow drums of distended hide, covered with bronze bells, and on these they beat all at once in many quarters, and the instruments give forth a low and dismal tone, a blend of wild beast's roar and harsh thunder peal. They had rightly judged that, of all the senses, hearing is the one most apt to confound the soul, soonest rouses its emotions, and most effectively unseats the judgement.

While the Romans were in consternation at this din, suddenly their enemies dropped the coverings of their armour, and were seen to be themselves blazing in helmets and breastplates, their Margianian steel glittering keen and bright, and their horses clad in plates of bronze and steel. Surena himself, however, was the tallest and fairest of them all, although his effeminate beauty did not well correspond to his reputation for valour, but he was dressed more in the Median fashion, with painted face and parted hair, while the rest of the Parthians still wore their hair long and bunched over their foreheads in Scythian fashion, to make themselves look formidable. And at first they purposed to charge upon the Romans with their long spears, and throw their front ranks into confusion; but when they saw the depth of their formation, where shield was locked with shield, and the firmness and composure of the men, they drew back, and while seeming to break their ranks and disperse, they surrounded the hollow square in which their enemy stood before he was aware of the manoeuvre. And when Crassus ordered his light-armed troops to make a charge, they did not advance far, but encountering a multitude of arrows, abandoned their undertaking and ran back for shelter among the men-at-arms, among whom they caused the beginning of disorder and fear, for these now saw the velocity and force of the arrows, which fractured armour, and tore their way through every covering alike, whether hard or soft.

But the Parthians now stood at long intervals from one another and began to shoot their arrows from all sides at once, not with any accurate aim (for the dense formation of the Romans would not suffer an archer to miss his man even if he wished it), but making vigorous and powerful shots from bows which were large and mighty and curved so as to discharge their missiles with great force. At once, then, the plight of the Romans was a grievous one; for if they kept their ranks, they were wounded in great numbers, and if they tried to come to close quarters with the enemy, they were just as far from effecting anything and suffered just as much. For the Parthians shot as they fled, and next to the Scythians, they do this most effectively; and it is a very clever thing to seek safety while still fighting, and to take away the shame of flight.

Now as long as they had hopes that the enemy would exhaust their missiles and desist from battle or fight at close quarters, the Romans held out; but when they perceived that many camels laden with arrows were at hand, from which the Parthians who first encircled them took a fresh supply, then Crassus, seeing no end to this, began to lose heart, and sent messengers to his son with orders to force an engagement with the enemy before he was surrounded; for it was his wing especially which the enemy were attacking and surrounding with their cavalry, in the hope of getting in his rear. Accordingly, the young man took thirteen hundred horsemen, of whom a thousand had come from Caesar, five hundred archers, and eight cohorts of the men-at-arms who were nearest him, and led them all to the charge. But the Parthians who were trying to envelop him, either because, as some say, they encountered marshes, or because they were manoeuvring to attack Publius as far as possible from his father, wheeled about and made off. Then Publius, shouting that the men did not stand their ground, rode after them, and with him Censorinus and Megabacchus, the latter distinguished for his courage and strength, Censorinus a man of senatorial dignity and a powerful speaker, and both of them comrades of Publius and nearly the same age. The cavalry followed after Publius, and even the infantry kept pace with them in the zeal and joy which their hopes inspired; for they thought they were victorious and in pursuit of the enemy, until, after they had gone forward a long distance, they perceived the ruse.

For the seeming fugitives wheeled about and were joined at the same time by others more numerous still. Then the Romans halted, supposing that the enemy would come to close quarters with them, since they were so few in number. But the Parthians stationed their mail-clad horsemen in front of the Romans, and then with the rest of their cavalry in loose array rode round them, tearing up the surface of the ground and raising from the depths great heaps of sand which fell in limitless showers of dust, so that the Romans could neither see clearly nor speak plainly, but, being crowded into a narrow compass and falling one upon another, were shot, and died no easy nor even speedy death. For, in the agonies of convulsive pain, and writhing about the arrows, they would break them off in their wounds, and then in trying to pull out by force the barbed heads which had pierced their veins and sinews, they tore and disfigured themselves the more.

Thus many died, and the survivors also were incapacitated for fighting. And when Publius urged them to charge the enemy's mail clad horsemen, they showed him that their hands were riveted to their shields and their feet nailed through and through to the ground, so that they were helpless either for flight or for self-defence. Publius himself, accordingly, cheered on his cavalry, made a vigorous charge with them, and closed with the enemy. But his struggle was an unequal one both offensively and defensively, for his thrusting was done with small and feeble spears against breastplates of raw hide and steel, whereas the thrusts of the enemy were made with pikes against the lightly equipped and unprotected bodies of the Gauls, since it was upon these that Publius chiefly relied, and with these he did indeed work wonders. For they laid hold of the long spears of the Parthians, and grappling with the men, pushed them from their horses, hard as it was to move them owing to the weight of their armour; and many of the Gauls forsook their own horses, and crawling under those of the enemy, stabbed them in the belly. These would rear up in their anguish, and die trampling on riders and foemen indiscriminately mingled. But the Gauls were distressed above all things by the heat and their thirst, to both of which they were unused; and most of their horses had perished by being driven against the long spears. They were therefore compelled to retire upon the men-at-arms, taking with them Publius, who was severely wounded. And seeing a sandy hillock near by, they all retired to it, and fastened their horses in the centre; then locking their shields together on the outside, they thought they could more easily defend themselves against the Barbarians. But it turned out just the other way. For on level ground, the ranks do, to some extent, afford relief to those who are behind them. But here, where the inequality of the ground raised one man above another, and lifted every man who was behind another into greater prominence, there was no such thing as escape, but they were all alike hit with arrows, bewailing their inglorious and ineffectual death.

Now there were with Publius two Greeks, of those who dwelt near by in Carrhae, Hieronymous and Nicomachus. These joined in trying to persuade him to slip away with them and make their escape to Ichnae, a city which had espoused the Roman cause and was not far off. But Publius, declaring that no death could have such terrors for him as to make him desert those who were perishing on his account, ordered them to save their own lives, bade them farewell, and dismissed them. Then he himself, being unable to use his hand, which had been pierced through with an arrow, presented his side to his shield-bearer and ordered him to strike home with his sword. In like manner also Censorinus is said to have died; but Megabacchus took his own life and so did the other most notable men. The survivors fought on until the Parthians mounted the hill and transfixed them with their long spears, and they say that not more than five hundred were taken alive. Then the Parthians cut off the head of Publius, and rode off at once to attack Crassus.

From *Lives*
by Plutarch

A Christian Martyr

This is a contemporary account of the martyrdom of a young Christian woman under the Sasanid king, Shapur II (AD309–379). It is one of many such accounts put together in Edessa, in northern Mesopotamia, which was then a great missionary centre of eastern Christianity on the frontier of the Sasanid Empire. It was written in Syriac, a version of Aramaic based on the dialect of Edessa, which became for several centuries the major literary language of much of the Middle East. The woman in question, Martha, was the daughter of King Shapur's master craftsman, Posi, who was an early victim of the Great Persecution of Christians begun by Shapur in AD339. Although a hagiography, the account is based on eyewitness reports and is probably a fairly accurate description of the interrogation of Martha, by the Zoroastrian high priest, the chief Mobed. It shows the Zoroastrian horror of Christian asceticism, and of vows of celibacy like the one Martha had taken, which were in direct opposition to the life-affirming values of Zoroastrianism.

Now the glorious Posi also had a daughter called Martha who was a 'daughter of the covenant'. She too was accused, and at the third hour on the Sunday of the great feast of the Resurrection she was arrested. They brought the blessed Martha, daughter of the glorious Posi, into the presence of the chief Mobed, who then went in to inform the King about her. The King bade him to go out and interrogate her, saying, 'If she abandons her religion and renounces Christianity, well and good; if not, she should be married off. If, however, she fails to follow either of these courses, she should be handed over to be put to death.'

So the chief Mobed went out and started to interrogate the glorious Martha as follows: 'What are you?' To which the blessed Martha replied derisively, 'I am a woman, as you can see.' Those who happened to be there in the presence of the chief Mobed blushed and bent down their heads when they heard the wise Martha's reply to his question. The Mobed's face became green with anger and shame, but he controlled his feelings and said, 'Reply to my question.' To which the wise Martha said, 'I did reply to the question I was asked.'

The Mobed then said, 'What did I ask you, and what reply did you give?' Martha said, 'Your honour asked "What are you?" and I replied, "I am a woman as you can see".'

'I asked you what is your religion,' said the Mobed. The glorious Martha replied, 'I am a Christian, as my clothing shows.' The Mobed went on, 'Tell me the truth, are you the daughter of that crazy Posi who went out of his mind and opposed the King, with the result that he was put to an evil death?' To this the blessed girl replied, 'Humanly speaking, I am his daughter, but also by faith I am the daughter of the Posi who is wise in his God and sane in the firm stand he took on behalf of the King of Kings, the King of Truth, the Posi who yesterday acquired everlasting life by means of his dying for his God. If only God would hold me worthy to be a true daughter of this blessed Posi, who is now with the saints in light and eternal rest, while I am still among sinners in this world of sorrows.'

The Mobed then said, 'Listen to me, and I will advise you what is your best course: the King of Kings is merciful and he does not desire anyone's death, but in his goodness he wishes all his friends to become fellow-religionists of his and so be honoured by him. So it was in the case of your father: because the king liked him, he honoured him and gave him advancement; but your father acted foolishly and said things that were quite out of place, whereupon the King of Kings urged him not to be stubborn, but to no effect. This was the reason why he was put to death. And now in your case, do not act stubbornly as your father did, but do the will of Shapur, king of kings and lord of all regions. As a result you will be greatly honoured, and whatever you ask for your own comfort will be granted by the king.'

The glorious Martha replied, 'May King Shapur live, may his graciousness never leave him, may his compassion continue; may his graciousness be preserved by his children and his compassion redound to himself and on the people who deserve it. May the life that he loves be accorded to all his brethren and friends, but let all who imitate my father meet the evil death you said my father died. As for me, a wretched handmaid, the dregs of the handmaids of God and of the king, why should any transient honour come to me? I have decided to become the object of abuse like my father for the sake of my father's God, and I will die like him because of my faith in God.'

The Mobed said, 'I am aware of the hardness of heart you Christians have – a people guilty of death. Furthermore, no obedient offspring is likely to come from a rebellious man like Posi. Nevertheless, simply so that I shall not be held guilty before God of not having done my best to warn you, I am taking all this trouble over you in order to bring you over to the religion of the excellent gods who care for this world.'

The holy Martha replied, 'You have said your part, and I have said mine – unless you are quite blind and are paying no attention to the true state of affairs that I have described. Otherwise you have both heard and seen which exhortation is profitable and which harmful; which leads to the kingdom of heaven, which leads to the fire of Gehenna, which provides life, and which engenders death.'

The Mobed went on: 'Listen to me and don't be stubborn and obstinate, following your own perverted wishes in everything. Instead, seeing that you are set on not giving up your religion, act as you like, but do this one thing only, and you shall live and not die: you are a young girl, and a very pretty one – find a husband and get married, have sons and daughters, and don't hold on to the disgusting pretext of the 'covenant'.'

The wise virgin Martha replied, 'If a virgin is betrothed to a man, does the natural law order that someone else should come along, attack her fiancé, and snatch away this girl who has already been betrothed? Or does it say that such a virgin should give herself up to marry a man who is not her fiancé?'

'No,' answered the Mobed.

The betrothed of Christ, Martha, then said, 'So how can your authority order me to marry a man to whom I am not betrothed when I am already betrothed to someone else?'

To which the Mobed said, 'Are you really betrothed, then?' And the blessed Martha replied, 'I'm in truth betrothed.' 'To whom?' asked the Mobed. 'Is not your honour aware of him?' said the glorious Martha. 'Where is he?' asked the Mobed. Wise in our Lord, she replied, 'He has set out on a long journey on business; but he is close by and is on the point of coming back.' 'What is his name?' inquired the Mobed. 'Jesus,' replied the blessed Martha.

Still not understanding, the Mobed went on, 'What country has he gone to? In which city is he now?' The splendid Marth replied, 'He has gone off to heaven, and he is now in Jerusalem on high.'

At this point the Mobed realised that she was speaking of our Lord Jesus Christ, whereupon he said, 'Didn't I say at the very beginning that this was a stubborn people, not open to persuasion? I will spatter you from head to toe with blood, and then your fiancé can come along to find you turned into dust and rubbish: let him marry you then.'

The courageous Martha replied, 'He will indeed come in glory, riding on the chariot of the clouds, accompanied by the angels and powers of heaven, and all that is appropriate for his wedding feast; he will shake from the dust the bodies of all those who are betrothed to him, wash them in the dew of heaven, anoint them with the oil of gladness, and clothe them in the garment of righteousness, which consists of glorious light; he will place on their fingers rings as the surety of his grace, while on their heads he will put a crown of splendour, that is to say, unfading glory. He will allow them to sit on his chariot – the glorious cloud– and will raise them up into the air bringing them into the heavenly bridal chamber that has been set up in a place not made by hands, but built in Jerusalem the free city on high.'

When the chief Mobed heard this, he left her in his palace and went in to inform the king of everything. The king then gave orders for the impudent girl and daughter of an impudent father to be taken outside the city and immolated on the very spot where her father had been killed.'

Holy Women of the Syrian Orient from the original *Syriac*
by Sebastian P. Brock and Susan Ashbrook Harvey

Zoroastrian Funerary Rites

As the Persians converted to Zoroastrianism, they gradually adopted the practice of exposing the dead, so as not to pollute the earth. By Parthian times it had become the norm for all except kings, whose bodies continued to be embalmed and placed in rock or stone tombs, like the Achaemenids. The practice is described in a history of his own time written by Agathias (c.AD532–c.581), a Byzantine lawyer and man of letters who lived in Constantinople. He begins by recounting how the body of the Persian general, Mermeroes, was disposed of.

Mermeroes' servants took up his body, carried it out of the city and, following their ancestral custom, left it uncovered and unattended to be devoured by dogs and by such loathsome birds as feed on carrion.

Persian funeral customs regularly take this form. Thus the flesh is picked away leaving the bones bare to rot scattered and dismembered on the plains. It is strictly forbidden for them to put their dead into any kind of tomb or coffin or even to cover them over with earth. And if the birds do not swiftly swoop down on a man's body or the dogs do not straightaway come to tear it up they think that he must have been utterly vicious and depraved and that his soul has become a sink of iniquity reserved as the exclusive haunt of the foul fiend. In that case his relations mourn still more bitterly for him since they consider him to be completely dead and to have no share in a better hereafter. But if a man is devoured on the instant then they bless him for his good fortune and they regard his soul with awe and wonder, considering it to be the most virtuous and god-like and destined to ascend to the place of bliss. If any of the rank and file happen to be afflicted with some grievous ailment when out on active service somewhere, they are taken away while still alive and lucid. When a man is subjected to this type of exposure a piece of bread, some water and a stick are set down beside him. As long as he is able to eat, and still has some small residue of strength left him he wards off attacking animals with the stick and scares away the prospective feasters. But if without actually destroying him the illness reduces him to a state where he can no longer move his arms, then the animals devour the poor wretch when he is not properly dead and is only just beginning to breathe his last, thus robbing him in advance of any possible hope of recovery.

There have in fact been many instances of people who recovered and returned home, presenting an appearance of deathly pallor and emaciation which was enough to frighten the life out of anyone who should chance to fall in with them and looking for all the world like characters on the tragic stage arriving from 'the portals of darkness'. If anyone returns in these circumstances everybody shuns him and treats him as a pariah since he is regarded as polluted and still belonging to the netherworld. Nor is he permitted to resume his place in society until the stain of pollution incurred by the imminence of death has been purged by the Magi in order that he may, as it were, embrace life anew.

From *The Histories* by Agathias
translated by Joseph D. Frendo

A Learned Barbarian? Impossible!

Agathias's work of contemporary history is notable for including a brief history of Sasanid Persia, for which he was able to draw on information from the Persian Royal Annals which were kept in the Sasanid capital of Ctesiphon on the Tigris. Agathias says that the Persian officials acceded to his request to allow a professional interpreter by the name of Sergius, who had occasion to visit Ctesiphon, to inspect the relevant documents on his behalf because they thought 'that it would enhance the prestige of their kings if the Romans too were to learn what kind of men they were'. But somewhat churlishly Agathias repaid this helpfulness on the part of the Persians with an intemperate attack on the reputation enjoyed by the Persian King of the time, Khosrow (or Chosroes) I (AD531–579) as a man of culture and learning who was well versed in Greek philosophy. In the passage that follows, the Stagirite whom Agathias refers to is the Greek philisopher Aristotle, the Paeanian orator is the great Athenian advocate and orator Demosthenes, and the son of Olorus is the Greek historian Thucydides.

Chosroes has been praised and admired quite beyond his deserts not just by the Persians but even by some Romans. He is in fact credited with being a lover of literature and a profound student of philosophy and somebody is supposed to have translated the works of Greek literature into Persian for him. It is rumoured moreover that he has absorbed the whole of the Stagirite more thoroughly than the Paeanian orator absorbed the works of the son of Olorus, that his mind is filled with the doctrines of Plato the son of Ariston and that not even the *Timaeus* (this, and the names that follow, are all works by Plato) bristling as it does with geometrical theorems and scientific speculations, would elude his grasp, nor for that matter the Phaedo or the Gorgias, or any other of the polished and more intricate dialogues, as for instance the Parmenides.

Personally, I could never bring myself to believe that he was so remarkably well-educated and intellectually brilliant. How could the purity and nobility of those time-honoured writings with all their exactitude and felicity of expression be preserved in an uncouth and uncivilized tongue? Moreover one may well ask how a man brought up from childhood in the glamorous atmosphere of the court, surrounded by pomp and adulation, and then succeeding to an utterly barbarous style of life of which battles and manoeuvres were a regular feature, could hope to achieve any real competence or proficiency in this branch of learning.

Yet if people were to praise him on the score that, in spite of being a Persian and in spite of being weighed down with the cares of empire and the responsibility of governing so many nations, he still showed some interest in acquiring a smattering of literature and liked to be considered something of a dilettante, in that case I should add my own voice to the general chorus and should not hesitate to regard him as superior to the rest of the barbarians. But those who attribute exceptional wisdom to him and call him the rival of all philosophers that have ever lived, claiming that, in the manner of the Peripatetic definition of superior culture, he has mastered every branch of science, thereby disclose the unreality of their pretensions and make it plain to all that they are merely echoing the ill-considered opinions of the crowd.

From *The Histories* by Agathias
translated by Joseph D. Frendo

2

The Lost Country

*W*ITH THE OVERTHROW *of the Sasanid Empire by the Muslim Arabs in the mid-seventh century, Persia ceased to exist as an independent state for approximately eight hundred and fifty years. During this time, it was either fragmented, with various states ruling parts of its territory, or else it was incorporated into a larger non-Persian empire. But it was during this period that the culture and demography of Persia, as it is today, was formed. A new Persian language emerged after the Arab conquest, using the Arabic script and with a large Arabic vocabulary. This resulted in a golden age of Persian literature, especially in the field of poetry. It was also a period that saw successive waves of invasions. The Arabs were followed by the Saljuq Turks and the hugely destructive invasions of the Mongols and Tamerlane. This added a large Turkish-speaking component to the population. As the newcomers were tribal nomads, it also greatly increased the proportion of nomadic or semi-nomadic tribespeople. This became a defining and potentially destabilising feature of Persia until well into the twentieth century.*

The first two centuries after the Arab conquest have been called 'the two centuries of silence', because there are no texts in Persian from this period and it is as if the Persian voice had been silenced. The country was very much under Arab domination and was ruled by an Arab Muslim caliphate, first from Medina in Arabia, then from Damascus in Syria, and lastly from Baghdad in Iraq. Arabic was the language of official communication and cultural expression, as well as the language of the new Muslim religion. Educated Persians quickly mastered Arabic and were soon making major contributions to Arabic language culture in many fields of learning. During these first two centuries most of the Persian population was converted to Islam, though Zoroastrian, Christian and Jewish communities continued to exist, subject to the payment of a special tax and certain restrictions. The Zoroastrians were less well treated than the other two communities, as a result of which some emigrated to India to form the Parsee community there. Zoroastrian festivals and customs, however, survived – most notably the *No Ruz* or New Year festival. The memory of the Sasanid kings and of Persia's legendary past also remained alive.

The Islamicisation of Persia included the emergence of scattered communities of Shiites who denied the legitimacy of the Sunni caliphate. They believed that God had entrusted the guidance of the Muslim community after the death of the Prophet Muhammad to his cousin Ali and his designated male descendants by his wife, Fatima, the Prophet's daughter. These early communities were formed by Arab Shiites fleeing persecution in Iraq. Some of them settled in the city of Qom in western Persia, which eventually became a wholly Shiite city and a major theological centre. A number of other cities came to have significant Shiite minorities. In the ninth century large parts of the Caspian region were converted, again by refugees from Iraq, to a politically militant form of Shiism, known as Zaydi Shiism. But overall Persia remained a predominantly Sunni country until the Safavids imposed Shiism in the sixteenth century.

The caliphate began to come under Persian influence, however, following a revolutionary movement in the middle of the eighth century, which brought to power a new dynasty of Arab caliphs descended from an uncle of the Prophet, and named the Abbasids after him. The early Abbasid caliphs depended largely on Persian troops, because the revolution had begun in the north-eastern Persian province of Khurasan. The transfer of the seat of the caliphate from Damascus to Baghdad also placed it firmly within the Persian cultural orbit. Persian influence was now felt in the bureaucracy, with the infiltration of Persian officials at the highest levels. In time, the caliphs themselves came to resemble the ancient Persian kings, behaving as autocrats, claiming to rule by divine right and surrounded by a magnificent court, rich in ceremony.

During the ninth century, however, the power of the caliphs declined as they fell under the domination of Turkish slave troops they had brought in to free them from dependence on their Persian soldiers. Outlying parts of their Empire began to break away, and in Persia a succession of independent dynasties emerged, owing at best only nominal allegiance to the caliph. The most important of these in terms of its lasting influence was that of the Samanids, who came from a Persian gentry background and ruled Khurasan and Transoxania[1] from their capital of Bukhara for the whole of the tenth century. The Samanids helped to forge a new Perso-Islamic culture, based on a revival of the Persian language which had been transformed under the influence of Arabic from the Middle Persian of the Sasanid era into the Persian or *Farsi* spoken today. They patronised Persian-language poets, and their rule saw the first flowering of the Classical Persian poetry that is one of the glories of Persian culture. One of these poets was Firdausi, who began writing his national epic, the *Shah-nama* (*Book of Kings*), which did more than anything to shape and perpetuate a Persian national consciousness. The Samanids also encouraged the translation into Persian of religious and historical works written in Arabic. They were supplanted in Khurasan at the end of the tenth century by a Turkish dynasty, the Ghaznavids, who had migrated from Central Asia and established themselves at Ghazna in eastern Afghanistan. Despite their Turkish origins, the Ghaznavids too patronised Persian-language poets and writers. Firdausi completed his great work at the Ghaznavid court, though he felt he was not adequately rewarded for his some fifty thousand couplets.

While the Samanids and the Ghaznavids were promoting a Perso-Islamic culture in the east, a Persian dynasty in the west, that of the Buyids was seeking to revive the ancient Persian monarchy. The Buyids, a Zaydi Shiite dynasty from the Caspian region, carved out an empire that at its height covered most of Persia outside Khurasan, together with Iraq and the seat of the Sunni caliphate, Baghdad. They did not attempt to remove the Caliph and impose

[1] The land between the Oxus and Jaxartes Rivers in Central Asia. Its principal cities are Bukhara and Samarqand (Samarkand).

Shiism, though they did promote Shiite schools, festivals and ceremonies. They also claimed descent from the Sasanids and adopted the ancient Persian title of 'King of Kings'.

Both the Ghaznavids and the Buyids were swept aside by the Saljuqs, a Turkish tribe that headed a large migration of Turkish nomads from Transoxania into Persia in 1035. While still in Transoxania, they had been converted by wandering dervishes from their original Shamanism to Sunni Islam. By around 1059, a Saljuq dynasty was ruling over Persia and Iraq and had established its capital in Isfahan, in west central Persia. The beautiful Friday Mosque in Isfahan dates from the Saljuq period. Like the kings of ancient Persia, the Saljuqs claimed to rule by divine right, describing themselves as 'the shadow of God on earth'. They were given the title of Sultan by the Caliph, whom they rescued from Buyid Shiite domination, and became something like the secular arm of the caliphate, dedicated to upholding Sunni orthodoxy. Saljuq power enabled the caliphate to withstand a serious challenge at this time from a rival Shiite caliphate – that of the Fatimids in Egypt. One form this took was a vigorous propaganda campaign by Fatimid missionaries. Among these missionaries was a Persian by the name of Hasan-e Sabbah who adopted a new tactic of targeted assassinations aimed at the Sunni establishment which were carried out by his devoted followers from the castle of Alamut high in the Elburz Mountains of northern Persia. His organisation, which soon broke with the Fatimids and which he extended into Syria, came to be known in Europe as 'The Order of the Assassins'. The mathematician, astronomer and poet, Omar Khayyam, was a contemporary of Hasan-e Sabbah, and legend has it that the two were fellow-students.

The arrival of the Saljuqs brought a fundamental change in the demography of Persia, by introducing a significant Turkish element into the population for the first time. Turkish tribesmen continued to move into Persia from Transoxania throughout the Saljuq period. They were also the first of a long line of Turkish or Mongol dynasties which would rule Persia almost continually until the coming of the Pahlavi dynasty in 1925. Turkish 'men of the sword' would generally provide the ruling house and its main military force, while the Persian 'men of the pen' would continue to run the bureaucracy.

The Saljuq sultanate went into a decline in the twelfth century and was eventually replaced in the east by the kingdom of the Khwarazmshahs, which is really only memorable for the fact that by slaughtering a caravan of merchants from Mongolia and then killing a Mongol ambassador, they precipitated the invasion of Persia by Chingiz Khan (Ghengis Khan) in 1219. This first onslaught lasted until 1223 and was confined to Transoxania and Khurasan, but in the course of it whole cities were razed to the ground and entire populations wiped out. The second attack came some thirty years later when Chingiz's grandson, Hülegü, captured and destroyed the seemingly impregnable castles of the Assassins, before marching on Baghdad and sacking the city, killing the caliph and much of the population. He then invaded Syria and Palestine, before being halted by the Mamluk regime in Egypt. This marked the limit of the Mongol advance.

Hülegü founded a Mongol kingdom centred on Persia, which he and his successors ruled until 1335. They were known as Il-Khans or 'subject khans', meaning that they were subject to the Great Khan in China, although in practice this subordination was purely nominal. They had different capitals at different times, but one of these was Tabriz in the north-western province of Azerbaijan, which until the middle of the sixteenth century came to be regarded as the natural capital of Persia.

The Mongols arrived as Shamanists, and toyed with Christianity and Buddhism before finally converting to Sunni Islam. They were tolerant in religious matters and tended to favour Islamic mystics, known as Sufis. These were increasing in numbers and becoming organised into orders with their own convent buildings where the 'master' instructed his disciples. A new Sufi order founded during the Mongol period was the Safavid order, which was to change the course of Persian history. The religious tolerance of the Il-Khans, combined with the end of the caliphate, created a climate favourable to the spread of the sort of unorthodox beliefs that would later be espoused by the Safavids.

The nomadic tribesmen who arrived in Persia in the Mongol armies were mainly Turks, not Mongols. They came in far greater numbers than under the Saljuqs, significantly increasing the proportion of tribal nomads in the country and forcing many peasants to flee their lands, thereby reducing the area under cultivation.

It was during the Mongol period that direct contacts between Persia and Europe were resumed. The Mongol invasions came at the time of the Crusades and the reported Christian sympathies of the new Mongol rulers of Persia raised hopes in Europe that they might prove to be the fulfilment of the legend of Prester John, the Christian emperor of Asia, who would help to defeat the Muslims. There were exchanges of ambassadors and talk – but nothing more – of an alliance against the Muslim Mamluk rulers of Egypt. The well-ordered Mongol Empire which stretched from China to the borders of Syria also attracted European merchants, like the family of Marco Polo. Marco and his father and uncle, who were Venetian merchants, travelled through Persia in 1272, on their way to the Court of the Great Khan – Coleridge's *Kubla Khan* – in his capital of Xanadu or Shang-Tu.

Less than half a century after the disintegration of the Il-Khanid state, Persia was subjected to a fresh invasion from beyond the Oxus River by another Mongol leader, Tamerlane. Between 1380 and 1396 Tamerlane invaded Persia three times, leaving a trail of devastation in his wake that was at least as destructive as that of the earlier Mongol invaders. He punished rebellions with acts of savage cruelty, burying thousands of men alive in the walls of new fortresses and erecting huge pyramids of human heads. His only constructive work was his capital of Samarqand (Samarkand) in Transoxania, which he filled with the loot of his conquests and embellished with magnificent new buildings, erected and adorned in large part by captive craftsmen. It is striking that the three greatest poets of Persia – Rumi (1207–1273), Saadi (c.1213–1292), and Hafez (c.1326–c.1390) – lived through these terrifying times. They had, however, the good fortune to be sheltered from the carnage, Saadi and Hafiz in Shiraz in the south of Persia, and Rumi by migrating from Khurasan to Konya in central Anatolia shortly before the Mongol onslaught.

Tamerlane died in 1405 at the age of seventy as he was setting out to conquer China. After a period of internecine fighting, his Empire was divided between two of his sons. The western half was soon lost to a Turkoman tribal confederation, known as the Black Sheep, which ruled Iraq and western Persia from its capital in Tabriz. The eastern half enjoyed a period of stability under Tamerlane's youngest son, Shah Rukh, who moved his capital to Herat in Khurasan, leaving his own son, Ulugh Beg, to govern Transoxania. Both were cultured men, who preferred to pursue their literary, artistic and scientific interests in peace. But after Shah Rukh's death in 1447, there was further turmoil, which resulted in the separation of Transoxania from Khurasan. While Transoxania broke up into a number of petty states ruled by rival Timurid princes, Khurasan enjoyed an Indian summer under Tamerlane's great-grandson, Sultan Husayn Bayqara (1470–1506), who was a great patron of the arts. His court at Herat is associated not only with some outstanding writers and poets, but also with a famous and influential school of miniature painting.

Meanwhile in western Persia another Turkoman confederation, that of the White Sheep, had established itself in Tabriz after overthrowing its Black Sheep rival in 1467. The White Sheep leader, Uzun Hasan, assumed the title of 'King of Iran'. He also forged an alliance, sealed by marriage, with the Sheikhs of the Safavid Sufi order, which had changed its nature dramatically since its foundation in Mongol times. It had acquired a military force of Turkoman tribesmen and adopted an extreme form of Shiism. These tribesmen, who were called 'Red-Heads' because of their distinctive headgear, worshipped their Safavid Sufi Sheikh as a divine incarnation of the first Shiite Imam, Ali, and as the Mahdi, the saviour-figure of Shiism. After the death of Uzun Hasan in 1478, the White Sheep dynasty began to decline and rival princes became engaged in a long-drawn-out power struggle. Relations with the Safavids deteriorated with the family being imprisoned for a time and then forced to take refuge with a Shiite ruler in the forests of Gilan, by the Caspian. From there the twelve-year-old Safavid Sheikh, Ismail, set out with a small band of followers in the summer of 1499. The following year he rallied his Turkoman tribesmen and in the spring of 1501 he defeated a White Sheep army on the banks of the River Araxes in Azerbaijan. Shortly afterwards he entered Tabriz where he crowned himself

Shah of Iran and declared Shiism the official religion of his new state. Over the next ten years he conquered the whole of Persia, restoring its old north-eastern frontier on the Oxus River and, in the west, capturing Baghdad and confronting the Ottomans in Anatolia.

Europe, meanwhile, was facing a growing threat from the Ottomans, who overran much of the Balkans in the latter part of the fourteenth century and captured Constantinople in 1453. This gave a new impetus to contacts between Europe and Persia, which had been brought to a temporary halt by the collapse of the Mongol state and the power struggle that followed. Both sides had an interest in cooperating against their common enemy, the Ottomans, but in practice this proved difficult to achieve. A number of European powers exchanged embassies with the new Mongol conqueror, Tamerlane, who inflicted a crushing defeat on the Ottomans at the battle of Ankara in July 1402. But the Ottomans soon recovered and, in the second half of the century, there was an exchange of envoys between Venice and Uzun Hasan, the ruler of the Turkoman White Sheep confederation, who was challenging the Ottomans from the east. Venice shipped badly needed guns to Uzun Hasan, but they arrived too late to save him from defeat by the Ottomans in August 1473. Attempts to build an anti-Ottoman alliance between European powers and Persia would go on.

Marco Polo in Persia

The Venetian, Marco Polo (1254–1324), passed through Persia with his father and his uncle on their way to and from China. Both on the way out, in 1272, and on the way back, in 1293, they passed through the port of Hormuz (or Hormos) on the Persian Gulf. It was situated on the Persian coast, just inside the mouth of the Gulf, and was ruled by an Arab dynasty which variously owed allegiance to the Il-Khanid governors of the Persian provinces of Kerman and Fars. Marco Polo's description of Hormuz is of great interest for what he has to say about its trade, about the local method of shipbuilding – something he knew a thing or two about, being a Venetian – and about the effects of the scorching, sand-filled wind that blasts the region during the summer months. A few years after Marco Polo left Hormuz for the second time, repeated attacks by Mongol tribesmen caused its ruler to transfer the entire population to a small island off the coast, where a town and port were built and named New Hormuz. Before long it was known simply as Hormuz and became the main trading entrepôt in the Gulf, famed in Europe for its legendary wealth. The text of Marco Polo's travels sometimes refers to him in the third person, because it was written down by a Pisan writer by the name of Rusticiano, to whom Marco Polo told his stories when they were both temporarily imprisoned in Genoa – Marco having been taken prisoner in a sea battle in which he commanded a Venetian galley. This was in 1298, three years after he returned from his travels.

The plain of which we have spoken extends in a southerly direction for five days' journey, and then you come to another descent some twenty miles in length where the road is very bad and full of peril, for there are many robbers and bad characters about. When you have got to the foot of this descent you find another beautiful plain called the Plain of Formosa.[2] This extends for two days' journey; and you find in it fine streams of water with plenty of date-palms and other fruit-trees. There are also many beautiful birds, francolins, popinjays, and other kinds such as we have none of in our country. When you have ridden these two days you come to the Ocean Sea, and on the shore you find a city called Hormos. Merchants come thither from India, with ships loaded with spicery and precious stones, pearls, cloths of silk and gold, elephants' teeth, and many other wares, which they sell to the merchants of Hormos, and which these in turn carry all over the world to dispose of again. In fact, 'tis a city of immense trade. There are plenty of towns and villages under it, but it is the capital. The King is called Ruomedam Ahomet. It is a very sickly place, and the heat of the sun is tremendous. If any foreign merchant dies there, the King takes all his property.

[2] A corruption of Harmuza.

In this country they make a wine of dates mixt with spices, which is very good. When any one not used to it first drinks this wine, it causes repeated and violent purging, but afterwards he is all the better for it, and gets fat upon it. The people never eat meat and wheaten bread except when they are ill, and if they take such food when they are in health it makes them ill. Their food when in health consists of dates and salt-fish (tunny (tuna), to wit) and onions, and this kind of diet they maintain in order to preserve their health.

Their ships are wretched affairs, and many of them get lost; for they have no iron fastenings, and are only stitched together with twine made from the husk of the Indian nut. They beat this husk until it becomes like horse-hair, and from that they spin twine, and with this stitch the planks of the ships together. It keeps well, and is not corroded by the sea-water, but it will not stand well in a storm. The ships are not pitched, but are rubbed with fish oil. They have one mast, one sail, and one rudder, and have no deck, but only a cover spread over the cargo when loaded. This cover consists of hides, and on the top of these hides they put the horses which they take to India for sale.[3] They have no iron to make nails of, and for this reason they use only wooden trenails in their shipbuilding, and then stitch the planks with twine as I have told you. Hence 'tis a perilous business to go a voyage in one of these ships, and many of them are lost, for in that Sea of India the storms are often terrible.

The people are black, and are worshippers of Mahommet. The residents avoid living in the cities, for the heat in summer is so great that it would kill them. Hence they go out (to sleep) at their gardens in the country, where there are streams and plenty of water. For all that they would not escape but for one thing that I will mention. The fact is, you see, that in summer a wind often blows across the sands which encompass the plain, so intolerably hot that it would kill everybody, were it not that when they perceive that wind coming they plunge into water up to the neck, and so abide until the wind have ceased. And to prove the great heat of this wind, Messer Mark related a case that befel when he was there. The Lord of

[3] Persian horses were always in great demand in India. In the seventeenth century the Safavid shahs limited the number that could be exported because of their military importance.

Hormos, not having paid his tribute to the King of Kerman,[4] the latter resolved to claim it at the time when the people of Hormos were residing away from the city. So he caused a force of sixteen hundred horse and five thousand foot to be got ready, and sent them by the route of Reobarles[5] to take the others by surprise. Now, it happened one day that through the fault of their guide they were not able to reach the place appointed for their night's halt, and were obliged to bivouac in a wilderness not far from Hormos. In the morning as they were starting on their march they were caught by that wind, and every man of them was suffocated, so that not one survived to carry the tidings to their Lord. When the people of Hormos heard of this they went forth to bury the bodies lest they should breed a pestilence. But when they laid hold of them by the arms to drag them to the pits, the bodies proved to be so baked, as it were by that tremendous heat, that the arms parted from the trunks, and in the end the people had to dig graves hard by each where it lay, and so cast them in.

The people sow their wheat and barley and other corn in the month of November, and reap it in the month of March. The dates are not gathered till May, but otherwise there is no grass nor any other green thing, for the excessive heat dries up everything.

When any one dies they make great business of the mourning, for women mourn their husbands four years. During that time they mourn at least once a day, gathering together their kinsfolk and friends and neighbours for the purpose, and making a great weeping and wailing. And they have women who are mourners by trade, and do it for hire.

Now we will quit this country. I shall not, however, now go on to tell you about India; but when time and place shall suit we shall come round from the north and tell you about it. For the present, let us return by another road to the aforesaid city of Kerman, for we cannot get at those countries that I wish to tell you about except through that city.

I should tell you first, however, that King Ruomedam Ahomet of

[4] The province and city of Kerman are in south-east Persia, to the north of Hormuz. The 'King of Kerman' must have been a semi-independent governor of the Mongol Il-Khans, who ruled Persia.
[5] The reference is to a district called Rudbar.

Hormos, which we are leaving, is a liegeman of the King of Kerman.

On the road by which we return from Hormos to Kerman you meet with some very fine plains, and you also find many natural hot baths; you find plenty of partridges on the road; and there are towns where victual is cheap and abundant, with quantities of dates and other fruits. The wheaten bread, however, is so bitter, owing to the bitterness of the water, that no one can eat it who is not used to it. The baths that I mentioned have excellent virtues; they cure the itch and several other diseases.

From *The Book of Ser Marco Polo, the Venetian*
translated and edited by Colonel Henry Yule, CB

Marco Polo Hears a Tale of the Assassins

Marco Polo was in Persia only sixteen years after the invading Mongols under Hülegü captured and destroyed the castles of the Assassins in the Elburz Mountains of northern Persia. The Assassins were Ismaili Shiites who waged a campaign of targeted assassination against the ruling Sunni establishment, first in Persia, and later in Syria as well. Marco Polo's account of how they were persuaded to carry out their suicidal missions by being drugged and given a material taste of Paradise seems to have had no foundation in fact and to have been put about by their enemies. But it soon became a firm part of the European legend of the Assassins. Marco Polo is also incorrect in calling the founder of the sect in Persia, whose name was Hasan-e Sabbah and not Aloadin, 'The Old Man of the Mountain'. That title belongs properly to the most famous leader of the Syrian branch of the sect, Sinan, and seems to have been coined by the Crusaders.

Mulehet[6] is a country in which the Old Man of the Mountain dwelt

[6] This seems to be a corruption of Alamut, the principal Assassin fortress in Persia in the Elburz Mountains, about thirty-seven miles (sixty kilometres) north of Qazvin. Marco Polo may also have confused it with 'mulhed', the Arabic word meaning heretic, which was a label frequently attached to the followers of Hasan-e Sabbah by their Muslim enemies.

in former days; and the name means Place of the Aram. I will tell you his whole story as related by Messer Marco Polo, who heard it from several natives of that region.

The Old Man was called in their language Aloadin. He had caused a certain valley between two mountains to be enclosed, and had turned it into a garden, the largest and most beautiful that ever was seen, filled with every variety of fruit. In it were erected pavilions and palaces the most elegant that can be imagined, all covered with gilding and exquisite painting. And there were runnels too, flowing freely with wine and milk and honey and water; and numbers of ladies and of the most beautiful damsels in the world, who could play on all manner of instruments, and sung most sweetly, and danced in a manner that was charming to behold. For the Old Man desired to make his people believe that this was actually Paradise. So he had fashioned it after the description that Mahommet gave of his Paradise, to wit, that it should be a beautiful garden running with conduits of wine and milk and honey and water, and full of lovely women for the delectation of all its inmates. And sure enough the Saracens of those parts believed that it *was* Paradise.

Now no man was allowed to enter the garden save those whom he intended to be his Ashishin.[7] There was a fortress at the entrance to the garden, strong enough to resist all the world, and there was no other way to get in. He kept at his court a number of the youths of the country, from twelve to twenty years of age, such as had a taste for soldiering, and to these he used to tell tales about Paradise, just as Mahommet had been wont to do, and they believed in him just as the Saracens believed in Mahommet. Then he would introduce them into his garden, some four, or six, or ten at a time, having first made them drink a certain potion which cast them into a deep sleep, and then causing them to be lifted and carried in. So when they awoke, they found themselves in the garden.

When therefore they awoke, and found themselves in a place so

[7] The Arabic word 'hashishi' (one who takes hashish) seems to have been a term of abuse used against the Syrian branch of the sect and to have been the origin of the term 'assassin'.

charming, they deemed that it was Paradise in very truth. And the ladies and damsels dallied with them to their hearts' content, so that they had what young men would have; and with their own good will they never would have quitted the place.

Now this Prince whom we call the Old One kept his court in grand and noble style, and made those simple hill-folks about him believe firmly that he was a great Prophet. And when he wanted one of his Ashishin to send on any mission, he would cause that potion whereof I spoke to be given to one of the youths in the garden, and then had him carried into his palace. So when the young man awoke, he found himself in the castle, and no longer in that Paradise; whereat he was not over well pleased. He was then conducted to the Old Man's presence, and bowed before him with great veneration as believing himself to be in the presence of a true Prophet. The Prince would then ask whence he came, and he would reply that he came from Paradise! And that it was exactly such as Mahommet had described it in the Law. This of course gave the others who stood by, and who had not been admitted, the greatest desire to enter therein.

So when the Old Man would have any Prince slain, he would say to such a youth: 'Go thou and slay So and So; and when thou returnest my angels shall bear thee into Paradise. And shouldst thou die, natheless even so will I send my angels to carry thee back into Paradise.' So he caused them to believe; and thus there was no order of his that they would not affront any peril to execute, for the great desire they had to get back into that Paradise of his. And in this manner the Old One got his people to murder any one whom he desired to get rid of. Thus, too, the great dread that he inspired all princes withal, made them become his tributaries in order that he might abide at peace and amity with them. I should also tell you that the Old Man had certain others under him, who copied his proceedings and acted exactly in the same manner. One of these was sent into the territory of Damascus, and the other into Curdistan.

Now it came to pass, in the year of Christ's Incarnation, 1252, that Alaü,[8] Lord of the Tartars of the Levant, heard tell of these great

---

[8] Hülagü (1217–1265), the grandson of Chingiz Khan (Ghengis Khan) and founder of the Mongol Il-Khan dynasty of Persia.

crimes of the Old Man, and resolved to make an end of him. So he took and sent one of his barons with a great army to that castle, and they besieged it for three years, but they could not take it, so strong was it. And indeed if they had had food within it never would have been taken. But after being besieged those three years they ran short of victual, and were taken. The Old Man[9] was put to death with all his men and the castle with its garden of Paradise was levelled with the ground. And since that time he has had no successor; and there was an end to all his villanies.

From *The Book of Ser Marco Polo, the Venetian*
translated and edited by Colonel Henry Yule, CB

Persia through Arab Eyes

Ibn Battuta (1304–1377) was one of the great travellers of the medieval world. An Arab from Morocco, he visited the cities of Isfahan, in west central Persia, and Shiraz, further to the south, in 1326. On his way home from China in 1347 he again spent some time in Shiraz, but only passed through Isfahan, which had lost much of the splendour and prosperity it had enjoyed as the capital of the Saljuq Empire. Isfahan had suffered not only from the Mongol invasion, with many of its inhabitants being massacred, but also, as Ibn Battuta makes clear, from endemic sectarian strife between Sunnis and Shiites. When Ibn Battuta arrived there in 1326 it was just beginning to make something of a recovery. Some of the things he remarks on, like the large number of pigeon towers which produced fertiliser from the pigeon droppings, and the excellence of its fruits, have been enduring features of the city. However, the people of Isfahan were later to acquire quite the reverse reputation to the extravagant generosity he observed, becoming known instead for their parsimony.

[9] Hasan-e Sabbah, founder of Order of the Assassins, died in 1124. His principal fortress surrendered to the Mongols in 1256 and the last of the Assassin leaders in Persia, Rukn al-Din, was murdered by the Mongols later that year.

We travelled on for the whole of this day between orchards and streams and fine villages with many pigeon-towers, and after the time of the '*asr* prayer (afternoon prayer) we reached the city of Isfahan, also called Ispahan, in Persian Iraq.[10] The city of Isfahan is one of the largest and fairest of cities, but it is now in ruins for the greater part, as the result of the feud there between the Sunnis and the Rafidis,[11] which continues to rage between them still to the present day, so that they never cease to fight. It is rich in fruits, among them being apricots of unrivalled quality which they call *qamar al-din*; the people there dry these apricots and preserve them, and their kernels when broken open disclose a sweet almond. Others of its produce are quinces that are unequalled for goodness of taste and size, delicious grapes, and the wonderful watermelons whose like is not to be found in the world, except for the watermelons of Bukhara and Khwarazm. Their rind is green, and the inside is red; they are preserved as dried figs are preserved in the Maghrib, and are exceedingly sweet. When anyone is not used to eating them, they relax him on his first experience of them – and so indeed it happened to me when I ate them at Isfahan.

The people of Isfahan have fine figures and clear white skins tinged with red; their dominant qualities are bravery and pugnacity, together with generosity and a strong spirit of rivalry between them in procuring [luxurious] viands. Some curious stories are told of this last trait in them. Sometimes one of them will invite his friend and will say to him, 'Come along with me for a meal of *nan* and *mast*' – that is bread and curdled milk in their language; then, when his friend goes along with him, he sets before him all sorts of wonderful dishes, with the aim of outdoing him by this [display]. The members of each craft appoint one of their own number as headman over them, whom they call the *kilu*, and so do the leading citizens from outside the ranks of the craftsmen. One company [for example] will be composed of young bachelors. These companies try to outdo one another and

[10] West central Persia was known as 'Persian Iraq', as opposed to Mesopotamia which was 'Arab Iraq'.

[11] Rafidi was a pejorative term used by Sunnis for Shiites.

invite one another to banquets, displaying all the resources at their disposal and making a great show in regard to the dishes and everything else. I was told that one company of them invited another, and cooked their viands with lighted candles, then the second company returned the invitations and cooked their viands with silk.

Shiraz, which the Mongol invaders had left untouched, greatly impressed Ibn Battuta. It was famous for its Muslim saints and scholars, its poets and its gardens. His first visit in 1326 was around the time of the birth of Persia's greatest poet, Hafiz, and only thirty-four years after the death of its second greatest, Saadi, at whose tomb Ibn Battuta paid his respects. The city was then ruled by the founder of the Inju dynasty of Fars, Mahmud Shah, who had been sent there by the Mongol Il-Khan. By the time Ibn Battuta returned in 1347, the Il-Khanid Empire in Persia had collapsed, Mahmud Shah's sons had fought over the succession, and his youngest son, Abu Ishaq, had emerged as the independent ruler of both Shiraz and Isfahan – though six years later he was to be driven out of Shiraz by a new dynasty, the Muzaffarids, and subsequently put to death. Ibn Battuta pays tribute to the qualities of Abu Ishaq, who was a generous patron of scholars and poets.

Shiraz is a city of solid construction and wide range, famous in repute and high in esteem; it has elegant gardens and gushing streams, sumptuous bazaars and handsome thoroughfares; and is densely populated, substantial in its buildings, and admirable in its disposition. Those engaged in each craft occupy the bazaar particular to that craft, no outsiders mixing with them. Its inhabitants are handsome in figure and clean in their dress. In the whole East there is no city except Shiraz which approaches Damascus in the beauty of its bazaars, fruit-gardens and rivers, and in the handsome figures of its inhabitants. It is situated in a plain, surrounded by orchards on all sides, and intersected by five streams; one of these is the stream known as Rukn Abad,[12] the

[12] The Ruknabad was a canal built by the Buyid ruler, Rukn al-Daula, in 949, which was much loved by both Saadi and Hafiz, who sang its praises in their poems.

water of which is sweet, very cold in summer and warm in winter, and gushes out of a fountain on the lower slope of a hill in those parts called al-Qulai'a.

The principal mosque of Shiraz, which is called the 'ancient mosque', is one of the largest of mosques in area and most beautiful in construction. Its court occupies a wide expanse paved with marble, and is washed down every night during the summer heats. The leading inhabitants of the city assemble in this mosque every night and pray the sunset and night prayers in it. On its northern side is a gate known as the Hasan Gate, leading to the fruit market, which is one of the most admirable of bazaars and to which I for my part would give the preference over the bazaar of the Courier Gate at Damascus.

The people of Shiraz are distinguished by piety, sound religion,[13] and purity of manners, especially the women. These wear boots, and when out of doors are swathed in mantles and head-veils, so that no part of them is to be seen, and they are [noted for] their charitable alms and their liberality. One of their strange customs is that they meet in the principal mosque every Monday, Thursday and Friday, to listen to the preacher, sometimes one or two thousand of them, carrying fans in their hands with which they fan themselves on account of the great heat. I have never seen in any land an assembly of women in such numbers...

...The Sultan of Shiraz at the time of my entry was the distinguished King Abu Ishaq, son of Muhammad Shah Inju.[14] His father named him Abu Ishaq after the Shaikh Abu Ishaq al-Kazaruni – God profit us by him! He is one of the best of sultans, handsome in figure and conduct and form, of generous character and good moral qualities, humble in manner yet a man of power, with an army numbering more than fifty thousand Turks and Persians. His most favoured supporters are the people of Isfahan; on the other hand, he places no trust in the people of Shiraz, will not take them into his service, nor admit them to intimacy, nor permit any man of them to carry arms, because they are men of bravery

---

[13] This means they were orthodox Sunnis.
[14] His name was in fact Mahmud Shah.

and great courage, and audacious against kings. Whosoever of them is found with a weapon in his hand is punished. I myself once saw a man being dragged by the *jandars* (that is the police troops) to the *hakim* (chief of police), after they had tied his hands to his neck. I asked what he had done, and was told that there had been found in his hand a bow during the night. So the sultan of whom we are speaking has made a practice of holding down the men of Shiraz and favouring the Isfahanis over them, because he is afraid that they may make an attempt on his life...

...Among the sanctuaries outside Shiraz is the grave of the pious shaikh known as al-Sa'di, who was the greatest poet of his time in the Persian language and sometimes introduced Arabic verses into his compositions. It has [attached to it] a hospice which he had built in that place, a fine building with a beautiful garden inside it, close by the source of the great river known as Rukn Abad. The shaikh had constructed there some small cisterns in marble to wash clothes in. People go out from the city to visit his tomb, and they eat from his table, wash their clothes in that river and return home. I did the same thing at his tomb - may God have mercy upon him.

From *The Travels of Ibn Battuta, 1325–1354*
translated by H. A. R. Gibb

A Spanish Knight at the Court of Tamerlane

A Spanish knight, Ruy Gonzalez de Clavijo, was sent in 1403 by King Henry III of Castile on an embassy to the great Mongol conqueror Tamerlane, or Timur Beg, at his court in Samarqand, in Transoxania. The name Tamerlane is a corruption of the Persian name he acquired of Timur Lang, meaning 'Timur the Lame'. A number of European rulers, as well as the Byzantine Emperor in Constantinople, exchanged embassies with Timur, whom they saw as a useful ally against the Ottomans, but Clavijo is the only one from whom we have an account of his experiences – and a fascinating and invaluable one at that. Calvijo's mission seems to have had no specific purpose beyond satisfying King Henry's curiosity and fostering good relations with the most powerful ruler in Asia and the Middle East. Diplomatic contacts had begun a year earlier when two of King Henry's envoys witnessed Tamerlane's victory over the Ottoman Sultan, Bayazid I, at the battle of Ankara, and were sent home by Tamerlane with rich gifts and an ambassador of his own. Tamerlane's ambassador returned to Samarqand with Clavijo. Among the things that impressed Clavijo as he travelled through Persia in 1404 was the system of post horses, which goes back to the Achaemenids and enabled Tamerlane to communicate rapidly with the most distant parts of his empire.

The Lord (Timur) had horses waiting at the end of each day's journey, at some places one hundred, and at others two hundred; and thus the posts were arranged, on the road, as far as Samarqand. Those whom the Lord sent in any direction, or who were sent to him, went on these horses as fast as they could, day and night. He also had horses placed in deserts, and uninhabited districts, as well as in places that were populous; and he caused great houses to be built in uninhabited places, where horses and provisions were supplied by the nearest towns and villages. Men were appointed to take care of these horses, who were called *anchos*. Thus, when ambassadors or messengers arrive, these men take their horses, take off their saddles, and place them on fresh horses, and one or two of these *anchos* go with them, to take care of the horses; and when they reach another post, they return with these horses. If any of the horses become tired on the road, and they meet another at any place, belonging to any other man, they take it in exchange for the tired horse. The custom is that when any one rides on a road, if he is a lord, or merchant, or ambassador, he must give up his horse for the service of any one who is going to the great lord, and if any one refuses, it costs him his head, for such are the commands of Timour Beg. They even take horses from the troops, and the ambassadors often took horses from the troops, for themselves and their men; and, not only can those, who are going to the great lord, take the horses of such people, but they can even demand them from the son or the wife of the great lord himself. They told the ambassadors that even the eldest son of Timour Beg had been obliged to give up his horse to ambassadors who were going to the great lord.

Not only was this road thus supplied with post horses, but there were messengers on all the roads; so that news could come from every province, in a few days. The lord is better pleased with him who travels a day and night for fifty leagues, and kills two horses, than with him who does the distance in three days.

The great lord, considering that the leagues were very long, in his empire of Samarqand, divided each league into two, and placed small pillars on the roads, to mark each league; ordering all his Zagatays[15] to march twelve, or at least ten of these leagues, in each day's journey. They call these leagues *moles*, because these turrets, which he caused to be built at the end of each league, and these leagues, the length of which he regulated, are in a country which is called Mongolia. The ambassadors travelled in the country, and saw the pillars, and each of the leagues was equal to two leagues of Castile.

In truth, it would scarcely be believed, unless it was actually seen, the distances which these fellows travel, each day and night; for they ride as far as their horses can carry them; and they do not only travel the distance which the lord has ordered, but they sometimes go over fifteen and twenty leagues in a day and night, without any consideration for the toil of their horses. When their horses are knocked up, they kill and sell them, if they are in an inhabited country; but we found many dead horses on the road, which had been killed by hard riding.

From *Narrative of the Embassy of Ruy Gonzalez de Clavijo*
to the Court of Timour at Samarqand, 1403–1406
translated by Clements R. Markham

[15] Chingiz Khan (Genghis Khan) bequeathed a Khanate in Central Asia to his second son, Chaghatai. The Zagatays, or more commonly Chaghatais, were the Mongol tribesmen of the Khanate, which Timur seized control of at the outset of his career. They provided him with his main fighting force.

Clavijo Becomes a Burden on the Peasantry

The unpopular practice, which Clavijo describes here, of making the local inhabitants provide for the needs of a foreign embassy wherever it stopped, continued well into the ninteenth century. Officials travelling on the king's business also had the right to live off the land in this way.

The custom was that at any place where they arrived, whether it was a city or a village, they were supplied with much food, fruits, and fodder for horses, being three times as much as they wanted; and men were made to watch the property and horses of the ambassadors day and night, and if any were missing, the people of the place had to make up the loss. If the people, when they arrived, did not bring what was required, they immediately received such a number of blows, with sticks and whips, that it was wonderful. The chiefs of the place were then sent for, and brought before these knights,[16] the first thing they heard of being about blows and whippings. They received a wonderful number, and were told that they knew it to be the command of the great Lord that, when ambassadors were on their way to him, they were to receive honour, and everything they required; that the said knights had arrived with these Frank ambassadors, and that they had not found anything ready for them; that the people should pay dearly for such neglect of the orders of the great Lord; and that they would know, in future, what to expect when ambassadors arrived, if everything was not ready.

When they arrived at any city or village, the first thing which the followers of the knights, who accompanied the ambassadors, did, was to ask for the *reis* or chief of the place; and they took the first man they met in the street, and, with many blows, forced him to show them the house of the *reis*. The people who saw them coming, and knew they were troops of Timour Beg, ran

---

[16] Timur's officers who accompanied the embassy from Castile.

away as if the devil was after them, and those who were behind their shops, selling merchandise, shut them up, and fled into their houses; and they said one to another, '*Elchee*', which means ambassador, and that, with the ambassadors, there would come a black day for them.

From *Narrative of the Embassy of Ruy Gonzalez de Clavijo*
to the Court of Timour at Samarqand, 1403–1406
translated by Clements R. Markham

Clavijo meets Tamerlane

Clavijo was received by Tamerlane at his palace outside Samarqand called Dilgusha or The Heart's Delight on Monday September 8th, 1404. He gives us a unique eyewitness description of the great and terrible conqueror in old age; Tamerlane was then about seventy and was to die the following year, shortly after setting off to conquer China. Tamerlane's anger towards the Ming Emperor of China, who had treated his embassies as those of a subordinate vassal, is reflected in his deliberate humiliation of the Chinese envoys now at his court, by ordering them to be placed below Clavijo and his companions. Tamerlane regarded himself as the ruler of the whole world and refers to King Henry III of Castile as his 'son'.

On Monday, the September 8th, the ambassadors departed from the garden where they had been lodged, and went to the city of Samarqand. The road went over a plain covered with gardens, and houses, and markets where they sold many things; and at three in the afternoon they came to a large garden and palace, outside the city, where the lord then was. When they arrived, they dismounted, and entered a building outside; where two knights came to them, and said that they were to give up those presents, which they brought for the lord, to certain men who would lay them before him, for such were the orders of the private *Meerzas*[17]

[17] The civil officials.

76

of the lord; so the ambassadors gave the presents to the two knights. They placed the presents in the arms of men who were to carry them respectfully before the lord, and the ambassador from the Sultan did the same with the presents which he brought. The entrance to this garden was very broad and high, and beautifully adorned with glazed tiles, in blue and gold. At this gate there were many porters, who guarded it, with maces in their hands. When the ambassadors entered, they came to six elephants, with wooden castles on their backs, each of which had two banners, and there were men on the top of them. The ambassadors went forward, and found the men, who had the presents well arranged on their arms, and they advanced with them in company with the two knights, who held them by the arm pits, and the ambassador whom Timour Beg had sent to the King of Castile was with them; and those who saw him, laughed at him, because he was dressed in the costume and fashion of Castile.

They conducted them to an aged knight, who was seated in an ante-room. He was a son of the sister of Timour Beg, and they bowed reverentially before him. They were then brought before some small boys, grandsons of the Lord, who were seated in a chamber, and they also bowed before them. Here the letter, which they brought from the King to Timour Beg, was demanded, and they presented it to one of these boys, who took it. He was a son of Miran Meerza, the eldest son of the Lord; who desired that the ambassadors should be brought before him.

Timour Beg was seated in a portal, in front of the entrance of a beautiful palace; and he was sitting on the ground. Before him there was a fountain, which threw up the water very high, and in it there were some red apples. The Lord was seated cross-legged, on silken embroidered carpets, amongst round pillows. He was dressed in a robe of silk, with a high white hat on his head, on the top of which there was a spinal ruby, with pearls and precious stones round it.

As soon as the ambassadors saw the Lord, they made a reverential bow, placing the knee on the ground, and crossing the arms on the breast; then they went forward and made another; and then a third, remaining with their knees on the ground. The Lord ordered them to rise and come forward; and the knights, who had held them until then, let them go. Three *Meerzas*, who stood before the Lord, and were his most intimate councillors, named Aoldalmelec Meerza, Borundo Meerza, and Noor Eddin Meerza, then came and took the ambassadors by the arms, and led them forward until they stood together before the Lord. This was done that the Lord might see them better; for his eyesight was bad, being so old that the eyelids had fallen down entirely. He did not give them his hand to kiss, for it was not the custom for any great lord to kiss his hand; but he asked after the King, saying, 'How is my son the King? Is he in good health?' When the ambassadors had answered, Timour Beg turned to the knights who were seated around him, amongst whom were one of the sons of Toktamish, the former Emperor of Tartary,[18] several chiefs of the blood of the late Emperor of Samarqand, and others of the family of the lord himself, and said, 'Behold! here are the ambassadors sent by my son the King of Spain, who is the greatest King of the Franks, and lives at the end of the world. These Franks are truly a great people, and I will give my benediction to the King of Spain, my son. It would have sufficed if he had sent you to me with the letter, and without the presents, so well satisfied am I to hear of his health and prosperous state.'

The letter which the King had sent was held before the Lord, in the hand of his grandson; and the master of theology said, through his interpreter, that no one understood how to read the letter except himself, and that when his highness wished to hear it, he would read it. The Lord then took the letter from the hand of his grandson and opened it, saying that he would hear it presently, and that he would send for the master, and see him in private, when he might read it, and say what he desired.

The ambassadors were then taken to a room, on the right hand side of the place where the lord sat; and the *Meerzas*, who held them by the arms, made them sit below an ambassador, whom the emperor Chayscan,[19] Lord of Cathay, had sent to Timour Beg to demand the

---

[18] Toktamish was a descendant of Chingiz Khan (Genghis Khan) and ruler of the Mongol power known as the Golden Horde which controlled much of present-day Russia and Ukraine. Originally a protégé of Timur's, he turned against his patron, but was eventually decisively defeated by Timur in 1395.

[19] The reference is to the Ming Emperor of China. Timur set off to conquer China in 1405, but only got as far as the Jaxartes River before he died.

yearly tribute which was formerly paid. When the Lord saw the ambassadors seated below the ambassador from the Lord of Cathay, he sent to order that they should sit above him, and he below them. As soon as they were seated, one of the *Meerzas* of the Lord came and said to the ambassador of Cathay, that the Lord had ordered that those who were ambassadors from the King of Spain, his son and friend, should sit above him; and that he who was the ambassador from a thief and a bad man, his enemy, should sit below them; and from that time, at the feasts and entertainments given by the Lord, they always sat in that order. The *Meerza* then ordered the interpreter to tell the ambassadors what the Lord had done for them.

This Emperor of Cathay is called Chayscan, which means nine empires; but the Zagatays called him *Tangus*, which means 'pig emperor'. He is the lord of a great country, and Timour Beg used to pay him tribute, but he refuses to do so now. As soon as these ambassadors, and many others, who had come from distant countries, were seated in order, they brought much meat, boiled, roasted, and dressed in other ways, and roasted horses; and they placed these sheep and horses on very large round pieces of stamped leather. When the Lord called for meat, the people dragged it to him on these pieces of leather, so great was its weight; and as soon as it was within twenty paces of him, the carvers came, who cut it up, kneeling on the leather. They cut it in pieces, and put the pieces in basins of gold and silver, earthenware and glass, and porcelain, which is very scarce and precious. The most honourable piece was a haunch of the horse, with the loin, but without the leg, and they placed parts of it in ten cups of gold and silver. They also cut up the haunches of the sheep. They then put pieces of the tripes of the horses, about the size of a man's fist, into the cups, and entire sheep's heads, and in this way they made many dishes. When they had made sufficient, they placed them in rows. Then some men came with soup, and they sprinkled salt over it, and put a little into each dish, as sauce; and they took some very thin cakes of corn, doubled them four times, and placed one over each cup or basin of meat.

As soon as this was done, the *Meerzas* and courtiers of the lord took these basins, one holding each side, and one helping behind (for a single man could not lift them), and placed them before the Lord, and the ambassadors, and the knights who were there; and the Lord sent the ambassadors two basins, from those which were placed before him, as a mark of favour. When this food was taken away, more was brought; and it is the custom to take this food, which is given to them, to their lodgings, and if they do not do so, it is taken as an affront; and so much of this food was brought, that it was quite wonderful.

Another custom is, that when they take any food from before any of the ambassadors, they give it to their retinue; and so much food was placed before them, that, if they had taken it away, it would have lasted them for half a year. When the roast and boiled meats were done with, they brought meats dressed in various other ways, and balls of forced meat; and after that, there came fruit, melons, grapes, and nectarines; and they gave them drink out of silver and golden jugs, particularly sugar and cream, a pleasant beverage, which they make in the summer time.

When dinner was finished, the men who bore the presents on their arms passed before the Lord, and the same was done with the presents sent by the Sultan of Babylon; and three hundred horses were also brought before the Lord, which had been presented that day. After this was done the ambassadors rose, and a knight was appointed to attend upon them, and to see that they were provided with all that they required. This knight, who was the chief porter of the Lord, conducted the ambassadors, and the ambassadors from the Sultan of Babylon, to a lodging near the place where the Lord abode, in which there was a garden, and plenty of water.

When the ambassadors took leave of the Lord, he caused the presents, which the King had sent, to be brought, and received them with much complacency. He divided the scarlet cloth amongst his women, giving the largest share to his chief wife, named Caño, who was in this garden with him. The other presents, brought by the ambassador from the Sultan, were not received, but returned to the men who had charge of them, who received them, and kept them for three days, when the Lord ordered them to be brought again: because it is the custom not to receive a present until the third day. This house and garden, where the Lord received the ambassadors, was called *dilkoosha*, and in it there were many silken tents, and the Lord remained there until the following Friday, when he went to another garden, where there was a very rich palace, which he had lately ordered to be built, called Bayginar.[20]

> From *Narrative of the Embassy of Ruy Gonzalez de Clavijo
> to the Court of Timour at Samarqand, 1403–1406*
> translated by Clements R. Markham

Clavijo Dines with Tamerlane's Women

Clavijo was awed by the huge quantities of meat and wine consumed at the banquets he attended. He found the women to be no laggards in this respect. Both the drinking of wine and the easy way the women mixed with the men violated Islamic norms but were typical of the way of life of the nomadic tribes, which Tamerlane and his court had not left far behind.

On Thursday, the 9th of October, Hausada, the wife of Miran Meerza, the eldest son of the Lord, gave a great feast, to which she invited the ambassadors, and it was given in the enclosure of tents which was set apart for her use, and which was very beautiful. When the ambassadors came near the tents, they found a very long row of jars of wine placed on the ground. The ambassadors were admitted into a tent, and ordered to sit down at the door, under an awning. The said Hausada, and many other ladies, were seated at the door of a large tent, under an awning.

On this day there was a marriage of one of her relations. Hausada herself was about forty years of age, fair and fat, and before her there were many jars of wine, and of a beverage of which they drink much, called *bosat*, made of cream and sugar.

[20] Bagh-e Chenar or The Garden of the Plane Tree.

There were also many knights and relations of Timour Beg, and jugglers, who were performing before her. When the ambassadors arrived, the ladies were drinking, and the way they drink is this: – an old knight, a relation of the lord, and two small boys, his relations, serve the cup, before Hausada, and before the other ladies, in this manner, – they hold white napkins in their hands, and those who pour out the wine, pour it into small golden cups, which they place on flat plates of gold. Those who serve the wine, then come forward, with the pourers-out behind, and when they have got half way, they touch the ground three times with their right knees. When they come near to the ladies, they take the cups, with their hands wrapped in the white napkins, so that they may not touch the cups, and present them kneeling, to the ladies who are going to drink. When the ladies have taken the cups, those who bring the wine, remain with the flat plates in their hands, and walk backwards, so as not to turn their backs to the ladies. As soon as they are at a little distance, they bend their right knees again, and remain there. When the ladies have finished drinking, the attendants go before them, and the ladies place the cups on the plates which they hold. You must not think that this drinking is of short duration, for it lasts a long time, without eating.

Sometimes, when these attendants are before the ladies, with their cups, the ladies order them to drink, and they kneel down, and drink all that is in the cups, turning them upside down, to show that nothing is left; and on these occasions they describe their prowess in this respect, at which all the ladies laugh.

Caño, the wife of Timour Beg, came to this feast, and sometimes the company drank wine, and at others they drank cream and sugar. After the drinking had lasted a long time, Caño called the ambassadors before her, and gave them to drink with her own hand, and she importuned Ruy Gonzalez for a long time, to make him drink, for she would not believe that he never touched wine. The drinking was such that some of the men fell down drunk before her; and this was considered very jovial, for they think that there can be no pleasure without drunken men.

They also brought great quantities of roasted sheep and horses, and other dressed meats; and they eat all this with much noise, tearing the pieces away from each other, and making game over their food. They also brought rice, cooked in various ways, and tarts made with flour, sugar, and herbs; and besides the meat brought in basins, there were other pieces on skins, for those who wanted them.

From *Narrative of the Embassy of Ruy Gonzalez de Clavijo
to the Court of Timour at Samarqand, 1403–1406*
translated by Clements R. Markham

3
The Splendour of the Safavids

*U*NDER THE SAFAVIDS *(1501–1722), Persia became a state again in its own right and one of the three great empires of the Muslim world – the other two being the Ottoman and Moghul empires. But it fractured the unity of the Muslim world by adopting Shiism. With the Safavids ruling for more than two hundred years, Persia also enjoyed its longest period of political stability since the Arab conquest. It became more prosperous as a result and opened up to the outside world as never before. Relations with Europe became much closer and more intensive, spurred in part by the lure of Persian raw silk which, as an export earner, was the crude oil of its day. Of all the Safavid kings, the one who more than any other left his mark on the country was Shah Abbas I (1588–1629) – the only Muslim ruler of Persia to have been called 'the Great'. The beautiful city of Isfahan, which he made his capital, is his lasting memorial. Later kings lacked his strength and ability, and a Safavid state that had grown weak, with a court that was riven by factionalism, was overthrown not by one of the great powers it had repulsed in the past, like the Ottomans, but instead by an army of Afghan rebels that could hardly believe their luck.*

The Safavids imposed Shiism on a country that was predominantly Sunni. They did this through a combination of violence and proselytising. In the early stages, many thousands of Sunnis who refused to convert were put to death, while many others fled to neighbouring Sunni states, mainly Ottoman Turkey and India. From early on Shiite clerics in the Arab centres of Shiism, like Lebanon, were invited to come and help propagate the new faith. In the course of the sixteenth century many such clerics settled in Persia, although at the start some had reservations because of the unorthodox Shiism espoused by the founder of the Safavid dynasty, Shah Ismail I (1501–1524) and his Turkoman followers, in particular their belief in his divinity. But this was soon played down by Ismail once he was in power and was abandoned altogether by his son, Shah Tahmasp I (1524–1576), who during his long reign was responsible for the main missionary drive. Shah Tahmasp's son, Shah Ismail II (1576–1577), tried to turn the clock back and restore Sunnism, but quickly ran into opposition and abandoned the attempt. By the beginning of the seventeenth century most of Persia had been converted to mainstream Twelver Shiism, so-called because of its belief in a line of twelve divinely-guided Imams descended from Ali, the cousin and son-in-law of the Prophet, through his son, Husayn. But there remained sizeable Sunni minorities in the outlying areas among, for example, the Kurds in the north-west, the Afghans in the east, and the Baluch tribesmen in the south-east.

Warfare with Persia's Sunni neighbours also strengthened Shiite sentiment until it became part of a new sense of national identity. These wars were mainly with the Ottoman Turks in the west and the Uzbeks in the east, the latter being a federation of Turkish and Mongol tribes which drove the descendants of Tamerlane – the Timurids – out of Transoxania.

The problem for the Ottomans was not just the Shiism of the Safavids. It was much more the fact that they presided over a militant Shiite Sufi order which drew much of its support from disaffected Turkoman tribesmen in Ottoman Anatolia. The Ottoman Sultans launched no less than five campaigns against Safavid Persia between 1514 and 1553, when a peace treaty brought a temporary halt to the conflict. They succeeded in driving the Persians out of eastern Anatolia and capturing Baghdad, but had no success in Persia itself, where the Safavid forces adopted a scorched earth policy. Later in the sixteenth century the Ottomans returned to the attack, taking advantage of a Safavid state weakened by factional in-fighting. Their motive now was more an economic one – the desire to control the lucrative trade routes and the valuable silk-producing region around the southern Caspian. They managed to seize a considerable area of the southern Caucasus and north-west Persia. But all this territory, together with Baghdad and much of Iraq, was recovered by the greatest of the Safavid kings, Shah Abbas I (1588–1629), in a series of campaigns between 1603 and 1625. The war continued under Shah Abbas's successor, Shah Safi I (1629–1642), until 1639 when another peace treaty was signed, which held until the fall of the Safavid Empire more than eighty years later. Persia was left in control of eastern Kurdistan, much of the southern Caucasus, including eastern Georgia and a large part of Armenia, but Baghdad and Iraq, which had been lost by Shah Safi, reverted to the Ottomans.

In the course of these wars the Christian countries of Georgia and Armenia were devastated and much of their population deported to Persia. Large numbers were resettled in towns and villages in Persia, including a sizeable Armenian community in Shah Abbas's new capital of Isfahan. Many of the young women ended up in the harems of the Shah and of Persian grandees, while a large number of the boys and young men were made to convert to Islam and trained for employment in various capacities, some at the court as pages or as eunuchs guarding the harem, many more as soldiers in the Safavid army. Although these Christian converts in the service of the Crown were known as 'slaves', they were generally well-treated and many rose to high office in the army and the administration. Christians who were resettled in new communities as merchants, artisans, or farmers didn't even have the status of 'slaves' and were simply treated as a religious minority. The Safavid shahs valued their skills and helped them to get established. This was particularly true of the Armenians in the Isfahan suburb of New Julfa, which was specially created for them and who enjoyed considerable prosperity as merchants, shopkeepers and craftsmen until the fall of the Safavid state. The more successful Julfa merchants became very wealthy indeed and controlled most of Persia's overland export of silk to Europe.

The Safavids often had to defend their eastern province of Khurasan from both plundering raids and full-scale invasions by the Uzbeks in Transoxania. During most of the sixteenth century the Khurasan capital of Herat was the seat of the Safavid crown prince, which was an indication of the importance they attached to holding the province. The Safavids were also periodically at war with the Moghuls in India over possession of Qandahar (Kandahar) in present-day Afghanistan, which changed hands a number of times. But relations with the Moghuls were frequently quite friendly, with the two powers exchanging grandiose embassies calculated to impress. The founder of the Moghul Empire, Babur, was in fact an ally of the Safavids and his son, Humayun, fled from his enemies to Persia where he received help in recovering his throne.

There were intermittent attempts to forge an anti-Safavid alliance, mainly between the Ottomans and the Uzbeks, but sometimes involving the Moghuls as well. These never came to anything. Nor, for that matter, did the attempts by the Safavids and some of the European powers to build a grand alliance against the Ottomans. But these led, for the first time, to extensive diplomatic exchanges between Persia and Europe. There were no permanent embassies, but the Roman Catholic missions which Shah Abbas I permitted to become established in Isfahan were valued by the Persians for their close association with particular European powers – the Augustinians with Spain and Portugal, the Carmelites with the Papacy, and the Capuchins with France. They were later joined by the Jesuits.

Direct trade between Persia and Europe also began under the Safavids. During the sixteenth century the Persian Gulf was controlled by the Portuguese, so the English Muscovy Company opened up a trade route through Russia via the Caspian, but this eventually proved too difficult and had to be abandoned. In 1622, however, the English East India Company was persuaded by Shah Abbas I to help him with its warships – an arm he lacked – to expel the Portuguese from their base on the island of Hormuz at the mouth of the Gulf, which they had captured just over a century earlier. The English then established themselves at the port on the mainland across from Hormuz, which they called Gombroon and the Shah named Bandar-e Abbas, 'the port of Abbas'. They were joined shortly after by the Dutch and much later by the French, while the Portuguese moved to the port of Kong, a little higher up the Gulf. All were given trading privileges and allowed to establish warehouses and offices with accommodation for their staff, both on the Gulf and in Abbas's new capital of Isfahan. Persia's principal European trading partners were the Dutch and English East India Companies, with the Dutch selling spices from Southeast Asia, and the English offering their cloth, which was useful in the cold winters in central and northern Persia. In return, both bought Persian silk, the country's most valuable export item. Although the English were the first to become established, the Dutch were dominant during the Safavid period. Individual European merchants offering high value goods, such as jewellery, also did business in Persia.

During the first half of the sixteenth century there was a further sharp increase in the nomadic population, as Turkoman tribes which had become followers of the Safavid Sufi order moved into Persia from Anatolia and as far afield as northern Syria. The nomadic population, which included the Turkish and Mongol tribes that had arrived earlier, as well as older Persian, Kurdish, Arab and Baluch tribal groupings, now accounted for as much as a third of the total population and remained at this level well into the twentieth century.

The early Safavid state was dominated by these Turkoman tribes and their chiefs or amirs. Although in theory they owed absolute obedience to the Safavid Shah as their Sufi 'master', it was not long before they began putting their tribal interests first. This led to factional in-fighting and civil war when the Shah was weak or a minor. Shah Abbas I was himself placed on the throne in 1587 at the age of sixteen in a coup by a powerful Turkoman amir. But he refused to be a pawn in the hands of the amirs and finally broke their power altogether by creating a large standing army of Georgian, Armenian and Circassian 'slave' troops, thereby greatly reducing the dependence on Turkoman tribal levies. He also deprived the Turkoman amirs of many of their provincial governorships, where they had ruled as petty kings. He had these governorships either brought under the direct control of the central government or put into the hands of Caucasian 'slaves', who had no power base of their own. These measures brought a welcome stability to the state, which was then run by an extensive and efficient bureaucracy headed by the grand vizier.

Shah Tahmasp I had moved the Safavid capital from Tabriz to Qazvin, which was three hundred and twelve miles (five hundred kilometres) away to the south-east, and therefore less exposed to Ottoman attacks. Shah Abbas I moved it further south again to Isfahan, which occupied a more central position. He expanded and rebuilt the city with a magnificence that reflected the power and prestige he had won for Persia and which it had not known since Sasanid times. The prosperity that came with political stability and efficient administration drew merchants from all over Europe and Asia to Isfahan, which became a wonderful, bustling city full of vitality. The Safavid court presented the most magnificent spectacle of all, becoming, as the seventeenth century wore on, ever grander, more lavish and ruled by an elaborate ceremonial. In the view of many European visitors, Isfahan outshone even Constantinople, the capital of the Ottoman Empire.

From the reign of Shah Abbas I until the fall of the Safavid dynasty there was a sizeable European community in Persia and a steady traffic of Europeans travelling back and forth. There were the embassies, the trading companies, the Roman Catholic missions, individual merchants, and travellers of independent means. There were also Europeans seeking employment at the Persian court as craftsmen, artists and soldiers, more particularly artillery officers, since the Persians, unlike the Ottomans, were never very good at handling artillery.

A spate of books about Persia, written by Europeans who had spent time there for one reason or another, were published in Europe during the seventeenth and early eighteenth centuries. Demand for these books was high and they were rapidly translated into other European languages. Europe was looking out beyond itself and its educated classes eagerly devoured books about other cultures. The scope of the subject matter is hugely impressive. It ranges from detailed descriptions of Isfahan, the court and government with all the secular and religious offices, to accounts of the system of education, of popular entertainments and of such refinements as the art of letter-writing. There are also vivid descriptions of palace receptions and of encounters with the various Persian rulers.

The authors saw Safavid Persia as different to Europe, but in no way inferior. They were critical of the despotic power of the Shah, of the political influence of the harem, of the extravagance of the grandees, and of the bigotry of some of the Shiite clergy. On the other hand, they were impressed by the magnificence of the court, the splendour of Isfahan, the thriving commercial world with its bazaars and caravanserais, and the high level of security that was maintained until the later years of Safavid rule. Above all, they were charmed by the educated Persians they came into contact with, by their innate curiosity and love of learning, by their tolerant outlook and their polished manners.

This comprehensive and generally balanced picture of Persia, highlighting its strengths as well as its weaknesses, contributed to a more positive attitude in Europe towards the Islamic world. It also encouraged Europeans to take a more critical look at their own beliefs and institutions, by showing them that a society with different ones could function just as well, if not better in some respects. This helped to bring about the European Enlightenment.

Not all of Shah Abbas I's policies, however, were good for Persia. To prevent royal princes heading rebellions, as he himself had done, he ended the practice of appointing them as provincial governors and instead confined them to the harem, until such time as one of them should be called upon to rule. This not only deprived his successors of any experience of government, it also put them too much under the influence of the eunuchs and women of the harem. This was particularly true of the last two Safavid shahs, Shah Sulayman and Shah Sultan Husayn, who had a special council of eunuchs and women in the harem, to which they paid more attention than to the council of state, presided over by the grand vizier.

The position of the ruler was further secured during most of the seventeenth century by the cruel practice of blinding all the brothers and nephews of a new shah, since under Islamic rules no blind prince could lay claim to the throne.

Towards the end of the seventeenth century serious problems began to emerge. The extravagance of the court contributed to a growing financial crisis, the government was divided by factional in-fighting, the army was no longer properly maintained, and the famed security on the roads became a thing of the past. On top of all this, the last Safavid ruler, Shah Sultan Husayn, who was naturally pious, allowed himself to be persuaded by the leading Shiite cleric to sanction the persecution of religious minorities with the aim of forcing them to convert to Twelver Shiism. This policy was a complete failure, caused huge resentment, and even helped provoke a number of revolts among the Sunni minority. One of these was among the Sunni Afghans of Qandahar province and in March 1722 an army of twenty thousand Afghan horsemen from the Ghilzai tribe, led by their chief, Mir Mahmud, defeated the Safavid army and laid siege to Isfahan. Seven months later the city was starved into surrender and on October 23rd Shah Sultan Husayn rode out to his unfinished palace at Farahabad, where he pinned the aigrette of sovereignty on the turban of the Afghan conqueror.

The overthrow of the Safavids removed a dynasty that enjoyed a unique legitimacy in the eyes of its Shiite subjects. Not only were the Safavids the founders of the Shiite state, they also claimed to be descended from the Shiite Imams and, on that account, to be the representatives of the only truly legitimate ruler in Shiite eyes, who was the Hidden Imam – the Twelfth Shiite Imam who had disappeared from sight in the ninth century. There were occasional Shiite clerics who disputed their right to rule, mainly on account of their fondness for wine, and who asserted instead the overriding authority of the most senior clerics, the *mujtaheds*. But generally speaking the Safavids could count on the support of their clergy. For a good half century after their demise, they continued to be regarded by much of the population as the only legitimate rulers of Persia.

A Less than Friendly Welcome for an English Merchant

One of the hallmarks of the Safavid period was the growth of direct trade with Europe, rather than through intermediaries in the Levant. English merchants keen to find new markets for English cloth were among the first into the field. In 1561 the Muscovy Company in London sent a Leicestershire merchant, Anthony Jenkinson (1529–1610/11), to explore the possibility of opening up direct trade with Persia through Russia. Jenkinson arrived in the then Safavid capital of Qazvin in November 1562 carrying samples of English cloth and letters of recommendation from the young Queen Elizabeth I, drawn up in Latin, English, Italian and Hebrew. Jenkinson, who had already made a harrowing journey to Bukhara through Russia, seems to have managed well enough to talk to the Shah in Turkish, which was the main language of the Safavid court.

He has left a memorable account of his reception by Shah Tahmasp I (1524–1576), which was distinctly hostile. The reason for this, however, lay less in Tahmasp's well-known Shiite piety, than in his desire not to damage relations with the Ottoman Turks, with whom he had just made peace. A Turkish ambassador was in Qazvin at the time and urged the Shah to reject Jenkinson's request for trading privileges, as it would damage the interests of Turkish merchants. Four years later, however, Shah Tahmasp granted these privileges to the Muscovy Company. Jenkinson is correct in saying that pious Shiites regarded Christians as unclean, but he is wrong in supposing that this was why he was made to put on slippers on entering the palace. It was a normal procedure to avoid dirtying the valuable carpets on which Persians sat and ate their meals.

The 20th day of November aforesaid, I was sent for to come before the said Sophie[1], otherwise called Shaw Thomas, and about three of the clock at after noon I came to the court, and in the lighting from

[1] The Safavid Shah was known in Europe as 'the Sophy' which was derived from 'Safi al-Din', the name of the ancestor of the Safavid Shahs, who founded the Safavid Sufi order in 1301.

my horse at the court gate before my feet touched the ground, a pair of the Sophie's own shoes termed in the Persian tongue *basmackes*, such as he himself weareth when he ariseth in the night to pray (as his manner is) were put upon my feet, for without the same shoes I might not be suffered to tread upon his holy ground, – being a Christian, and called amongst them *gower*, that is, unbeliever, and unclean: esteeming all to be infidels and pagans which does not believe as they do, in their false filthy prophets Mahomet and Murtezallie.[2] At the said court gate the things that I brought to present his majesty with, were divided by sundry parcels to sundry servitors of the court to carry before me, for none of my company or servants might be suffered to enter into the court with me, my interpreter only excepted. Thus coming before his majesty with such reverence as I thought meet to be used, I delivered the Queen's majesty's letters with my present, which he accepting, demanded of me of what country of Franks[3] I was, and what affairs I had there to do: unto whom I answered that I was of the famous city of London within the noble realm of England, and that I was sent thither from the most excellent and gracious sovereign Lady Elizabeth, Queen of the said realm, for to treat of friendship, and free passage of our merchants and people, to repair and traffic within his dominions, for to bring in our commodities, and to carry away theirs, to the honour of both princes, the mutual commodity of both realms, and wealth of the subjects, with other words here omitted. He then demanded me in what language the letters were written, I answered, in the Latin, Italian, and Hebrew: well said he, we have none within our realm that understand those tongues. Whereunto I answered that such a famous and worthy prince (as he was) wanted not people of all nations within his large dominions to interpret the same. Then he questioned with me of the state of our countries, and of the power of the Emperor of Almaine, King Philip, and the great Turk,[4] and which of

[2] Murtaza, meaning 'the chosen one,' was one of the titles of Ali, the cousin and son-in-law of the Prophet Muhammad and the first Shiite Imam.

[3] The Persians called all Europeans 'Franks'.

[4] The Emperor of Alamiane is the Habsburg, Ferdinand I, who was Emperor of the Holy Roman Empire. King Philip II of Spain was his nephew. The great Turk is the Ottoman Sultan, Sulayman the Magnificent.

them was of most power: whom I answered to his contention, not dispraising the great Turk, their late concluded friendship considered. Then he reasoned with me much of religion, demanding whether I were a *gower*, that is to say, an unbeliever, or a *Muselman*, that is, of Mahomet's law. Unto whom I answered, that I was neither unbeliever nor Mahometan, but a Christian. What is that said he unto the king of Georgia's son, who being a Christian was fled unto the said Sophie, and he answered that a Christian was he that believeth in Jesus Christus, affirming him to be the son of God, and the greatest prophet: 'Doest thou believe so?' said the Sophie unto me: 'Yea, that I do' said I: 'Oh thou unbeliever' said he, 'we have no need to have friendship with the unbelievers,' and so willed me to depart. I being glad thereof did reverence and went my way, being accompanied with many of his gentlemen and others, and after me followed a man with a basanet (basin) of sand, sifting all the way that I had gone within the said palace, even from the said Sophie's sight unto the court gate.

From *Early Voyages and Travels to Russia and Persia*
by Anthony Jenkinson and other Englishmen

Shah Tahmasp: A Mean Old Recluse

Vincenzo Degli Alessandri (died after 1595) was a Venetian diplomat who was sent to Persia in October 1570, when Cyprus, a Venetian possession, was under attack by the Ottomans. His mission was to persuade Shah Tahmasp I to join the Christian princes in an anti-Ottoman alliance. D'Alessandri reached Qazvin in August 1572, after travelling on foot through Ottoman territory disguised as an Armenian merchant. He stayed in the Persian capital for some time waiting for an audience with the Shah, but this was steadily refused and he had to content himself with delivering his letter from the Doge of Venice to one of the Shah's sons, who was sympathetic to the alliance proposal, before returning home. By this time Cyprus had been lost, but the Christian powers had also won their first great victory over the Ottomans at the naval battle of Lepanto, off the west coast of Greece, in October 1571. In September 1574 D'Alessandri delivered a report on his mission to the council of Venice, which provides a valuable picture of Shah Tahmasp in old age, consumed by avarice, as well as of his court, his council of state, and the peculiar reverence in which the Safavid monarch was held.

The King is in the sixty-fourth year of his age, and the fifty-first of his reign, is of middling stature, well-formed in person and features, although dark, of thick lips, and a grisly beard; he is more of a melancholy disposition than anything else, which is known by many signs, but principally by his not having come out of his palace for the space of eleven years, nor having gone once to the chase nor any other kind of amusement, to the great dissatisfaction of his people, who according to the customs of that country, not seeing their King, can only with the greatest difficulty make their petitions, and cannot have a voice in the decisions of justice; so that day and night they cry aloud before the palace for justice, sometimes a thousand, more or less. And the King, hearing the voices, usually orders them to be sent away, saying that there are judges deputed in the country, with whom rests the administration of justice, not taking into consideration that these things are against the tyrannical judges and sultans, who usually wait in the street to assassinate the people, seen by me as well as by many other people. I have been told as a fact, that in the book of lawsuits there are written more than ten thousand persons who have been killed during the last eight years. This evil comes principally from the Cuzzi,[5] who, as they do not receive pay, are forced to take bribes, and do so the more, as they see that in the matter of law affairs the King takes no thought or care. Hence it arises that throughout the kingdom the roads are unsafe, and in the houses themselves one runs great dangers, and the judges nearly all allow themselves to be corrupted by money.

The King's service is divided into three classes; first, the women, daughters of sultans, bought by the King, or received as presents into his harem, which is thus called from them, the Seraglio, as the abode of the women. They are all Georgian and Circassian[6] slaves, and he is attended by them when he sleeps in the palace. When he sleeps out,

[5] Qazi: an Islamic judge who applies the Sharia, or Islamic law.
[6] Circassia was a region in the north Caucasus.

he is attended by slaves in the lower duties, as in dressing and undressing; these number of forty or fifty, and keep in order the tents and the larder. The third class of people who attend him are the noble sons of sultans, who do not sleep in the royal palace, but come morning and evening from their houses to their attendance, and generally are about one hundred in number. The King is served by them in turn, by handing water to him, by presenting to him his robes, and by following him when he walks in the gardens. Pay is given by the King to the servants who attend him, from fifteen years of age to twenty-five and even thirty, as long as they have no beard. In this manner, in proportion to their service, he lends some twenty, some twenty-five, and some fifty thousand *scudi*, at twenty per cent, to some for ten, and others for twenty years, receiving for himself the interest from year to year. They then lend it on good security, at sixty and eighty per cent to nobles of the court who are in expectation of receiving rank and appointments from the sovereign, and if it happens that those who have borrowed the money do not compound for the capital with him who has advanced the money, they sell their houses and possessions, nor is any compensation to be had afterwards.

The rewards of service of the nobles are the appointments of the court as centurions and captains of the King's guard, also sultanates, which mean governorships of the provinces; these all belong to the service of the person of the King. The council is really one body, in which the King is the sole president, with the intervention of twelve sultans, men of long experience in affairs of state. It is remarkably well attended by those sultans who from time to time come to the court, and who all enter the council, which is held every day except when the King goes to the bath, or has his nails cut; the time of this council in summer as well as winter is from the twenty-second hour of the day, and according to the matters in hand, continues till the third, fourth, and sixth hour of the night. The King sits upon a Masthean, not very high from the ground, and behind his shoulders his sons sit when they are at court, especially Sultan Caidar Mirise,[7]

[7] Haydar Mirza, the third son of Shah Tahmasp. He was held in high regard by Tahmasp and considered himself the natural successor, but was killed in the succession struggle that followed Tahmasp's death in 1576.

who, as lieutenant of his father, does not leave the King's sight. The sultan councillors, who are four in number, named viceroys, sit in front. The King introduces the subjects, and discourses about them, asking their opinions from the sultans, and each one as he states his opinion, rises, and comes near the King, speaking aloud, that he may be heard by his colleagues. If, in the course of argument, the King hears anything which strikes him, he has it noted by the grand councillors, and very often takes a note of it with his own hand; and thus in their order in which the King inquires of them, the sultans give their opinions. When the King has no doubt about the matter in question, it is settled at the first council; and if he has doubts, he hears the arguments of the full council, and then settles it after private consideration. In the number of the consulting sultans is included the *Curzibassa,*[8] chief of the King's guard, although he may not be a sultan. The grand councillors have no vote, and can say nothing unless they are called upon by the King; they, although of great dignity, cannot rise to the rank of sultan, nor to any other appointments belonging to the military service, even if they are nobly born.

The reverence and love of the people for the King are incredible, as they worship him not as a King, but as a god, on account of his descent from the line of Ali,[9] the great object of their veneration. Those who are in sickness or hardships do not call to aid the name of God so much as that of the King, making vows to present him with some gift, and some go to kiss the doors of the palace, that house being considered fortunate which is able to get some cloth or shawl from the King, or else some water in which he has washed his hands, which they consider a preventive of fever. To pass over many other things I might say about this matter, I will only mention that not only the people, but his own sons and the sultans speak to him as if they could not find epithets worthy of such greatness, saying, 'Thou art the living faith, and in thee we believe.' And not only in the neighbouring cities can one observe these signs of reverence, but also in the distant towns and places many hold that besides having the prophetic spirit,

[8] Qurchi-bashi: commander of the Qurchis, a kind of household cavalry.
[9] The Safavids claimed descent from Ali through the Seventh Shiite Imam, Musa al-Kazim (745-799). The claim has since been shown to have been bogus.

he has the power of raising the dead and of working other like miracles, saying that, as Ali, their chief saint, had eleven male children, this King has received from the Majesty of God, the same favour as Ali.

From *A Narrative of Italian Travels in Persia in the 15th and 16th Centuries* by Charles Grey

Shah Abbas I Welcomes Two Elizabethan Adventurers

Among the most remarkable English visitors to Safavid Persia were two Elizabethan adventurers, Sir Anthony Sherley and his brother Robert, who arrived in Qazvin in December 1598 to seek their fortune with Shah Abbas I. Anthony, the eldest, had considerable military experience. The mission he gave himself – it had no sanction whatever from Queen Elizabeth I – was to persuade the Shah to join in an alliance with the Christian princes of Europe against the Ottomans, their common enemy (though not, in fact, the enemy of England) – and to promote trade between Persia and England. Shah Abbas eventually agreed to both these proposals, although the military alliance proved as elusive as ever. Both the Sherleys, but particularly Robert, acted at different times as the Shah's envoys to Europe. Robert also spent several years in Persia helping Shah Abbas to refashion his army and died there in 1628, broken-hearted at apparently losing the Shah's favour. George Manwaring was one of the gentlemen in the Sherley brothers' suite and has left this colourful account of their first encounter with Shah Abbas, who was returning to Qazvin in buoyant mood after winning a decisive victory over the Uzbeks, his principal enemy on his eastern frontier. Abbas's energy and ebullience comes across strongly.

The King, some two days before he entered into Casbeene (Qazvin), sent a courier or post before him to his lord steward, to furnish us with the best horses he could get, and that we should meet him four miles forth of Casbeene, accompanied with the governor and himself, which was very gallantly performed by them both. In this sort was Sir Anthony and we of his company appointed: first, Sir Anthony himself in rich cloth of gold, his gown and his undercoat, his sword hanging in a rich scarf to the worth of a thousand crowns, being set with pearl and diamonds, and on his head a turban according, to the worth of two thousand dollars, his boots embroidered with pearl and rubies; his brother, Mr Robert Sherley, likewise in cloth of gold, his gown and undercoat, with a rich turban on his head; his interpreter, Angelo, in cloth of silver, gown and undercoat; four in cloth of silver gowns, with undercoats of silk damask; four in crimson velvet gowns, with damask undercoats; four in blue damask gowns, with taffety (glossy silk) undercoats; four in yellow damask, with their undercoats of a Persian stuff; his page in cloth of gold; his four footmen in carnation taffety. And thus we set forward: Sir Anthony and his brother riding together; the lord steward on the right hand and the governor on the left; the rest came after two by two, myself directly before Sir Anthony, with a white staff in my hand, for it pleased him to make me his marshal, for in that country every great man hath his marshal to ride before him.

So after we were half a mile forth of the city we saw such a prospect as is not usually seen, which was, twelve hundred soldiers, horsemen, carrying twelve hundred heads of men on their lances, and some having the ears of men put on strings and hanged about their necks; next after these came the trumpeters, making a wonderful noise; because they are contrary to our English trumpets, these trumpets being two yards and a half in length, with the great end big, and so much compass as a hat. Next after them came the drummers, their drums being made of brass, and carried upon camels; then after them came his six standard bearers; then after them came his twelve pages, bearing every one a lance in his hand; then a good distance after them came the King, riding alone with a lance in his hand, his bow and arrows, sword and target[10] hanging by his side, being a man of low stature, but very strongly

[10] A light, round shield.

made, and swarthy of complexion. Next after the King came his lieutenant-general of the field, and all his bows in rank like a half-moon; and after them came his officers in the wars, to the number of twenty thousand soldiers, all horsemen.

So at our first encounter of the King, Sir Anthony and his brother did alight off their horses, and came to kiss the King's foot; for it is the fashion of the country, be he never so good a man he must kiss the King's foot at the first meeting; after that was performed the King did look upon them both very stately, and afterward did look upon us all, giving never a word to Sir Anthony, but bid the lieutenant-general place him according as he had given him direction, and so the King set spurs to his horse, and did ride away for the space of an hour; Sir Anthony being placed in the King's place, with his brother Mr Robert Sherley, the lieutenant-general on the right hand, and the lord steward on the left. After the King was departed, the lord steward told Sir Anthony it was the fashion to entertain strangers in that fashion, but willed him to have patience awhile, and he should see the event; so within an hour the King returned back again as fast as his horse would go, and having following him sixteen women on horseback richly attired, and when he came close to Sir Anthony the women did holloa, and gave such a cry, much like the wild Irish which did make us wonder at it; then after they had made an end, the King came and embraced Sir Anthony and his brother, kissing them both three or four times over, and taking Sir Anthony by the hand, swearing a great oath that he should be his sworn brother, and so did he call him always, and so the King marched along, putting Sir Anthony on his right hand.

It was a wonderful sight to see the multitude of people that there were that day; and still as the King did pass along the people would kneel down and kiss the earth; but before we came into the city, there was proclamation made that, upon pain of death no soldier should enter into the city, but such as were born there, for fear of making any uproar; and so they were all discharged and departed every one to his own country for that time. So after we had entered the city, we marched through every street and in the end came to a banqueting house of the King's; where the King brought Sir Anthony up into a very fair chamber richly trimmed; in which chamber Sir Anthony delivered a speech to the King, which was the occasion of his coming, with a discourse of our wearisome journey, and of our usage in Turkey, and other accidents which did happen unto us by the way, which the King did harken very attentively unto, and when Sir Anthony had ended his speech, the King stood up and replied: 'Brother, I do grieve to hear of thy sore adventures and troubles by the way, but I do much rejoice to see thee here in safety at our court; for be thou well assured I will place thee on my head.' This was his meaning, that he would advance him to great honour; then there was a great banquet brought in, with music before it, where they passed away the time for the space of two hours, with great joy; after the banquet was ended, the King requested Sir Anthony to look through the window to behold their sports[11] on horseback.

Before the house there was a very fair place to the quantity of some ten acres of ground, made very plain; so the King went down, and when he had taken his horse, the drums and trumpets sounded; there was twelve horsemen in all with the King; so they divided themselves six on one side, and six on the other, having in their hands long rods of wood, about the bigness of a man's finger, and on the end of the rods a piece of wood nailed on like unto a hammer. After they were divided and turned face to face, there came one into the middle, and did throw a wooden ball between both the companies, and having goals made at either end of the plain, they began their sport, striking the ball with their rods from one to the other, in the fashion of our football play here in England; and ever when the King had gotten the ball before him, the drums and trumpets would play one alarum (call to arms), and many times the King would come to Sir Anthony to the window, and ask him how he did like the sport.

So when the sport was ended Sir Anthony sent me down of some business, and as I went down the stairs it was my chance to meet the King, who, when he saw me, took me by the arm, and caused me to return back again with him, and brought me to the chamber where the Turk's ambassador was, and did lead me along to the upper end of the chamber, and put me above the Turk's ambassador, bidding me sit down there, by reason they have no stools, but sit on carpets. I could ill

[11] Despite this encounter with the game of polo, which had been played in Persia since ancient times, it was not introduced into England until the nineteenth century – and then from India.

sit cross-legged after their manner, but did kneel on my knees; then the ambassador told the King it was the fashion of England to sit on stools, for he had been oft-times in the English merchants' houses in Constantinople. When the King had heard those words, he presently went into the next room, and caused one of his pages to bring forth a little form (bench), which they did use to set bottles of wine[12] upon, and throwing a carpet of gold upon it, caused me to sit down; then he called for some wine, and did drink a health unto me, and used these words: 'I do esteem more of the sole of a Christian's shoe, than I do of the best Turk in Turkey.' And then he asked me if I would serve him. I answered him, in regard I was a subject in his country, I must be at his command, yet I was loath to leave my old master, in regard he loved me well; at which words the King did take me about the neck and kissed me three or four times, and said, 'I do highly commend thy constancy; nevertheless I will entreat my brother, thy lord, for thee, that thou shalt be my servant so long as you stay in my country.'

Then after some few words more he went forth of the room to Sir Anthony and and told him that he must needs have one of his servants from him; he answered that it did not lie in his power to give any of them, but if it pleased him, he might command any of them to do him what service they were able; the King thanked him very heartily, and told him that he should command all his servants to do the like; then after some few words' parley the King brought Sir Anthony to his house and told him he would take no leave of him, for he did purpose to see him before he did sleep. So after we had supped at our own house, Sir Anthony, not thinking the King would have seen him any more that night, because it waxed late, he determined to have gone to his rest, but he was disappointed, for the lord steward came for him, with sixteen torches and some twenty gentlemen to attend him, to bring Sir Anthony and all his company to the King, to spend that night with him, but when we came where the King was, such a spectacle we did behold which did almost ravish us with joy to see it; you shall understand that in the middle of the city of Casbeene there is a place which they call the *bussard* (bazaar) made in fashion

[12] Most of the Safavid kings enjoyed drinking wine, and some did so to excess, despite the Islamic prohibition.

like the Exchange in London, though not so beautiful, yet three times so big, where they keep shops of all manner of trades; for that time the shopkeepers had set forth their commodities in the best manner, and themselves apparelled very gallantly. In the middle of that place standeth a round thing made with a seat, set up with six pillars, ... on which place they used to sell apparel and other commodities; that being bravely trimmed with rich carpets, both of gold and silver and silk, and the King's chair of estate placed in the middle, the chair being of silver plate set with turkies (turquoises) and rubies very thick, and six great diamonds, which did shew like stars, the seat being of rich scarlet embroidered with pearl, and the multitude of lamps hanging abut it were innumerable. The King, when he came unto it, did cause Sir Anthony to ascend up into that princely throne, and, standing by the chair with his viceroy and other of his nobility, did take Sir Anthony by the hand, and willed him to sit down in his chair of estate; but Sir Anthony, falling on his knee, desired the King to pardon him, for so princely a place did not become him, in regard he was but a subject himself. The King swearing a great oath, which was by the soul of Mortasolee,[13] that he should sit in the chair, and if the best Persian of them all did greve at it, he would presently cut off his head; and taking Sir Anthony by the hand, made him sit down without fear, which Sir Anthony did, and when he was set, the King kissed him, and said, 'Brother, thou dost well become this place'; then he called for a stool for Mr Robert Sherley, which was presently brought, and he sat him close by his brother Sir Anthony, and placing all us of Sir Anthony's company round about the throne, sitting on carpets cross-legged, according to the country fashion; then there came in a royal banquet with drums and trumpets sounding before it, which was brought in by twenty-four noblemen, and when the drums and trumpets were departed, the music came in playing, with twenty women very richly apparelled, singing and dancing before the music.

...So when the banquet was ended the King arose, taking Sir Anthony by the arm, and so they walked, arm in arm, in every street of the city, the twenty women going before, singing and dancing, and his noblemen coming after, with each of them one of our company by

[13] Murtaza Ali.(See note 2 pg 94)

the hand, and at every turning there was variety of music, and lamps hanging on either side their streets of seven heights one above another, which made a glorious show; and thus for the space of eight days and nights did we spend the time in sporting and banqueting with all the pomps they could devise.

> From *George Manwaring, Gent: A True Discourse of Sir Anthony Sherley's Travel into Persia*, in *Sir Anthony Sherley and His Persian Adventure* by Sir E. Denison Ross

A Banquet with Shah Abbas I

The European visitors to Safavid Persia provide us with very human portraits of the Safavid kings that, for obvious reasons, are not to be found in the Persian court chronicles. One of the most vivid and engaging portraits of Shah Abbas I is provided by the cultured Roman aristocrat, Pietro Della Valle (1586–1652) who decided to go to Persia on his way back from a pilgrimage to the Holy Land in 1616. Like so many others, he seems to have wished to promote an anti-Ottoman alliance. He also entertained plans to establish a colony of Nestorian Christians from southern Iraq in Shah Abbas's new capital of Isfahan – the result of his marriage to a Nestorian Catholic lady while he was in Baghdad on his way to Persia. Della Valle reached Isfahan in February 1617 and remained in Persia until 1622, writing up his experiences and everything he learnt about the country in a series of voluminous letters to a learned friend in Naples. They are a treasure of information about Shah Abbas and the Persia of his time. Della Valle had to wait a year for his first meeting with the Shah, which took place not in Isfahan, but at a great banquet in the palace at Farahabad on the southern shore of the Caspian Sea, where Abbas was in the habit of spending the winter. Della Valle was able to talk to Shah Abbas in Turkish.

On the next day the vizier repaired to my house, and found me already drest and waiting for him; but as it was yet early, he remained with me till the hour at which he expected I might be admitted to an audience. At length we mounted our horses and repaired in company to the palace, the principal gate of which fronts a very handsome and long street; arrived at which we alighted. We did not enter by a large meadow before the palace, but rounded it, ascending by a large square joining the palace on one side, to which one passes by a garden that no one is allowed to enter on horseback.

I found here a number of Georgians who waited upon the King to abjure their religion and become Mahometans; this induced a conversation between the vizier and myself; in which I learnt that liberty of conscience was allowed throughout the kingdom; and that the King was wholly indifferent to what religion his subjects professed, holding all as good, either the Mahometan, the Christian or Jewish faith; but these people, added he, are continually pestering His Majesty to become Mahometans.

At one end of the square, near the palace, there is a beautiful tree of great height at which the first *corps de garde* is stationed. Here the vizier left me in the shade to give advice of my approach, and receive the necessary orders; and after some time he returned to inform me, the King had ordered him to conduct me to the *divan khanè* (audience hall) of the garden, where the principal officers about the court awaited him. The floor of the *divan khanè*, raised only two steps from the ground, was covered with beautiful carpets, on which the officers of the court already assembled were seated. The Khan of Astarabad; the *corchibashi*, or chief of the soldiery, called *corchi*; Muharrab Khan; Delli Muhammad, surnamed Delli from his facetiousness, that word signifying sportive; a sultan from the frontiers next to India; with several others of consideration. Besides these, on the opposite side, Sarù Kogia Bey, and Effendiar Bey, a particular favourite of the King; and on the side fronting the west, that of least esteem among them, were several musicians with various instruments, such as violins, cymbals, lutes, and others, but varying in shape from ours, the strings of which were not only of catgut, but also of silk covered with wire.

On my entrance I was led to sit between the Khan of Astarabad, and the *corchibashi*, as the most honourable station, the Vizier of Mazandaran remaining at the door; those officers in greatest familiarity with the King never sitting at his audience, but remaining standing to obey orders. The rest of the assemblage kept their seats as on my arrival. After remaining seated thus for some time we were served with dinner. What was prepared for us was brought by the garden-gate, the dishes being carried by as many persons following each other after the *maitre d'hotel*, of from eighteen to twenty years of age, without beards, who act as the King's pages, and drest in the costume of Mazandaran; that is to say, in pantaloons, with a tight round frock fitting the body and reaching to the middle of the thighs; no turban, but instead a fur cap with the hair outwards, and the skin turned up at bottom to shew the cloth with which it is lined.

These kind of caps, called in Persia *bork*, are very common here, and are the same as for convenience-sake are worn in the house in lieu of turbans. The pages do not wear liveries, such not being used at all in these parts, but each was clad in a different colour to the other, according to fancy, and in various kinds of cloth, some embroidered with gold and others with silver, the *bork* being generally of a different colour from the pantaloons, and these again varying from that of the frock.

The dishes they carried were large as our basons (basins), with high covers, either round or steeple-shaped, to cover the pyramids of pilao and other messes (servings of food). The dishes were some of silver but mostly of gold, and in order to make the greater shew, they were intermixed.

The *maitre d'hotel* on reaching the *divan khanè*, knelt and spread before me and my two neighbours a cloth of moderate size of an octagonal shape, of gold brocade fringed, with gold tassels of different shapes and colour. On this cloth every thing placed was served in dishes of gold, and the meats they contained, notwithstanding it was seasoned after the country fashion, was truly a feast for a King. Besides these dishes, near each of us was a large porringer of the capacity of a small pipkin (small pot), full of acids, extracted from different matters, of which spoonfuls are occasionally taken during the repast, either to assist digestion or sharpen the appetite; to serve which, in each porringer, which like the dishes were of gold, a deep new spoon was put, made of aromatic wood, with a very long handle; these, however, serve but for one meal, never being used a second time.

Although we were not long at dinner, wine was served twice round to all the company according to rank; as I objected to a second cup I was much importuned, as those about me being prohibited the use of wine by their religion, and aware that no such injunction withheld me, considered my abstinence as a reproach.

While diverting ourselves in conversation the musicians kept playing continually, but in such gentle tones and so low as to be scarcely heard, so as to afford no interruption.

While talking, the cup which was of gold and the salver the same, kept continually moving, the quantity drank at each time, however, was small, and the Persians accustomed to these entertainments have good heads.

It was now late, when the King attended by some favourite officers of state, such as the *agamir*, the chief of the eunuchs, and some others, entered by the garden gate opposite to us. As well as the others, he was dressed in a very fine cotton vest of a lively green colour, laced over the breast; for, notwithstanding it be customary to lace them on the side, as I have elsewhere noticed, they are sometimes laced in front with orange laces. His drawers, or trowsers, were of violet coloured cloth, his shoes of orange shagreen[14] or zigri, and his turban red and silver, striped. His broad sash was of various colours, as well as that above it, and the sheath of his scymitar of black shagreen, the hilt of bone, probably the tooth of some fish.

His walk was stately; his left hand on the guard of his sword, the point of which towards the sky, and the concave bend upwards according to the custom of the country. From caprice he is used to wear the wrong side of his turban before, which except himself, none is allowed to do.

As soon as we perceived the King at a distance, we incontinently (immediately) rose on our feet, but without leaving our places. He advanced towards us with a measured pace, unsupported, at the head of those who followed him, according to a general practice, whether on foot or on horseback. He is of middling stature, not

[14] A kind of untanned leather with a rough surface.

lean but delicate, well built and proportioned, and of dignified port (bearing), notwithstanding he be now near nine and forty years old. Whether he speak, he walk, or simply look at you, he has constantly the appearance of great animation and vivacity; nevertheless, in spite of his perpetual restlessness, and his natural capriciousness, he constantly maintains somewhat of serious and grave, which plainly indicate majesty. His face is rather handsome than otherwise, but his complexion is very dark, either naturally or owing to his frequent exposure to the sun. His hands are constantly dyed of a very dark colour with *alcana* (henna). His nose is aquiline; his whiskers, which are long and hang down, as well as his eyebrows, are black: he wears no beard. His eyes are lively, sparkling and smiling, and as well as the rest of his countenance expressive of that greatness of mind and genius, in which he surpasses the whole of the princes of his kingdom.

On the King approaching, the sultan I before mentioned as being with us, who had come from the country over which he was appointed governor,[15] on the frontiers of India and Jagatay,[16] with four or five of the chiefs from those parts who accompanied him, advanced and kissed his foot, as is usual when sultans or khans repair to court from a distant country, and when they take their leave. This homage on the part of the sultan was imitated by those with him, after which it was repeated by the sultan and the rest, and again a third time, every one each time making a mysterious circle round the King. This ceremony being finished, the sultan and those who accompanied him returned to the *divan khanè* and resumed his place. The King entered also, and, as did the others, left his shoes on the steps of the *divan khanè*; not so much as a mark of respect as for cleanliness sake.

Their shoes have heels to them, and are in consequence much more comfortable, and pleasant of wear than our flippers without, and not being tied are as easily disengaged without stooping.

On the King's entering the *divan khanè*, my neighbours gave

[15] He was governor of Qandahar, now in Afghanistan.
[16] The area covered by the former Chagatai Mongol khanate of Central Asia which, by this time, was occupied by Uzbek, Kazakh and Kirghiz tribes.

me a hint, upon which I left my place accompanied by the *corchibashi* who was at my left, and retained that station, putting his hand under my arm as if to support me. The King seeing me advance, stood still; on getting near I made him a profound bow according to our custom, and kneeling on my right knee stooped, in view of kissing the hem of his garment, but he presenting me his hand and hindering me, I kissed it, and touched it with my forehead. On rising, while returning to my station accompanied as before, the King enquired whether I spoke their language, and understanding from those with whom I had conversed that I did, he turned to me with a smile, and said '*chosk ghieldi, safa ghieldi*' (truly welcome, very welcome); after which he resumed his place at the anterior part of the *divan khanè*, on the left hand as you enter, in the same spot in which Saru Kogia was before. The King being seated here by himself, and Saru Kogia opposite to him, we resumed our former position. Almost all the officers of rank who accompanied him standing about his person without the *divan khanè*, with some of those who before the arrival of His Majesty were seated with us.

The King at first kneeled down and sat upon his heels, which is considered the most respectful and humble posture, but which soon tires; after which he changed it for that manner of sitting peculiar to our tailors. After His Majesty had set us the example, we changed our previous uncomfortable posture also, and sat with our legs across. After this he pulled off his turban and remained bare headed, notwithstanding it was night and the apartment open. This, I understood, is his usual practice, whether alone or in conversation. In this, we did not imitate him, it being considered an incivility to sit without a turban, not only when among persons of higher rank, but even among strangers or your equals. He afterwards ordered wine to be brought; this the Effendiar Bey, who stood without the *divan khanè*, preparing in a hurry to present to the King, fell into a small reservoir of water at the foot of the steps leading to the place, which excited a hearty laugh at his expense, redoubled when upon his recovering himself, and again advancing, he broke the glass decanter which contained the wine against the joists of the door.

The King having drank, two or three pages standing in the room served us each according to rank, one after the other as before; the cups from which we drank being of gold, and that of the King of glass. On the cup being presented to me, the King noticing I did not take it with the same eagerness as the rest, observed, 'perhaps he does not drink wine.' I answered, 'that I was little accustomed to do so, but felt it a duty since I understood it to be His Majesty's pleasure that I should, and that in mere momentous matters I was desirous of shewing him my readiness to submit to His Majesty's will.' I thereupon emptied my cup, which was very small, for the second time that day; the wine, however, notwithstanding it was pure, was neither very strong nor very good.

In the mean time, a number of people came with the presents made by the sultan on occasion of his visit to court. This custom appears to be of very great antiquity, the King of the Medes according to Philostrates[17] never being visited even in the time of Apollonius without receiving presents. This custom is general throughout the East among all ranks. Equals for what they give receive an equivalent; where the value tendered for that received be greater, it is considered an acknowledgement of superiority, where less, an assumption of the same on the reverse. Vassals make presents to their lords, who give back little in return. When princes of similar power and equal authority make them, the quality and nature of what is tendered is reconverted on each side. The sovereign who receives them from an inferior prince gives little or nothing in return. Thus the Turks, wont to receive from the King of Persia, render but a trifle; and the present war, as I conceive, originates from the Shah disliking to give without an equivalent; and notwithstanding the expense of the war infinitely surpasses the value of the annual boon, peace is prevented by the pertinacity of the King in refusing the annual donation.

After the presents had been passed in review, to which His Majesty paid little attention, unless indeed to some falcons,

[17] Flavius Philostratus (born c.170 AD), the Greek author of a number of philosophical works, including *The Life of Apollonius of Tyana*, a philosophising mystic of the first century AD.

arrows, and instruments of war, he employed the remainder of the day in the expediting of various affairs, giving different commissions and writing several letters; he also listened to the reading of several by the agamir in so loud a tone of voice that we distinctly heard every syllable; among these was one from my former *mehmandar*[18] Tochta Bey, now Governor of Hispahan, informing of the arrival of an ambassador expected from Spain.

His Majesty enquired of the courier, as is his general custom, respecting the ambassador,[19] and where he was lodged; of me also, if he were the man of rank designated; on which point I satisfied him, informing him, that although he was personally unknown to me, I knew his family to be one of the most noble in Spain; and in answer to his question, whether a Castilian or Portuguese, acquainted him that notwithstanding he had possessions in both countries, he was a true Spaniard.

In this manner the King dispatched his various affairs, conversing first with one, then with another, the wine passing round all the while; I availed myself, however, of his being so closely engaged to pass my turn. At length lights were brought in; these were large iron pots into which rags and grease were put, at the end of sticks, and which when kindled give much more light than our torches. These are peculiar to persons of high rank; four of them were placed without the *divan khanè* in the open air, and wherever three or four are visible it is an infallible sign that either the King is on the spot or his haram (harem). Within the *divan khanè*, a row of wax candles were disposed in gold and silver sticks, and a lamp of grease, such as I have before described.

Immediately after a collation was served, consisting only of provocatives to drinking, as without wine in this country there is no conversation. These, at the same time, very much prevent the wine from affecting, as by my own experience I am well enabled to ascertain. The entertainment continued thus till past one o'clock in the morning, the King all the time conducting himself with

[18] The *mehmandar* was the court official charged with looking after a foreign guest.
[19] The Spanish ambassador, Don Garcias de Silva Figueroa, was on his way to the court of Shah Abbas.

great familiarity, yet constantly preserving his dignity. After some time, the King called Delli Muhammed Khan, the jester, to come and divert him, condescending so far as to tell him, that if too idle to move, he would himself come to him. The guests upon this perceiving the Shah disposed to unbend (as such perhaps is the custom) withdrew one after the other, without any ceremony whatsoever, and making as little noise as possible.

For my part, a novice in these matters, I waited some time, expecting they might return, as I noticed that all were free to go and come back; I remained some time; at length, fearful of being the only one left at table, I withdrew, and as I waited some time on the steps for my slippers, the *agamir* on one side, and the Governor of Mazandaran on the other, came to acquaint me that the King enquired for and wished to see me.

I returned immediately upon this intimation, and having entered the *divan khanè*, knelt down in order to sit opposite to the King near Delli Muhammed Khan, but soon as the King perceived me, he told me he wished to confer with me, and made a sign for me to be seated on his right, with which I complied. Notwithstanding we were no more in the saloon (the *divan khanè*) than the King, Delli Khan, and myself, the musicians still continued to play in the same manner as before described, so as not to hinder conversation.

When seated, the King made many enquiries of me respecting myself, my profession, my family, and object in travelling; of the countries through which I passed; of Europe; its politics; its religions; the power and views of Spain, respecting its ambassador; and many other subjects, reasoning upon my replies on the latter, and shewing himself in his conversation perfectly well informed of the religions, customs, and interests of Europe, a very widely-informed man and a consummate politician. He detailed to me in return the cause of his wars with Gourgistan, as Georgia is called here; he told me of Trimuraz,[20] who had excited the Turks to war with him, having sought for assistance from the

[20] Taimuras was a Georgian prince who led a rebellion against Safavid rule over eastern Georgia.

Tatars, but 'what can they do with their arrows, which go *ter, ter,*' said he, 'let them come, let them come, I shall speak and do,' putting his hand to his sword and assuming a menacing aspect; when recollecting himself, and apprehensive of too much presumption, he turned his eyes towards heaven and rebuked himself, exclaiming, *toba, toba,* expressions of regret and resignation to God; then turning the conversation to tactics, he shewed himself well acquainted with war, its instruments, the fittest for cavalry and infantry, and the various manoeuvres in battle.

The lessons which he gave to the attendants about him on these subjects were listened to with minute attention and much approbation; for my part I observed, that it was only for masters to give such lessons, and that he was certainly qualified to teach from so much experience, and such great success as he had ever had. The King smiled at the compliment, modestly observing that what he had ever done was but of little value.

You must not, however, imagine that our discourse (which, as it embraced so many subjects, was consequently of long duration) passed without frequent reference to the cup; a practice common with the King, less with him for its being the custom of the country than to allow his penetrating mind to work into the recesses of the hearts of those with whom he converses, and with courtesy and the assistance of Bacchus to draw from them their most secret thoughts.

After continuing thus conversing, and drinking sometime to a great excess yet without ill consequence to myself, Delli Khan, upon the cup passing with greater briskness, knowing it to be the signal for departure, withdrew so silently that I saw his place empty before I noticed his retreat. Yet, seeing the King did not rise, I thought it improper to do so before him. At length he made a sign, observing longer sitting was superfluous, and putting on his turban leaned against a pillar of the *divan khanè*, where he was surrounded by the musicians, who continued to play very gently. Hereupon the Vizier of Mazandaran, who was on his feet as well as the other officers, beckoned me to retire, which I did without saying a word, making a slight bow as I passed the King, which was dispensed with by the courtiers. The vizier assigned me some of his people to see me home, remaining with the King, who is wont to continue in this posture, a prey to an habitual melancholy,[21] listening to the music: sometimes when he thinks of it, retiring to the haram.

Extracts from the *Travels of Pietro Delle Valle in Persia* in *A General Collection of the Best and Most Interesting Voyages and Travels in all Parts of the World* by John Pinkerton

Ram Fights and Bull Fights

Among the most popular entertainments in Safavid Persia were ram fights and bull fights. One of the best descriptions of these is given by the Spanish ambassador to the court of Shah Abbas, Don Garcias de Silva Figueroa (1550–1624). He arrived in Persia via the island of Hormuz in the Persian Gulf, then a Portuguese possession, in October 1617 and witnessed the ram and bull fights in the town of Kashan, about one hundred and twenty miles (two hundred kilometres) north of Isfahan, as he was on his way to meet the Shah. Figueroa, who remained in Persia until 1619, refers to himself as 'the ambassador'.

The next day the governor (of Kashan) and several other people of rank came to collect the ambassador, to conduct him to the Maidan,[22] where they planned to divert him for some hours. After dismounting in front of the royal palace, they first showed him the seraglio (the harem) and the garden, and asked him if he would like to climb up to a gallery, or if he wished to watch the fights with which he was to be entertained from down below. These were to be between several rams and bulls, which were reputed to fight well. As

[21] Shah Abbas is said to have felt deep remorse for having his eldest son murdered in February 1615, after suspecting him, almost certainly unjustly, of plotting to seize the throne.
[22] Maidan or Maydan is the Persian word for a town square. European writers are usually, as in this case, referring to the main square, where the palace of the shah or his governor was also to be found.

he said he preferred to watch from where he was, a place was immediately made for him among a large number of people of all sorts, even including several women, enveloped and hidden in their white veils, who stood near to where the fight was to take place.

Some men immediately entered from either side, accompanying two others, each of whom was leading a powerful ram, loaded with hats and garlands of flowers around the necks and the horns. After animating them for the fight, by whispering words into their ears, they set them loose, and the rams immediately began to crash against one another with the violence one normally sees in these kinds of combats. But these rams fought with an extraordinary courage and fury. And while there was not much amusement to be had in that, there was pleasure nonetheless in seeing the demonstrations of joy or sadness made by their owners, according to whether or not they had the advantage. The partisans of the victor showed by their cries the share they took in his satisfaction, and the sad silence of the others revealed the affliction they shared with the loser, while during the fight they laid very considerable bets.

This first fight being over, there entered the owners of two powerful bulls, which were bigger than those one normally sees in Persia, but their horns and their height were smaller than those generally used in bull-fights in Madrid, which are a foot taller, but otherwise the same colour, for the most part black. They arrived loaded with flowers and ribbons of every colour, and their owners were much better accompanied than the owners of the rams. As soon as they appeared, all the people of the town divided into two factions for the fight, filling most of this huge square.

All the men had sticks in their hands, the size of a pilgrim's staff, except for the owners of the bulls. But there was so great an ill-humour and concern in their faces, that it seemed as if they themselves would have to enter the lists and fight, because they believe there is no disgrace or affront which approaches the grief of seeing their bull defeated. For while these bull-fights are very common in all the provinces of Persia, Kashan is special in that they are the normal entertainment of its inhabitants, and that there are men who have such a passion for them that they travel all over the kingdom to find bulls which have some reputation for valour, in which they rest all their honour.

And as factions and taking sides are so common among the men, they are particularly so in the big towns, where people are often divided not only over matters of importance, where honour is at stake and where one is in some way obliged to feel the affront one has received, but also over matters of no substance, of entertainment, in which one cannot help showing more liking for one lot than for the other, and above all if one is already committed to the party by other considerations. Just as in Rome in the past, where the whole town was either for the Prasini or for the Veneti, so it is in Kashan where all the people are divided in favour of one or other of the two bulls that are fighting. The same passion appears in the ram fights, but not with the same animosity as with the bull-fights where they often come to blows and do not leave off before several among them have had their heads broken. And what aggravates them the most and drives them to fight among themselves, to treat each other badly in this way, although they have no other weapons than sticks, is the fact that very often the victory is uncertain, and the fight between the bulls so stubborn on either side, that neither flees, or in withdrawing leaves the field to the more valiant. Each of the owners, who are always by them as they fight, talks up his bull, praising it and preferring it to the other. From that they come to blows just between themselves, punching and kicking, and thus insensibly they draw in their partisans, who first of all lend their man verbal support, and then lay about one another with sticks, with such animosity that neither the authority of the governors, nor the efforts of their officers and soldiers, are capable of separating them. The women who watch from a little further away don't fight among themselves, but aid their friends with cries of joy or disappointment.

The bulls finally arrived at the place of combat, charged at each other, locked horns and pushed each other, urged on by their owners and supporters. But the most remarkable thing was the noise made by the women who, although some distance away and seated in a row and veiled, did not cease supporting their side. After a while the bulls separated, sweat pouring off them and their heads bleeding from wounds. The ambassador thought they had done their duty and wanted to press a sum of money on their owners. But these said loudly that they didn't want money and they didn't believe the ambassador wanted to give them an affront. The tumult was such that the governors were obliged to let them continue the combat, telling the ambassador there would be serious fighting between the two sides if there was not a clear winner.

While the bulls were relaxing, their owners crawled gently towards them and squatting on their heels at their sides, they made many gestures with their arms and head, and in such a quiet voice that nobody could hear, they incited them to return to the fight. From what one could judge from their gestures and expressions, they spoke with such affection that it seemed that their intention was to touch the bulls with compassion, by remonstrating to them about the affront they would receive if they were so cowardly as to withdraw, or so weak as to let themselves be defeated, because they, the owners, would lose the money they had paid for them, the expenditure they had had in feeding them and the cost of the *galans*[23] they wore. The bulls resumed the fight and eventually the one that was a little stronger put the other to flight. Then the supporters of the victor, both men and women, surrounded the owner and the victorious bull and led them home with great cries of joy.

From *L' Ambassade de D. Garcias de Silva Figueroa en Perse*

A Description of Shah Abbas's capital of Isfahan

Shah Abbas transferred the Safavid capital from Qazvin to Isfahan in 1598, and embarked on a massive development programme to make the city a worthy capital of his Empire. Magnificent mosques, palaces, bazaars and whole suburbs were built, and new squares, avenues and parks laid out. By the end of his reign Isfahan bore comparison for elegance and vitality with Constantinople, the capital of the rival Ottoman Empire, and the saying became current in Persia that 'Isfahan

[23] I have been unable to discover the meaning of this French word – Ed.

is half the world'. Someone who saw the city at this point was a young Englishman by the name of Thomas Herbert (1606–1682) who accompanied the first official English embassy to Persia in 1628. The embassy, which was sent by King Charles I, stopped in Isfahan on its way to meet Shah Abbas at another of his palaces on the southern shore of the Caspian, this time at Ashraf. Herbert had time to explore the city and in the account he later wrote of the embassy he guides the reader around the sights of Shah Abbas's Isfahan in his characteristically florid and ebullient style.

Isfahan, metropolis of the Persian monarchy, is seated in the Parthian territory (now called Ayrac)[24] and as umbilic (central) to that spacious body which at this day is awed by the Persian sceptre. She is in compass at this day about nine English miles, including towards seventy thousand houses, and of souls (as may be conjectured) contains about two hundred thousand; for, besides natives, there are merchants of sundry nations, as English, Dutch, Portuguese, Pole, Muscovite, Indian, Arabian, Armenian, Georgian, Turk, Jew, and others, drawn thither by the magnetic power of gain. It hath several good buildings; but the most observable are the Maydan, *mechits* (masjids or mosques), *hummums* (public baths), and palaces; as be the gardens, monuments, and Jelphey (Julfa), a suburb adjoining.

Isfahan is most pleasant in its situation, elegant as to building, populous for inhabitants, rich in trade, and noble by being the usual residence of the court; eminent for all sorts of exercise, sufficiently watered by the Sindery,[25] fruitful in its soil; and for air so pure and quick that I very well remember we found it much warmer in more northern cities which had greater latitude. And, seeing Quintus Curtius saith of Persia, '*Regio non alia in tota Asia salubrior habetur,*'[26] I may in praise of this place add, than the air of Isfahan no part of Persia is more healthy. Howbeit, the town is of no great strength, yet has a mud-wall about it; and towards the outside of the city, a large castle, unflanked but moated about; and

[24] Persian Iraq. See footnote on page 69.
[25] Zayandeh-Rud, the name of the river that runs through Isfahan.
[26] 'There is no kingdom in all Asia that is healthier'.

118

several houses within, which guard the treasure, arms, and ice there stored.

Let me lead you into the Maydan;[27] into which ere I can bring you, we pass over a well-built arched bridge of hewn stone, which is towards the southwest end of the city, supported by five-and-thirty pillars, through which the Sindery (or Zindarout) from the mountains streams gently; spreading in rainy seasons here well-nigh so broad as the Thames, but very shallow. For in summer her channel is contracted, and so shallow that children usually wade or pass through it, for that the citizens for the better watering of their gardens by sluices drain and divide it into many rivulets, insomuch as the course of the river is spoiled, and (which is strange) lost in some valleys not many leagues distant thence, where 'tis drunk up without ever emptying itself (like other streams) into any sea or ocean: especially by the pipes which feed the two great and famous gardens belonging to the King, called Nazer-jareeb and Cherbaugh,[28] which for beauty contend with all others in Asia.

The Maydan is without doubt as spacious, as pleasant and aromatic a market as any in the universe. It is a thousand paces from north to south, and from east to west above two hundred, resembling our Exchange, or the Place-Royal in Paris, but six times larger. The building is of sun-dried brick, and an uninterrupted building, the inside full of shops, each shop filled with wares of sundry sorts; arched above (in cupolas), terrace-wise framed at top, and with blue plaster pargeted (plastered). And, being the noblest part, is placed as it were in the heart of this city. The King's palace, or Chonna-Potshaugh, conjoins it upon the west side possessing a large space of ground backwards, but juts not to the street further than the other buildings, which are uniform to the street so as to passengers it gives not any bravery, her greatest gallantry being in the outward trim; for it is pargeted and painted with blue and gold, embroidered with posies of Arabic, which after the grotesque manner makes it show very pleasant. Within, the

[27] This is the main square of Isfahan, known as the Royal Square until the Islamic Revolution of 1979 when it was renamed the Square of the Imam.
[28] The Chahar Bagh or Four Gardens, the famous tree-lined avenue in Isfahan with a central water channel and fountains laid out by Shah Abbas I.

rooms (according to the common form there) are arched, enlightened by trellises; the rooms embossed above, and painted with red, white, blue, and gold; the sides painted with sports and landscape; the ground, or floor, spread with carpets of silk and gold, without other furniture; terraced above, garnished with a *pharoe* (tall tower) overtopping many mosques; and the garden, or wilderness, behind the house made fragrant with flowers, filled with airy citizens privileged from hurt or affrights, and for which they return their thankful notes in a more melodious concert and variety than if they were in the exactest *vollyere* (aviary) in the universe. Within the hippodrome many of the cavalry use to ride (according to the ancient custom, as Xenophon in the *Life of Cyrus* instances); so do the Persians at this day, daily repairing to the court-gate, mounted, with lances in their hands, *shamsheers* or swords and quivers by their side; where, after they have pranced awhile, they depart, unless the King prepare to go abroad; for then they give their due attendance.

The north aisle of the Maydan hath eight or nine arched rooms, usually hung with lamps and latten candlesticks, which being lighted (as 'tis usual, especially at the Festival of Lights, which they call *Ceraghan*) give a curious splendour. Thither the Potshaw (*Padeshah*, the King) and others frequently resort for pastime, as tumbling, sleight of hand, dancing girls, and painted catamites (that *nefandum peccatum* being there tolerated). At the furthest end north is the mint, where we saw one day silver coined, gold the second, and next day brass. Not far thence are the cooks' shops, where men use to feed the helpful belly, after the busy eye and painful feet have sufficiently laboured.

Afore the King's door are one-and-thirty demi-cannons of brass and twelve iron culverins (a large cannon) unmounted, brought thither (as I suppose, after some overthrow they gave the Portuguese or Turk) from Ormus[29] or Babylon.[30] Opposite to this palace is a fair temple, or *Jewma Mechit*,[31] but that at the south end is the most

[29] Hormuz: the island at the entrance to the Persian Gulf which Shah Abbas captured from the Portuguese in 1622, with naval help from the English East India Company.
[30] Here means Baghdad.
[31] 'Masjid-e Jome', the Friday Mosque. Herbert refers to the mosque of Sheikh Lutfullah, described by Robert Byron on pp.321-323.

noble.[32] The outside is stone: not formed according to the Cross (the hieroglyphic of our salvation) as ours be, but round as were the Jews'. Within this here is distinguished into aisles; the walls are lined fifteen foot high from the sole (ground) with white, well-polished marble; cupolaed, compassed with walls, and open to the air, the aisles excepted where the people resort to prayer and prostrations, which are covered; and without are some seats to rest in. In the centre is a large tank, and at the portal another, octangular, filled with pure water, which first glides round the inside of the Maydan through a stone course, or channel, six foot deep and as many broad, which, after a pleasant murmer, drills (trickles) into this tank, whence it is sucked out by subterranean passages and distributed into private houses and gardens for use and refreshment. Within the Maydan the shops be uniform, trades usually having their shops together; of which, some be mercers (textile merchants), lapidaries some, and (not the fewest) such as sell gums, drugs, and spices, showing also greater variety of simples[33] and ingredients of medicines than ever I saw together in any one city of Europe; and such as may give encouragement to physicians both to view and judge both of their nature and quality, as well as temperature of the climes they come from, which such as are ignorant cannot distinguish.

Other mosques (here called *dear* and *zunae*) are orbicular for shape, and part thereof have large cupolas for sight, but low and indifferently pleasant, a great part being open to the air; and some have their *alcoranas* (minarets), high, slender, round steeples or towers, most of which are terraced near the top, like the Standard in Cheapside, but thrice the height, for the better conveniency of the boys at the accustomed hours to sing aloud in, and for placing lights at the *Ceraghan*, or Feast of Lights, which is annual. The materials of these *mechits* (mosques) are sun-burnt bricks, varnished on the outside and beautified with painted knots and fancies: few are without their tanks, or cisterns, of water, wherein Mussulmans (Muslims) wash their hands, arms and eyes, having formerly bathed

[32] Refers to the Masjid-e Shah, or Royal Mosque, renamed the Mosque of the Imam after the Islamic Revolution of 1979.
[33] Plants used for medicinal purposes.

their face, ears, breast and feet, as an operative work to purge away sin, if not to confer holiness. The female sex during worship use to approach no nearer than the door of the *mechit*.

Hummums in this city be many and beautiful; some are four-square, but most be globous (globe-shaped). The stone of which they are built is for the most part white and well-polished; the windows large without, crossed and inwardly made narrow; the glass (where glass is) is thick annealed (toughened by heating) and dark; the top or outside covering round, and tiled with a counterfeit turquoise, which is perfect blue, very beautiful and lasting. The insides of these hot-houses are divided into many cells and concamerations (chambers), some being for delight, others for sweating in, all for use; for the truth is, bathing with these is (as it was with the Greeks and Romans) no less familiar than eating and drinking, yet the excess doubtless weakens the body, by making it soft and delicate, and subject to colds. Howbeit, they may better there use it than we in Europe, by reason that they drink water, eat much rice (*pelo*) and like food of easy digestion, which makes their bodies solid and hard, so as little fear is that bathing will make them frothy: besides, their much sitting and little exercise makes them sweat less and need more bathing. These baths are of pure stone, paved with black and chequered marble: men frequent them commonly in the morning, women towards night: the price for bathing is very small, but so much used as makes the gain the more abundant. 'Tis accounted a catholicon against most diseases, especially colds, catarrhs, phlegm, ache, agues, *lues venera* (syphilis), and what not. The women's being there is known by a linen cloth, usually displayed afore the door, which serves to forbid men any approach during the time they stay there.

The city is built upon a level ground, and of oval form, having many streets, and scarce any house but is accommodated with large gardens full of cypress-trees. The city-wall is of no force against cannon: but of use against horse, and shock of any lance: some parapets and bulwarks it has of more ornament than use, the Persian magnanimity ever choosing to die rather than be besieged. It has a dozen portresses or gates, of which four are lately shut up, which are lately made the entrance into a royal garden.

Palaces here are few: the King's house is in the Maydan; that also where we lodged belonging to the King, but made ready for our ambassador; Conna Meloeymbeg,[34] Mir-Abdula, Tamas-Koolibeg, and Haram Beguna[35] were all that I saw worth the remembering. The first is low built, pargeted and painted without, but gilt within and spread with carpets, the usual furniture of this country; all which have large gardens beautified with flowers, being plentifully watered. The last, which is the royal *seraglio* (harem), is famous for the treasures and beauties it contains; of which (being dangerous to inquire, and much more to view) we will be silent. The castle is large, strongly walled and moated: made defensive with some pieces of brass, but more by a troop of lean-faced, beardless, memberless eunuchs, who though Cyrus made such esquires of his body, now, like so malignant *sagittaries* (centaurs), have no other duty save to guard the ladies. The battlements it has are pleasant to look upon; but the horizontal plain, which is easily discovered from thirty rising turrets there, yields most pleasure.

Gardens here for grandeur and fragour (fragrance) are such as no city in Asia outvies; which at a little distance from the city you would judge a forest, it is so large; but withal so sweet and verdant that you may call it another paradise: and, agreeable to the old report, '*Horti Persarum erant amoenissimi*'.[36] At the west end of Isfahan is that which is called Nazer-jareeb,[37] a garden deservedly famous. From the Maydan if you go to this garden you pass by Cherbaugh, through an even street near two miles long and as broad as Holborn in London, a great part of the way being garden walls on either side the street; yet here and there bestrewed with *mohols*, or summer-houses; all along planted with broad-spreading chenaer (plane) trees, which, besides shade, serves for use and ornament. Being come to the garden, or rather fruit-forest, of Nazer-jareeb, you find it circled with a high wall, which is about three miles in compass, entered by three

[34] Khaneh-ye Mulaim Beg: 'The house of Mulaim Beg', who was the Shah's factor, responsible for negotiating with the English and Dutch East India companies.
[35] Haram-e Begumha: The Harem of the ladies.
[36] 'The gardens of the Persians were very picturesque'.
[37] The Hezar Jareeb, or Park of a Thousand Jareebs, a jareeb being a unit of measurement that varied considerably from place to place.

gates that are wide and well built. From north to south it was a thousand of my paces; from east to west seven hundred; and the prospect from one end to the other easily and fully discovered by reason there is a fair open aisle (like that in Fontainebleau) which runs along, and is formed into nine easy ascents, each surmounting or rising above the other about a foot, all being very smooth and even. In the centre, or middle of the garden is a spacious tank, formed into twelve equal sides, each side being five foot, set round with pipes of lead, which spout the liquid element in variety of conceits; and that sort of pastime continues to the north gate, which is raised a pile for prospect and other sort of pleasure, anticly (grotesquely) garnished without, and within divided into six rooms: the lower part is adorned with tanks of white marble, which fume out a cool breeze by quaffing so much crystalline water as makes it bubble there by a constrained motion; the aqueduct being brought by extraordinary charge and toil thither from the Coronian Mountain. The higher rooms are beautified with variety of landscapes, which represent their manner of sport, hawking, fishing, riding, shooting, wrestling, courting, and other fancies. The roof upon the parget (ornamental plaster work) was gilt, and painted with blue and other colours. In this summer-house by some gentlemen who were *coozelbashaws*[38] of the Georgian nation I was invited to taste some Shiraz wine. They expressed very high civility, and gave me leave to drink what I pleased; nevertheless I was sorry to see them in that exercise so over-liberal, which the custom of the place reproves not; but, professing themselves Christians, have for their instruction that of the Psalmist, *Vinum laetificat cor; in jucunditatem creatum est, non in ebrietatem*, etc.[39] Nevertheless it was worthy my observation and commendation that, being over-charged, they never quarrel, nor amidst their cups lash out in discourse to the just offence of any, whereas in other countries excess in wine has too often contrary effects. But what seemed the most pleasant was the view we enjoyed from her terrace: that afforded us

[38] Qizilbash: literally 'Red-heads'. The term was originally used to denote the Turkoman tribesmen who brought the Safavids to power, on account of their red bonnets. Here used more generally to denote the Safavid soldiery.
[39] Ecclesiastes.xxxi.28.

a curious prospect into a great part of the city, which (save at Rustam's tomb,[40] upon a hill two miles thence) elsewhere by reason of the level cannot well be obtained. This garden is replenished with trees of all sorts, for medicine, shade, and fruit; which are all so green, so sweet and pleasant, as may well be termed a compendium of sense-ravishing delights, or Abbas his Paradise.

From *Travels in Persia 1627–1629*
by Thomas Herbert

Celebrating the End of Winter

The No Ruz or New Year festival is not the only Zoroastrian festival that has survived the Islamicisation of Persia and has continued to be celebrated nationally. Just before No Ruz, which is at the spring equinox, there is the festival of 'Chahar Shanbeh Suri', which marks the end of winter. This ancient festival was witnessed in 1637 by an embassy sent by the German princeling, Duke Frederick of Holstein-Gottorp, who had the extravagant idea of diverting the entire export of Persian silk to his north German principality via Russia. The scheme never got off the ground and was later abandoned. The embassy travelled through Russia and crossed to the southwest shore of the Caspian, to the Persian province of Shirvan with its capital of Shamakhi, where the embassy was entertained by the Safavid governor and where, shortly after its arrival, 'Chahar Shanbeh Suri' was celebrated. The form the celebrations took is described by the secretary to the embassy, Adam Olearius.

The third of March (1637), the Persians celebrated another feast, which they call *Tzar Schembesur*, that is, the fourth sad Sabbath, and it is the next Wednesday before the vernal equinox, by which they begin their year; of which they are perswaded, that this Wednesday

[40] Rustam is the legendary Iranian hero of Firausi's *Shah-nama* (*Book of Kings*). The Hezar Jareeb Park was built on the lower slopes of a mountain called 'Rustam's Throne.'

is the most unfortunate day. And this, they say, they know not only by tradition, but also by experience, which hath discover'd to them, that there never happend any thing but misfortune to them that day. Thence it comes, that they do not any business that day, they keep their shops shut, swear not, nor make any debauches; but above all things, take they an especial care, not to pay away any money that day, out of a fear, they should be oblig'd not to do any thing else all the year after. There are some who spend the whole day in telling what money they have in their houses: others go, without speaking a word by the way, to the river, for some water, wherewith they sprinkle their houses and houshold-stuff, thinking by that means to divert the misfortune which might befall them. If they meet with any one of their acquaintance, as they return home-wards, they cast some water into his face with their hands, or haply, pour the whole pitcher full upon him: but this is a kindness they do only to their best friends, out of a perswasion, that those who are so served, and have their cloaths all wet, cannot fail being happy all the year after. Young people that are not married, find also their divertisement at this solemnity, which is, to walk up and down the streets or along the river side, playing upon certain timbrels of bak'd earth, which they carry under their arms. Others carry great staves in their hands, and go up to their knees in the river, to dash those who come to fetch water, either by casting it at them with their hands, or taking hold of them, to wet them, or to rub their faces with the borders of their wet garments, or haply they break the pitchers with their staves. These last are look'd upon as ill-presaging birds, so that those who can keep out of their clutches, think they have avoided many misfortunes that should have happened to them that year. Upon which accompt (account) it is, that there are some, who to avoid meeting with them, go and fetch in their water before day: but all these fopperies are done only in the morning, for as soon as it is after-noon, they go a-walking and bestow the time in any of their other ordinary exercises.

A Fireworks Display

The Safavid kings and their governors had a great love of fireworks displays. One such was enjoyed by the Holstein embassy in the city of Ardabil, south of Shirvan, as it continued its journey to Isfahan. Somewhat surprisingly, and to the anger of many of his subjects, the governor of Ardabil laid on the fireworks, normally reserved for a joyful occasion, on the day known as Ashura, which is the most sacred day in the Shiite calendar. It is the anniversary of the martyrdom of the Imam Husayn, the Third Shiite Imam, and the climax of ten days of mourning ceremonies, which the governor of Ardabil had invited the principal members of the Holstein embassy to join him in watching. Adam Olearius, who wrote an account of the embassy, greatly admired this display of Persian skill in pyrotechnics.

After these ceremonies, the governour entertain'd the ambassadors with noble fire-works; which most of the Persians took very ill at his hands, and thought it not over religiously done of him, to give such divertisements to the Christians during the time of their *Aschur*, which ought to represent only things conducing to sadnesse and affliction.

These fire-works consisted of several very excellent and ingenious inventions, as of little castles, towers, squibs, crackers, etc. The castle, to which they first set fire, was three foot-square, the walls of paper, of all sorts of colours. They lighted first several small wax candles about the moat of it, which discover'd the figures painted on the paper. There came out of it squibs and crackers for an hour and a half, or better, before the castle itself took fire. Then they set fire to another invention, which they call *Derbende*. It was a kind of saucidge (sausage), about six inches thick, and three foot long, casting, at first, at both ends, a shower of fire, and afterwards several squibs and little serpents, which falling among the people, set their cotton garments on fire; while they fir'd several sorts of crackers, which in the air, were turn'd to stars and other figures. They set fire also to several boxes; but what we most admir'd was a great kind of fire-work, which was fasten'd to the ground with great iron chains, and cast out fire at the mouth, with so dreadfull noise, that we were afraid it would have burst at last, and scatter its fiery entrails among the company. This fire-work they call *kumbara* (a mortar).

There were some, who carry'd paper-lanthorns upon long poles, which were also fill'd with squibs and crackers: but what diverted us most of all, was that, out of those lanthorns, there came a piece of linnen, which, being folded together, and ty'd up in knots, had, in each of those knots, several squibs, crackers and serpents, which having much ado to get out, made an admirable shew, by the windings which the fire made through all the folds on that piece of cloath. Others carried in their aprons, a certain composition, into which some that pass'd by let fire fall, as it were negligently, whereupon, he who carried it shaking his apron, there came out a great number of stars, which burnt a long time upon the ground.

Hunting with the Shah

The Holstein ambassadors – Otto Bruggman, a Hamburg lumber merchant, and Von Krusenstiern – reached Isfahan in August 1637. They had an audience and banquet with Shah Abbas I's grandson and successor, Shah Safi I, who would make no commitment on the Persian silk exports, but who invited them to join him on a hunting expedition. Olearius was included in the party and has left an entertaining account of the various hunts the ambassadors were taken on.

The 17th (October 1637) betimes in the morning, there were horses brought for the persons and camels for the baggage. The ambassadors got on horse-back, with Father Joseph, and about thirty persons of their retinue. The *mehmandar* conducted them into a spacious plain, whither the King came soon after, attended by above three hundred lords, all excellently well mounted, and sumptuously cloath'd. The King himself was in a vestment of silver brocado, with a turbant adorn'd with most noble heron's feathers, and having led after him four horses, whereof the saddles, harness, and covering cloaths were beset with gold and precious stones. The King at his coming up very civilly saluted the ambassadors, and ordered them to march near him on his left hand.

The other *chans* (khans) and great lords, march'd after the King, with so little observance of order, that many times the servants were shuffled in among their masters. There was, among the rest, in the King's retinue, an astrologer, who always kept very close to him, and ever and anon observ'd the position of the heavens, that he might prognosticate what good or ill fortune should happen. These are believ'd as oracles. We rode up and down that day above three leagues, the King taking occasion often to change his horse and upper garments, which he did every day while the hunting lasted. The morning was spent in hawking, the hawks were let out at herns (herons), cranes, drakes, sometimes at crows, which they either met with by chance, or were set purposely upon. About noon we came to an Armenian village, where we found a great number of tents of divers colours, pitch'd after an odd kind of way; which yet made a very pleasant prospect. After the King had been brought by his grandees into his tent, they came for the ambassadors, who with some of their gentlemen and officers dined with him. There was nothing extraordinary; fruits and conserves were brought in first, and afterwards the meat, upon a kind of bier, or barrow, which was cover'd all over with plates of gold, and it was serv'd in dishes of the same metal.

In the after-noon, the *mehmandar* carried the ambassadors to be lodg'd in another village, about a quarter of a league from the place where the King had his tents. The inhabitants of those villages are Armenians, and they are called *Desach*, and *Werende*, from the countrey, where they liv'd before, near Iruan (Erivan), whence they were heretofore translated by *Schach-Abas*, to the end, that, living near Ispahan (Isfahan), they might be employ'd about the vines. When they understood we were Christians, they entertain'd us much more kindly, and made us several presents of fruits and wine. *Seferas-beg,* and some other lords gave the ambassadors a visit, to be merry, and participate of a collation with them. They brought along with them two of those fallow deer, which the Persians call *ahu*s, and some herns, which we sent to Ispahan. The King, coming to hear that the *mehmandar* had lodg'd us in another village, was very much displeas'd at it, and commanded that we should be brought the same night, to be quarter'd in the next house to that where he was lodg'd himself; which was accordingly done, and our supper was brought us out of the King's kitchin, in dishes of gold.

The 18th (October) betimes in the morning, the King sent the ambassadors word, that he would go with very few persons about him, a-crane-hunting, intreating them that they would bring along with them onely their interpreter, out of this respect, that the cranes might not be frighted by the great number of people, and that the pleasure of the hunting might not be disturb'd by too much noise. The ambassadors took onely Father Joseph along with them: but the sport was no sooner begun with the day, ere they sent for all the retinue. They had made a great secret way underground, at the end whereof there was a field, about which they had scatter'd some wheat. The cranes came hither in great numbers, and there were above fourscore taken. The King took some of their feathers, to put into his *mendil* or turban, and gave two to each of the ambassadors, who put them into their hats. That done, they rode up and down the fields, and spent the time in hawking, till that drawing towards noon, the King went to take his repast in the same house, where he had dined the day before, and was in a very good humour. They had sent for his musick thither.

At night, he sent to entreat the ambassadors to come onely with six persons along with them, to the hunting of the drake and wild-goose, at a place, half a league from the village. They all alighted within two hundred paces of the place where they expected the sport, and went into a great hut built of earth, near which they had hidden the nets upon the side of a small brook, where there is abundance of fresh-water fowl. The King caus'd us to sit down all about the walls of the hut, and oblig'd us to help him off with some bottles of excellent wine, which was all the divertisement we had that day. For, not so much as one bird appearing, we return'd to our quarters, where the King sent us cold mutton, boyl'd and roasted, sowr sheeps milk, which they account a great delicacy, cheese, and several vessels full of citrons, and other fruits, raw and preserv'd.

The next day was our greatest day for sport, the King having ordered to be brought to the field, a great number of hawks, and three leopards taught to hunt, but very few dogs. Having spent some time in beating the bushes up and down, and found nothing, the King carried us into a great park, which was bout two leagues about. The Persians call it *hazartzirib*, that is, a place where a thousand bushels of wheat may be sown. It was compass'd with a very high wall, and divided into three partitions. In the first were kept harts, wild-goats, deer, hares, and foxes. In the second were kept that kind of deer, which thy call *ahus*; and in the third, wild asses, which they call *kouhrhan*. The King first commanded the leopards to be let in among the *ahus*, and they took each of them one. Thence we went to the wild asses, and the King seeing one of them at a stand, spoke to the Ambassador Brugman, to fire his pistol at it, and perceiving that he miss'd it, he took an arrow, and though he rid in full speed, shot it directly into the breast of the beast. Another he took just in the fore-head, and afterwards he wounded others in several places. He never fail'd, though he always shot riding in full speed. He was as well skil'd at his sword as at his bow; for perceiving one of the wild asses could hardly go, he alights, and going directly to the beast, gave it a blow with his sword over the back, with which single blow he cleft it down to the belly. He struck another with his cymitar over the neck, with so much strength and flight, that there wanted not an inch of his having cut it clear off. One of the *chans* took the King's sword, wip'd it clean, and put it into the scabbard. Then we all went to another small partition, that was in the middle of the park.

At the entrance of this inclosed place, the King commanded one of the two huntsmen who carried his fowling-piece after him, to shoot at a wild asse, which had before been wounded with an arrow. The ancienter man of the two thinking it a disparagement to him, that the command was directed to the younger, would needs prevent him, shot at the beast, and miss'd. The company laugh'd at him, which put him into such madness, that suffering the King to go on, he returns to his camerade, drew his sword upon him, and cut off the thumb of his right hand. The wounded party makes his complaints to the King, who immediately commanded the other's head to be brought him: but upon the mediation of several of the grandees, his punishment was changed, and he had only his ears cut off. The executioner, I know not upon what inducement, cut off but part of the ear; which the grand-master, Mortusaculi-Chan perceiving, and thinking the man had foul play done him to have ought of his ears left, alighted, took out his own knife, and cut off what the executioner had left; to the great astonishment of all of us, who were not accustomed to see persons of that quality turn common executioners.

Within the enclosed space I spoke of, there was a little building much after the fashion of a theatre, into which the King brought us, to a collation of fruits and conserves. That done, there were driven into the place thirty-two wild asses, at which the King discharg'd some shots with the fowling-pieces, and shot some arrows, and afterwards permitted the ambassadors, and the other lords to shoot at them.

It was pretty sport to see those asses run, having sometimes ten or more arrows shot into their bodies, wherewith they incommodated and wounded the others when they got in among them, so that they fell a biting one another and running one at another after a strange manner. Having knock'd down all those that were wounded, there were let in thirty wild asses more, which they also kill'd and laid them all in a row before the King, to be sent to Ispahan (Isfahan), to the court kitchin. The Persians so highly esteem the flesh of these wild asses, that they have brought it into a proverb in their *Kulusthan*.[41]

This kind of hunting being over, dinner was brought in at the same place. Here it was, that the Ambassador Brugman was pleas'd, upon his own account, to present the King of Persia, with his Highness the Duke of Holstein's picture, in box all beset with diamonds, as also with a very fair steel looking-glass, polish'd on both sides, and embellish'd with several figures, grav'd by that famous artist, John Dresde, and done after an excellent way, whereof he himself had been the inventor.

After dinner, we retir'd into some houses thereabouts, to take our midday's repose. The King sent us thither ten *ahus*, and a very fair stagg, the horns whereof had twelve brow-ancklers: but ere we were well laid down, word was brought us, that the King was got on horse-back, in order to have some further sport. We immediately follow'd, and found him a-hawking. He soon gave over that sport, and taking along with him nine persons of his own retinue, and six of ours, he went into a spacious low walk at the end whereof

[41] *The Gulestan* or *Rose Garden* is the title of one of the best-known works by the Persian poet, Saadi.

there was a place for the keeping of wild-ducks: but instead of hunting, he must needs fall a-drinking, and was so dispos'd to mirth, that the noise we made, kept the ducks and geese from coming near the place.

The 21st (of October), the King sent betimes in the morning to invite us to go a pidgeon hunting. We were carried up to the top of a great tower, within which there were above a thousand nests. We were plac'd all without, having in our hands little sticks forked at the ends. The King commanded our trumpets to sound a charge, and immediately there were driven out of the tower or pidgeon-house, great numbers of pidgeons, which were most of them kill'd by the King and those of his company. This was the end of that kind of hunting, after which we took our way towards the city: but ere we got into it, the King carried us into one of his gardens, called Tzarbach (Chahar Bagh), which is no doubt the fairest of any we have seen in Persia, where we had another magnificent treatment. As soon as we were got to our lodgings, there were brought us, from the King, twelve wild drakes, and as many pidgeons; but they were provided, it seems, only for the Ambassador Brugman and his ladies.

Some daies afterwards, it was published by the *tzartzi* or publick crier, all over the city, that all should keep within their houses; and that none should presume to come into the street; the King being to go that way abroad, to give the court ladies the divertisement of hunting.

The custom of the country is, that the King's wives and concubines should not go abroad, unless it be in certain chests or cabinets, which are cover'd all over, and carried by camels. All which notwithstanding, they permit not, that, while they are passing by, there should be any one in the streets, or that any men should come within musket-shot of the field where they are, upon pain of present death. The King goes before, and the ladies follow about half an hour after, accompany'd by their women and a great number of eunuchs. When they are come into the field, they get on horse-back, carry hawks on their fists, and use their bows and arrows as well as the men.

Only the King and eunuchs stay among the women; all the rest of the men are about half a league from them, and when the sport is begun, no man is to come within two leagues of them, unless the King send for him by an eunuch. The lords of the court in the mean time hunt some other way. The King returned from his hunting, Nov. 26 so drunk, as were also most of his lords that they could hardly sit their horses.

Persian Poets

As librarian to the Duke of Holstein, Olearius had a keen interest in literature and was impressed by the Persian love of poetry. Then, as now, this was not confined to an elite, but was shared by everyone. Olearius took the trouble to acquire some knowledge of Persian while he was in the country, though whether it was enough to justify the judgements he passes on the poetry is open to doubt. But he was certainly better informed on the subject than most Europeans who visited Persia.

There's no nation in the world more addicted to poetry than the Persians. There you have poets in all the market-places, and in all houses of good fellowship, where they entertain and make sport for such as frequent them, as the mountebanks, and such as shew tricks of legerdemain do in Europe. All bear with them, and the great lords think they cannot give their friends a better entertainment than by diverting them, while they are at dinner, with the recital of some poem. The King himself, and the *chans* (khans) have, among their other menial servants, their poets, whose only business it is to find out somewhat for their diversion by whom they are maintain'd, and which they are not to communicate to any other, without the consent of their patrons. The poets are known from others by their habit, which is the same with that of the philosophers; to wit, a long white coat, but open before, with great broad sleeves, and they have at their girdle a kind of a hawking-bag, in which are their books, paper, and an ink-horn, that they may give copies of their verses to such as desire them. Their under garment hath no sleeves, and would be a perfect cloak, if it had but a cape. They wear no stockings; their breeches come down to their feet, like pantaloons, and in winter, they wear such as reach but to the ankles. Instead of *mendils* or turbans, they wear a kind of caps. Those who put off their productions in the market places and at taverns, wear skarfs of several colours, which come about their bodies just above the waste, and passing over the right shoulder fall down under the left arm. Most of these take for the subject of their poetry the religion of the Turks and their saints (i.e. Sunnism), which they are pleased to rail at and make sport withall.

It may well be imagin'd, that, among so many poets, there must also be some poetasters, and that there, as well as in other places, a man must expect to find but few Homers and Virgils. Nay there are some so modest as to vent only the works of other men, and finding in themselves such a barreness of wit as will not produce any thing, make it their business to disperse their productions who are in repute. Persia hath this in common with France, as indeed it hath many other things, that it hath hardly any author excellent at an epick poem, and that some few poets laid aside, who are in great reputation, the rest are rather to be pittied. The best, and such as may justly be accompted good poets, are Saudi (Saadi), Hafis (Hafiz), Firdausi, Fussuli, Chagani (Khaqani), Eheli (Ahli), Schems (Rumi), Naway (Nava'i), Scahidi (Shahidi), Ferahsed (?), Deheki (Daqiqi), Nissimi (Nizami), etc. Their poetry is suitable to the modern way, and they will keep up the rime though they are not very exact in observing the number of the syllables. Nor do they think it much to use the same words to keep the rime, as imagining it no breach of the rules of their Prosodia (prosody). They also delight much in equivocations, and many times very handsomely begin the subsequent verse with the word that ended the precedent.

From *The Voyages and Travels of the Ambassadors* sent by Frederick Duke of Holstein, to the Great Duke of Muscovy, and the King of Persia, begun in the year 1633 and finished in 1639, written originally by Adam Olearius, secretary to the embassy

Doing Business with the Shah

*French jewellers were prominent among the European merchants who
did business in Persia during the Safavid period. One such was Jean-
Baptiste Tavernier (1605–1689), a Parisian and a Protestant, who
visited Persia nine times between 1632 and 1668. He undertook his
first journey to Persia more out of a simple desire to travel, which he
acquired from his father, who was a cartographer. But he soon proved
to be a hard-headed and successful merchant. On his return from his
last visit to Persia he was ennobled by Louis XIV, and retired to a
country estate to write about his experiences. He is an invaluable
source of information about Safavid Persia, as in this enjoyable
account of how he negotiated the sale of jewels to Shah Abbas II at the
court in Isfahan.*

I arrived in Isfahan for the sixth time on the 20th of December
1664. As soon as the *nazar* or grand-master of the royal household
was informed, he sent the head of the Armenian community, who
is called the *kelonter*, with seven or eight of the leading men of that
nation, to congratulate me on my arrival and to offer me, on his behalf,
all the services I could wish for. I thanked them, as I ought, for their
goodwill, but I easily perceived that their main aim was to try to get
admitted to the court through me, and to get a look at what I was
bringing so that they could profit from it.

The next day the *nazar* sent the same Armenians to me again with
four horsemen, to inform me that the King wished to see what I had
brought, and the *kelonter* was ordered to provide me with men for this
business, which was done with great splendour, as when the presents of
some ambassador are carried in ceremony. All the Europeans who were
in Julfa, where I was staying, mounted their horses to accompany the
large pieces, which were great mirrors enriched with precious stones,
chandeliers of rock crystal, and other things of this kind. The
Armenians also proceeded to follow, but I thanked them for the trouble
they wished to take, and seeing that they persisted in wanting to come
in spite of everything I could say to dissuade them, I finally let them
know that I had no need of them, that I was quite capable of

conducting my business myself, and that if they came to the court I would not show the King the half of my jewels. Had I not spoken to them a little sharply, I should not have been able to get rid of them.

As soon as they had left I mounted my horse and, accompanied by two of the horsemen the *nazar* had sent me, I made my way with speed to the convent of the Capuchin Reverend Fathers, where I had left my jewels, as being a safer place than my house in Julfa. The Reverend Father Raphaël is the superior of this convent and of the Capuchin mission in Persia. He has a perfect knowledge of mathematics and there are several lords of the court who have instruments he has made. As he has been more than twenty years in Persia, he speaks the language very well, and it is on this account that he has acquired much credit at the court, and is very well known to the King, who usually summons him to act as his interpreter in the dealings he has with the French.[42] At the same time as the horsemen had come from the King to summon me, two or three had also been sent after Father Raphaël, who was not then in his convent, which is in Isfahan. As it was Christmas eve, he had gone to Julfa[43] to see some Roman Catholics who live there, and who were preparing to perform their devotions. These horsemen ran from house to house, among the Europeans, in search of the Reverend Father, because it is the custom that when the *nazar* sends for someone to be found for the King, the horsemen who are sent to him absolutely have to bring him to the court, otherwise they would be in danger of losing their lives. They eventually found him, and he arrived at the palace a little before me.

As soon as I had arrived with my jewels, I was ushered into the place where the great ambassadors are given audience, and there I found the *nazar* with Father Raphaël and all the Europeans who had accompanied my large pieces of gold and silver plate. The *nazar* had already had everything laid out, so that the King only had to

[42] The French Capuchin, Father Raphaël du Mans, resided in Isfahan, from 1647 until his death in 1696. He had close contacts with the court and was considered the best informed European resident on Persia. He wrote a report on the country for Louis XIV's minister, Colbert, which led to the foundation of the French East India Company.

[43] Julfa was the suburb of Isfahan established by Shah Abbas I for Armenians he deported from Julfa in Armenia in 1605 as part of the scorched earth tactics he used against the Ottomans.

cast his eyes over it when he entered this hall. All my jewels were also on show, and the *nazar*, with his own hand, arranged everything on the floor, on a carpet of silk and gold thread. He considered all the pieces attentively, and with such admiration that he remarked several times to some courtiers who were present that no one had ever brought such beautiful things to Persia as I had, nor in such great quantity. He then begged me to conceal nothing from His Majesty, from whom I would receive much honour and favour. After I had protested that I had nothing more to show him other than what was on view, he ordered everyone to leave the hall, except for the two of us.

A quarter of an hour later, the King entered through a door that opens onto the hall from his apartment, followed only by thirteen eunuchs as his guard, and by two venerable old men, whose office is to take off the King's shoes when he enters rooms covered with carpets of silk and gold thread and to put them back on when he leaves. The King was wearing only a simple pair of taffeta breeches with little red and white checks, which came half-way down his legs, his feet being bare, and a little waist-length *hongreline*, with a big cloak of cloth of gold, lined with beautiful sable, with sleeves hanging down to the ground. The first piece the King cast his eyes upon was a large lustre or rock crystal chandelier. I had had it hung from a pole supported by two pillars and it was assuredly the richest and most beautiful piece of this kind that it was possible to see. He then turned to look at a rich tapestry hanging depicting human figures which I had also brought, and which he admired. The *nazar* made me step forward to do my reverence to the King, who, recognizing me, said to the *nazar*, 'There is that European gentleman who sold me lots of beautiful things five or six years ago, when Muhammad Beg was grand vizier.' While the King was speaking in this way, Father Raphaël was sent in, and was made to stand for a short time beside a pillar. Then the *nazar* had him taken to salute the King, who told him that he was very pleased by everything that he saw, and that he did not wish me to take anything back, provided that I priced the things reasonably. His Majesty then asked me where I had gone after leaving his empire, and I replied that I had gone to India. He wanted to know further whom

I had sold the rest of my precious stones to, and for how much; I replied that Shasta Khan had bought the lot for 120,000 rupees.

While the King was putting such questions to me, all the time standing up, the *nazar* showed him all the pieces one after another. Through Father Raphaël, I begged His Majesty to accept my large steel mirror as a gift. The Father explained to him its merit and effects, in the search of which several famous mathematicians had spent much time and study. As Father Raphaël has the reputation of being one of the most learned and expert people, his reasoning much pleased the King, who coming and standing in front of the mirror was surprised to see his face so extraordinarily large. He had it placed in front of one of his eunuchs, who had a monstrously big beaked nose, and as the mirror made it considerably longer and bigger; the King could not help laughing. This occupied him for a quarter of an hour, after which he went into his apartment, leaving me alone with the *nazar* and the Reverend Father. The *nazar* then said to Father Raphaël in Persian, 'This European gentleman has brought the King so many rarities, and so many kinds of jewels and beautiful gold and silver plate, that it has delighted the King's heart.' The *nazar*, a man of great judgment and very methodical, fearing lest some of my jewels go astray, forbade any Persian to go near them, and told me that I could only bring those Europeans into the hall whom I trusted to help me put away all the pieces. I summoned three or four, and together with Father Raphaël we put all the jewels back in their cases, and they were then locked up in a chest on which the *nazar* wished that I place my seal, after which he had it carried to a safe place in one of the rooms of the King's apartment. As for the big pieces of gold and silver plate, the mirrors, the chandelier, and the tapestries, he made me deposit the lot with one of the principal officers of the guard.

The sun had set by the time the *nazar* dismissed us with warm compliments, and assuring us that the King had been very satisfied with everything he had seen. The Reverend Father Raphaël came with us to Julfa in order to attend the following day to the devotions of Christmas Day. But the sun had barely risen when four horsemen came to look for him in his convent. Three others were sent at the same time to bring me from my house in Julfa, where they found me with the Reverend Father, and without giving us a moment, they made us follow them and go with haste to the King. The *nazar* was waiting for us impatiently and as soon as we arrived the chest containing the jewels was brought in. The *nazar* made me check my seal to see if it was intact, because these people wish all things to be done fairly and take great precautions in their affairs. The chest was then opened and the jewels taken out, the *nazar* again asking me if anything was missing. Then he ordered a secretary to write down in Persian the name, nature and price of each piece, as I called them out to Father Raphaël.

When this task was complete, the *nazar* brought in the chief goldsmith. It is necessary to point out that in Persia each profession has its head, who is an officer of the King and maintained by him. The head of the goldsmiths, moreover, receives two percent of the price of all the jewels that one sells to the King or to the lords of the court, and this two percent should be given to him by the person from whom the jewels are bought. However, I can say that the chief goldsmith has never had anything from me. For on all the voyages I have made to Isfahan, before showing anything to the King, I have always insisted to the grand vizier or to the *nazar* that I absolutely did not want to give anything to the chief goldsmith. Some jewellery merchants were also summoned to value the pieces, one giving the value of the diamonds, another of the pearls, another of the rubies, and another of the emeralds, each of them according to his expertise. However, the *nazar* spoke to me very obligingly, as did the other officers of the King who were present, and orders were given to bring the Reverend Father and myself the food which was usually eaten in the morning: bread, cheese, milk, cream, and grapes and melons as fresh as in the autumn, although we were now at the end of December. One would have said that the grapes and melons had just been gathered, and of the latter there were three sorts: red, green and almost white. In addition we were served four kinds of liquid jam and two kinds of sugared almonds, all in bowls and on plates of fine gold, for in Persia no other gold is worked. We were brought three of these gold bowls, each containing five or six of these fruit plates and they were put down in front of us on the carpet, as is the custom. While we were eating the *nazar* asked me two or three times if I wanted some wine, but I thanked him and told him that I normally only drank in the evening. He immediately ordered four large bottles of the same wine that was served to the King to be taken to my house, and that very evening I treated my friends to it.

All the time after lunch was spent in estimating the value of the jewels, and several times I argued with the valuers, because there were pieces that they estimated at less than half their worth. In the evening, they gave their prices to the *nazar,* and I gave him mine, and there was a considerable difference between the two. The *nazar* immediately took the two sets of prices to the King together with all the jewels, and on his return from His Majesty, seeing that the sun had set, he dismissed us with great compliments. The Reverend Father Raphaël retired to his convent, and I to Julfa, and I found at my lodging three French friends waiting for me impatiently. We supped together and drank the King's wine which the *nazar* had sent me and which was excellent.

Early the following day the *nazar* again sent out horsemen, three to seek out Father Raphaël, and four to fetch me from my house. When I arrived at the palace, I found the *nazar* and the Father waiting for me. The *nazar* gave me a warm welcome as usual and said laughingly that I was a lazy fellow. I let him know that it was not so much my fault as his, if I was coming later than he wished, and that the good wine which he had sent me had obliged me to celebrate for a part of the night with my friends, drinking his health and that of the King. He burst out laughing again and assured me that the King had found all my jewels very acceptable, but that the price I had put on them was too high, and that I should show myself more reasonable if I wanted the King to honour me with his favours, and to be welcoming out of regard for me to all the Frenchmen who would come to Isfahan in the future. He said many other obliging things to me and I begged the Reverend Father Raphaël to return the compliments on my part, and to let him know at the same time that I could take nothing off the price which I had put upon my jewels. Some days passed without us being able to reach an agreement. Horsemen were sent every morning to the Father's home and mine to bring us to the palace, which was very inconvenient at a time of snowfalls, and in a town full of mud like

Isfahan. At last, after several comings and goings, the *nazar* told me that in putting a fair price on my jewels on the basis of what they cost me, the King would give me a profit of twenty-five per cent, and that he would only take the gemstones, leaving me the pearls, which, he says, would be worth more to me in India. I could not resist accepting this offer, and the *nazar* wanted me to sign the agreement, which was taken at once to the King. His Majesty, having read it, ordered the *nazar* to ask me what favour I wished from him, and to tell me that he wanted me to be a court jeweller; that out of consideration for me all the Europeans who would come to Persia would be well received by his whole state, and as for me, since I was going to India where he believed there was no wine, he wanted me to be provided for until my return. To satisfy the royal command, I had a request drawn up, in which I entreated His Majesty to have me sent a command in the correct form with his seal attached, which would permit me to do business throughout his state in such merchandise as I wished, without being obliged to pay any customs duty. I also explained to him that, being an old man, I had brought my nephew to Persia, and had left him in Tabriz in the hands of the Reverend Father Gabriel de Chinon to learn the Turkish and Persian languages and to make himself capable, when he takes over my business and my journeys, of serving His Majesty, whom I entreated to take him under his protection.

Matters having proceeded in this way, the King had a letter written to the *khan* (governor) of Tabriz in favour of my nephew, saying that he considered him henceforth as one of his servants, and that he expected him to receive every kind of satisfaction during his stay in Tabriz, the more so as he was still young. For my nephew was still only ten to eleven years-old, a very suitable age to learn languages.

[Two days later] I was back with the *nazar* who had sent to find me early in the morning, and he told me that not only did the King agree to my demands, but that on top of that he wanted to give me the full robe of honour, which is only given as a great honour to the *khans* or provincial governors, and that he had also commanded that I be paid. On receipt of this news I returned to Julfa and Father Raphaël to his convent to await the orders of the King, but we had scarcely arrived when some horsemen rode up at full pelt to take us back to the court, where the *nazar*, the grand treasurer, and several other officials were waiting for me in the treasury chamber with the money which I was to be given in sealed bags. The *nazar* told me which pieces the King had kept, and that on the basis of the price I had placed on them, the whole lot would come to 3,460 *tomans*,[44] as I could see in my account book, which was correct. The grand treasurer then asked me if I wished to count it out *toman* by *toman*, or to count out one bag and then weigh all the others, since there were fifty tomans in each. So I took two of the bags, and having weighed the money *toman* by *toman*, I was then content to weigh the whole bags, which I found quite fair. But out of the 3,460 *tomans* which I ought to receive, I was only given 3,300, and the treasurer told me that it was the custom to withhold five per cent of everything which was sold to the King for those who served in the treasury chamber. I strongly disputed this point and told the treasurer that if the matter followed this course, I would leave him the money and take back my jewels; that the King had promised me twenty-five per cent profit, and that by his account it would be no more than twenty per cent, which I in no way wanted to hear about.

The *nazar*, seeing that I was very determined and that I was leaving the treasury chamber without taking the money, had the records examined to see how I had been treated on previous journeys. He recognised that I had always been given everything that the King had promised without any discount, and turning towards me with a laughing air, he said that there was no need to lock horns with the treasury people, and that the favours the King wanted to do for me would be worth more than another thousand *tomans*. In the end, not wishing to offend the *nazar*, I settled for half of what they were asking from me, which amounted to eighty-two and a half tomans, which the treasurer was satisfied with. Meanwhile sixteen porters were summoned, and the *nazar* ordered that the name and address of each of them be written down, for fear lest some bag go astray on the way. But as I saw that it was very late, I begged the *nazar* to postpone the matter to another time. Knowing that my money was ready, I did not hurry to collect it, and I spent the following day enjoying myself out

[44] One toman was worth approximately three pounds and six shillings sterling.

hunting with a party of Europeans. In a short time we had a good hunt, because the country is always full of game, as it is almost only the King's people who hunt, and on our return we entertained ourselves until two or three o'clock in the morning. That caused us to sleep later than usual, and I was awoken by the great noise made at my house by four horsemen sent by the *nazar*.

They were angry to the point of saying harsh words to me, for not wanting the King's word to take effect and for not having taken my money on the day that His Majesty had ordered me to be paid. In this respect, one must admit that there is no country in the world where it is easier to receive one's payment from the court than Persia, and in a large sum one sees no false coins, because all the money paid out comes from the treasury and is inspected by many people whose job it is. The money is then put into leather bags, each holding fifty *tomans*, and the chief inspector, by placing his seal on them, is answerable to the person to whom the payment is made for the number and quality of the coins. He also receives one and a half *abassis* for his trouble and for the bag he provides.

So I promptly had to follow the horsemen to the palace, where I found the *nazar* who was waiting for me, and who had my money delivered to me in the same hour. I had it carried to the house of the Dutch, because Mr Roothals, who was then in charge of the business of the Dutch East India Company, knowing that the order had been given for my payment, had Father Raphaël request me to lend him two or three thousand *tomans*. I only lent him 2,200, having promised the balance to some Armenian merchants who would return them to me in Surat,[45] just as Mr Roothals was having the sum which I had lent him returned to me at Hormuz, which will provide subject-matter for a little history which I am keeping for my journey to Hormuz. These transferences of money are practical for the merchant, who thereby avoids the expenses of carriages and all evil accidents. Together with my payment, I took back the rest of my jewels and

[45] A port on the northwest coast of India much frequented by European merchants. It was the main regional base of the English East India Company from 1612 to 1698, when it was replaced by Bombay.

my other merchandise, which I found in good condition. And that is in detail how all things happened in the sale I made to the King of Persia.

From *Voyages en Perse* by Jean-Baptiste Tavernier

The Royal Harem

The harem was and remains a subject of perennial fascination to Europeans. It was not easy to obtain information about the harem of the Safavid kings, but one European visitor who succeeded better than most was another Parisian jeweller and merchant, Sir John Chardin (1643–1713). He wrote the finest of all European accounts of seventeenth century Persia in terms of its range, detail and intrinsic interest, after spending long periods there in the 1660s and 1670s. Like Tavernier, Chardin was a Protestant and shortly after his last visit to Persia in 1680, he moved permanently to London to escape the growing persecution of Protestants in France. He was received with acclaim in his new homeland, where he was made a member of the Royal Society, an assembly of the most learned and distinguished people, and was knighted by King Charles II, possibly for services to the English East India Company.

In 1686, he brought out the first edition of his Voyages, *which made a deep impression in Europe and became the main inspiration for Montesquieu's* Lettres Persanes, *one of the seminal works of the European Enlightenment. Chardin says he set out 'to give an exact and trustworthy account' of Persia, bearing in mind 'what would merit the curiosity of us Europeans'. In pursuit of this aim, he was helped by a good knowledge of the Persian language and by his many Persian contacts, particularly at the court, to which he had privileged access through his appointment as a royal jeweller by Shah Abbas II. All this he put to good use in uncovering the secrets of the royal harem.*

It is very difficult to know anything for certain about what goes on in the harems or apartments of the women, which one can call an

145

unknown world, particularly those of the royal palace. Out of curiosity, I have constantly gathered information on the subject during the twelve years I have been visiting Persia. I believe, if I may be so bold, that I have had more experience of the country than any European before me, but I have not been able to learn any more on the way the royal *seraglio* is governed than what I am about to report. This is also, in my opinion, more or less everything that one can know, for I can affirm that even the great lords know no more. It is true that the eunuchs say something about it to the palace officials, as the occasion arises; but apart from it being of little import, these lords keep so secret what is confided to them, and are so discrete, that one never hears them talk of it except on some pressing occasion.

The women's apartment is usually the most magnificent and voluptuous part of the palaces of Persia, because that is where the lord is most frequently, and where he spends most of his life, in the bosom of his family. As for its government, I have learnt that the harem has the same offices as the court, in other words there are women invested with the same titles as the officers of the royal household, and having the same functions. There are those who fulfil the office of great and little equerry, who carry the King's weapons; others who perform the office of captain of the gate, of captain of the guards, and of the bodyguard; others who bear the title of usher, of serving gentleman, in a word, who exercise all the royal offices. I have even been assured that there are offices of war, a general of the musketeers, and the rest; but I don't know this as precisely as my report that follows. What is also certain is that there are women who carry out the ecclesiastical offices, like leading the public prayer, and who teach how the religious duties should be discharged. One can well imagine that these are not the youngest, or the most recent arrivals. There are, in addition, offices for all the necessary things of life, like dressmakers, shoemakers, artisans; there are also older women who practice medicine and prepare medications; there are mosques and a cemetery in these places; there is everything that there is in a town; in a word, a harem is on a big scale all that the largest convent of nuns is on a small scale.

There are three kinds of titles for the women of the harem. The women who are born there are called *begum*, which is the feminine of *beg*, meaning lord; it is the title of princesses of the blood royal. Those who have borne the King children, those who are his mistresses, and those who hold the high offices are called *khanum*, which is the feminine of *khan*, meaning duke, and is the title of provincial governors. The others, who are of lesser rank, have the title of *khatun*, which is to say, lady. The rest are all called slaves.

The royal harem is divided into various parts of a building or into palaces, which have no communication with one another. When the King dies, the women who have been his wives are put in a separate quarter, and cloistered there for the rest of their days. Normally, a guard of eunuchs is stationed at their gate, which only permits entry to those carrying messages and supplying the personal needs of the ladies. This is why the news of the King's death throws the *seraglio* into the most dreadful despair, and provokes cries which pierce the heavens. This does not come at all from love of the King, but because his mistresses are deprived of the hope of ever leaving that place, and because they are going to be shut up for life. The chief eunuch of one of the King's aunts told me, in 1675, that the *seraglio* of Shah Safi I, the grandfather of the present King, was still in existence, to the number of eighteen or twenty persons, who were separated and shut up in a section of the harem.

When the King has a son or a brother old enough to make love, he gives him a mistress of his choice, or several mistresses, depending on the indulgence he has for him, the necessary servant-girls and eunuchs, with a separate lodging in a quarter of the harem, to which he is relegated. His mother normally retires there, with all her retinue, to keep him company; and they can only have contact with the rest of the harem by special permission of the King. This poor captive prince is there, watched, subjected and constrained, like a convent novice, and much worse, because he is told that his life depends on conducting himself as the King pleases; and as the lives of his mother and the eunuch who runs his household are even more at stake, there is no one on earth who is less free. He does not even dare to look at women he has not been allowed to possess; and if he is surprised in an affair with some woman, even if it is only a matter of exchanging glances, the affair will be fatal to the whole household, particularly to the woman. I have heard tell that they often pay with their lives for these encounters and that girls are buried alive without warning for permitting an amorous look. As for the girls of the blood royal, when they have reached marriageable age, their mothers use such credit as they enjoy to get them married, which depends on the power they have over the King and on his liking for the princesses. But they are usually only married after the fire of their youth has passed, so that they are wiser and live better with their husband.

Each quarter of the harem has its own governor, as I have just indicated, and the whole *seraglio* is governed by a eunuch with the rank of *daroga*, or provost, which is the title of the governors of the big cities. This eunuch is always some old slave, deformed and grotesque, under whose supervision you can imagine the extent to which the young beauties live in a state of martyrdom. It is said that the order, silence and obedience of the harem is unbelievable. When the King is out of town, there is still a lieutenant of the King in the *seraglio* who has command over the whole palace all the time that the King is absent, and even over his children and his women. The eunuch who was governor of the palace in my time was called Aqa Shapour. I have had business with him several times: he was learned, and when he realised that I was somewhat well-read he gave a more favourable welcome to me than to most of those who approached him. His office made him much respected and feared in the city, and a recommendation from him was worth quite as much as an order from the prime minister.

The harem of the King of Persia is incomparable as far as the beauty of its women is concerned, because the most beautiful women of the kingdom are continually being sent there. Only virgins are admitted. When a woman of perfect beauty is found, wherever it is, she is requested for the harem, and that is never refused. On the contrary, it is a cause for happiness to have something that is pleasing to the King, and above all when it is a girl of quality, because the family is delighted to have a relation who can promote their interests with the Shah. When a girl enters the *seraglio*, her closest male relation is given a present and receives a pension for as long as she lives. The smallest pension is 250 francs, the biggest are 3,000 *écus* and the usual ones are 2,500 *écus*. If the girl gains the favour of the sovereign, either as confidante or as mistress, the pension increases; and if the King has children from her who survive, this relation is made a great lord and all the rest of the family are raised up. There are daughters of provincial governors and the greatest lords of the kingdom in the *seraglio*; but the largest number are Georgians, Circassians, and other peoples of these surrounding provinces, where it seems that beauty spreads its charms more liberally than anywhere else in the world.

The royal *seraglio* is commonly a perpetual prison, from which one only leaves by a stroke of chance; barely one girl in six or seven is so fortunate. The women who have had children never leave, if the child has survived for some time; because, as soon as it is born, the mother and the child are provided with a separate apartment and are given a retinue according to the sex of the child and also whether the King has more or less children.

But the loss of freedom is not the worst thing that happens in these *seraglios*. It is generally reported that the most horrible abominations in the world are committed there, pregnancies extinguished, forced abortions, life taken from the little creatures newly born, by refusing them milk or in some other fashion. Among all the women who become pregnant, only the one who bears the first son can bless her lot, because one day she will have the rank, the authority and the good fortune of a mother of the sovereign; but as for the rest, they are relegated to a corner of the *seraglio*, each with her child, where they live in the perpetual agony of seeing them deprived of life or sight, by the order of the sovereign, be he the father or brother of the child, which is a misfortune which hardly ever fails to happen to them. That is why all these favourites fear to have children, once the King has a son. The goal or the happiness to which they all aspire is to be married off; and it is what they attain by assiduous and long services to the mother of the King, or to the mother of the eldest son, or to the King himself. The mother of the King always has intrigues of more or less importance with most of the ministers and state officials, depending on her talent and her credit. They hardly ever fail to ask her for a girl from the harem for themselves or for one of their sons, as a means of gaining her favour. Sometimes these beautiful captives are given to great lords, without them thinking about it, as a signal favour to them.

Thus the first time that I was at the Persian court, the King sent a girl from the harem, and his favourite to boot, to the grand superintendent of his household, one night when the latter was not thinking or caring about it, as he was old and burdened with the weight of his ministry. However, either through policy and subservience, or otherwise, he did not leave his harem for three days to see the King, spending all the time with this new mistress. Happy is she who is given in this way to a great lord! For she becomes a legitimate wife and mistress of the house, and she is honoured and treated as if she were a daughter of the King. These *seraglio* girls are also married off to relieve the burden on the palace, when there are too many of them. In that case they are given to army officers and aides-de-camp and doorkeepers, who are, as in France, lower ranking gentlemen who attend the King and ushers. As, however, women with living children are never given in marriage, and those who have had children, or have only been pregnant, are rarely given, most of these women fear the favours of the King more than they desire them, and they are in despair when they feel their effect. The tricks they use on the one hand to avoid pregnancy, and the enormities they commit on the other to prevent childbirth, are the subject of a thousand tales. I have heard it asserted that the late King, Shah Abbas II, had one of these beautiful women burnt alive, simply because this fear of hers was noticed. One night when she was on duty he summoned her to come alone; she replied that she was having her 'female inconvenience', and that she dared not approach him in this state. The next day, he went to find her in her room; seeing him enter, she threw herself at his feet to prevent him touching her, inconvenienced as she assured him she was. The King, whose love made him suspicious, had her examined, and learnt that what she was saying was false. Beside himself with rage, he had her tied up inside a fireplace, wood placed around her and burnt alive.

Just as these beautiful people are married off as a reward for their good services, or as a favour to those to whom they are given, so they are also sometimes married off out of rancour, in order to punish them, and with the intention of making them unhappy. For that, they are given to people of low condition, either in the capital, Isfahan, or in the court. One gets news from the *seraglio* from these women, much more easily than from the eunuchs. As for me, I have learnt most of what I am reporting from the eunuch of the King's aunt, who spent a long time in the *seraglio* in the service of his mistress. I had become friendly with him through doing business with this princess, whose agent he was. I had an opportunity to draw him out on this subject; and as I had made him understand that my curiosity had no other purpose than to inform the people of Europe about the ways of the Persians, which were so unknown there, he spoke to me on this subject with more ease and confidence than he would have for anything else.

Information about this very private place is also obtained from the matrons who are brought there when the births are difficult, which does not happen very often. Because giving birth is very easy in Persia, as in the other hot countries of the Orient, there are no midwives. The old and most solemn female relations fulfil this office, but as there are hardly any elderly matrons in the harem, they are summoned from outside should they be needed. Finally, information is provided by the wet nurses; since the children of the King are never suckled by their mothers. The King's physicians have the task of finding the wet nurses, and care is taken to see that they are young, tall, slim, have black hair and have not had long illnesses.

The *seraglio* guard is composed of three different bodies. The first is the white eunuchs; they guard the exterior without coming near to the women or going so far into the harem as to be seen. They arouse jealousy, despite their impotence, because, among other things, the women of the *seraglio* can judge by the colour of these eunuchs that there are more handsome men than the one to whom they belong, which makes them love him less. I pass over the stories that the eunuchs, despite being completely castrated, are still capable of giving and receiving pleasure in relations with women, because shame forbids one even to recall what one has heard on such a subject. The second body is that of the black eunuchs, not the blacks of Abyssinia and Ethiopia, but of the Malabar coast [of

India], where the colour is grey-brown rather than black. They have their lodgings around the second enclosure, where they are present and from where they are summoned, as they are needed. The old and decrepit are used for coming near to the women and carrying their messages; the others are employed outside, that is to say, to come and go, to carry and to work. The third guard body is that of the women, as I have said. The King's favourites and his mistresses belong to this body, and there are always six of them on guard day and night, who serve in turn once a week, with an old woman, who acts as their mother, to govern them.

The women are accommodated on their own, or at the most two in a room, one young and one old, and are not able to visit another room without permission. They each have their allowance paid in money and in fabrics, their food cooked and prepared, and up to four or five servant girls and two eunuchs aged under ten or over fifty. Their allowance varies depending on their employment, the favour they enjoy and the rank of the person who gave them; beyond that, they are all treated in the same way. They are closely watched out of fear, it is said, lest they intrigue or plot against their rivals, or fall in love with one another. Oriental women have always been regarded as lesbians. I have heard it affirmed that they are so often and by so many people, and that they have ways of mutually satisfying their passions, that I consider it quite certain. They are prevented from doing this as far as possible, because it is claimed that it diminishes their charms and makes them less responsive to the love of men. The women who have been in the *seraglio* report surprising things about the passion with which the women make love to one another, of the furious jealousy that enters into it, like that which the favourites also feel for one another; of their hatreds, their treacheries and their nasty tricks. They accuse one another and reveal each other's faults. Those who enjoy the King's favour, like those who please him most with their singing, dancing or conversation, are the target of the envy and loathing of the others. Each has her rivals, and the most extreme are those who no longer hope to leave the harem, and in despair are thus reduced to seeking the King's favours, as the one and only good that remains to them in life. These jealousies have the cruellest consequences. The King, who finds neither love nor sincere attachment among all these perfidious women, degrades some, turning favourites into slaves, who are sent to serve in the lowest employments in distant quarters of the *seraglio*, and punishes others with beatings; some he has killed, even burning them or burying them alive.

From *Voyages du Chevalier Chardin en Perse et autres Lieux de l'Orient*

The New Year Festival

The most popular festival in Persia was then, as it remains today, the ancient Zoroastrian New Year festival of No Ruz, *which is celebrated at the spring equinox, on or about March 21st . Chardin would have witnessed the celebrations several times, probably most often in Isfahan. Here he describes the customs associated with* No Ruz, *in particular at the Safavid court.*

The New Year is announced to the people by *salvos* of artillery and musket fire in the capital and other large cities. The astrologers, magnificently clothed, come to the royal palace or the palace of the local governor, one or two hours before the equinox to observe the moment. They do this on a terrace or platform with an astrolabe, and as soon as they give the signal the *salvos* are discharged, and the musical instruments – the kettle-drums, horns and trumpets – make the air echo with their sound. In Isfahan, every day of the festival music is played before the King's gate with dances, fireworks and shows, as at a fair, and everyone spends the eighth day in an indescribable state of joy. Among other names, the Persians call this 'the festival of the new clothes', because even the poorest people put on a new set of clothes, and those who can afford it put on new clothes every day of the festival. It is the best time to see the court because there is more pomp and magnificence than at any other time, with everyone trying to outdo one another with their finest and richest apparel. Large numbers of people take part in excursions to different places out of town on each of the eight days. Everyone exchanges presents and from the evening before people send each other painted and gilded eggs. There are eggs that cost up to three gold ducats each. The King distributes about five hundred of these in his *seraglio*, in beautiful bowls, to the principal ladies. The egg is covered with gold and has four very fine little figures or miniatures on the sides. It is said that the Persians have always given one another eggs like that at the New Year, because the egg marks the origin and beginning of things. The quantity of eggs sold for this festival is unbelievable.

After the moment of the equinox has passed, the grandees go and wish the King a happy new year, each with the *taj* or royal bonnet[46] on his head, loaded with precious stones, in the most impressive attire they can afford, and each gives him a present of jewellery or precious stones, or cloth, or perfume, or rarities, or horses, or money, depending on his employment and his means. Most give gold, excusing themselves for not finding anything in the world beautiful enough for His Majesty's wardrobe. He is usually given between 500 and 4,000 *ducats*. The grandees employed in the provinces also send their compliments and their presents. Nobody is exempt, the aim being to outdo others and to surpass what one has done oneself in previous years. As a result, the King receives great riches at this festival, part of which he then spends in distributing New Year's gifts to everyone in the *seraglio*. The King entertains the great lords magnificently all the days of the festival from ten o'clock in the morning until one o'clock in the afternoon when he returns to the *seraglio*, and the grandees do the same in their residences, where they spend the rest of the day receiving visits and also the presents of their dependents, because that is the invariable custom of the Orient, the inferior giving to his superior, and the poor giving to the rich, from the peasant up to the King.

From *Voyages du Chevalier Chardin en Perse*
et autres Lieux de l'Orient

[46] This was the elaborate headgear peculiar to the Safavid court. It consisted of a red felt bonnet with twelve folds to symbolise the twelve Shiite Imams, a magnificent turban of coloured or striped brocade wound around the lower part and a red stick protruding from the top. The bonnet was believed to have been introduced by Sheikh Haydar, the father of the first Safavid Shah, Ismail I, and was known as the *Taj-e Haydari*, or Haydar's Crown.

The Shiite Mourning Ceremonies of Muharram

The main event in the Shiite calendar is the commemoration of the death of the Imam Husayn, the Third Shiite Imam, in October 680. He was the younger son of the Imam Ali, the First Shiite Imam, who was the cousin and son-in-law of the Prophet Muhammad and the Fourth Caliph of Islam. Ali was murdered in January 661, after which the Arab Umayyad clan established themselves as a caliphal dynasty in Damascus. Ali's followers, the Shiites, believed that God had intended the caliphate to remain in the hands of Ali's male descendants and they regarded the Umayyads as usurpers. Ali's son, Husayn, died in a vain attempt to take back the caliphate. On the tenth day of the Muslim lunar month of Muharram – the day that is called 'Ashura', the Arabic word for 'tenth' – Husayn and his small band of followers were slaughtered on the plain of Karbala in southern Iraq by the much larger forces of the Umayyad caliph, Yazid.

The commemoration of what Shiites regard as Husayn's passion and martyrdom extends over the first ten days of Muharram and reaches a climax on Ashura. It became a great public spectacle during the seventeenth century, presided over by the Shah in Isfahan and by the local governor in the provincial capitals, and incorporating ever more dramatic elements. Although Husayn's elder brother, Hasan, the second Imam, was not at the battle at Karbala, and had in fact come to terms with the Umayyads, he is included in the commemoration, as Shiites believe that the Umayyads poisoned him. Because the Muslim year is a lunar one, Muharram, like Ramadan, falls at different times in the solar year. Chardin was among a number of Europeans invited by the new king, Shah Safi II, later to be recrowned Shah Sulayman I, to watch the Ashura parades through the Royal Square in Isfahan at the end of June and beginning of July 1667.

During these ten days no trumpets or kettle-drums are sounded at the accustomed hours. Pious people shave neither the face nor the head, do not go to the bath, do not travel and, generally speaking, do very little business. Many wear black or violet clothes, which are the colours of mourning. All adopt a sad comportment and expression, and each contributes to the appearance of a public mourning. From morning to evening during these ten days, groups of the meanest sort of people are found throughout the town, some naked but for a loin cloth and blackened all over, some stained with blood, and some armed from head to foot with a sword in their hand. Yet others can be seen going through the streets knocking two stones together, their tongues hanging out like people who have fainted, assuming the postures and contortions of people in despair. They cry out with all their strength, 'Husayn! Hasan!' Those who are stained black, wish to portray the burning thirst and heat suffered by Husayn, which was so great, they say, that he became black and his tongue hung out. Those who are stained with blood wish to show that he received so many wounds that all the blood had drained from his veins before the soul left his body. This rabble run through the streets demanding alms at every shop and from every person of distinction they meet. No one refuses them at least a modest sum, but when they meet a Jew or an Armenian, or above all a heathen Indian, they do not fail to make him give them four or five times as much, saying, 'It is you who have killed our prophet, give us something for his blood.' This causes these poor heathens, who are easily recognisable by their costume, for they would not dare to dress like the Persians, to keep to their homes during these ten days and to go out as little as possible. The children who see them go by at this time also never fail to shout out to them, and to any foreigner, 'Cursed be Omar!', imagining that all those who are not of their country take a great interest in the memory of Omar,[47] and are greatly displeased to hear him cursed, as, indeed, is the case with the Turks, for whom it is one of the most stinging insults.

During these days of mourning a kind of temporary altar is set up on the corners of the main streets, at crossroads and in the squares, with a pulpit surrounded by many benches. All of this is covered in brocade, while the sides are hung from top to bottom with shields, all kinds of firearms and pointed weapons, drums, kettle-drums, trumpets, ensigns, pennants, lion and tiger skins, and with steel

[47] Omar was the second caliph of Islam. Although the first three caliphs before Ali are regarded as upsurpers of by Shiites, Omar, who was stabbed to death by a disgruntled Persian slave in 644, became a particular hate-figure in Safavid times.

armour for men and horses; it is like being in an arsenal. In amongst this are crystal and paper lanterns, lamps and candlesticks in quantity, which are lighted an hour after sunset.

The common people of the quarter go there in procession and immediately some Sufi or some other grave and pious person starts to talk to them about the festival until the preacher comes. The latter begins by reading a chapter from the book *El-Qatl* (*The Killing*), which contains the life and death of Husayn in ten chapters for the ten days of the commemoration. He then preaches on the subject for two hours, exciting the people to groan – I remember a preacher who told them, among other things, 'that a tear shed during this commemoration wipes out a pile of sins as big as Mount Sinai' – and also filling them with resentment towards the enemies of the saint and their adherents. I would never have believed the grief the people show; it is unimaginable. They beat their breasts; they shriek and howl, especially the women, tearing at themselves and sobbing. I have been present at these sermons and I admired the attentiveness of the audience, which could only come from an intense piety, although the preacher was very moving.

The sermon over, the people cry out with all their strength, 'Husayn! Hasan!' until their voice and their lungs fail them. Their cries are accompanied by the sound of small drums and of that instrument known as the *tintinnabula*, which makes for a lugubrious music, as the cries are long, low and plaintive. These blackened rascals, who knock two stones together, make this harmony even more sombre and strange. There is something very horrible about all that the first time one sees it. When the assembly can shout no longer, each person returns to his home, still crying out, 'Husayn! Hasan!' That is what the common people do. The grandees mark the festival more modestly in their homes. They invite many skilful clerics of their acquaintance who go to them every day at four o'clock in the afternoon. The conversation turns on the present subject, each person relating the finest literary passages, with their own thoughts on the matter. At seven o'clock, they read the chapter of the day, on which the most learned of the company comment, and at nine or ten o'clock there are refreshments and the party breaks up till the next day.

And so it goes on until the last day, which is the great festival, and the night before which is passed in prayer. I have seen it in Persia seven or eight times, but the most solemn was the one I saw in 1667. The King had recently ascended the throne, which is as much as to say that he had recently come into the world, having never left the harem during the lifetime of his father, who had died towards the end of the previous year. Never, therefore, having witnessed this festival, he ordered that it be celebrated with pomp.

This is what happened. It was June. The King and all the court went every evening, at six o'clock, to a great hall called the Hall of the Stable, which can easily hold five hundred people and which opens onto a beautiful garden with a large sanded parterre in the middle, where there is room for more than two thousand - not to mention the numbers that can be accommodated at the back and sides of the hall. This was lit up from top to bottom and there was an infinite number of lamps and lanterns in the garden, so that at eight o'clock in the evening, when the whole place was illuminated, it was brighter than during the day. A pulpit with seven steps and covered in black cloth had been set up on the parterre, close to where the King was sitting in the hall.

As soon as the King gave the order, the processions from each quarter of the town were brought in, each composed of four to five hundred men, shopkeepers and tradesmen, all armed to the teeth, some with helmets and coats of mail, others with armbands and cuirasses. Just as some were covered in iron, others were naked, their bodies oiled like wrestlers and gladiators. Almost all had a tiger skin on their backs and a shield on top; some held a sword in their hand, others carried lances or pikes, axes or maces. In the middle of the procession was a naked man, covered in blood, with the points of arrows and pieces of lances attached to his skin, as if they had passed through his body; he represents the saint of the festival. At the front were carried the standards of the troupe, made of satin or silver brocade, with the initials of Ali on one side and the emblem of Persia on the other. After this came the drums and trumpets, then the people beating the stones together like castanets, followed by a crowd of young boys intoning the names of Husayn and Hasan, and behind them marched the armed men.

There were ten such processions every evening. They came into the palace at a rapid pace, with big movements and clattering of arms to represent the fury with which Husayn's army fought that of Yazid.

On the great day of the festival these processions were much more magnificent. First of all, at the head of each troupe were carried twenty standards, several pennants, steel crescents and hands,[48] with the initials of Muhammad and Ali, attached to long pikes. These were the sacred standards of the Muhammadans, in their first wars, which they carried in the middle of their armies, as the Romans carried their eagles. They are still carried into battle today; but there is not as much faith as there was then. When they are carried in procession they are covered with a clear blue gauze to indicate that there is no intention of actually fighting. These were followed by several beautiful horses on leads, richly harnessed and carrying defensive arms attached to the saddle, such as steel armour, shields, and many other things, some gilded and others adorned with precious stones. After them came musicians, then black or blood-stained men, beating stones together, then these people covered with blood and arrows, and finally the machines that are the great adornment of the funerary pomp. These consist firstly of something resembling *catafalques*, covered with blue cloth and ornamented with pieces of brocade and a thousand knick-knacks which are hung around them as the fancy takes the people who make them; then there are coffins, also covered with velvet, or with black or coloured brocade, with a turban on top and arms attached to the top and the sides. The men who carry these machines do light jumps and turns in the middle of the procession.

Then came the big *catafalque*, carried by eight men, where Husayn was represented. Some of these resemble an ornamental bed, where Husayn and his brother are represented by two little boys, who say 'Husayn! Hasan!' to one another, others are like a cabinet of weapons, being adorned inside and out with bows and arrows, swords, shields, daggers, maces, with a boy in the middle,

[48] The hand is a Shiite emblem because its five fingers represent the five most sacred figures in Shiism: the Prophet Muhammad, his daughter Fatima, his cousin Ali who was married to Fatima, and their children, Hasan and Husayn.

fully armed, ready for battle, all shining in gold and silver. These *catafalques* are made at the expense and with the labour of the whole quarter of the town. Other *catafalques* represented mausoleums. On others a man was stretched out, his clothes blood-stained and bristling with arrows, his head all bloody, representing the saint in death. Branches of trees were carried around all these machines to protect them from the sun.

After these *catafalques* came more blood-stained men, this time riding horses covered with dust to represent the soldiers of this prince. The people of the procession followed behind them in a crowd, to the number of two or three hundred, making a horrible noise as they cried out 'Husayn! Hasan!' They are always armed, but for the most part only with big staves and they run instead of marching. They stop from time to time, to give their machines a chance to move forward, and at that point they jump, turn, and thrash about like men possessed, making themselves dizzy by constantly shouting out those names that are repeated so often.

Besides these processions, there were two extraordinary ones 'for the love of the King'. One was composed of Sufis, who guard the King's person and his palace, who are considered the most exemplary devotees of all the Muhammadans, and who are the most illustrious members of the Shiite sect.[49] The special feature of their procession was two men, each stretched out on a very narrow plank covered in blood, who imitated the dead very well, and ten asses, each bearing three little boys who were reciting the verses of the festival. The other procession was that of the Indian Muhammadans of the sect of Ali, and that was the most beautiful of all. It was led by five elephants carrying little towers in which were children singing the praises of Husayn and by six led horses of great price, with harnesses of gold or precious stones. Their *catafalque* was an ornamental bed eight foot square, carried by twelve men. It was of gold brocade with great gold fringes. There is nothing so beautiful to be seen on such an occasion. In the middle of the bed were two tombs, covered with gold embroidered cloths, and with four children at the corners, two

[49] These were members of the original Safavid Sufi order, which had otherwise become more or less defunct.

singing the praises of Hasan and Husayn, and two driving away the flies with fans of feathers. Behind the *catafalque* were two machines drawn by oxen, one representing the mosque of Mecca, the other the mosque of Medina.

All these processions went on in the middle of the Royal Square, watched by the King from the hall above the great portal (of the palace). The grand-provost was in the middle of the square, with thirty mounted guards and as many footmen, to prevent any disorder. For as Isfahan has been divided into factions since ancient times, it often happens that on such days the town quarters have a real fight with one another, which turns the festival into a wild disorder.

I would never finish if I were to report all the details of the festival. I shall only remark that on the last day of that festival, at which the King was present, he went to the hall at seven o'clock in the morning and first heard the sermon of the day, delivered by the preacher who had preached before him on the other days. His throne was on a great platform which joins the hall and which was covered with a rich tent. Around it were a great number of clerics and at the back were the Sufis. After the sermon, a hymn was sung in praise of Husayn and his family. It was sung by two groups, each one singing with all its might. After that, the square and its surroundings echoed to curses on Yazid and his adherents, followed by blessings on the King. When the action was over, forty costumes were given to the clerics and three hundred écus to the preacher. But as these costumes were given as alms and not as an honour, those who received them did not go to kiss the King's feet, as is the custom.

I must not forget that during this festival the Persians give much in the way of alms to the poor. They believe that it is a crime not to give what one can. The rich have great jugs of iced water with a cup inside placed in front of their doors, so that no one should suffer the thirst of which Husayn died; for they recount that, being without water, he threw himself in despair on his enemies who were besieging him. There are also water-carriers who go through the streets with a big goatskin on their back and offer large cups of iced water to everyone. It is their custom, when giving this water, to cry out, 'May he who will pay for this water be blessed until the seventieth generation.'

During the ten days of this festival, the King gave supper to all the people taking part in the processions, of whom there were more than four thousand, and, in addition, every day he sent twelve hundred pounds of bread, fifty dishes of meat and fifty francs in money to the great mosque to be distributed to the poor.

From *Voyages du Chevalier Chardin en Perse
et autres Lieux de l'Orient*

An Encounter with the Highway Police

The security that prevailed on the roads in Persia for most of the Safavid period – it broke down towards the end – was frequently remarked on by Europeans and made the country an attractive destination for merchants. This security was maintained by special guards on the roads known as rahdars. *The French traveller, Jean de Thévenot (1633–1667), discovered just how watchful they were shortly after he crossed into Persia with a caravan from Baghdad in August 1664. Thévenot and his companion, a merchant by the name of Monsieur Jacob, together with their servants, became separated from the rest of the caravan and were stopped by two* rahdars *and taken away for questioning. A man of private means who travelled for pleasure, Thévenot spoke good Turkish and learned some Persian as well. He stayed for five months in Isfahan and died on his way home through Persia.*

As I passed within a few steps of three huts made of canes, I saw two men in Persian habit, of whom he that seemed to be the chief had a close bodied coat of silk-stuff with large flowers of gold. They came towards us whilst I minded nothing, and spoke to me though I did not heed it: in the mean time finding that I listened not to what they said to me, one of them with a hooked stick, took hold of my horse's bridle and stopt him; which made me pull out a pistol, and to consider the men more attentively. I perceived that they made no shew of offering any violence, though they were armed each of them with a quiver full of arrows, a bow, an axe by their side and a cymetre; and indeed, it had not been their best course, I and they who followed me having our fire-arms all in readiness, which made me a little wonder at the boldness of the men.

At the same time Monsieur Jacob who saw their action, advanced towards them, with a design to fire, calling them in Turkish a hundred rogues and rascals, as if they had been robbers: my man came also with a musketoon presented, but perceiving that the men seemed not concerned, and did not so much as lay a hand upon their swords; but that on the contrary the chief of them calling me *cardash*, (that's to say brother,) civilly asked me to give him the hearing; I prayed Monsieur Jacob to hold his hand, and they very courteously told us that they had orders not to suffer us to pass. That surprised us a little, because we knew not the reason of it; but being informed of that, we would not proceed against their will, though we might have done it. These men are *rahdars*, (that's to say guards of the road,) of which there are many in several places, especially upon the frontiers, not onely of Persia, but also of every *khanlick* or province to secure the high-ways; and for wages they have a due of some *bistis*[50] of every loaded horse or mule.

They stop all that are not in the caravan, if they know them not. And the reason why they stopt us, was because we were not only a little separated from the caravan, but that a man who went before us, had told them, that in our caravan there were two unknown Franks (Europeans): the *kervan-basha*[51] being informed that we were stopt, came and spoke to them; but they told him that they would not suffer us to pass, because if they did they would lose their places. We might have easily forced them, (as I have said;) but it would not have lookt well to have committed violence upon our first entry into a countrey; for at this place begin the territories of the King of Persia. At length (by the council of the *kervan-basha*) we followed them to their huts, where they spread a carpet, on which we sate down together like good friends.

In the mean time they unloaded our goods, and several of their men came into the place where we were. Their master bid us lay by

---

[50] A *bisti* was a small denomination silver coin.
[51] The leader of the caravan.

our swords; which we freely did, and he drew them one after another. We had some thoughts that he intended to be revenged for our offering to fire upon him; but after he had look'd upon them, he put them up again. He told us a second time that his office was to suffer no man to enter into Persia unless he were known, least some might come and make their escape there, when they had committed villanies elsewhere; I made him answer that many Franks had past that way before, without being stopt, but he assured me of the contrary; and indeed, I believe that the ordinary way is somewhat more towards the north, than Mendeli.[52] In short, he protested that he would not let us goe, unless those of the caravan would answer for us, wherefore we sent our *muletor* (muleteer) with one of the Persians to the camp, which was half an hours walk from thence. In the mean time, that man complained several times to my servant, that we should have offered fire at him, and give him bad language as if he had been a rogue.

Nevertheless, he civilly ordered our dinner to be brought which consisted of a great bowl of bread; two bowls of sower milk, two plates of new made butter; and a wooden dish wherein there were about two eggs prepared with a sauce, which I think can hardly be found in any book of cookery; and that was for about a dozen of men. We fed a little and drank water in wooden cups. Then the man must needs see our trunks, he handled the watches of Monsieur Jacob one after another; I opened also my *sepet*; but finding that he had a mind to see all things onely out of curiosity, and to make *tamascha*[53] as he called it, I told him that he had no right of demanding custom, nor by consequence of viewing our goods, that it required much time to do them up again, and that therefore he might undoe what he thought fit, and do them up again himself; but that if any thing were lost, he should be made accountable for it, and that made him suffer me to make all fast again. Afterwards the man whom we sent with our *muletor* arrived, and brought him a paper signed by several of our caravan, who vouched

[52] Mendeli (modern Mandali) was the last town on the Turkish side of the frontier.
[53] To look at something for amusement or merely out of curiosity.

for us, and who indeed threatened, that if the least wrong were done unto us, they would complain of it, and that if we went and complained to the *chan*,[54] it would certainly bring them into trouble. Immediately they dismissed us, and we turned to the caravan.

From *The Travels of Monsieur Jean de Thévenot*
by Jean de Thévenot

Trouble in the Bath

Strict Persian Shiites regarded anything that had been touched by a Christian or other infidel as 'unclean'. Thévenot discovered this through an embarrassing but amusing incident shortly after he arrived in Persia.

They suffer no Christians to enter into their coffee-houses, nor their *bagnios*, because they (say they) are *medgis*, that is to say, impure. Whereupon I had a pretty pleasant adventure, when I was coming from Bagdad to Hamadan; being as yet ignorant of that custom; I very fairly went one day to one of their *bagnios*; they not knowing me to be a Christian, suffered me to strip, and enter the *bagnio*, where there were a great many Persians and Turks; but some among them knowing me, presently whispered the rest that I was a Christian; at which being extreamly startled, they acquainted the master of the *bagnio* with it, who to dismiss me civilly, came and told me that the vizier, or lieutenant of the *chan*, desired to speak with me. I, who understood nothing of their intrigue, made him answer that I would wait upon him so soon as I had done in the *bagnio*, and though he told me that he stayed for me, I would not go; but at length perceiving that the servants attended all the rest, and left me to look after myself, I went to my cloaths, and quarelled with the master, because they had not served me; which he suffered without making answer. Whereupon one of those who was in the *bagnio*, told me that the *bagnio*-master must wash all the bath over, as being polluted by my entring into it; and I heard no more of the viziers orders. The Persians hate the Turks no less, and hold them to be as impure as the

[54] The Khan, being the local governor.

165

Christians, but dare not tell them so as they do the Christians, to whom there are some *moulas*[55] that will not so much as teach the Persian tongue for love nor money, but there are others who are not so scrupulous.

From *The Travels of Monsieur Jean de Thévenot*
by Jean de Thévenot

Town Comforts

The hamam or public bath and the coffee house have been two great Persian institutions. Both were particularly flourishing in Safavid times. Coffee is thought to have been introduced into Persia early in the Safavid period, in the second half of the sixteenth century. It remained a favourite beverage until well into the nineteenth century when Russian and British influence led to it being replaced by tea. The two institutions are described with zest and appreciation by John Fryer (1650–1733), a surgeon in the English East India Company, who spent about eight months in Persia in 1677. Fryer writes in a somewhat florid style, reminiscent of Sir Thomas Herbert.

Their *balneos* or *hummums* are the most sumptuous, which are in all their cities, always hot; and it is lawful for every one of both sexes, on stated times of the day to bath for a small price. The prepositor of each house gives notice to all comers by blowing an horn, when the houses are ready to attend them; of which there are innumerable destined to these uses, each striving to outshine the other; insomuch that no time either of day or night passes, but you shall hear perpetual noises of horns to invite you to them; for no sooner is the fire kindled under them, but they let every one know by those loud instruments.

In which places the treatment is alike to all; for as before was said in the church and inns, so in the hot-houses all things are common to all. Wherefore if any one desire to be freed from the vulgar rout, he must hire an house for a whole day.

[55] Mullas: Muslim clerics.

These houses are beneath the earth, only some little round globes embellish'd with painted glass peep out above the ground to give light, and are well clos'd, lest the ambient air should offend by too forcible a ventilation through any neglected crevise. They are built with divers distinct cells one from another, in which men sit, are rubbed, and cleansed. Immediately within the porch is the greatest cell, or rather a large room, where they doff their cloaths, and being undressed leave their garments; in the middle of this place is a cystern of cold water coming into it by several pipes. All the other cells are so conveniently framed, that every one may breathe a different air as to the degrees of heat, such as may suit with the divers temperaments of several bodies.

The pavements are all marble, on which, the more hot water is thrown, the more it increases the heat, although at the same time the subterranean fire be as hot as it can be. On these marble floors they at last extend themselves, when they think they have tarried in long enough, that the barbers, whose business it is, should wind and turn every limb and joint of the body, before, behind, and on every side, with that dexterity and slight, that it is admirable to behold them perform it; whereby they leave no muscle, nerve, or superficial joint, either unmov'd, or not rubb'd: Then with a coarse hair-cloth and hot water they scrape off all the filth and sweat; and last of all by a depilatory they take clean away all manner of hairs growing either in secret parts, or any emunctuary to cause either nasty smells, or troublesome chafing.

When they retire to put on their cloaths (this is to be only understood of great men) there waits them a collation of fruit, sweetmeats, and variety of perfumes, as rosewater, rackbeet (willow water), and the like, with all befitting attendants, besides the usual servitors, to administer either coho (coffee), tea, tobacco, or brandy, if faint. When they are dress'd, they emplaister their feet and hands with a red paste, which wonderfully help sweaty and moist palms, as also stinking feet.

These things being premised, the benefits coming from the use of these are, when the body is inflamed and dried by immoderate heat, it is finely refreshed by sweet water, and the pores become moisten'd; the farther prosecution of which advantages having been spoken of before, I refer you thither, and proceed to the other houses of resort, which are only for the men, and not for the women.

Their coffee-houses, where they sell *coho*, better than any among us, which being boiled, has a black oil or cream swimming at top, and when it has not, they refuse to drink it. Hither repair all those that are covetous of news, as well as barterers of goods; where not only fame and common rumour is promulgated, but poetry too, for some of that tribe are always present to rehearse their poems, and disperse their fables to the company … They are modelled after the nature of our theatres, that every one may sit around, and suck choice tobacco out of long malabar canes, fasten'd to chrystal bottles, like the recipients or bolt-heads of the chymists, with a narrow neck, where the bole or head of the pipe is inserted, a shorter cane reaching to the bottom, where the long pipe meets it, the vessel being filled with water. After this sort they are mightily pleased; for putting fragrant and delightful flowers into the water, upon every attempt to draw tobacco, the water bubbles, and makes them dances in various figures, which both qualifies the heat of the smoke, and creates together a pretty sight.

At night there are abundance of lamps lighted, and let down in glasses from the concave part of the roof, by wires or ropes, hanging in a circle.

From *A New Account of East India and Persia*
being Nine Years' Travels
by John Fryer

A Sign of Royal Favour: the Robe of Honour

The most common way for the Shah to show his favour to a loyal servant was by sending him a robe of honour. This usually consisted of an under-garment, a long gown often lined with fur, a belt and a turban. Great lords were usually also given a sword and dagger of solid gold, adorned with precious stones. This would cost the recipient more than it was worth in gifts to both the Shah and the person entrusted with delivering the robe of honour. But it was still much sought after, because it increased the standing of the recipient in the eyes of those under him. The Dutch artist, Cornelis de Bruyn (1652–1726/27), who arrived from Russia at the Persian port of Darband on the Caspian in July 1703, witnessed the reception of a robe of honour by the local governor, the Khan of Shamakhi. The khan, who had ordered four days of public rejoicings, rode out in the midst of a magnificent procession to receive the robe of honour in a garden outside the town.

First there appeared a number of persons on horseback, succeeded by ten camels, adorned with two little red standards to the right and left. Upon six of these there were kettle-drums, which the Persians call *tambalpaes*, of which four were of extraordinary size, pointed at bottom, which a drummer upon one of the camels struck from time to time. Four trumpeters stopt at intervals on the wayside to sound their *karamas* or trumpets, which are very long, wide at bottom, and according to my ear, make a very disagreeable noise. At some distance after these came four *hautbois* (oboes), which they call *karana-nasier*. The camels were also followed by twenty musqueteers differently habited, some in green, some in purple and some in grey, and after these came six of the *khan*'s or governor's menial servants; after these appeared their master himself upon a fine chestnut horse most beautifully caparisoned. This nobleman, who was in a short kind of vest, and with a large turban on his head, after the Persian mode, was followed by four eunuchs, some tawny, others black, richly habited and well mounted.

After these appeared the most considerable personages of the place, and a great number of others on horseback; then nine led horses of the *khan*'s, sumptuously caparisoned, with each a small drum on the right side of the saddle. Most of the personages of distinction had the like, which from time to time they struck with their fingers. They were almost all of silver, like those of the khan. Besides all this a great number of soldiers were ranged along the garden, on the right hand towards the mountains, and each of these soldiers had a feather in his cap; and in short, two horses, upon which were two men covered from head to foot with a gown quilted and wrought with all sorts of colours, representing monkeys; and as they were well broke to the tricks and play of that creature, they drew the eyes of everybody upon them, and kept at the distance of twenty paces from each other, with musicians near them.

When they had reached the garden, the *khan* and the great men who had attended him dismounted from their horses at the fore-gate, which was large and built of stone. He there robed himself with his royal vestment, and in half an hour mounting his horse again, he returned to the town in the same order he came out of it. This robe was pretty long, and of gold brocade, and upon his head he had a golden cap, in the nature of a crown. This cavalcade was attended by a great number of servants on horseback, who rode and pranced about on the sides of the procession, with a *kalijan*, or smoking bottle, in their right hand for the use of their masters. These bottles are of glass, adorned with gold or silver at the top, and extremely neat. Other of these servants had a little pot full of fire at the pommel of their saddles, for their masters to light their pipes by, but there was no tobacco smoked upon this occasion.

Many of these great men diverted themselves along the way with darting the *ayner*, which is a kind of cane. Everybody had run out of the town to see this cavalcade, some on foot, and others on horseback, a sight agreeable enough to the eye, because of the variety of objects: others came from the villages, of which the country about is full, from the tents of the Arabs,[56] and from the gardens which are seen on all sides. The *khan*, before he assumed his robe, covered himself with the gold cap just mentioned, which was adorned with precious stones, closed at top, and carried at a small distance before him on horseback. They pretend that this cap represents the arms of the prophet Ali, who was wont to wear such a one. The *khan* took it off when he put on his robe, and it was carried before him in going back, as it had been in coming. This cavalcade took up two hours.

From *Travels into Muscovy, Persia, and part of the East Indies*
by M. Cornelius de Bruyn

[56] Here the word 'Arabs' is simply used to denote nomadic tribesmen.

Bandar Abbas: the European Trading Station in the Persian Gulf

De Bruyn travelled on to Isfahan where he remained for almost a year, doing valuable drawings of places and people, including a fine portrait of Shah Sultan Husayn. He returned to Europe by sea from the Persian Gulf port of Bandar Abbas, or Gombroon as the English called it. Situated just inside the mouth of the Persian Gulf, opposite the island of Hormuz, Bandar Abbas contained the main 'factories', or trading houses, of the English and Dutch East India companies. Unbearably hot in the summer, it was not a very pleasant place to live, as is clear from de Bruyn's description.

This city is a small league in circumference: it is likewise open, and extends itself along the sea-shore from east to west, or from northeast to west-southwest. It has no considerable buildings, and most of the houses have a very mean appearance on the outside. The best are those which belong to the English and Dutch factories, that of the governor being but indifferent. It is very incommodious for strangers to reside there: the common sort have only a set of wretched huts, and even the bazar itself is but a mean place. There are, indeed, four structures which have the name of castles; but they are low, small, and ruinous. That of the four which is farthest in the city, has some pieces of cannon to salute the ships. The poor people dwell there in cottages made of boughs, and covered with the leaves of the palm-tree, of which there is great plenty in that city. The principal houses are furnished with machines to draw and receive the wind. They are made like square towers of a considerable height, and are accessible to the wind on all parts, except the middle, which is closed up. Those two sides, which are most exposed, have two or three openings, which are long and narrow, and those of the other two sides are less. There is likewise between each opening a small advanced wall, which receives the wind, and turns it back into those apertures, by which means the houses are always rendered airy, when there is the least gale of wind. The inhabitants generally take a short

171

nap about noon, and pass the night upon the terrasses during the hot seasons, which would otherwise be very incommodious. But when these are over, they lie in chambers, as in other places. These towers, for the reception of wind, are very ornamental to the city.

A flag is always streaming upon the houses of the English and Dutch India companies, and serves for a signal to their ships. The house which belongs to our company, is the most beautiful structure in the city, and is built on the edge of it toward the east. The first foundation was laid there in 1698, by Mr Hoogkamer, the company's minister. It is very large, and furnished with fine magazines; the chambers too are handsome, and of a considerable height. There is likewise a very magnificent and beautiful hall in the middle of the apartments above, whose windows, as well as those of the director's, and his deputy's lodgings, have a prospect to the sea, from whence these apartments are refreshed with the most agreeable air in the world; but this house is not finished as yet.

The Europeans are buried in a tract of ground to the north of the city; and it is filled with lofty tombs covered with domes. One need not be surprised at the great number of them, since the air is very unhealthy, and the excessive heats carry off a vast multitude of people. But nothing is more pernicious than the burning fevers, which are there more common than in any other place, and frequently prove fatal in the space of twenty-four hours. The months of October and November are not less dangerous; for the air is then either very damp, or exceeding dry. The latter is the least dangerous, and the water is fresher, and better to drink than in a rainy season, the humidity giving it an ill flavour, and rendering it very unwholesome. Camels are sent for water to Eysien upon the mountains, about four leagues from the sea, and this is the wholesomest water in all the country. The inhabitants likewise send for it to Nayban, which is a league from the city, near the sea; but this latter is not so good.

We had tolerable weather during my continuance there: but the heat lasted longer than usual, and was extremely incommodious. It is sometimes insupportable; and I have been assured, that it has even melted sealing-wax. In this extremity they throw off all their upper garments, and cause themselves to be sprinkled over with water. Our

172

interpreter had a well in which he passed a great part of the day. These immoderate heats always occasion severe distempers, as I have already observed, and happy are those who escape them. But even these are not exempted from great inconveniencies, of which one of the most remarkable is the worms which eat into the arms and legs of persons, and which are not drawn out without their being exposed to apparent danger, by breaking them in the flesh. In a word, one could not find a more rigorous punishment for malefactors than confining them in a place like this. One, however, seldom fails of finding some people of merit and distinction here; whom interest, and the hopes of raising a great fortune, have drawn thither and whom death often snatches away before they have attained to the height of their desires.

From *Travels into Muscovy, Persia, and part of the East Indies*
by M. Cornelius de Bruyn

A Dangerous Russian Embassy is Received With Ceremony

In the early years of the eighteenth century, as the Safavid state began to show signs of decay, the Russian Tsar, Peter the Great, began to cast covetous eyes on Persia's Caspian provinces, with their lucrative silk farms. He sent an embassy to the court of Shah Sultan Husayn in 1715, officially to conclude a commercial treaty, but also to find out everything about conditions in Persia and its military strength – all of which was carried out by the ambassador, twenty-eight-year-old Artemii Volynsky, who encouraged Peter the Great's invasion of Persia's Caspian provinces a few years later. Attached to the Russian embassy was a Scottish surgeon, John Bell, who has left a striking account of the splendour and ceremony surrounding its reception by Shah Sultan Husayn.

May 4th, (1717) the ceremonial part of the ambassador's intro-duction to the Shah being previously agreed on, he was this day to have his first audience. In the morning horses were sent from the

King's stables, all of them magnificently equipped, with grooms to attend them; many of the saddles and bridles were garnished with gold and silver.

We marched in the same order as at our entry, only the dragoons had not their swords drawn. After passing through several streets we came into the great market place called Bazar, and then to a gate called Alla-Capy, i.e. God's Gate,[57] where we dismounted. Across this gate is hung a chain, and none are permitted to enter on horseback, except the Shah himself. We walked through the guards, drawn up on each side, to an inner court, and thence to an arched gate, surrounded with benches, and spread with carpets. Here the ambassador was desired to sit down till the Shah was ready to receive him. We waited at least two hours, during which time all the ministers of state, and officers of the household, passed us in great state. After them came a large elephant, mounted by his keeper, and adorned with gold and silver stuff; then two large lions, led by their keepers with chains of massy gold.

When this parade was over, an officer informed the ambassador that the Shah waited for him. Whereupon, proceeding immediately through the gate, we entered a spacious garden. The first thing that presented was a noble view of twenty horses standing in a row, richly caparisoned, having all their saddles and bridles ornamented with gold and silver, and some of them set with sapphires, emeralds, and other precious stones of great value. The horses were all tied to a rope fixed to the ground, at the extremities, by a stake of gold, near which lay a mallet of the same metal for driving it, according to the custom of Persia; the hind-feet were also fastened to a rope, to prevent kicking. This is an excellent precaution; for, though they were all stoned horses, they could neither hurt one another, nor any thing else: the chains that bound their hind-feet, with the stakes, and mallets were also of gold. The Persian horses are well managed; neither do I think them so vicious as those in Europe: whether they are naturally more gentle I shall not determine, perhaps it is entirely owing to the milder treatment of their grooms. At each end of the

[57] It is actually 'Ali Qapu', which means 'Lofty Gate'.

row stood a large vessel of gold full of water, for the horses to drink.

Approaching nearer to the hall of audience, we passed the two lions, chained to the ground, one on each side of the passage, near them were placed two basons of gold, filled with water for drink. Next to the lions stood the elephant, with his keeper on his back. As the ambassador passed, both the lions couched, and the elephant bent his fore-knee, at a word pronounced by the keepers. We now turned to the left, and had a full view of the hall of audience, about a hundred yards distant. It seemed to stand by itself in the middle of the garden; it is indeed contiguous to the *seraglio*, on the south, but is quite open to the north. Before the entry is a large fountain of pure water, which springs upward in three pipes, and falls into a bason filled with roses, jessamine (jasmine), and many other fine flowers.

When we came to the stair we were desired to put off our slippers, and our servants were no farther admitted. The ambassador only and six of his retinue (among whom I was) entered the hall. We ascended by eight steps of marble, the whole breadth of the hall. From the roof hung a canvas which was stretched out over the stair, and shaded the whole inside of the edifice. The hall is a spacious square building, with a terrace roof. The ceiling is very magnificent, being all arched, and set with mirrors of different magnitudes till within three feet of the floor; which is quite covered with silk carpets, interwoven with branches, and foliage, of gold and silver. In the middle were two basons, into which several pipes, each about eight feet high, spouted water, which, falling upon roses and other flowers, has a fine effect on a hot day. The farther end of the hall is a semicircle. Here sat the Shah upon a sofa, raised about a foot from the floor, which was elevated four steps above the rest of the hall. He was attended by twenty eunuchs; one carried his sabre, another his bow, a third the quiver with arrows, a fourth the calianne, or tobacco pipe, so that each had his office of state.

The ambassador was received in the hall by the master of ceremonies, called Ish-aggan Basha, to be by him introduced to the Shah. He continued sitting upon his sofa, with his legs across, while all his ministers of state stood in their places, clothed magnificently in their robes; which they never wear except on solemn days; and when these are over they leave them in a wardrobe at court, appointed for keeping them. I must confess the appearance was very splendid, and put me in mind of the accounts left us by the ancients, of the magnificence of the Kings of Persia.

At our entry into the hall we were stopped about three minutes at the first fountain, in order to raise the greater respect; the pipes were contrived to play so high that the water fell into the bason like a thick rain. Nothing could be distinguished for some time, and the Shah himself appeared as in a fog. While we moved forward, every thing was as still as death. The master of the ceremonies took the ambassador by the arm and conducted him within six yards of the throne, who, offering to advance, in order to deliver his credentials, was prevented by the *etmadowlett*,[58] or prime minister. This minister received the credentials, and laid them before the Shah, who touched them with his hand, as a mark of respect. This part of the ceremony had been very difficult to adjust. For the ambassador insisted on delivering his letters into the Shah's own hands. The Persian ministers, on the other hand, affirmed, that their kings never received letters directly, from the ambassadors of the greatest emperors on earth.

The ambassador now made a short speech, which the Sophy (Shah) answered, through the *etmadowlett*, in very obliging terms. He then enquired after his Czarish majesty's health, and asked several questions about the Swedish war; and whether the ambassador had suffered any hardships on the road during so long a journey? To all which he returned answers suitable to the occasion. At last, he was desired to take his seat, to which he was led by the master of the ceremonies. It was about a foot high, and placed at the distance of ten yards from the King. A little behind the ambassador were placed his attendants, on seats nearly of the same height. During all this ceremony, musick played; consisting of a variety of instruments, which are not unharmonious, and the mufty or high-priest, read, without intermission, chapters of the Koran.

Before the ambassador was seated, the presents from his Czarish majesty to the Sophy, carried by fifty men, were brought to the entry,

---

[58] The grand vizier had the title of Etemad al-Daula, meaning 'Trusty Support of the State'.

and received by the proper officers. They consisted of sables, and other valuable furs, falcons, a variety of fine tea, musical clocks, gold-watches set in diamonds, etc. As soon as the ambassador had taken his seat, all the ministers of state sate down on their hams, on both sides of the hall, in rows; for none are allowed to sit cross legged in presence of the Sophy. There was now placed before the company little tables, on which were set all kinds of sweet-meats, and confections; and before the ambassador was laid a golden calianne, or tobacco-pipe; which the Persians reckon an high instance of respect.

The musick continued playing, and the mufty (Muslim cleric) still continued reading; but every thing else was very silent. Several messages passed between the King and the ambassador, by means of the master of the ceremonies, and our interpreter. The King spoke the Persian language, and the ambassador the Russian, while the other two used the Turkish. In the mean time some pure water, with a bit of ice in it, was brought in golden basons to drink. About an hour after, victuals were brought by a number of servants, who carried them on their heads, in large square baskets. First the Shah was served, and next the ambassador with his retinue, then all the officers of state that sat in the hall. The grand steward of the household waited on the King, and his assistants on the rest of the company, according to their different ranks. At the same time our servants were entertained in the garden.

The entertainment consisted mostly of different kinds of rice boiled with butter, fowls, mutton, boiled and roasted lamb. The whole was served in large gold or china dishes, and placed in the baskets, which stood on a long cloth spread above the carpet. The dishes were interspersed with saucers filled with aromatic herbs, sugar and vinegar. But, according to the custom of the country, we had neither napkins, spoons, knives nor forks; for the Shah himself eats with his fingers, and every one followed his example. There were indeed, besides the common bread, some very large thin cakes, which we used instead of napkins, to wipe our fingers. They are made of wheat-flower, the Persians sometimes eat them, they are not disagreeable. Our drink was sherbet, and water cooled with ice. Formerly it was usual, on such occasions, to drink wine, and have women to dance and sing. But the present Sophy, being a sober and devout prince, thought it proper to abolish a custom productive of so many indecencies, and directly contrary to the rules of the Koran. We had therefore only men to sing, and no dancing.

The ambassador, and all the gentlemen who were admitted into the hall, continued with their heads covered during all the time of the audience. They only, on entering the royal presence, uncovered once and bowed to his majesty. When the entertainment was over, the ambassador took his leave and returned to his lodgings, conducted by the Maymandar Basha,[59] in the same manner as in the morning. The streets were lined with the Sophy's guards to prevent any inconvenience from the vast crowds of people.

From *Travels from St Petersburg in Russia
to Diverse Parts of Asia* by John Bell

The Fall of the Safavids

It was the capture of Isfahan by Afghan rebels in 1722 that brought down the Safavids, after a rule of more than two centuries. The head of the Jesuit mission in Isfahan, Father Tadeusz Krusinski, stayed in the city right through the nine-month siege and wrote a graphic account of it. This is his moving description of the terrible famine that finally forced the capitulation of the city, of Shah Sultan Husayn's distress when he realised the suffering he had brought upon his people, and of the Shah's pathetic last ride to the camp of the Afghan chief, Mir Mahmud, to surrender his sovereignty.

This scarcity was also a consequence of the King's and his ministers' ill policy, who if they had been directed by the Ahgvans (Afghans) themselves how to behave most for their Advantage, could not have done otherwise than they did.

For, as if they thought there was not people enough in Ispahan to consume the provisions there as fast as might be, the first ordinance that was published on the arrival of the Aghvans, even before the passages were clos'd, and one side of the city lay open, was a general

[59] Mehmandar-bashi, the chief official responsible for looking after foreign guests.

prohibition that none should leave the capital; not only citizens who had houses there, but foreigners, and all those that were there upon occasion. This first fault was not the worst; the next was still greater; which was an order to admit the inhabitants of the neighbouring towns and villages, driven thither by the fear of war, and they were there very welcome: which so fill'd it with useless mouths, and all sorts of rabble, that tho' the city is very great, and the streets very wide, there was hardly any passing in it.

Though such a vast multitude must make a prodigious consumption, the hope of succours to free the city in a little while, hinder'd the taking of any precautions for supplies, and provisions continu'd at a reasonable price till the end of May. They grew dearer in time, yet the price was still tolerable. In July and August the citizens began to eat camels, mules, horses and asses, and there was no other meat in the markets. A horse's carcass at the end of August was worth 1,000 crowns. In September and October they eat dogs and cats, of which so many were devour'd, that one would have thought the very species was lost there ... Corn failing in September, a pound of bread was sold for thirty shillings, and in October for above fifty.

The city of Ispahan being so full of trees, that according to Tavernier it looks more like a forest than a city, part of them was fell'd in the famine time, and the leaves and bark sold by the pound. The roots of herbs made into meal were eaten. Shoe-leather being boil'd was for a time the common food; at last they came to eat human flesh, and the streets being full of carcasses, some had their thighs cut off privately. For this inhumanity was not tolerated; and some being taken eating human flesh, they were bastinado'd[60] for it. But the fear of punishment did not hinder the increasing of the evil, which grew at last to an horrible excess. For several children were stolen and eaten, half dead as they were of famine; and that the most monstrous barbarities, which we read with so much horror in the relations of the most cruel famines, might not be wanting in that of Ispahan, there were mothers who kill'd and eat their own children.

[60] The bastinado was a beating on the soles of the feet. It was the most common punishment.

The mortality, which is the inevitable consequence of the like Calamities, was answerable to the excess of misery in Isfahan. It was so great, that no care was taken to bury the dead corpses, which were flung out into the streets in so great numbers, that there was no going without passing over them, to which people at last accustom'd themselves. But notwithstanding this disorder, which any where else would have caus'd a plague, Ispahan was preserv'd by the serenity of the air of the climate. However, there being such heaps of carcasses in every street, the citizens threw them time after time into the River Senderou, on that side where it runs nearest to the city. The quantity so thrown in was so great, that the water of the river was totally infected by it, and so corrupted, that it was a whole year before it was drunk, or any of the fish eaten that was taken in it. People of quality suffer'd as much as the vulgar; and one may judge of their sufferings in general by the streights to which a Persian lord was reduced. This lord having sold all he had by piece-meal to subsist his family, finding there was no more food to be had, he resolv'd to deliver himself and them from a cruel famine, for which he saw no remedy; and having order'd a dinner a little more sumptuous than ordinary, he privately poison'd all the meat, so that himself and all his family, even to the meanest domestick, found an end to their miseries; none of them, himself excepted, knowing how it came.

When Myrr-Maghmud[61] was inform'd by his spies, that he had nothing to apprehend on the King's part, who was depriv'd of all means of doing him hurt by the divisions at court and ill councils; that the city was every day more and more weaken'd by the mortality and the desertion of the inhabitants; and that the eunuch Achmet-Agha, the only man he fear'd, was dead, he thought of nothing but strengthening his posts and securing the avenues to Ispahan, to hinder any succors entring the place. And as he doubted not but he should soon reduce it by famine, so he made no attack for two months together. He sent back those Persians that had yielded themselves to him and sometimes he massacr'd them to strike terror into the rest. Nevertheless, he still

[61] Mir-Mahmud, the Afghan chief besieging the city.

carry'd on a negotiation with the King for the surrender of the city: and tho' this prince consented to every thing, even to his abdication, Maghmud spun out the business into length, purely to augment the misery of the citizens.

'Tis true, he might have forced the city in the beginning of October, if he had storm'd it, as his principal officers wou'd have had him do, representing to him that the consternation which would seize all Persia on the news of the sack of the capital would very much facilitate the conquest of the rest of the kingdom: and that besides, he could have no better title, according to the laws of the *Alcoran* (the Koran), to mount the throne, than by conquering sword in hand. But Myrr-Maghmud, who knew well that he ran no hazard by delaying, and was not willing to abandon the King's and grandees' treasures to pillage, which must have been done, had the city been taken by storm, put it off on various pretences whatever instances were made to him to give the assault. Sometimes he pretended a regard for his troops, which were too dear to him to be needlessly expos'd; and at other times, that somebody at least shou'd be left alive for them to command in Ispahan.

While he was thus eluding the sollicitations of his chief captains, the negotiations with the court were still carry'd on; and the extremity of the famine having at last taken hold of the King's palace, as well as the rest of the city, necessity reduc'd that Prince to sollicit the conclusion of a treaty, the first article of which was his own dethronement, which he seem'd more eager about, than Myrr-Maghmud himself.

In fine, on the 28th of October, Shah-Hussein, who had nothing left in his palace for his subsistence, came to his final resolution; and to prepare mens minds for it, after having cloath'd himself in black, he went out of his palace, and ran thro' the principal streets of the city of Ispahan, deploring his and his kingdom's misfortunes with sighs and groans. The misery and desolation to which he saw the people reduc'd, touch'd him when it was too late. He did his utmost to comfort them, telling them that the new King would govern them better; excusing his own ill conduct by the advice of his ministers, for which he appear'd mightily troubl'd. The melancholy words, and the fall of a Prince who was driven from his throne after a reign of twenty-eight years, had all the effect one can imagine on his subjects, who never had an aversion to him; and by his extreme humanity, a virtue little known to his predecessors, he had always made them bear with him, tho' they despis'd his indolence and his slavish subjection to his eunochs. But whatever reason there was to condemn his misgovernment, and tho' by his weakness and carelessness, he had dug the pit into which he was falling, yet his faults were forgotten, and their hearts were wholly taken up with his misery. The greatness of his disgrace, swallowed up all other reflections; and the people being more troubl'd for their King than for themselves, abandon'd themselves to lamentation, and made more piercing cries, than all the horrors they had endur'd during a long siege cou'd force from them; which were heard even as far as Zulfa (Julfa).

In the midst of this dreadful desolation, Shah-Hussein return'd to his palace; and the next day, the 22nd of October, he dispatch'd plenipotentiaries to the camp of the Aghvans, to conclude and sign the articles of capitulation, which were agreed on and signed the same day.

And on the day following, the 23rd of October, remarkable for so strange an event, the Aghvans sent horses for the King, and his principal officers; there being not one left in Ispahan, where all were eaten during the famine. Shah Hussein and his train mounted the horses the Aghvans had sent, and went thro' the city towards their camp. Tho' the people had been prepared for this ceremony, they had much ado to support themselves at the sight of it. They did not burst out into cries, as they had done two days before. A sullen, doleful silence express'd more sorrow, and was more moving than their loud laments. And in their wondring, ghastly looks one might see that such astonishment, pity, consternation, and despair had seiz'd their hearts, as stifled all complaints. In the mean time, Shah Hussein had advanced sorrowfully to his fine house at Farahabad, in an equipage very different from the royal pomp with which he was wont to go to that palace of pleasure, adorn'd with all that cost and art could produce to render it delightful. It was the only house whose preservation he had at heart, and the first which his rebel subjects took from him. His ministers and officers griev'd more for their master's disgrace than he did himself; because they foresaw better the dismal consequences of it They follow'd him with down-cast looks, and an air of confusion and despair; in which might also be discovered the secret indignation of mortify'd pride reduc'd to creep to barbarians, whom the least subalterns at court were wont to treat with the utmost contempt and insolence.

While Shah-Hussein was drawing near the camp of the Aghvans, the chiefs of that nation endeavoured, tho' in vain, to prevail with Myrr-Maghmud to go forth and meet him; which was decent for him to do, inasmuch as the King was to be his father-in-law: But Myrr-Maghmud, as is common with persons advanced on a sudden above their natural sphere, who are always fearful of doing too much, was not gain'd by their representations, but proudly resolv'd to expect the King in one of the halls of the palace; and when he enter'd, would hardly move a step or two to receive him.

Shah-Hussein, on the contrary, no sooner saw him, than he ran to him with open arms, and after having embrac'd him, and kiss'd him with great tokens of friendship, he took his crown out of his bosom, and put it on his head, declaring him, in the presence of the grandees of both nations, his successor to the throne, to the exclusion of his own children and their posterity. He then pray'd him, according to the conditions of the treaty, to regard him for the future as his father; not to meddle with his wives; to treat the princes of the blood royal as his younger brothers, and to take care that they wanted nothing in the haram, where they were to be shut up according to the custom of Persia.

He also recommended to him the good government of the kingdom; an exact distribution of justice; not to overburthen the people with extraordinary taxes, and to content himself with what they had been accustom'd to pay.

Whether it was that Myrr-Maghmud observ'd that his haughtiness had displeas'd the grandees of his own nation, or that the King's humbling himself and yielding up the royalty so frankly, had mollify'd his hard heart, he began to shew a little more humanity, and invited Shah-Hussein to sit down with him on a sopha; where he took a lower seat for himself, and gave him the left hand, which is the place of honour in Persia. Shah-Hussein, after this, deliver'd to him a writing sign'd by himself and all his ministers, which transferr'd the sovereignty to him and his family; without stipulating any thing more for the King and his children, than the preservation of his own honour and the lives of his children. Upon which the *mufti*, or chief priest of the Aghvans, advanc'd; and having said some prayers over the depos'd King and the new one, both bending before him, he pronounc'd a set form of curses and execrations which he threaten'd should fall on the head of either of the two who broke the articles both had agreed upon.

> *The History of the Late Revolutions of Persia*
> from the Memoirs of Father Krusinski

4
The Worst of Times

*T*HE PERIOD FROM *the fall of Isfahan to the Afghans in 1722 and the restoration of much of the former Safavid Empire under a new Qajar dynasty in 1796 was one of the cruellest in the long history of Persia. It was marked by almost ceaseless warfare, much of it in the form of civil war, by terrible acts of violence and by the dominance of the nomadic tribes. Three figures stand out. The first is Nadir Shah, who put an end to the brief period of Afghan rule, seized the crown of Persia and went on to invade India and carve out a new but ephemeral Persian Empire. He transferred the capital from Isfahan to Mashhad in the north-east and tried to make Persia a Sunni country once again. The second figure of note is Karim Khan Zand, a tribal chieftain who later ruled over about two-thirds of the country from his capital of Shiraz in the south-west. His relatively humane rule is the one ray of light in the whole period. The third figure is Aqa Muhammad, chieftain of the Qajar tribe in the north. He was cruel and ruthless, but a clever tactician. He put an end to the civil war, reunited most of the country, and made the northern city of Tehran the capital of his Qajar kingdom which was to endure for over a century.*

The Afghan occupation was short-lived. Shah Mahmud found himself in possession of Isfahan, but little else. Surrounded by a hostile population, he became increasingly paranoid. At the end of January 1723 thousands of members of the Safavid establishment in Isfahan were put to death over the course of three days. Two years later the Safavid princes – there were up to one hundred and eighty of them – were brought out from the palace in Isfahan, their hands tied behind their back, and slaughtered in cold blood. Shortly afterwards Mahmud, now thoroughly deranged, was murdered by his cousin, Ashraf, who replaced him as shah. Meanwhile both Russia under Peter the Great and Ottoman Turkey had invaded Persia and seized extensive territory – Russia along the western and southern shores of the Caspian, and Turkey along a broad front in the west. In a treaty signed in 1724, they recognised each other's conquests.

Ashraf feared that the Turks intended to restore Shah Sultan Husayn to the throne and had him killed. He then checked the Turkish advance, but was defeated in the north by one of the Shah's sons who had escaped from Isfahan during the siege, assumed the title of Shah Tahmasp II and recruited a brilliant general by the name of Nadir Quli Khan. Ashraf fell back on Isfahan, where he had about three thousand Shiite clergy massacred before he was again defeated and fled to Shiraz. Defeated once more outside Shiraz in December 1729, Ashraf fled east and was killed with his few remaining followers some months later by a band of Baluch tribesmen. His death marked the end of the Afghan occupation.

For the next twelve years Persia was dominated by the extraordinary figure of Nadir Quli Khan, or Nadir Shah as he would soon become. Starting from humble origins as a member of the Afshar tribe in Khurasan – one of the Turkoman tribes that brought the Safavids to power – he had managed through his own energy and ability to assemble an army which he rewarded handsomely through plunder or through heavy exactions on the civilian population. He deliberately mixed peoples and religions, so that the army was united only in loyalty to him.

After putting an end to the Afghan occupation, Nadir drove out the Turks and got the Russians to leave of their own accord. In the meantime, he deposed Shah Tahmasp II and installed his infant son in his place, with the title of Shah Abbas III and himself as viceroy. Four years later he took the final step to the throne in a stage-managed event that would have done credit to any twentieth-century dictator. In February 1736 he assembled thousands of civil, military and religious officials at a great encampment in Azerbaijan, which was filled with his loyal soldiers, and had them beg him take the crown. This he graciously agreed to do on condition that the

Persians abandoned their Shiite faith and reverted to Sunnism as followers of a new school of Sunni law. No doubt thoroughly intimidated, the assembly consented to this, as well as to two further demands: that they remain loyal to him and give no support to a Safavid. Nadir seems to have had no religious convictions at all and is thought to have made the break with Shiism mainly in order to deprive the Safavids of their legitimacy. It has also been suggested that he had ambitions to become the new caliph of the Muslim world, which was predominantly Sunni. At all events, he spent the rest of his reign attempting unsuccessfully to get the existing caliph, the Ottoman Sultan, to recognise the new school of Sunni law.

The infant Shah Abbas III was sent to join his father in confinement in Khurasan and Nadir was crowned at the encampment with much celebration on March 8th, 1736. His action in deposing the Safavids provoked a number of tribal revolts which he crushed, putting the leaders to death, deporting thousands of tribal families to his home province of Khurasan, and sometimes incorporating large numbers of the tribesmen into his army. The Persian people, who had welcomed his liberation of the country, were now beginning to suffer under the heavy taxes he imposed to pay his troops. He also confiscated the revenues of the Shiite clergy, many of whom fled to India and to the Shiite shrine cities in Iraq, where they laid the foundations of a Persian clerical presence, beyond the reach of the Persian government. This was to be a significant factor in clerical agitation against the Qajar and Pahlavi monarchies in the nineteenth and twentieth centuries.

Nadir next turned his attention to recovering Qandahar (Kandahar) from the Afghan tribal rebels who had overthrown the Safavids in the first place. After a year-long siege, he captured the famously impregnable fortress, razed it to the ground and moved the entire population to a new town he built nearby, called Nadirabad. The escape of some of the rebels into India and the failure of the Moghul emperor, Muhammad Shah, to return them, as Nadir requested, gave him the excuse to invade the Moghul Empire and lay hands on its fabled wealth. Brushing aside Moghul resistance, he occupied Delhi in March 1739, and sacked the city when its inhabitants began attacking his troops in the narrow streets. After exacting a huge tribute, he handed back sovereignty to Muhammad Shah and returned to Persia laden with booty, including the Peacock Throne, which was later broken up, and the Kuh-i Nur diamond, which ended up with the British crown jewels. Passing through Kabul on his way back, he recruited forty thousand Afghan troops into his army. On his arrival in Herat the first strains appeared in his relations with his eldest son, Reza Quli Khan, when he discovered, to his anger, that the prince had had Shah Tahmasp II and his two sons, Abbas and Ismail, murdered. The prince had done this to remove possible rivals to the succession following rumours that Nadir had been killed in India. Nadir's next campaign was in the north-east, where he restored Persia's ancient frontier on the Oxus River. He also recruited thirty thousand Uzbeks into his army, which was now predominantly Sunni.

He established his capital, in Mashhad, in his home province of Khurasan, thereby further emphasising the break with the Safavids. It was the centre of an important caravan trade with Central Asia and India, and Nadir did much to promote its prosperity.

His campaign in the north-east was followed by one in the north-west, against the Lezgian tribesmen of Daghestan in the northern Caucasus, whom he wished to punish for killing his brother, Ibrahim, three years earlier. On his way there in the spring of 1741, as he was riding through a forest, a shot was fired at him which missed and killed his horse. The assailant got away, but Nadir suspected that his son, Reza Quli Khan, was behind the attack. The following year the man was caught and brought before Nadir. Whatever he said seems to have convinced Nadir that his suspicions were justified and he had his son's eyes torn out.

Nadir's army suffered heavy losses in the Daghestan campaign which continued with little success until 1743 when war was then renewed with Turkey which refused to recognise the Persians as Sunnis, as Nadir had demanded, and was harassing Persian merchants and officials. A peace treaty was finally signed in September 1746, which recognised the frontiers agreed under the Safavids, without making any significant concession to Nadir on the religious front.

In the last years of his reign Nadir became increasingly tyrannical, using ever more violence to extract money from the civilian population and finding disloyalty at every turn, which he punished with instant death. He showed every sign of becoming mentally unbalanced. Rebellions broke out all over, which he put down with the savagery of Tamerlane, carrying out mass executions and erecting huge pyramids of human heads. The end came in June 1747 when he was on his way to put down a rebellion of Kurds in Khurasan. On the evening of June 19th he summoned his loyal Afghan commander, Ahmad Khan Abdali, and ordered him to arrest the officers of his Persian guard, whom he no longer trusted, but not to do so until the morning. The officers got wind of what was afoot and burst into Nadir's tent later that night, where they found him sleeping with one of his favourite women. He leapt up and tried to defend himself with his sword, but was cut down and his head severed from his body.

Nadir's assassination plunged the country into a terrible civil war. Almost all his progeny were immediately killed with only a grandson, Shah Rukh, who was blinded in the power struggle, surviving to rule in Mashhad over western Khurasan. He became the puppet of Nadir's Afghan commander, Ahmad Khan Abdali, who as Ahmad Khan Durrani, carved out an Afghan kingdom for himself centred on Qandahar. He incorporated much of eastern Khurasan, with Herat, into this kingdom and established a protectorate over the rest of eastern Persia. Elsewhere, the civil war continued without interruption until 1763 when one of the contestants, a tribal leader by the name of Karim Khan Zand, succeeded in defeating his rivals.

Karim Khan Zand ruled most of Persia outside Khurasan. He made the southern city of Shiraz his capital, but he also used Tehran as his base in the north, laying the foundations for its future role as the country's capital. He fostered a gradual recovery of his impoverished and devastated territories, by giving them a period of peace and orderly government, with fair taxation and investment in infrastructure, such as the bazaar and caravansaries he built in Shiraz, and through encouragement of foreign trade. The English East India Company, which pulled out of Persia for a time after the death of Nadir Shah, was given trading rights at Bushire, near the head of the Persian Gulf. It became the major commercial power in the Gulf after the withdrawal of the Dutch in 1765. Many of the people who had fled Persia now began to return, including some of the Shiite clergy, although Karim was not pious and regarded most of them as parasites.

Since the Saljuqs all the rulers of Persia had been Turks or Mongols. Even the Safavids, who were of mixed descent, continued to use Turkish as their first language. Karim was the first native Persian, and there would not be another until Reza Khan Pahlavi in the twentieth century. Even today he is regarded with a special affection in Persia on account of the care he had for his people, his modesty and his sense of justice. He ruled in the name of a Safavid puppet shah whom he kept in comfortable confinement until his death in 1773, after which Karim adopted the title of 'Advocate of the People'. But he was capable of ruthlessness when he felt it necessary, as when he ordered the execution of the thousands of Afghan troops left behind in Persia after Nadir Shah's death on the grounds that they were a destabilising element. He fought one major foreign campaign, laying siege to Basra in April 1775 over the harassment of Persian residents and pilgrims by the Ottoman authorities. The city surrendered a year later, but was given up by the Persians on Karim's death in March 1779.

This was followed by a renewed civil war as Karim's male relatives fought over the succession. None of them, however, possessed his abilities and their internecine quarrels only benefited another contender for power, the chief of the Qajar Turkoman tribe, Aqa Muhammad. A great-nephew of Karim's, Lutf Ali Khan Zand, put up a last desperate fight but was finally defeated and brutally put to death by Aqa Muhammad in 1794. Two years later Aqa Muhammad assumed the crown as the first shah of the Qajar dynasty which ruled Persia until 1923.

Not surprisingly, contacts between Persia and Europe, which had greatly increased under the Safavids, fell off sharply during the turbulent years of the eigteenth century. So European accounts of Persia during this period are comparatively few.

A Cruel and Bloody Tragedy

The terrible bloodshed that characterises so much of the eighteenth century in Persia began within months of the Afghan capture of Isfahan in September 1722. In January 1723 the citizens of the northern city of Qazvin rose up against an Afghan army that was occupying their city and drove it out, killing many of the Afghan troops. The Afghan leader who was now sitting on the Safavid throne, Shah Mahmud, was terrified that there would be a similar explosion of popular fury in Isfahan, where the Afghans were heavily outnumbered by the Persian population. To prevent this, he instituted a massacre of whole sections of the Safavid establishment. This was witnessed by Father Tadeusz Krusinski, the head of the Jesuit mission in Isfahan, who served Mahmud as he had the Safavid Shah as an interpreter and left this chilling account of what happened. Father Krusinski returned to Europe shortly after Mahmud's death in April 1725.

The remains of this broken army returned to Ispahan (Isfahan) in January 1723. The consternation which seiz'd the Aghvans (Afghans) on the news of this defeat, and of the sad condition which the few soldiers who sav'd themselves were in, was so great, that if the Persians of Ispahan had known how to make their advantage of it, they were able to have destroy'd their conquerors by a general rising: But there being no body to head them, and each man jealous of his neighbour, and all betraying one another, they gave the Aghvans time to look about them, and recover out of the fright they were in; after which Maghmud (Mahmud) acted the most cruel and bloody tragedy that ever was known.

This usurper, who saw with a glance of his eye the danger he was in, and that he ow'd his safety only to the cowardice and baseness of the Persians, perceiv'd that with the few Aghvans he had, who were not the tenth part of the people of Ispahan, he was every day expos'd to destruction, if they should ever come to the knowledge of their own strength, or any Persian lord have zeal and resolution enough to undertake any thing: This consideration struck him so home, that not thinking himself safe in Ispahan, as long as there were Persians enough left there to make head against him, if they had a mind to it, he resolved to massacre them, as we are about to relate.

He chose the 25th of January for this strange execution. In the morning he sent to invite three hundred Persian lords and chief citizens to a royal festival, and as fast as they came they were murder'd, and their dead bodies, after they were stripp'd, flung naked into the square or *meidan*, just before the King's palace. None of the massacred Persians was more pity'd than the son of Mirza Rostom, of the house of the princes of Georgia. He was a youth of about twelve years of age, who had been adopted even by one of the Aghvans. He threw himself into the arms of some of the chiefs of that nation, conjuring them with tears to save his life. They kept him in the middle of them, and would have sav'd him, but he was snatch'd from them, and as he stuck to a tree, the cruel butchers slew him without mercy.

Maghmud was not contented with the death of the Persian lords; that there might remain none of their race, he caus'd their children to be also massacred with the same barbarity, or greater if possible. There were about 200 young gentlemen, as well Persians as Georgians, who were bred up in a college to acquire learning, and the knowledge of military exercises. These were taken thence, and led out of the city; and when they were in the country, the Aghvans let them go, and bad them run for their lives; which the poor lads endeavouring to do, those barbarians follow'd them, as if they had been hunting of game; kill'd them in sport, and strow'd the field with their carcases. The pretence for such horrible cruelty was a sham plot said to have been formed by these young gentlemen against the life of Maghmud; but the usurper's aim was to secure his usurpation by the extinction of all the nobility.

The unmerciful fury of this barbarian stopp'd not there. There remain'd about three thousand Persian soldiers of Schah Hussein's guards, and others who had sworn fidelity to the usurper, and had been incorporated in his troops. He was afraid these men would upon occasion turn against him; and to free himself from that danger, he order'd them to be drawn up in one of the courts of the palace, under colour of receiving a bounty, which the kings of Persia were wont to give their guards, and consisted of a feast of pilau, rice and meat mixed together; and while they were eating it, their arms were taken from them, and then the Aghvans fell upon them and slew them all. 'Tis certain, the usurper ran a great risk here; and if those wretches, knowing they were to be disarm'd, had defended themselves, 'twou'd have caus'd an insurrection in the city, and probably have ended in the death of every Aghvan in it.

This was what happen'd on the 25th of January; but on the following days there was a continual search made after the Persian soldiers, and all Persians fit to bear arms; of whom so great a number were massacred, that many houses were left empty; and as the carcasses were always flung out into the gardens, there were none even in the most by-places which were not full of them.

The History of the Late Revolutions of Persia
from the Memoirs of Father Krusinski

The Last Conqueror of the East

The extraordinary career of Nadir Shah (reigned 1736–1747), the humble tribesman who rescued Persia from the Afghans, sacked Delhi and carved out an ephemeral empire, caught the European imagination. The first account in English of his career was published by a former employee of the East India Company, James Fraser, as early as 1742, while Nadir was still on the throne and at the height of his power. Although Fraser learnt Persian in India he never went to the country and obtained most of his information from the representative of the East India Company in Isfahan, William Cockell, who had personal dealings with Nadir. This is Cockell's description of Nadir in the early years of his reign, before the cruel, suspicious and rapacious side of his nature got the better of him.

Nadir Shah is about fifty-five years,[1] upwards of six foot high, well-proportion'd, of a very robust make and constitution, his complexion

[1] Historians differ over Nadir's date of birth, with some favouring 1698 and others 1688. Either way, Nadir must have been younger at the time Cockell described him, as Fraser returned to England in 1740.

sanguine and inclining to be fat, but the fatigue he undergoes prevents it; he has fine large black-eyes and eye-brows; and, in short, is one of the most comely men I ever beheld. The injury the sun and weather have done to his complexion only gives him a more manly aspect. His voice is so uncommonly loud and strong, that he frequently, and without straining it, gives orders to his people at above a hundred yards distance. He drinks wine with moderation but is extremely addicted to women, in which he affects great variety, and yet never neglects his business on their account; his hours of retirement among the ladies are but few, seldom entering their apartments before eleven or twelve at night, and is up and in public by five in the morning. His diet is simple, chiefly pillaw and plain dishes; and, if public affairs require his attendance, he neglects his meals, and satisfies his hunger with a few parched pease (of which he always carries some in his pockets) and a draught of water.

In the camp, or in the city, he is almost constantly in public, and if not, he may be sent to, or spoke with by any person. He musters, pays and cloaths his army himself and will not suffer any perquisites to be taken from the soldiers by his officers, on any pretence whatever. He has monthly accounts transmitted to him of the state of affairs in all parts of his dominions, and holds a correspondence with his several private spies in every place: besides, in every province and city there is a person called *hum calam*, appointed to inspect into the governor's actions, and keep a register of them; no affair of any consequence can be transacted but in the presence of that officer, who, besides the account the governor is obliged to send monthly, transmits his journal by a separate conveyance whenever he thinks proper, without permitting the governor to peruse it; he has no settled salary or gratuity for his trouble, but is rewarded or punished just as Nadir Shah finds he deserve. This extraordinary caution in a great measure prevents the governor's oppressing the people, or entering into conspiracies or rebellions against him.

He is extremely generous, particularly to his soldiers, and bountifully rewards all in his service, who behave well. He is, at the same time, very severe and strict in his discipline, punishing with death those who commit a great offence; and with the loss of their ears, those whose transgressions are of a slighter nature; he never pardons the guilty, of what rank so ever, and is highly displeased, if, after he has thoroughly examined the affair, any person presumes to intercede in their behalf, before which they may give their sentiments with freedom.

When on a march, or in the field, he contents himself to eat, drink, and sleep like a common soldier, and enures all his officers to the same severe discipline. He is of so hardy a constitution, that he has often been known, of a frosty night to repose himself upon the ground in the open air, wrapt up in his cloak, with only a saddle for his pillow, especially when, upon an extraordinary enterprise which required expedition, he has been obliged to out-march his baggage, by which means he has fallen upon the enemy when they least expected him. He is never happy but when in the field, and laments the time he is obliged to stay in a city to refresh his troops, in which (as in all things else) he uses the utmost despatch. His meals are over in less than half an hour, after which he returns to business; so that the servants who attend him standing are changed three or four times a day. He never indulges himself in any kind of pleasure in the day-time, but constantly at sun-set retires to a private apartment; where, unbending himself at once from business, he sups with three or four favourites, behaving all the time in the freest and most facetious manner. In this private conversation no person is allowed to mention any thing relating to public business; nor, at other times, must they presume upon this intimacy to behave with more familiarity than their equals. Two of his evening-companions, happening to transgress in that point by taking the liberty to advise him in public, he immediately ordered them to be strangled, saying: 'Such fools were not fit to live, who could not distinguish between Nadir Shah and Nadir Kuli.'[2]

His mother entreated him for some time after he seized Tahmasp[3] to restore him and said Tahmasp would certainly make sufficient amends by creating him generalissimo for life. Did she

[2] Nadir Kuli (Quli), meaning 'Slave of the Unique' was Nadir's original name before his rise to power. Nadir is saying that now that he is shah, people should not treat him as if he was the ordinary person he was then.

[3] The Safavid Shah, Tahmasp II, who was deposed by Nadir in Isfahan in September 1732 and kept in detention in Khurasan until 1739, when he and his sons were murdered.

really think this? 'Yes,' she said. He replied: 'If I was an old woman, perhaps I might be inclined to think so too,' and desired her to give herself no trouble about state affairs.

Among Nadir Shah's extraordinary faculties, his memory is not the least to be admired, there being few things of moment that he ever said or did, but what he remembers; and can readily call all the principal officers in his numerous army by their names. He knows most of the private men who have served under him any time, and can recollect when and for what he punished and rewarded any of them. He dictates to one or two secretaries, and gives orders about other affairs at the same time, with all the regularity and promptness imaginable.

In time of action, I'm told, he is equally surprising, it being scarce credible how quick he is in discerning the odds on either side, and how active in succouring his troops. If any of his general officers give ground without being greatly overpowered, he rides up and kills him with a battle-axe (which he always carries in his hand) and then gives the command to the next rank.

From *The History of Nadir Shah* by James Fraser

Nadir Shah's Encampment

An English merchant, Jonas Hanway (1712–1786), who was employed in St Petersburg by the London-based Russia Company, was sent to Persia in 1743 to investigate trading possibilities. But an exploratory caravan of English woollen goods which he was taking to Mashhad was looted by rebels in Astarabad, on the south-east corner of the Caspian Sea, and he himself threatened with being carried off by Turkoman tribesmen to shepherd their flocks. After he had managed to extricate himself he went to seek compensation from Nadir Shah, who was preparing to resume the war with Ottoman Turkey and was encamped with his army near the city of Hamadan in north-west Persia. Hanway arrived there on 28th March 1744 and stayed for ten days. In the end he received partial compensation, but he returned to Russia later that year somewhat disillusioned about the prospects for trade. His subsequent account of his experiences in Russia and Persia, which appeared in 1753, was a considerable publishing success. One of the most valuable passages is this detailed description of Nadir's encampment.

In placing the camp a general regularity is observed, as far as is agreeable to the size and shape of the ground; it being a rule constantly pursued, to place the tents of certain principal ministers and officers in the front, or to the right or left of the Shah's quarters, that some of them may be always near him. The circuit of the quarter allotted to the Shah's own tents is very large: the entrance consists on one side of a line of uniform tents, serving for guard-rooms; and the other, of the tents in which the affairs of the chancery, and the like public concerns, are transacted. About two hundred yards beyond this avenue is the pavilion in which the Shah usually sits, to give audience and transact business: it is oblong, supported by three poles, adorned with gilded balls at the top; the covering is of a cotton cloth of a brick colour, and the lining of clouded silk: the floor is covered either with carpets or cloths, and the body of the pavilion has on each side a kind of alley, through which the attendants may walk round; sometimes the Shah sits upon a large sopha, or chair; cross-legged, and sometimes on the floor. The hind-part of this tent is divided into small apartments, where the officers who do not appear in his majesty's presence, attend: there is nothing sumptuous in this pavilion, the front of which is always open, even in the worst weather; however when it is extremely cold, several pots of lighted charcoal are placed in the middle. At a considerable distance behind were placed the Shah's private tents, to some of which he retired at his meals: and in order to render them warm, he had Indian panels, which were occasionally set up, and formed the linings of two small apartments. To these were admitted only his secret emissaries, when they had any remarkable intelligence to communicate; but in the last years of his life he had no familiarity with any of them.

Almost contiguous to these were the tents of the Shah's ladies, which differed from the others in having several curtains that formed separate compartments one within another. The boundaries of the

Shah's quarter were occupied by his eunuchs and female slaves, and almost this whole circuit, especially towards the residence of the women, was surrounded by a strong fence of net-work, round which the night-guard patrolled, and severely punished all intruders. As there were no lights in these parts, nor any tents near them, it frequently happened that people, coming to the camp by night, ignorantly straggled thither, and were sure to be ill-treated when this happened.

I observed, that none but the officers in immediate waiting were admitted into the royal pavilion; for the officers of state, and people in business, stood in the open air in all weathers, forming a semicircle in front of the tent: if they were brought to answer for their conduct, they were held under the arm by proper officers, to prevent their escape, or committing any acts of violence. The same ceremony, with very little difference, was observed also towards foreign ambassadors, or great men; the last indeed was under pretence of respect, but it also served to prevent any accident; an attempt having been once made on the Shah's life.

The Persians use a certain glazing in their cotton tents, which, in some degree, prevents their being penetrated by water. The tents of persons of distinction are of various shapes, but most commonly oblong, and supported by three poles: the outside is always of coarse cotton cloth, and the inside is either lined with the same, or with woollen, or silk, according to the different seasons of the year, and circumstances of the owners: the ground is spread with a thick cotton cloth, or mat, and over that is laid a carpet, or woollen printed cloth of several colours; besides this covering, the square of the floor is laid round with felts, as already described, and these supply the place of bedsteads and feather-beds; though some have their beds raised a little above the damp of the earth. The top and sides of the tents of great officers are sometimes lined with panels, which are wrought with flowers and variety of figures: large tents are often divided into two rooms, or apartments, by panels or curtains; the back part is appropriated for the use of the women; but such grandees as have several women, place a set of tents for them at a distance from their own, which are surrounded with cotton cloths, to prevent their being seen: they have also, at a convenient nearness to their tents, a hole dug, enclosed by a cotton screen of four folds, to answer the necessary purposes of nature.

That part of the camp called in Turkish the *ordubazar* or camp-market, begins at the end of the square fronting the guard rooms, and is about half a mile long: it consists of tents on each side like a street, running as direct as the nature of the ground will admit: these tents are often supplied with a variety of provisions, apparel, horse-furniture, and other necessaries, which are brought hither for sale; not to mention the continual change of property arising from the daily confiscations made by the Shah. The care of this market is committed to an officer called *ordubazari*, who often rides up and down to keep order; and when any disputes arise, they are brought before the *deroga bazar*, or superintendant of the market, who acquires a considerable income from rents, fees, presents, and extortions. Many of the shop-keepers were little better than common sutlers; but such as carry on great business are under the protection of some of the principal courtiers, who are the grand dealers in flour and rice, of which there is always a great consumption: and as these courtiers have many supernumerary servants, camels and mules, they send them to the distant provinces that produce rice, which they bring to the camp for sale, and make great profits. But if the shop-keepers, or other traders, interfere with them in these branches of trade, they generally mark them out for destruction.

Nadir often enquired into the price of necessaries, and reduced them as he thought proper, fining the market-people upon every transgression: but the most notorious instance of injustice to the shop-keepers, was his obliging them, when his tents and their appurtenances were grown old, to take them, and pay him the value of new ones.

The two imperial standards were placed on the right of the square already mentioned: one of them was in stripes of red, blue, and white, and the other of red, blue, white, and yellow, without any other ornament: though the old standards required twelve men to move them, the Shah lengthened their staffs, and made them yet heavier; he also put new colours of silk upon them, the one red and yellow striped, the other yellow edged with red: they were made of such an enormous size, to prevent their being carried off by the enemy, except by an entire defeat. The regimental colours were a narrow slip of silk sloped to a point, some were red, some white, and some striped: several hours before the moving of the camp, one of the standards was taken down by way of signal, and carried forward to the place where the new camp was to be pitched. The Shah's set of tents, and those of the great men went with it attended by a convoy. The bulk of the army often marched an hour or two before the Shah; for in removing from one encampment to another, he sometimes galloped the whole way.

The Shah had about sixty women, and very near the same number of eunuchs, who generally rode near his person, and kept pace with him: before him were his *shatirs* (running footmen), preceded by the *chiaux* (chanters), and before them the *keshikchi* (watch-guards), being the foremost of his bodyguard, who were best acquainted with the track the Shah was to take: these spread a mile or two before him and terminating in a kind of angle, gave notice of the Shah's approach, by crying out in Turkish, '*yerrie*', or make way: this is called the *kouruck*, which is always troublesome, and sometimes fatal to such as cannot get out of their way; for when they meet with people in the Shah's rout, rivers, precipices, and rocks are no excuse; they drive at them with their maces, and make all before them fly at their approach.

When Nadir travelled with his women, the army was kept at almost a mile distance; but when he went without them, people were permitted to come nearer. In the latter part of his reign he seldom did travel without them; probably the better to avoid any evil designs against his person. The Shah's women, and indeed others of distinction, rode on white horses, in the manner as men ride; but when they did not go in his company, they were usually carried on camels, seated in machines resembling a covered wagon, and hung like panniers over a pack-saddle. On these occasions they were entirely concealed under a covering of crimson-cloth; and in this manner they rode one on each side, conducted with the usual pomp: the motion is very disagreeable, and apt to create a disorder, not unlike the sea-sickness. The sick ladies, and female servants of the court, were always concealed in the same manner, under a covering of crimson cloth: other women, of no particular distinction, rode on horses or mules; these mixed among the crowd, but had a linen veil over their faces, and wore great coats, resembling those of the men; but the poorer sort had a white veil, which covered their whole body. The women belonging to the Ousbeg Tartars were not so scrupulous about hiding their faces as the Persians. The number of women in the camp, except upon perilous enterprises, in proportion to the men, is generally one to ten.

The Shah when sick used to be carried in a horse-litter: other people of fashion were seated, or laid on mules upon a large flat pack-saddle, bolstered up: but the common way of carrying their sick men, is to fix two poles to meet in the middle over the neck of the horse, at the point of the saddle, the breast and shoulder resting between the interstices of the poles.

Upon extraordinary occasions the rear-guard was said to be very numerous, consisting of eight thousand *yesaul*: their business was not only to secure the rear of the army, but to prevent straggling or desertion; therefore they examined every one who quitted the camp; and if there was the least ground of suspicion, they would not suffer even a stranger to go about his business without a bribe. If the beasts belonging to travellers happened to tire while the camp was removing; these fellow, instead of assisting them, frequently drove the owners away, and converted the cattle and baggage to their own use.

In marching, the greatest part of the soldiery, as well as the *yesaul*, kept in a collected, but irregular body: the followers of the camp covered several miles. The elephants and camels were employed only in carrying great burthens: the last are of several kinds, but the most serviceable is that called the *maje*, which have two bunches on their backs. They are generally fed with balls of meal; and though very hardy, they frequently die of epidemical distempers.

From *An Historical Account of the British Trade over the Caspian Sea with a Journal of Travels from London through Russia into Persia* by Jonas Hanway, Merchant

Persian Fashions

European visitors were always struck by the attention the Persians paid to their appearance and dress. Even amid the horrors and the incessant warfare of the eighteenth century this continued to be the case, as is clear from this description by Hanway of what men and women wore and how they looked.

With regard to their persons and dress, the men in most parts of the country shave their heads very close; the young ones have often a lock on each temple, which hangs pendant, and serves as an ornament to their faces, somewhat in the manner of European beaus some years since. Their cheeks are shaved, but the beard on the chin reaches up to their temples: the men for the most part are tall, and of good shapes, their complexions swarthy, particularly in the southern parts, and their eyes and hair black. Most of them have caps of cloth, which rise ten or twelve inches, and terminate on the top in four corners: they have a shorter cap for summer, faced with grey Bokharian lambskins; their ears, which are very large, are always left bare, and generally hang down, in consequence of the weight of the caps resting upon them, and many are proud to show that their ears are not cut off. Crimson is a colour they much affect in their caps, as well as in their outward garments; and it makes a grand appearance: deep blue, which one seldom sees worn, except in coarse cloths, is their mourning colour. The better sort of people wear a sash of Kermania wool, wrapped about their heads as turbands; some of these are so exceeding fine as to cost one hundred crowns, and the common price for such as are good is eight or ten crowns: their heads are thus kept very warm, and the more so as they seldom pull off their caps, but wear them even in the presence of their King.

The outward garment of the common sort of people is a slight cotton: in general they wear two or three light vestments, which reach only to their knees; so that their dress gives them a great advantage over the Turks, who wear long effeminate robes. Besides their cloth garments of the ordinary sort, which are much esteemed, some have them lined with furs, as ermins, squirrels, or sables, which are worn for warmth, and very often for state also; for it is common to see a great man sit in his sable-coat in the height of summer: but it must be observed that these coats reach no farther than the waist; thus demonstrating a judicious distinction not to load themselves with a superfluous weight of cloaths. Silk is worn in summer by men of fashion, especially for under-garments; but these as well as their cotton and woollen under-garments are quilted, which renders them very warm without being heavy. Under the sash round the waist they carry a long pointed knife in a case of wood, which is mounted with gold or silver. Their shirts, for the most part, are made of checkered silk and cotton: these have neither wrist band nor collars, for they always go bare-necked. The sleeves of their upper garments reaches down to their fingers; they sometimes wear cloth-stockings, which set loose like boots but for the most part they use only socks of wool, which reach over the ankles. They wear slippers like women's shoes without quarters; these are of shagreen made with the skin of horses rumps, which are prepared hard and rough like a seal's skin: the heels being high, they are calculated to carry one out of the dirt, but are extremely uneasy to those who are not accustomed to them. Their drawers, or rather trowsers are more convenient than breeches in a hot country, being without any tight ligaments: for this reason their cloathing in general seems to be more conducive to health and strength than that of the Europeans; the sash, round the waist, may however keep their loins too warm; but girding up the loins is indeed a part of dress the most ancient we read of. Their writers carry their ink and pens about them in a case which they put under their sash, or in their pocket under their arm.

The dress of the women in Persia is simple, differing from the men rather for the distinction of sexes, than by affecting any form shocking to nature: they adorn their arms with bracelets after the manner of some Europeans, and their heads with jewels of several kinds: one of these is composed of a light gold chain-work, set with small pearls, with a thin gold plate pendant, about the bigness of a crown piece, on which is impressed an Arabian prayer: this is fixed to the hair at the upper part of the temple, and hangs upon the cheek below the ear. They have large ear-rings, and some are said to wear gold rings set with pearls in their nose, which is incomparably the worst taste they have; the poorer sort wear the same thing in baser metals: their hair hangs in tresses; their shirts, as well as the men's, are of a thin manufacture of silk and cotton; but these are open at the breast in the manner of men's shirts in Europe, whilst the men's are supported on the left shoulders by a small button; the women also wear drawers and slippers as the men.

The Persians observe an outward decency in their cloathing; their very religion seems to exact it of them, and the simplicity of their customs contributes to the same end. They are neat in their houses; and even the meanest sort are usually very clean in their cloaths, which have seldom any rent; but if it was not for their repeated bathings, the want of changing their shirts would render their persons indelicate.

> From *An Historical Account of the British Trade over the Caspian Sea with a Journal of Travels from London through Russia into Persia* by Jonas Hanway, merchant

Nadir's Cruelty

During the last years of his reign, Nadir's physical and mental health deteriorated and he became increasingly suspicious, brutal and rapacious. The French Jesuit, Father Bazin, was his physician from 1741 until his assassination in 1747, and left a record of some of the terrible scenes he witnessed, as in this account of the forty-five days Nadir spent with his army in Isfahan in the winter of 1745–1746. Nadir unleashed his soldiers on the city and the surrounding area to terrorise the inhabitants and extract as much money as they could.

During this time terrible cruelties and injustices were committed by his (Nadir's) orders, or else without any punishment on his part. His army spread through the town and the neighbouring countryside, bringing disaster everywhere. Angry soldiers could be seen running along the roads and the streets, leading with heavy blows groups of twenty or thirty wretches who had been unable to satisfy their greed. All one heard everywhere were shrill and piercing cries of dismay and despair. If someone fled his house, his neighbour's house was pillaged; if a village was abandoned by its inhabitants, the nearby town was made to pay; everything was in a state of confusion and alarm; a town taken by assault and left to the fury of the conquering army does not witness scenes more horrible than those in Isfahan during the stay of the usurper. His fears increased with his acts of cruelty; each day was the last for some family; I never left the palace without seeing twenty-five or thirty corpses of men strangled by his order or battered to death by his soldiers.

Before he left, he wanted to do an inventory of all the precious furnishings of his palace. A carpet that served as ornament for the throne had been missing for about three years. The suspicion fell first on the keeper of the crown jewels. He denied the charge and, after being severely bastinadoed, declared that his predecessor had sold the carpet. 'To whom?' demanded Nadir. 'Who would have the temerity to buy the furnishings of my palace?' The accused man asked for time to make searches. He returned a few days later and denounced as buyers eight merchants - two Indians, two Armenians and four Jews. They were arrested and after being interrogated each had an eye torn out. They were then chained together by the neck. The following morning a huge fire was lit on Nadir's orders and they were all thrown into it together.

From *Lettres Édifiantes et Curieuses écrites des Missions Étrangères, Vol 4, Paris 1780. Mémoire sur les dernières années du règne de Thamas Kouli-Kan, et sur sa mort tragique, contenus dans une lettre de Frère Bazin, de la Compagnie de Jésus au Père Roger, Procureur général des Missions du Levant*

A Persian Gymnasium

For most of the second half of the eighteenth century the city of Shiraz, in south-west Persia, was an oasis of peace, especially under the benevolent rule of Karim Khan Zand, who controlled it from 1754 until his death in 1779. A young ensign with the East India Company in India, William Francklin (1763–1839), spent nine months in Shiraz in 1786 and 1787, when it was still under Zand rule, although this was not to last much longer. Francklin, who became an Oriental scholar in later life, was intrigued by much of what he saw and experienced, such as this Zur-Khaneh, or House of Strength, where men performed traditional gymnastic exercises and engaged in wrestling. As Francklin suggests, this Persian institution, which still exists today, may well have its roots in pre-Islamic times.

There are places in Shirauz (Shiraz) distinguished by the name of *Zoor Khana* (*Zur-Khaneh*), the house of strength or exercise; to which the Persians resort for the sake of exercising themselves. These houses consist of one room, with the floor sunk about two feet below the surface of the earth, and the light and air are admitted to the apartment by means of several small perforated apertures made in the dome. In the centre is a large square terrace of earth, well beaten down, smooth, and even; and on each side are small alcoves raised about two feet above the terrace, where the musicians and spectators are seated.

When all the competitors are assembled, which is on every Friday morning by day-break, they immediately strip themselves to the waist; on which each man puts on a pair of thick woollen drawers, and takes in his hands two wooden clubs of about a foot and a half in length, and cut in the shape of a pear; these they rest upon each shoulder, and the music striking up, they move them backwards and forwards with great agility, stamping with their feet at the same time, and straining every nerve, till they produce a very profuse perspiration. After continuing this exercise about half an hour, the master of the house, who is always one of them, and is distinguished by the appellation of *pehlwaun*, or wrestler, makes a signal, upon which they leave off, quit their clubs, and, joining hands in a circle, begin to move their feet very briskly in union with the music, which is all the while playing a lively tune. Having continued this for a considerable time, they commence wrestling; but before the trial of skill in this art begins, the master of the house addresses the company in a particular speech, in part of which he informs the candidates, that as they are all met in good fellowship, so ought they to depart, and that in the contest they are about entering into, they should have no malice or ill-will in their hearts; it being only an honourable emulation, and trial of strength, in which they are going to exert themselves, and not a contentious brawl; he therefore cautions them to proceed in good humour and concord: this speech is loudly applauded by the whole assembly.

The wrestlers then turn to their diversion, in which the master of the house is always the challenger; and, being accustomed to the exercise, generally proves conqueror, by throwing each of the company two or three times successively. I have sometimes, however, seen him meet with his equal, especially when beginning to grow fatigued. The spectators pay each a *shahee*, in money, equal to three-pence English, for which they are refreshed during the diversion with a *calean* (water-pipe) and coffee. This mode of exercise, I should suppose, must contribute to health, as well as add strength, vigour, and a manly appearance to the frame. It struck me in its manner of execution to bear some resemblance to the gymnastic exercises of the ancients.

From *Observations Made on a Tour from Bengal to Persia
in the years 1786–1787* by William Francklin

The Tomb of Hafiz

Shiraz has long been known as 'the city of poets', having been the home of Persia's two greatest poets, Saadi (c.1215–1292) and Hafiz (c.1325–1389). Francklin gives a charming description of how the people of Shiraz would make a pleasurable outing to Hafiz's tomb, which had just been rebuilt by Karim Khan Zand and was then about two miles outside the city walls; the city has since spread out around it. Unfortunately the tomb built by Karim was destroyed by Reza Shah Pahlavi in 1938 and, in the view of many, a less attractive one built in its place.

The tomb of the celebrated and deservedly admired Hafiz, one of the most famous of the Persian poets, stands about two miles distant from the city walls, on the northeast side, and nearest the gate Shah Meerza Hamza. Here the late Vakeel Kerim Khan has erected a most elegant *ivan* or hall, with apartments adjoining: this building is executed in the same style as the *dewan khana* (*divan khanè*), nor has any cost been spared to render it agreeable: it stands in the middle of a large garden; in front of the apartments is a stone reservoir in the centre of which is a fountain. In the garden are many cypress trees of extraordinary size and beauty, as well as of great antiquity: I take them to be the same as those described by Sir John Chardin. Under the shade of the trees is the tomb of the poet Mahomed Shems ad deen Hafiz, of fine white marble from Tauris (Tabriz), eight feet in length and four in breadth: this was built by order of Kerim Khan (Karim Khan Zand), and covers the original one: on the top and sides of the tomb are select pieces from the poet's own works, most beautifully cut in the Persian *nustaleek*[4] character. During the spring and summer seasons, the inhabitants visit here, and amuse themselves with smoking, playing at chess, and other games, reading also the works of Hafiz, who is in greater esteem with them than any other of their poets, and they venerate him almost to adoration, never speaking of him but in the highest terms of rapture and enthusiasm: a most elegant copy of his works is kept upon the tomb for the purpose, and the inspection of all who go there. The principal youth of the city assemble here, and shew every possible mark of respect for their favourite poet, making plentiful libations of the delicious wine of Shirauz to his memory.

From *Observations Made on a Tour from Bengal to Persia in the years 1786–1787* by William Francklin

[4] A form of Persian calligraphy.

Persian Manners

While he was in Shiraz, Francklin stayed with a Persian family with whom he was very friendly. This gave him, as he says, 'an opportunity of seeing more of the nature and disposition of the middling sort of people, and their manners and customs, than perhaps has fallen to the lot of most travellers.' Here he gives a generally affectionate and admiring account of Persian manners, as he experienced them.

The Persians, with respect to outward behaviour, are certainly the Parisians of the East. Whilst a rude and insolent demeanour peculiarly marks the character of the Turkish nation towards foreigners and Christians, the behaviour of the Persians would, on the contrary, do honour to the most civilized nations: they are kind, courteous, civil and obliging to all strangers, without being guided by those religious prejudices so very prevalent in every other Mahomedan nation; they are fond of enquiring after the manner and customs of Europe; and, in return, very readily afford any information in respect to their own country. The practice of hospitality is with them so grand a point that a man thinks himself highly honoured if you will enter his house and partake of what the family affords; whereas going out of a house, without smoking a *calean*, or taking any other refreshment, is deemed, in Persia, a high affront; they say that every meal a stranger partakes with them brings a blessing upon the house; to account for this, we must understand it as a pledge of faith and protection, when we consider that the continual wars in which this country has been involved with very little cessation, since the extinction of the Sefi (Safavid) family, have greatly tended to an universal depravity of disposition, and a perpetual inclination to acts of hostility. This has lessened that softness and urbanity of manners for which this nation has been at all former times so famous; and has at the same time too much extinguished all sentiments of honour and humanity amongst those of higher rank.

The Persians in their conversation use such extravagant and hyperbolical compliments on the most trifling occasions, that it would at first inspire a stranger with an idea, that every inhabitant of the place was willing to lay down his life, shed his blood, or spend his money in his service; and this mode of address (which in fact means nothing) is observed not only by those of higher rank, but even amongst the meanest artificers, the lowest of which will make no scruple, on your arrival, of offering you the city of Shirauz and all its appurtenances, as a *peishkush* or present. This behaviour appears at first very remarkable to Europeans, but after a short time becomes equally familiar.

Freedom of conversation is a thing totally unknown in Persia, as that walls have ears is proverbially in the mouth of every one. The fear of chains which bind their bodies has also enslaved their minds; and their conversation to men of superior rank to themselves is marked with signs of the most abject and slavish submission; while, on the contrary, they are as haughty and overbearing to their inferiors.

The Persians in their conversation, aim much at elegance, and are perpetually repeating verses and passages from the works of their most favourite poets, Hafiz, Sadi, and Jami;[5] a practice universally prevalent, from the highest to the lowest; because those who have not the advantages of reading and writing, or the other benefits arising from education, by the help of their memories, which are very retentive, and what they learn by heart, are always ready to bear their part in conversation. They also delight much in jokes and quaint expressions, and are fond of playing upon each other; which they sometimes do with great elegance and irony. There is one thing much to be admired in their conversations, which is the strict attention they always pay to the person speaking, who they never interrupt on any account. They are in general a personable, and in many respects a handsome people: their complexions, saving those who are exposed to the inclemencies of the weather, are as fair as Europeans.

From *Observations Made on a Tour from Bengal to Persia in the years 1786–1787* by William Francklin

[5] Jami (1414–1492), the last of the great classical poets of Persia.

The Beauties of Shiraz

Living in a family with which he was on such close terms, Francklin had a rare opportunity for a European man to get to know Persian women. These seem to have cast their usual spell over him.

The women at Shirauz (Shiraz) have at all times been celebrated over those of other parts of Persia for their beauty, and not without reason. Of those whom I had the fortune to see during my residence, and who were mostly relations and friends of the family I lived in, many were tall and well-shaped; but their bright and sparkling eyes was a very striking beauty: this, however, is in a great measure owing to art, as they rub their eye-brows and eye-lids with the black powder of antimony (called *surma*), which adds an incomparable brilliancy to their natural lustre. The large black eye is in most estimation among the Persians, and this is the most common at Shirauz. As the women in Mahomedan (Muslim) countries are, down to the meanest, covered with a veil from head to foot, a sight is never to be obtained of them in the street; but from my situation, I have seen many of them within doors, as when any came to visit the family where I lived, which many did, directed by their curiosity to see an European, understanding I belonged to the house, they made no scruple of pulling off their veils, and conversing with great inquisitiveness and familiarity, which seemed much gratified by my ready compliance with their requests, in informing them of European customs and manners, and never failed to procure me thanks, with the additional character of a good natured *feringy* (the appellation by which all Europeans are distinguished).

Francklin was critical of the subordination of Persian women in marriage, but added this delightful observation.

The Persian ladies, however, during the days of courtship, have in their turn pre-eminence; a mistress making no scruple of commanding her lover to stand all day long at the door of her father's house, repeating verses in praise of her beauty and accomplishments; and this is the general way of making love at Shirauz; a lover rarely being admitted to a sight of his mistress, before the marriage contract is signed.

From *Observations Made on a Tour from Bengal to Persia in the years 1786–1787* by William Francklin

Persian Prayers and Meals

Francklin describes how the life of his Persian family was regulated by the prayers which Muslims are obliged to say five times during the day. Three of these prayer-times were followed in turn by breakfast, lunch and dinner, and Francklin gives an interesting account of the different foods served at each meal by his 'middling sort of people', and how they relaxed after dinner, poetry again providing a major diversion.

The mode of living of the Persians is in general as follows: They always rise at day-break in order to perform their devotions. Their first prayer is denominated *numaz soobh*, or the morning prayer; it is said before sun-rise, after which they eat a slight meal, called *nashta*, or breakfast; This consists of grapes, or any other fruits of the season, with a little bread, and cheese made of goat's milk; they afterwards drink a cup of very strong coffee, without milk or sugar; then the *calean*, or pipe, is introduced. The Persians, from the highest to the lowest ranks, all smoke tobacco.

Their second hour of prayer is called *numaz zohur*, or mid-day prayer, and is always repeated when the sun declines from the meridian. Their dinner, or *chasht*, which is soon after this prayer, consists of curds, bread, and fruits of various kinds; animal food not being usual at this meal.

The third hour of prayer is called *numaz 'asur*, or the afternoon prayer, said about four o'clock.

The fourth hour of prayer is *numaz sham*, or evening prayer, which is said after sunset; when this is finished, the Persians eat their principal meal, called *shami*, or supper. This generally consists of a pilau, dressed with rich meat-sauces, and highly seasoned with various spices: sometimes they eat kibaab, or roast meat. When the meal is ready, a servant brings notice thereof, and at the same time presents a ewer and water; they then wash their hands, which is an invariable custom with the Persians, both before and after eating. They eat very quick, conveying their food to their mouths with their fingers; the use of knives and forks being unknown in Persia. Sherbets of different sorts are introduced, and the meal concludes with a dessert of delicious fruits. The supper being finished, the family sit in a circle, and entertain each other by relating pleasant stories (of which they are excessively fond), and also by repeating passages from the works of their most favourite poets, and amusing themselves at various kinds of games.

The fifth and last prayer is styled *numaz akhir*, the last prayer; or sometimes *numaz sheb*, or the night prayer, repeated about an hour after supper.

From *Observations Made on a Tour from Bengal to Persia in the years 1786–1787* by William Francklin

A British Tribute to the Shiraz of Karim Khan Zand

The short-lived but popular Zand dynasty (1750–1794) had an ardent British admirer in the representative of the English East India Company in Basra and Baghdad and later British ambassador to Persia, Harford Jones (later Sir Harford Jones Brydges). During nearly twenty years in Baghdad and Basra, he made two visits to Persia, learnt the language and watched with dismay as his hero, Lutf Ali Khan Zand, the last of the Zand rulers, was overcome by the chief of the Qajar Turkoman tribe, Aqa Muhammad Khan Qajar. Here he describes the various ways in which the founder of the Zand dynasty, Karim Khan Zand, improved and embellished his capital of Shiraz.

Perhaps no monarch, in the same space of time, ever bestowed on a city more useful, more ornamental, and, according to the taste of the Persians, more beautiful buildings than the *vakeel*[6] erected at Shiraz. He was aware, that a large army, unemployed, is always dangerous; and that if 'idleness is the parent of evil', be a proverb applicable in the case of an individual, it is not misapplied when predicated of an army like his own. The walls of Shiraz, the excavation of its deep and broad fosse, the beautiful bastions by which this latter was commanded, and its well-arranged and strongly-built gateways, exhibited a perfect specimen of Oriental fortification; and on this great work the troops were employed.

The *vakeel* found employment for the poor, by the erection of a noble and regularly-built bazaar, extending, in length, something between a quarter and half a mile; in the midst of which was placed a splendid caravanserai, serving at once as a custom-house, lodging for merchants, shops to hold their wares, and, in some measure, as an exchange. At one end of a very spacious square stood a citadel, provided with a deep ditch and draw-bridge; in which were contained a treasury, the mint, the palace, and the seraglio. On the opposite side of this square was a large and commodious gallery for the royal *nokara*, or military music; on the left hand was the *divan khoneh*, or hall of audience; on the right, the entrance to the *bagh shah*, or royal garden, in which stood a highly-ornamented building called the *koolah fringee*, or European's hat; because, being triangular, it had some resemblance to that absurd and comical covering for the head, a cocked-hat. Besides these, Shiraz was indebted to the *vakeel* for a noble mosque, not quite finished when he died; a spacious and splendid bath; and an *umbar* or reservoir, of water, capable of supplying in summer the whole city with that necessary element, in its purest and most limpid state.

Such works were conducive, either to the safety and comfort of the citizens, or to the dignity of the government. But the benevolent mind of the *vakeel* stopped not here. Without the walls, he laid out gardens, and erected buildings, in which the citizens might recreate

[6] Vakil, meaning 'viceroy', was the modest title Karim Khan Zand gave himself. He never assumed the title of 'shah'.

and amuse themselves; and all these were constructed with such beautiful bricks and correct masonry, that if equalled, they were not surpassed, in Europe, by either materials or workmen.

Amongst these resorts for rural enjoyment, might be reckoned the tomb of Hafiz, the tomb of Saadi, the *heft tun*,[7] and the garden called Dilgushay. I had the pleasure of seeing all these buildings in 1787, nearly in the same state as they were in at the death of the founder, before the scoundrel treachery of Hajy Ibrahim[8] had delivered the beautiful *divan khoneh* to be plundered of its rich furniture; and before the arrival of the ferocious eunoch,[9] who disfigured or destroyed almost every building in the city erected by the *vakeel*, under the idea, that by carrying away the grand pillars and beautiful marbles with which some of them were adorned, he adopted a means of destroying that which time alone could effect – the memory of the benefits bestowed on Shiraz by the *vakeel*; and who, when his savage and vindictive heart expressed satisfaction in bursting open and destroying the beautiful tomb which held the mortal remains of Kureem (Karim), ordered the bones of that great man to be burnt before him in a chafing-dish and scattered his ashes to the wind! forgetting, that it was by the noble and merciful spirit which once animated those reliques that his own life for many years had been spared. It is painful to add, that whatever part of these buildings the vengeance of the eunoch spared, or the good taste and mild nature of his nephew, the present king, took pleasure in repairing and restoring, the wrath of heaven, by an earthquake, has within these few years nearly engulphed or demolished.

From *The Dynasty of the Kajars*
by Sir Harford Jones Brydges

[7] The Haft Tan, or Seven Bodies, was a building erected by Karim, just north of the tomb of Hafiz, in memory of seven dervishes who took up their abode on that spot, each burying the other until all had died.
[8] Hajji Ibrahim was the influential mayor of Shiraz who gave invaluable support to Lutf Ali Khan Zand, but was then instrumental in bringing about his downfall by deserting him for Aqa Muhammad Khan Qajar.
[9] Aqa Muhammad was castrated in the first days of the power struggle that broke out after the assassination of Nadir Shah in June 1747.

The Vizier's Supper Parties

Harford Jones became a good friend of Mirza Muhammad Husayn, who was vizier or chief minister to the later Zand rulers, and often attended his suppers in Shiraz. His engaging account of these musical and literary soirées reveals the life-style of a cultured grandee of the bureaucratic class.

The *Mirza* was a man of unbounded liberality and generosity; and he made a point, as his nephew Mirza Bazurg[10] afterward did, to render it apparent to every body that he lived up to the full extent of his means, and put by nothing: the only expensive possession the Mirza had was books, and he was considered to possess the finest and rarest library ever collected by an individual in Persia.

At these suppers there were generally assembled from twenty-five to thirty persons, a very mixed company, consisting of men of the law, men of the sword, and some of the principal merchants who either were resident in the city or were visiting it in the way of their business. The first were disagreeable and solemn; the second were sometimes men of very high rank, and consequently of great pretensions; whilst the last were shrewd intelligent persons, who had seen a great deal of the Oriental world, and were excellent and instructive companions. The *Mirza* himself was an elegant poet, under the name of Wafa, or 'the Grateful': he was acknowledged to be the best hand in Persia at a *lateefa*, joke or pun; and he did the honours of his house incomparably well, giving to each of his guests his full proportion of conversation and attention, and always directing the first to such subjects as he imagined those he addressed to be best acquainted with.

The guests assembled a short time after the hour appointed for the *nemauz-el-ash*, or evening prayer; so that we were never disturbed, as in many other houses, by one or more getting up

[10] Mirza Bazurg (or Bozorg) became the very capable vizier of the Qajar Crown Prince, Abbas Mirza, when the latter was governor-general of Azerbaijan (1799–1834) under Fath Ali Shah.

ostentatiously to repeat their prayers. The entertainment began as usual, with *caleans* (water-pipes), coffee, sweetmeats, and what the Persians call sweet-tea, which is a strong decoction of different spices much sweetened with sugar. There were seated at the lower end of the room three or four persons possessed of the best voices in Shiraz, and the most celebrated performers on the *kemooncheh*, or Persian lyre, who were to be procured. Before the supper was brought in, these persons, at intervals, were called on to sing and play some of the odes of Hafiz, or some of the *Mirza*'s own lyric compositions. About nine the supper was produced, which was always excellent; and nothing delighted the *Mirza* so much as to see his guests doing honour to it. When the supper was removed, the room was perfumed, and the *caleans* again brought in. The *Mirza*'s reader, who had an excellent voice, then came forward, and read portions either from the Shah Nameh or from prose histories of Persia and Arabia, until the Mirza called out 'Bareekulla', 'well done'; which was the signal for the reader to leave off, and the guests to depart, except such as wished to speak to him privately on any business with the government, this being the time he always gave private audience to such suitors. Twice, I think, I saw Mirza Bazurg's children brought in, after supper, to entertain the company with what is called capping verse;[11] and the quantity of Persian poetry these children could repeat, appeared to me quite astonishing.

From *The Dynasty of the Kajars*
by Sir Harford Jones Brydges

A Sad Encounter

The last of the Zand rulers, Lutf Ali Khan Zand, whom Harford Jones so much admired, was decisively defeated by the founder of the new

[11] Capping verse has been a favourite entertainment of educated Persians, who until recently learnt a vast amount of poetry by heart. Each person has to recite a verse beginning with the last letter of the verse recited by the previous person. Players drop out as they fail to come up with an appropriate verse.

Qajar dynasty, Aqa Muhammad Khan, in a battle near Persepolis, in July 1792. Harford Jones later recalled a touching encounter he had shortly before that battle with Lutf Ali Khan's young son, for whom a terrible fate lay in store.

The evening before the King (Lutf Ali Khan) marched, I happened to go into the garden of Koulah Fringee, to which I had free admittance; and there I saw the King's son, a boy about seven years old, with his tutor or *lala*. I would willingly have avoided the little prince; but he sent one of his attendants after me, to desire me to come to him. On coming up to him, and saluting him, he said: 'you are the *fringee*[12] my father so often talks of. You brought him a pretty musical clock: did you bring nothing for me? I shall be king tomorrow, whilst my father is away; and you must come to see me, as you were used to visit him.' I was delighted with the child, and replied, 'What does your highness wish for?' '*Lala*,' he replied, 'tells me the best penknives are made in your country: do give me one. And my *dy* (i.e. my nurse) says the scissors you make are better than ours: pray give me also a pair of scissors for *dy*.' I happened to have a very fine penknife in my pocket, which I immediately presented him; and told him, that when I went home I would send him two or three more, and scissors for his *dy*. The child, in the gaiety of his little heart, exclaimed, 'O! you are a good man!' He kept me walking and talking with him near an hour; and I never saw a prettier-behaved, handsomer, or more intelligent child. Strange to tell, the next time we met was in Azarbaijan; himself a shrivelled eunoch, and a slave; myself the accredited minister of my country, to the successor[13] of the destroyer of his father's house and throne.

From *The Dynasty of the Kajars*
by Sir Harford Jones Brydges

[12] Farangi, the Persian word that had long been used to describe all Europeans, was derived from 'Frank' (ie. Frenchman).
[13] Fath Ali Shah, the nephew of Aqa Muhammad.

5

Foreign Hegemony and the Challenge of the West: the Qajars

*T*HE PERIOD OF Qajar rule (1796–1925) brought a welcome peace *and* stability after the anarchy of the eighteenth century. But *Persia's weakness relative to the West was exposed by her defeat in two successive wars with Russia which led to the loss of territory in the Caucasus. Russia and Britain, then assumed an increasingly dominating role as their rivalry in Central Asia – the Great Game – led them to compete for influence in Persia.*

The Qajars made a number of half-hearted attempts at modernisation which achieved little. The religious revolution attempted by the Babis – the forerunners of the Bahais – in the mid-nineteenth century, which might have been a catalyst for radical change, was crushed by an alliance of throne and mosque. Subsequently, popular discontent with foreign political and economic domination as well as with the corrupt and arbitrary rule of the Qajars found expression in a series of protest movements which culminated in the Constitutional Revolution of 1906–1907. In all these movements, the Shiite clergy played a prominent role. Hopes raised by the securing of a constitution and a representative parliament were disappointed by the chaos that followed, which led to a resurgence of tribal power. In the meantime, Britain acquired a new interest in Persia through the discovery and exploitation of its oil resources.

The condition of the country worsened dramatically during the First World War when the various combatants fought one another on Persian soil and effective government more or less ceased. After the war, the continuing lawlessness and the threat from local insurrectionary movements supported by the Bolshevik government in Moscow, prompted a coup in 1921 by an officer of the Persian Cossack Brigade, Reza Khan, with the encouragement of British military commanders in northern Persia. The Qajar monarchy was abolished four years later.

The Qajars were one of the Turkoman tribes that brought the Safavids to power. They were based around Astarabad, known today as Gurgan, on the south-east corner of the Caspian Sea. It was a Qajar chief, Fath Ali Khan, who first lent his support to Shah Tahmasp II in his fight back against the Afghan invaders, only to be executed by Tahmasp at the instigation of his new general, the future Nadir Shah. The Qajars made a bid for power in the civil war that broke out after Nadir's death. At the outset of this, the future founder of the Qajar dynasty, Aqa Muhammad, was captured and castrated, in a vain attempt, as it turned out, to disqualify him from ascending the throne. After his father was defeated and killed in a struggle with Karim Khan Zand, Aqa Muhammad became a hostage at Karim's court in Shiraz where he was well treated, but nursed a burning resentment towards the Zands and an absolute determination to win power.

This he achieved after Karim's death, when he managed to escape back to his tribal homeland in the north. He overcame rival Qajar chiefs, defeated the Zands, and reunited much of the former Safavid realm under his rule. He deliberately presented himself as the heir to the Safavids. At his coronation in March 1796, he girded himself with the sword of Shah Ismail I, thereby committing himself to defend and support the Shiite faith. He was pious in his religious observance and generally respectful towards the Shiite clergy, more of whom were returning to Persia from Iraq.

Where the Zand capital had been in Shiraz in the south-west, Aqa Muhammad established his in Tehran, close to the Qajar tribal lands in the north. But he spent little time there. He remained very much the tribal chief, ruling from the saddle with a minimal administration. His achievement in reuniting the country and restoring order has tended to be overshadowed by his reputation for brutality, the most notorious example of which is his punishment of the citizens of Kerman for supporting the last of the Zands. He had all the adult males of the city put to death or blinded, and the women and children given as slaves to his soldiers.

Aqa Muhammad's determination to recover the former Safavid possessions in Georgia, Armenia and the southern Caucasus led to confrontation with Russia. He sacked the eastern Georgian capital of Tiflis in 1795, after the kingdom became a Russian protectorate and refused to return to its Persian allegiance. Russia had no troops on hand at the time, but two years later a Russian army moved into Georgia and much of the southern Caucasus, though it was withdrawn after Catherine the Great's death in November 1796. Aqa Muhammad was on his way to reassert his authority in Georgia when he was murdered in his tent on the night of June 17th 1797 by three of his servants.

He was succeeded by his nephew, Fath Ali Shah, during whose reign Persia began to be drawn into the conflicts and rivalries between the European powers, beginning with the conflict between Britain and France in the Napoleonic wars. First Britain, then France and then again Britain made alliances with Persia – Britain because it wanted to block a possible French attack on its possessions in India, and France because it wanted to open the way to such an attack. But because of the shifting alliances in Europe, neither Britain nor France fulfilled promises they made to help Persia against Russia, which invaded and occupied Persian territory in the southern Caucasus. As a result, Russia was able to defeat Persia in two successive wars and deprive her of all her possessions in the southern Caucasus. The Treaty of Turkomanchay of 1828 which ended the second war also saddled Persia with a huge indemnity and forced her to grant Russian merchants very favourable trading terms as well as special immunities and privileges, known as capitulations. These were later extended to the subjects of other European countries and became a major source of grievance.

Popular resentment towards Russia burst out into the open the following year when a Tehran mob, incited by a Shiite cleric, attacked and killed all but one of the forty-five members of a Russian mission. The mob had become inflamed after the mission took under its protection one of the Shah's principal eunuchs, who was a former Armenian Christian, and two Armenian women from the harem of the prime minister.

The wars with Russia made Persia painfully aware of Europe's military superiority and prompted the first attempt at a modernising reform. With the enthusiastic support of the Crown Prince, Abbas Mirza, who led the Persian campaigns in the Caucasus, French and then British military advisers were brought in to train and equip a new army corps on European lines. Abbas Mirza also sent the first young Persians to study in Europe, in this case in England. One of them, on his return, set up the first printing press in Persia.

By the end of Fath Ali Shah's reign, Persia began to feel the impact of a growing Anglo-Russian rivalry in the region, which came to be known as the Great Game. Britain saw Russia as an expansionist power in Central Asia with possible designs on India, which she could more easily pursue if she were allowed to become dominant in Persia. Consequently, throughout the nineteenth century Britain and Russia jostled for influence in Persia, each seeking to advance its interests and to undermine the other. An attempt by Abbas Mirza to recover Herat – once the seat of the Safavid crown prince – was strongly opposed by Britain, for fear that the Persians would let in the Russians, bringing them an important step closer to India. But any immediate danger of an Anglo-Persian conflict over Herat was averted by Abbas Mirza's premature death in 1833, which put an end to the campaign. Fath Ali Shah died the following year, having appointed Abbas Mirza's son, Muhammad Mirza, as his successor.

Under Fath Ali Shah, the Qajars made the transition from tribal chieftains to traditional Persian monarchs. He sought to emulate the splendour and ceremony of the Safavid court, appearing on formal occasions in a blaze of jewels. He also identified with the Sasanid kings of ancient Persia by depicting himself in a number of rock reliefs, often close to those carved out by the Sasanids. He embellished his capital Tehran with new buildings and gardens, was a generous patron of the arts and crafts, and fostered an important literary revival. The most colourful of the Qajar monarchs, with his handsome figure, his wasp-like waist and his long black beard, he had at least a thousand wives and concubines and demonstrated an astonishing virility, producing some two hundred and sixty children. Only very rarely did he display his uncle's cruelty. The worst instance was early in his reign when he became resentful of the influence of his grand vizier, Hajji Ibrahim, whom he had inherited from his uncle, accused him, almost certainly falsely, of treason, and had him blinded and his tongue cut out before putting him to death, along with several of his closest male relatives.

One Safavid practice Fath Ali Shah did not imitate was that of confining the royal princes to the harem. Instead he appointed them to provincial governorships, where they ruled as petty kings. On his death, two of them opposed the succession of Muhammad Mirza. But Britain and Russia, increasingly the arbiters of Persia's fate and united in their desire to maintain internal stability, stood firmly behind the Crown Prince. After the British envoy provided him with the money to pay his troops, he was able to crush his opponents and ascend the throne as Muhammad Shah.

One of the new Shah's first actions, however, was to lay siege to Herat, despite strong British objections. But he was unable to overcome the Afghan resistance and was forced to withdraw after the British broke off diplomatic relations and occupied the Persian island of Kharg at the head of the Persian Gulf. He was also compelled to accept a commercial treaty granting Britain the same favourable terms already granted to Russia.

Tensions between the Qajar monarchy and the Shiite clergy appeared for the first time during the reign of Muhammad Shah. He had fallen under the influence of a Sufi mystic, Hajji Mirza Aqasi, who had been his tutor. Soon after his accession he had his prime minister strangled and appointed Aqasi in his place. The Shiite clergy detested Sufism, which they saw as a challenge to their authority, and deeply resented the favour that was now extended to Sufis. They were further antagonised by measures taken by Aqasi to enlarge the area of secular law and to limit the right of sanctuary, which mainly applied to mosques, shrines and the homes of senior clerics. Despite the difficulties they had faced during the eighteenth century, the Shiite clergy retained a strong hold on the population, who regarded them as their defence against tyranny. Their influence had been further enhanced by the triumph of a school of thought which gave the most senior clerics, the *mujtaheds*, the power to interpret Shiite law and obliged the faithful to follow their rulings. There were a number of clashes between Muhammad Shah and the clergy, and the traditional Shiite view, that in the absence of the Hidden Imam all government lacks legitimacy, began to gain ground.

The most serious challenge to Shiism, however, came from a messianic movement that grew out of Shiism itself. Known as the Babi movement, it was founded by a young merchant from Shiraz, Sayyed Ali-Muhammad, who in 1844 announced that he was the *Bab* or 'Gate' to the Hidden Imam of Twelver Shiism, whose reappearance as the Mahdi he expected imminently. He accused the secular and religious establishment of corruption and called for economic and social reforms, including a degree of female emancipation. He attracted a considerable following, mainly among lower-ranking Shiite clergy and merchants and craftsmen, but also including many women. Then, early in 1848, he made the much more sensational claim from prison that he, himself, was the Imam and had a new revelation which rendered the laws of Islam invalid. This made him an apostate in the eyes of the orthodox Shiite clergy and set off a number of violent Babi uprisings, which only subsided after Sayyed Ali-Muhammad was executed in Tabriz on July 9th 1850.

Two years later, however, there was a Babi attempt on the life of the new Shah, Nasir al-Din, as a result of which about fifty Babis were put to death with great cruelty. Some years later the Babi movement split, with a small group remaining faithful to the original revolutionary message of the *Bab* and a much larger one, that of the Bahais, following yet a further revelation which preached a peaceful, humanitarian creed.

The smooth accession of Nasir al-Din after his father's death in September 1848 was again ensured by the firm support of Britain and Russia. His reign, which lasted until 1896, was the longest of any Qajar monarch. It was marked by increased rivalry between Britain and Russia, by mounting popular resentment at foreign political and economic domination, and by growing pressure for reforms to strengthen Persian independence.

The Persian economy underwent some fundamental changes in the second half of the nineteenth century, which caused hardship and discontent. Foreign trade was dominated by Europeans, who only had to pay a flat import duty, while Persian merchants remained subject to many internal road tolls and dues as well. The commercial treaties with European countries also prevented the Persian government from imposing any protectionist tariffs, with the result that many of the traditional handicraft industries were virtually wiped out by cheap manufactured imports. The textile industry was particularly hard hit. Furthermore, the flood of imported European goods meant that Persia's foreign trade moved heavily into deficit. In 1864 a silkworm disease had devastating consequences for the country's most valuable export item, silk. Opium production took its place, which led to a reduction in wheat cultivation in favour of the opium poppy, and contributed to an increased occurrence of famine. From the 1870s there was also inflation, caused by a collapse of the world price of silver on which the Persian currency was based.

Egged on by Russia, Nasir al-Din Shah made another attempt to recover Herat, but although he captured the city in 1856 he was forced to withdraw and renounce all claims to Afghan territory after a British expeditionary force landed on the Gulf coast, marched inland and won an easy victory over the Persian army.

Nasir al-Din Shah had a fitful interest in reforms and appointed two reforming prime ministers – Amir Kabir from 1848 to 1851 and Mushir al-Daula from 1871 to 1873. Both attempted to put the state finances on a sound footing and to attack corruption but both ran up against vested interests that contributed to their downfall. Amir Kabir also aroused the young Shah's fears of an over-powerful minister and was dismissed and then brutally murdered at the Shah's behest. His most lasting memorial was a European-style college of education in Tehran, where teachers from Europe taught a modern curriculum. Mushir al-Daula survived his downfall, which his enemies were able to bring about after he granted a sweeping economic concession to Baron Julius de Reuter, a naturalised Briton of German origin who had created the Reuters news agency. The concession gave Reuter a monopoly of all new industrial undertakings, including the construction of roads and railways, and of virtually all the natural resources of the country for the next seventy years, together with the farm of the customs for twenty-five years. In return, the Shah received an immediate payment of forty thousand pounds sterling and the promise of more to come. Mushir al-Daula hoped the concession would not only promote the rapid economic development of the country, but would also commit Britain to defending Persia's territorial integrity against any future threat from Russia. As it turned out, the British government was unenthusiastic, Russia was predictably furious, and there was strong opposition at home – all of which persuaded the Shah to cancel the concession and dismiss his prime minister.

Nasir al-Din Shah was the first Persian ruler ever to travel abroad. Initially encouraged by Mushir al-Daula in the belief that it would strengthen his support for reform, the Shah made three visits to Europe and Russia in 1873, 1879 and 1889, where he was the object of much excited curiosity. His second visit led to the formation of a Persian Cossack Brigade, numbering only a few hundred men to begin with, but rising to fifteen hundred by 1900 and to several thousand ten years later. The brigade was made up of Persian troopers, trained, clothed and equipped like their Russian counterparts, with Persian and Russian officers, the Russians occupying the most senior positions. The Shah had this set up, despite British protests, after he had been impressed by the Cossack detachment which escorted him in Russia. It quickly established itself as by far the most effective unit in the Persian army.

These costly European tours added to the government's financial difficulties. In order to plug the widening gap between revenue and expenditure, the Shah resorted increasingly to the sale of offices and of economic concessions, despite the discouraging experience of the Reuter concession. This attracted a horde of European fortune-hunters who descended on Tehran in much the same way that Western businessmen were to do during the oil boom of the 1970s. In 1890 the Shah granted another British subject, a Major Talbot, a fifty-year monopoly over the production, sale and export of a commodity dear to almost all Persians – tobacco. The resulting protests made the opposition to the Reuter concession look like a storm in a teacup.

For the first time the agitation was nationwide, which owed much to the new telegraph network. This made it possible to communicate rapidly with all the main urban centres in Persia as well as with the Shiite holy cities in Iraq. The protests were initiated by the merchant community but were quickly taken up by many of the Shiite clergy, who had the ability to bring large crowds onto the streets. They were encouraged by nationalist and reformist intellectuals as well as by the Russians, who made clear their opposition to the concession at the outset. From the spring of 1891 there were mass demonstrations in one city after another. The climax was reached in December 1891 when a *fatwa* prohibiting the sale or use of tobacco was issued in the name of the most senior Shiite *mujtahed*, Hajji Mirza Hasan Shirazi, who was beyond the reach of the government, in Iraq. The ban was observed even by the women of the royal harem. The Shah, deeply alarmed by the scale of the opposition, cancelled the concession the following month. The compensation that had to be paid to the English company forced the government to raise the first of many foreign loans.

Nasir al-Din Shah was assassinated on May 1st 1896 and succeeded by his son and heir apparent, Muzaffar al-Din, who was already old and in poor health. The government faced growing financial difficulties, as it struggled to meet the interest on foreign loans and to find the money for the new shah to take the waters at European spas. New loans were taken out, including two from the Russians for which they extracted further commercial concessions. To increase the customs revenue, Belgian administrators were brought in and a Belgian, Joseph Naus, was put in charge of the whole operation. Revenue was increased, but at the price of further antagonising Persian merchants. More concessions were granted, including one given in 1901 to another British citizen, William Knox D'Arcy, to explore for and exploit oil resources. The concession covered all of Persia except for the five northern provinces, where Russia was sensitive to any British intrusion.

There was a revival of opposition activity with the formation of semi-secret societies in Tehran and other cities. The members were mainly middle-ranking clergy with progressive views (some of them secret Babis), merchants, civil servants and intellectuals. They met to discuss European political ideas, and ways of ending despotic government and foreign domination. They gained encouragement from the Japanese defeat of Russia in 1905 and the abortive Russian revolution of the same year.

The opposition came out into the open in December 1905 after the governor of Tehran had a number of sugar merchants bastinadoed for raising their prices. The incident sparked months of agitation in support of various demands, the most significant of which was for the election of a constituent assembly. The agitation was led by the same alliance of Shiite clergy, merchants, and intellectuals, which had been the driving force behind the opposition to the tobacco concession. The difference was that this time the agitation was supported by Britain and opposed by Russia. A major feature was the Persian tradition of taking sanctuary, which had been extended to foreign legations. The turning point came in July 1906 when fourteen thousand people took sanctuary in the grounds of the British legation in Tehran.

The Shah gave in to demands for the dismissal of the prime minister and the election of a constituent assembly. Elections on the basis of a limited franchise were held at the end of September and the first national assembly, or *majlis,* met in October. A committee of the *majlis* drew up a constitution in two parts, the first of which was signed by Muzaffar al-Din Shah on his deathbed in December 1906 and the second part by his successor, Muhammad Ali Shah, the following October. The constitution described the Shah's power as deriving, not from God, but from the people, and left the executive, represented by the Shah and his ministers, very much at the mercy of the legislature, consisting of the *majlis* and an upper house, the senate, although it was to be many years before the senate would be set up. The legislature had to approve any measure of importance and could appoint, investigate and dismiss the Shah's ministers. While the constitution declared Twelver Shiism to be the official religion and said that legislation must accord with its teachings, it also enshrined such liberal principles as the equality of all under the law, regardless of religion, and freedom of speech and the press, with the exception of anti-Islamic statements. The constitution, much of which was pushed through in the face of opposition from religious conservatives, remained, at least theoretically, in force until the Islamic Revolution of 1978–1979.

In the freer climate that now prevailed, radical newspapers and political societies proliferated, mainly in Tehran and Tabriz, which were the two main centres of the constitutional movement. But the euphoria was somewhat marred when, in August 1907, Britain signed an agreement with Russia dividing Persia into spheres of influence. The two powers had decided to end their rivalry in the face of the growing threat from Germany. The agreement created a Russian zone in the north which included most of the major towns, a British zone in the south-east, and a neutral zone in the middle. The constitutionalists who had looked to Britain for support felt badly let down and were more determined than ever to free the country from Anglo-Russian domination.

Meanwhile Muhammad Ali Shah, who had Russian advisers, was determined to throw off the fetters of the constitution. He received encouragement from some members of the Shiite clergy who had supported the constitutional movement but believed it had become anti-Islamic. They found further evidence of this in the anti-clerical tone of some of the newspapers. There were also many ordinary working people in Tehran who depended on the court for their livelihood and who saw this threatened by the austerity policies of the *majlis*, which refused to raise any more foreign loans.

The Shah made his move in June 1908, using the Cossack Brigade under its Russian commander to crush the small body of volunteers defending the *majlis*, or parliament building. The *majlis* was then closed down and many prominent constitutionalists arrested and executed, while others fled abroad.

To begin with only Tabriz resisted the royalist coup. But it managed to hold out against the Shah's forces for several months until Russian troops moved in. By that time revolts were breaking out elsewhere and in July 1909 an army led by leftist revolutionaries moved against Tehran from the Caspian province of Gilan, while another army of Bakhtiyari tribesmen advanced from the south. When they entered the capital, the Shah fled to the Russian legation. An ad hoc grand assembly was set up which deposed Muhammad Ali and installed in his place his twelve-year-old son, Ahmad, with the head of the Qajar tribe as regent. Leading royalists were tried and five of them executed, including a prominent Tehran *mujtahed*, Shaykh Fazlallah Nuri, who had turned against the constitution, insisting that only God could legislate. The franchise was widened and a new parliament elected which was inaugurated in November 1909. Meanwhile an agreement was reached with Britain and Russia for the ex-shah to go into exile with a pension and with a guarantee from the two powers that he would be restrained from all political agitation.

Two political groupings emerged in the parliament – the conservative Moderates, who were the larger of the two, and the Socialist-oriented Democrats, who drew their main strength from Tabriz with its strong ties with the Russian Socialist movement. Relations between them were tense, with each party having armed supporters outside parliament who carried out periodic assassinations.

Both parties, however, enthusiastically supported the appointment of a team of American financial experts led by Morgan Shuster to reform the country's finances. Shuster arrived in Tehran in May 1911, and was given wide-ranging powers with the title of Treasurer-General of Persia. But he antagonised the Russians by attempting to enforce his authority in their northern sphere of influence. In November they presented an ultimatum to the Persian government, demanding the dismissal of Shuster and an undertaking not to engage foreigners without Russian and British consent. They warned that if no satisfactory answer was received within forty-eight hours Russian troops, who were present in Azerbaijan in large numbers, would march on Tehran. The parliament rejected the ultimatum, but the government gave in and forcibly dissolved the parliament.

Earlier in the summer, despite the guarantee given, the ex-shah entered Persia from Russia at the south-eastern corner of the Caspian Sea. While his commander-in-chief advanced on Tehran with an army of Turkoman tribesmen, two of his brothers led revolts in the northwest. But after his general was defeated and executed near Tehran, Muhammad Ali fled back across the Caspian to Russia.

To meet this threat, the Bakhtiyari tribal chief who had helped to oust Muhammad Ali in the first place, was appointed prime minister, and after the dissolution of the parliament Persia was largely run by Bakhtiyari chiefs. They abandoned any attempt to restore the country's finances, instead making heavy demands on the treasury to support their tribesmen. At the same time they were unable to combat the lawlessness and tribal disturbances that were afflicting much of the country, particularly in the south. The regular army had virtually ceased to exist apart from the Persian Cossack Brigade, which was effectively a Russian instrument. A gendarmerie force with Swedish officers had been set up in 1911, but it was not yet strong enough to take on powerful and well armed tribes.

Britain moved Indian troops into the south to secure the trade routes and to protect the new oil installations in Khuzistan. D'Arcy had struck oil there in commercial quantities in 1908 and had set up the Anglo-Persian Oil Company the following year. The oil became a vital British interest in 1912 when it was decided that the British fleet should go over from coal to oil. Two years later the British government bought a controlling interest in the company.

Ahmad Shah was freed of the regency in July 1914 when he was crowned at the age of 17. The following month the First World War broke out. The Shah and his government declared Persia's neutrality, but were unable to prevent the country becoming a battleground. Turkish troops invaded and occupied much of Kurdistan and Azerbaijan, where they became locked in war with the Russians. The Germans sent agents into Persia and had considerable success in stirring up some of the southern tribes against the British. They also gained the active support of the gendarmerie under their pro-German Swedish officers. Probably a majority of the urban and educated population hoped for a German victory to put an end to the Anglo-Russian domination. A third parliament was convened in Tehran in December 1914, but dissolved a year later and many of the deputies rallied around an alternative nationalist government which was set up with German support in Kermanshah. When the Russians recaptured Kermanshah some of the members of this opposition government made their way to Berlin. The British meanwhile managed to restore their position in the south by raising a Persian force called the South Persia Rifles.

After the Bolshevik Revolution of October 1917, the Russian forces in Persia were withdrawn. In a popular move, the Bolshevik government announced the cancellation of almost all the concessions obtained by Tsarist Russia and repudiated the 1907 Anglo-Russian agreement. Soon it was lending assistance to the nationalist and reformist movements that were gaining ground in the north of the country. Discontent was universal. By the end of the war Persia's economy and infrastructure had been severely damaged, lawlessness was widespread, and tens of thousands were dying of famine and disease. The government tried to present a claim for reparations at the Versailles peace conference, but was told that as a non-belligerent it could not be heard.

Britain was now heavily subsidising the Persian government and even paying for the upkeep of the Persian Cossack Brigade, which still had its Tsarist officers. Britain had also established a military base in the northern city of Qazvin to counter Bolshevik activity, but was unable to prevent Bolshevik forces from moving into the Caspian province of Gilan to join with a local insurrectionary movement in setting up a Soviet Socialist Republic. This discredited a grandiose scheme devised by the British foreign secretary, Lord Curzon, to make Persia effectively a British protectorate and a bulwark against any threat to British India. The Persian government signed up to Curzon's Anglo-Persian Agreement after being heavily bribed, but the parliament refused to ratify it.

By 1921 the British were preparing to withdraw their troops from Persia and were concerned, as were many Persian leaders, that a weak government in Tehran would be unable to prevent pro-Bolshevik forces from seizing power. British military officials in Persia – but not the British government – then encouraged and facilitated a coup that was already being planned by the Persian commander of the Cossack division in Qazvin, Reza Khan (all the Russian officers having been dismissed the previous October) and a nationalist journalist, Sayyid Ziya al-Din Tabatabai. The commander of the British troops in northern Persia, General Ironside, was particularly impressed by Reza Khan, who had distinguished himself in recent fighting with Bolshevik forces in Gilan, and saw him as the strong man Persia needed. On the night of February 20th-21st 1921, Reza Khan and Sayyid Ziya entered Tehran with over two thousand Persian Cossacks, who swiftly took control of all the key points in the city. Martial law was declared, many representatives of the old order were arrested and Sayyid Ziya, promising a programme of major reforms, was appointed prime minister by the Shah. Reza Khan became commander-in-chief of the army, though it was soon clear that he was the dominant figure. Ahmad Shah would reign for another four years, but it was effectively the beginning of a new era.

. European accounts of Persia, of which there had been relatively few since the fall of the Safavids, began to appear again in increasing numbers with the restoration of internal peace and stability under the Qajars and the growing political and economic ties between Persia and Europe. But Europe's political advances, and its overwhelming technological and economic strength, meant that Europeans and Persians no longer met as equals, as they had in Safavid times. European writers tended now to be more critical of Persian ways, as they sought reasons for Persia's relative backwardness.

Many of the British accounts were written by diplomats and soldiers and reflected the increased British political interest in Persia, arising out of concern for the defence of India. Some of the soldiers were sent on arduous journeys through remote tribal areas to provide information that would be helpful in foiling any hostile Russian initiatives. British travellers, too, were occasionally commissioned by their government to provide reports on particular parts of the country.

The interest taken in the nomadic tribes was new. Although they constituted a third of the population, they had been largely ignored by the seventeenth century travellers. The interest was driven not only by strategic needs, but also by a certain romantic outlook which found the tribes, for all their feuding and plundering habits, more honourable than the often devious, corrupt and extortionate representatives of the Qajar government. This romanticism extended beyond the tribes to the sights and sounds of immemorial Persia - like the long caravans of camels and mules bearing pilgrims to the Shiite shrine city of Mashhad, described so eloquently by the young Englishman and future Viceroy of India, George Nathanial

Curzon. This romantic view was shared by much of the reading public in Europe, which lapped up exotic tales of the Orient, some of them written by travellers to Persia.

Besides the accounts written by diplomats and soldiers and others who had business in Persia of one kind or another, a growing number were written by travellers with nothing more than a personal interest in the country, like Sir Robert Ker Porter, James Baillie Fraser and Sir Henry Layard. From around the middle the nineteenth century European women began to record their impressions of Persia. One of the earliest was Lady Sheil, the wife of the British Minister in Tehran, but before long women were also present as independent and often intrepid travellers, of which there is no finer example than Isabella Bird. Their accounts of the country have an added interest in that they were able to penetrate the secretive world of the harem and to meet Persian women.

A landmark publication at the end of the nineteenth century is Curzon's *Persia and the Persian Question*, which is the last truly encyclopaedic work on Persia conveying, as it does, a vast amount of information about the country. Writers thereafter are inclined to have a narrower focus, and perhaps also to strive more after a literary effect, as Gertrude Bell does very successfully in her description of the charming and hospitable King of Merchants in his magical garden outside Tehran.

Hard Times for the Tribes

The restoration of central government authority by the Qajars was a blow to the nomadic tribes which had been able to give full rein to their predatory instincts during the anarchy of the eighteenth century. This is amusingly highlighted by Sir John Malcolm (1769–1833) who led three diplomatic missions to Persia between 1800 and 1810 for the government of British India, which was then in the hands of the English East India Company. Malcolm, who concluded the first treaties between Britain and Persia in January 1801, was a fluent Persian speaker who vowed to spend 'every leisure hour in researches into the history of this extraordinary country, with which we are but little acquainted.' The outcome was his two-volume History of Persia, *from which the following passage is taken and which remains an extremely readable and valuable work, particularly for the picture it gives of Persian life and institutions in Malcolm's own time.*

The wandering tribes are all plunderers; and glory in acknowledging it. They are continually recounting their own successful acts of depredation, or those of their ancestors; and from the chief to the lowest man, they boast openly of deeds for which men would be capitally punished under a better ordered government. Every sentiment that escapes them evinces their attachment to their predatory habits. They often regret the tranquillity of their country; and speak with rapture of those periods of confusion, when every man who 'had a horse, a sword, and a heart, could live in comfort and happiness'. When on the march towards the royal camp at Sooltaneah,[1] I asked a chief of a tribe, what ruins those were on the right of the road? His eyes glistened. 'It is more than twenty years,' he said, 'since I accompanied my uncle in a night attack to plunder and destroy that village, and it has never been rebuilt. Its inhabitants are a bad race, and our enemies; however, they have settled near it, and are again become rich. I trust in God,' he added with emphasis, 'that the present tranquillity will not last; and if old times return, I will have another blow at these fellows before I die.' A still more remarkable instance occurred on my first mission. When hunting one day near the line of march, we came to a deep ravine: as we were crossing it, an old Persian of the tribe of Lac, then in my service, turned round, and said to me with a smile:- 'In this ravine, sir, about twenty years ago, I and ten others of my tribe, lay in wait for a caravan. We attacked them, and killed five or six useless fellows of merchants and mule-drivers: the rest ran away, and we found plenty of plunder. I lived gloriously for some years on the produce of the shawls that fell to my share; but all my cash is gone, and I am now a poor old fellow. Yet, after all, it is some consolation to think one has had a taste of the good things of this world.'

[1] Fath Ali Shah regularly passed the summer months encamped with his court and troops at Sultaniyeh in north-west Persia, where he spent the time hunting.

This race, as may be concluded from these anecdotes, are strangers to the causes which promote civilisation and improvement, and insensible to the blessings of security and good order. They view every thing through the medium they have been accustomed to; and power only possesses charms in proportion as it ministers to their passions. But this observation may perhaps be applied with equal justice to their superiors. The reigning King (Fath Ali Shah), when I endeavoured to explain to him the nature and operation of the various checks in the British government, exclaimed, after listening with great attention, 'Your king then appears to be no more than the first magistrate of the state! So limited an authority may be lasting, but can have no enjoyment! My power is very different: it is real enjoyment! I can elevate or degrade all the high nobles and officers you see around me at pleasure: but then, it is true, there is no security for my family possessing the throne. Right in Persia always has and always will belong to the sword.'

It is not surprising that the military populace, where the monarch professes these sentiments, should measure their title to consideration, and their power of attaining enjoyments, by their means of pillaging and oppressing. If a prince or chief of high rank evince a contrary disposition, his conduct excites very opposite feelings to admiration. A man of one of these tribes, who was sent to accompany two English gentlemen through a part of Persia, contended that a prince of the blood whom he served had better claims to the crown, because he was more dreaded than one of his royal brothers, whom they had extolled for his humanity, virtue, and intelligence. 'You see,' he said, 'that small village before us. If the prince you praise were where we are, the inhabitants would be at this moment running to meet him, and be eager to pitch his tents: whereas, if my master were here, so great is the terror of his name, they would already have fled to the summit of the neighbouring hills. Now, I ask you, which is the most proper of these two to govern Persia?' The same person, who was an intelligent man of his class, was very inquisitive about the conditions of England; and, after listening with delight to their accounts of the richness of is fields, the beauty of its towns, and the great wealth of its inhabitants, he exclaimed, 'What a number of plunderers you must have there!' On being informed that the laws restrained men from plundering, he asked with astonishment, 'What then can be the occupation of so numerous a population?'

Though the members of the military tribes are proud of being called plunderers, they hold the name of thieves in abhorrence. Force implies strength, fraud weakness. There are, however, some of the lesser clans whose occupation is avowedly theft; but even these pretend to honour. When the British mission passed through Kurdistan, the camp was one day pitched near the huts of some families of the tribe of Ghishkee. The women were employed in baking, spinning, and weaving carpets; while the men were, as usual, wandering idle, or in search of game. The English gentlemen, who had been told that this tribe were the greatest thieves in Persia, and that the children were beat daily by their mothers to accustom them to pain, that when they were caught stealing they might not be intimidated by blows into confessing their accomplices, asked an old man if these accusations were true. 'We are abused,' he said, 'more than we deserve; for, after all, our theft is only a kind of war. We never rob or steal, except from those with whom our ruler, the Waly of Sennah, is on bad terms. When Persia is in confusion, then is our harvest: but now these Kajirs (Qajars) have every thing their own way, and we are likely to be ruined.' Some suspicion being expressed as to the truth of his statement, the old man said with animation, 'that his tribe had been appointed to guard the English camp, and that we should have an opportunity of judging of their honesty, when trust was reposed in them, by their manner of performing that duty.' He had a right to boast that they were faithful guards, for not an article was lost while they attended the mission.

From *The History of Persia* by Sir John Malcolm

The Shiite Clergy

Malcolm makes an interesting observation on the Shiite clergy, drawing a distinction between the outlook of the senior clerics and that of the lower orders.

The religious orders are divided into several classes. The few who attain very high rank, are usually men of learning, of mild temper, and retired habits. They are very careful to preserve the respect they enjoy, by cherishing the impression entertained of their piety and humility. It is rare to see them intolerant, except where they deem the interest of that religion, of which they are the head, in danger. The lower classes of the priesthood are commonly of a very opposite character. With little knowledge, and great pretensions, they demand a respect which they seldom receive; and so are among the most discontented of the community. The general disposition of the Persians to treat strangers of a different religion with kindness and hospitality, is a subject of constant irritation to them. They rail at all communication with infidels, and endeavour to obtain an importance with the lower orders by a display of their bigotry and intolerance. This class are often accused by their countrymen of indulging the worst passions. To say a man hates like a moollah, is to assert that he cherishes the most inveterate hostility.

From *The History of Persia* by Sir John Malcolm

The Irrepressible Persians

The Persians have long been famous for their readiness to criticise their rulers, however despotic, and for their ready wit. The two are combined in this entertaining anecdote recounted by Malcolm. As he points out, such outspokenness was generally tolerated and even enjoyed by the rulers and their representatives – so long, of course, as it posed no particular threat.

The citizens of Persia are not subdued by their situation into a submissive temper. They are easily inflamed into passion, and act, when under its influence, like men careless of the result. A stranger, unacquainted with the nature of the government, and the latitude of speech which it permits in the persons it oppresses, is surprised to hear the meanest inhabitant of a town venting imprecations against his superiors, nay, sometimes against the King himself. These extraordinary ebullitions of passion, which are very common among the lower orders, generally pass unheeded. Sometimes they may provoke a reproof, or a few blows; but they never receive consequence from the unwise interference of power.

Many of the inhabitants of the principal cities are men of some education: but even those who are not so, are remarkable for the fluency of their language. They express themselves with a freedom and boldness not always restrained by the disparity between them and the person they are addressing. Hajee Ibrahim, formerly prime minister, who gloried in the name of citizen, used to delight in relating a dialogue between his brother, who was *beglerbeg*, or governor of Isfahan, and a seller of vegetables in that city. An extraordinary impost having been laid on every shop, the latter forced himself into the governor's presence when he was giving public audience, and exclaimed, that he was totally unable to pay the tax. 'You must pay it, or leave the city,' was the reply. 'I cannot pay it,' said the man; 'and to what other place can I go?' – 'You may either proceed to Shiraz, or Kashan, if you like those towns better than this,' said the governor. 'Your brother,' replied the shopkeeper, 'is in power at one of these cities, and your nephew at the other: what relief can I expect in either?'– 'You may proceed to court,' said the ruler, 'and complain to the King, if you think I have committed injustice.'– 'Your brother, the Hajee, is prime minister,' said the man. 'Go to hell!' exclaimed the enraged governor, 'and do not trouble me any more!' – 'The holy man, your deceased father, is perhaps there,' said the undaunted citizen. The crowd could not suppress their smiles, and the governor, who shared the general feeling, bade the complainant retire, and said he would attend to his case, provided he would not bring a curse upon his family, by insisting that they shut him out from all hopes of justice, both in this world and the next.

From *The History of Persia* by Sir John Malcolm

English Revenue-Raising Measures Excite the Shah

One of the most amusing writers on early Qajar Persia is the British diplomat, James Morier (1780–1849). He is best known for his satirical novel of Persian life, The Adventures of Hajji Baba of Isfahan. *But he also wrote lively accounts of the two British diplomatic missions he accompanied as secretary in 1809 and 1811-1814. The second of these was led by Sir Gore Ouseley, who concluded a treaty of alliance with Persia in March 1812. During his stay in Tehran, Ouseley had a number of informal conversations with the Qajar monarch, Fath Ali Shah, who was notoriously avaricious, though not without a certain charm. Morier records one conversation in the presence of the grand vizier or prime minister, Mirza Shafi, in which the Shah was keen to learn what English practices would increase his revenue.*

The ambassador, during the winter, had frequent interviews with the King, who conversed with him in the most familiar manner, upon all sorts of subjects. It happened one day that His Majesty was in high spirits, or as the Persians would say, *damaughish chauk bud*, and sent for the Ambassador to converse with him. The grand vizier Mirza Sheffea was also present. After using many flattering expressions, His Majesty said to the ambassador 'That he had been informed by his viziers, that in England we had a variety of modes of increasing the revenue of the country, of which they were totally ignorant in Persia – Now tell me, what might be done here, as you do it in England?' The ambassador answered, 'That one of the things which he thought might be established in Persia, useful to His Majesty's subjects, and beneficial to his treasury, was a post for the transmission of letters.' He then explained the nature of an English post, its advantages and its profits. 'Aye, aye,' said the King, 'I perfectly comprehend you.' Then turning to the grand vizier, he said, 'Now, Mirza Sheffea, I'll tell you exactly how it is. You, for instance, have a correspondent at Ispahan (Isfahan). Of course you can't afford to give a messenger ten *tomauns*[2] every time you have something to say, which on urgent occasions you are now obliged to do: but if you had an opportunity of communicating with him every day, which the post would give you, you would write to him constantly, and your concerns would go on well. Now, that is the utility of the thing. As for the profit, it is thus. We will say, two hundred letters are to be sent to Ispahan, for each of which one *real*[3] will be charged by the post. Now there are about ten stages from here to Ispahan. The men who carry the letters from stage to stage will be contented to receive a *real* a-piece; therefore giving ten to the carriers, 190 will remain clear profit to the Shah, – '*Be Ser Shah*, By the head of the King,' exclaimed His Majesty, 'this is excellent. But,' turning to the Ambassador, 'you have more expedients still. Tell me what is there besides the post, that we have not in Persia?'

His Excellency would have been happy to drop the subject, for he felt that the information which would be drawn from him might be disagreeable to the grand vizier; but the King being very urgent, he informed His Majesty, that one of the great sources of our revenue (but which was resorted to only on particular emergencies), was the income tax, the principles of which he explained, endeavouring to impress upon the King's mind that it was intended to bear more upon the rich than the poor; a principle which the English government kept constantly in view, when the exigiencies of the state required the levying of new taxes. 'What do you say to that?' said the King to his grand vizier: 'These English are extraordinary people!'

The ambassador, in continuation, said, 'We have also taxes, that are more particularly levied upon the rich. If a man keeps more than a certain number of horses, he is taxed in progressive ratio

[2] In Morier's time a *tomaun*, now written *toman*, was worth about eleven shillings sterling. This compares to its exchange value of over three pounds sterling in Safavid times.

[3] A *real*, now written *rial*, is a unit of currency worth one-tenth of a *toman*. It is the main currency unit in Iran today.

for every supernumerary horse; the same for servants, for carriages, &c.' 'Did you hear that, Mirza Sheffea,' exclaimed the King. 'I am your sacrifice; I am ready to pay whatever your Majesty pleases,' said the vizier. 'That's right,' returned the King; 'but there is a great deal of policy as well as profit in what the ambassador says: for instance, a Governor-General of India makes an immense fortune, and returns home richer than a *shazadeh* (a King's son). He sets up great state, and eclipses all the princes; it is of course very proper that he should be made to pay for such advantages.' The King then requested the ambassador to make a written note of the different details which he had already given in conversation, and hoped that he might be enabled to realise them in Persia.

From *A Second Journey through Persia, Armenia, and Asia*
Minor to Constantinople between the years 1810 and 1816
by James Morier

The Sounds of Persia

This is a wonderfully atmospheric passage from Morier on the sounds to be heard as day breaks in a Persian town or city.

There are noises peculiar to every city and country; and none are more distinct and characteristic than those in Persia. First, at the dawn of day, the *muezzins* are heard in a great variety of tones, calling the people to prayers from the tops of the mosques; these are mixed with the sounds of cow-horns, blown by the keepers of the *hummums*, to inform the women, who bathe before the men, that the baths are heated, and ready for their reception. The cow-horns set all the dogs in the city howling in a frightful manner. The asses of the town generally beginning to bray about the same time, are answered by all the asses in the neighbourhood; a thousand cocks then intrude their shrill voices, which, with other subsidiary noises of persons calling to each other, knocking at doors, cries of children, complete a din very unusual to the ears of an European. In the summer season, as the operations of domestic life are mostly performed in the open air, every noise is heard. At night, all sleep on the tops of their houses, their beds being spread upon their terraces, without any other covering over their heads than the vault of heaven. The poor seldom have a screen to keep them from the gaze of passengers; and as we generally rode out on horseback at an early hour, we perceived on the tops of the houses, people either still in bed, or just getting up, and certainly no sight was ever stranger. The women appeared to be always up the first, whilst the men were frequently seen lounging in bed long after the sun was risen.

From *A Second Journey through Persia, Armenia, and Asia Minor to Constantinople between the years 1810 and 1816* by James Morier

The Splendour of the King of Kings

The Qajar monarch, Fath Ali Shah, is famous for his love of splendour and ceremony. This is magnificently captured by the English artist, Sir Robert Ker Porter (1777–1842), who spent two years in Persia from 1817 to 1819 and witnessed the Shah's appearance at the No Ruz (New Year) ceremony in the palace in Tehran. The ceremony took place in the gardens of the palace, which was within the citadel. Later Fath Ali Shah sat for Ker Porter, while the artist drew his portrait.

After passing over an open space, we crossed the bridge of the citadel, and thence were conducted into a very large square. A dome-shaped building of wood open to the eye, appeared in the middle of the place; and under its roof stood the enormous brass cannon, which Chardin mentions having seen in the Maidan-shah at Ispahan. It was brought from that capital several years ago, and stationed here, on a huge, and apparently immoveable carriage. Old guns, of various calibre, all equally awkward and unmanageable, and mingled with a few of modern fabrick, stand round the sides of this central structure. Not far distant, about two hundred swivels[4] lay in rows on the ground. They belonged to the camel corps, who were on duty to salute the King on his entrance into the great assembly of his people. And, indeed, it might well have that title; for persons of all ranks were thronged together, within the walls of this outer court.

Persians of the lowest orders, some decently attired, others in the rags of mendicity; khans in *kaalats* (the robe of honour) covered with gold and brocade; servants in gorgeous coats; and soldiers in their military garbs; all pressed on each other in one equalising mob. It was not practicable to get our horses through such a mass of human beings; so we dismounted at the entrance of the square, and following the necessity of shouldering our way to the opposite egress, tried by that wedge-like motion, to make a passage to the royal portal. Awe of the chief heads-man, did not widen the path an inch; neither did the hard-plied stick of the chargé d'affaires' domestics in front, effect the slightest breach; they might as well have battered a wall. However we got through at last, with no small impression made upon our court apparel, and the shawls of our waists rent into as many strips as we had tugs in our passage. Leaving the throng behind we turned under a narrow and dark arch-way, to a low and very small door, and entered through it at once upon the quarter of the palace. It shewed a spacious area, shaded with trees and intersected by water. In the centre, stood the splendid edifice where his Majesty was to sit to receive the homage of his subjects. We were led towards the southern aspect of this place, the grand saloon fronting that way, where the ceremony of royal presentation was to be performed, and were carefully stationed at the point deemed the best for seeing and hearing the Great King. Before his Majesty appeared, I had time to observe the disposition of the scene, in which this illustrious personage was to play so conspicuous a part.

Rows of high poplars, and of other trees, divide this immense court, or rather garden, into several avenues. That which runs along the midst of the garden is the widest; enclosing a narrow piece of

---

[4] A swivel gun was a light cannon that was mounted on the back of a camel and fired when the camel was lying down.

still water, stretching from end to end, and animated here and there, with a few little *jets d'eau*; the margins of which were spread with oranges, pears, apples, grapes, and dried fruit, all heaped on plates, set close together, like a chain. Another slip of water, faced diagonally the front of the palace; and its fountains being more directly in the view of the monarch, were of greater magnificence and power, shooting up to a height of three or four feet! a sublimity of hydraulic art, which the Persians suppose cannot be equalled in any other country. Along the marble edges of this canal and fountains were also placed fruits of every description, in pyramids; and between each elevated range of plates, with these their glowing contents, stood vases filled with flowers, of a beautiful fabric, in wax, that seemed to want nothing of nature, but its perfume. In a line, beyond these, were set a regular row of the finest china bowls, filled with sherbet. So far, the refreshments of the fete.

The company was thus disposed: in two parallel files, down the sides of the wide centre avenue, stood the khans and other Persians of rank; many of whom we had been constrained to elbow, in our way to the place of ceremony. They were arrayed in their most costly attire, of gold or silver brocades; and some of them wearing, in addition, the royal *kaalat*, which usually consists of a *pelisse* lined with fine furs, and covered with the richest embroidery. Their heads were bound with Keshmere shawls, of every colour and value. All these persons had been arranged in their places, by the master of the ceremonies or rather, according to his own consequence, we might style him grand-marshall of the palace; for the duty he performed, was much in the way of our ancient heraldic officers at royal feasts; and besides, he was of such high personal dignity in himself, as to be son-in-law to the King. He was preceded in the exercise of his office, by a man bearing before him an enameled wand, surmounted by a bird of the same delicate construction.

The royal procession made its appearance. First, the elder sons of the King entered, at the side on which we stood: Abbas Mirza taking the left of the whole, which brought him to the right of the throne. His brothers followed, till they nearly closed upon us. Directly opposite to this elder rank of princes, all grown to manhood, their younger brothers arranged themselves on the other side of the transverse water. They were all superbly habited, in the richest brocade vests and shawl-girdles, from the folds of which glittered the jewelled hilts of their daggers. Each wore a sort of robe of gold stuff, lined, and deeply collared with the most delicate sables, falling a little below the shoulder, and reaching to the calf of the leg. Round their black caps, they too had wound the finest shawls. Every one of them, from the eldest to the youngest, wore bracelets of the most brilliant rubies and emeralds, just above the bend of the elbow. The personal beauty of these princes, was even more extraordinary, to the eyes of a traveller, than the splendour of their dresses; there was not one of them, who might not have been particularised any where else, as most eminently handsome. A fine line of features, large dark eyes full of lustre, graceful stature, and a noble mien, made them, indeed, an object of admiring wonder in themselves.

At some distance, near the front of the palace, appeared another range of highly-revered personages; moullahs (Muslim clerics), astrologers, and other sages of this land of the East, clothed in their more sombre garments of religion and philosophy. Here was no noise, no bustle of any kind; every person standing quietly in his place, respectfully awaiting the arrival of the monarch. At last, the sudden discharge of the swivels from the camel corps without, with the clangor of trumpets, and I know not what congregation of uprorious sounds besides, announced that His Majesty had entered the gate of the citadel. But the most extraordinary part of this clangour, was the appalling roar of two huge elephants, trained to the express purpose of giving this note of the especial movements of the Great King.

He entered the saloon from the left, and advanced to the front of it, with an air and step which belonged entirely to a sovereign. I never before had beheld anything like such perfect majesty; and he seated himself on his throne with the same undescribable, unaffected dignity. Had there been any assumption in his manner, I could not have been so impressed. I should then have seen a man, though a king, theatrically acting his state; here, I beheld a great sovereign feeling himself as such, and he looked the majesty he felt.

He was one blaze of jewels, which literally dazzled the sight on first looking at him; but the details of his dress were these: A lofty tiara of three elevations was on his head, which shape appears to have been long peculiar to the crown of the Great King. It was entirely composed of thickly-set diamonds, pearls, rubies, and emeralds, so exquisitely disposed, as to form a mixture of the most beautiful colours, in the brilliant light reflected from its surface. Several black feathers, like the heron plume, were intermixed with the resplendent aigrettes of this truly imperial diadem, whose bending points were finished with pear-formed pearls, of an immense size. His vesture was of gold tissue, nearly covered with a similar disposition of jewellery; and, crossing the shoulders, were two strings of pearls, probably the largest in the world. I call his dress a vesture, because it sat close to his person, from the neck to the bottom of the waist, showing a shape as noble as his air. At that point, it devolved downwards in loose drapery, like the usual Persian garment, and was of the same costly materials with the vest. But for splendour, nothing could exceed the broad bracelets round his arms, and the belt which encircled his waist; they actually blazed like fire, when the rays of the sun met them; and when we know the names from such excessive lustre, we cannot be surprised at seeing such an effect. The jewelled band on the right arm was called The Mountain of Light; and that on the left, The Sea of Light; and which superb diamonds, the rapacious conquests of Nadir Shah had placed in the Persian regalia, after sacking Delhi, stripping Mahomed Shah, the eleventh emperor of the Moguls, of his dominions, and adding to Persia all the provinces of Hindostan, north of the Indus.

The celebrated throne which Nadir Shah tore from under the Mogul emperors, was not brought forth at this festival; and that from which Futteh Ali Shah viewed his assembled subjects, was better suited to the benignant nature of the meeting, than such a trophy. That was gorgeous with Indian magnificence, and, might we not say, red with the blood of its defeated princes. This was a platform of white marble, an apt emblem of peace, raised a few steps from the ground, and carpeted with shawls and cloth of gold, on which the King sat in the fashion of his country, while his back was supported by a large cushion, encased in a net-work of pearls. The spacious apartment in which this simple seat of majesty was erected, is open from the roof of the building to the earth, on the side opposite to the assembled people; and supported, in front, by two twisted columns of white marble, fluted with gold. The interior of the saloon was profusely decorated with carving, gilding, arabesque painting, and looking-glass; which latter material was, in a manner, interwoven with all the other wreathing ornaments, gleaming and glittering in every part from the vaulted ceiling to the floor. Vases of waxen flowers, others with rose-water, &c. were arranged about the apartment; though they could scarcely be seen from the close ranks of the very young princes, who crowded near their royal parent.

While the Great King was approaching his throne, the whole assembly, with one accord, continued bowing their heads to the ground till he had taken his place. A dead silence then ensued; the whole presenting a most magnificent, and indeed awful appearance; the stillness being so profound, amongst so vast a concourse, that the slightest rustling of the trees was heard, and the softest trickling of the water from the fountains into the canals. As the motionless state of every thing lasted for more than a minute, it allowed me time to observe particularly the figure of the Shah. His face seemed exceedingly pale, of a polished marble hue; with the finest contour of features; and eyes dark, brilliant, and piercing; a beard black as jet, and of a length which fell below his chest, over a large portion of the effulgent belt which held his diamond-hilted dagger. This extraordinary amplitude of beard appears to have been a badge of Persian royalty, from the earliest times; for we find it attached to the heads of the sovereigns, in all the ancient sculptured remains throughout the empire.

In the midst of this solemn stillness, while all eyes were fixed on the bright object before them, which sat, indeed, as radiant and immoveable as the image of Mithrus itself, a sort of volley of words, bursting at one impulse from the mouths of the moullahs and astrologers, made me start, and interrupted my gaze. This strange outcry, was a kind of heraldic enumeration of the Great King's titles, dominion, and glorious acts; with an appropriate panagyric on his courage, liberality, and extended power. When this was ended, with all heads bowing to the ground, and the air ceased to vibrate with the sounds, there was a pause for about half a minute, and then His Majesty spoke. The effect was even more startling than the sudden bursting forth of the moullahs; for this was like a voice from the tombs, so deep, so hollow, and at the same time so penetratingly loud. Having thus addressed his people, he looked towards Captain Willock, the British chargé d'affaires, with whom I stood; and then we moved forward to the front of the throne. The same awful voice, though in a lowered tone, spoke to him, and honoured me with a gracious welcome to his dominions. After His Majesty had put a few questions to me, and received my answers, we fell back into our places; and were instantly served with bowls of a most delicious sherbet, which very grateful refreshment was followed by an attendant presenting to us a large silver tray; on which lay a heap of small coin called a *shy*, of the same metal, mixed with a few pieces of gold. I imitated my friend in all these ceremonies, and held out both my hands to be filled with this royal largesse; which, with no difficulty, we passed through our festal trappings into our pockets.

When the rest of the gratulatory compliments of the day, had been uttered between the monarch and his assembled nobles, the chief executioner, our former herald, gave us the signal that all was over for the morning.

From *Travels in Georgia, Persia, Armenia, Ancient Babylonia*
by Sir Robert Ker Porter

The Turkoman Slavers

For most of the nineteenth century the most dangerous Persian frontier to be anywhere near was the north-eastern frontier with what is now Turkmenistan. The steppelands beyond the frontier were occupied by Turkoman tribesmen who regularly carried out raids into Persia in search of slaves to sell in the markets of Khiva and Bukhara. This was only finally ended by the Russian capture of the Turkoman stronghold of Geok-Teppe, close to the Persian frontier, in January 1881. Up till then, Persian villagers within striking distance of the frontier as well as travellers on the road between Tehran and Mashhad were at constant risk of being carried off by the Turkomans.

Their way of operating is well described by the Scottish traveller, artist and writer, James Baillie Fraser (1783–1856) who took the road from Tehran to Mashhad in 1821.

Although these tribes originally were and still continue in most of their habits a pastoral people, yet robbery and plunder is the Toorkoman's (Turkoman) true profession; his flocks and herds indeed afford continual occupation, and maintenance to his family; but to plunder it is that he looks for riches, and all extraordinary indulgences; and so far from considering it as a crime, he looks upon it as the most honourable and praiseworthy of all employments. They unite together in larger or smaller bodies, according to the nature and remoteness of their object, under some leader, whose known conduct and courage has inspired them with confidence, and who for the time is absolute in his authority; and carrying a stock of barley for their horses, and bread for themselves, equal to the very sparing consumption of seven or eight days, they sally from their haunts in the desert, often upwards of two hundred miles beyond the inhabited country; and ascending the passes, move with astonishing celerity, probably at least two hundred miles more, upon the point to be attacked, which may be in the neighbourhood of Shahrood, Subzawar, Nishapore, or even at a much greater distance. They lie in wait near the gates of the village (if such be their object), and wait in perfect silence until morning dawns, and the unsuspecting inhabitants come forth from the gates, to labour, to drive their cattle afield, or for other purposes; when they start from their lurking place, seize all they can catch, murder those who resist, rapidly plunder the village, and binding their booty upon such cattle as they may have secured, hastily retreat before the neighbourhood have caught the alarm.

If their object be a caravan, they conceal themselves in some hollow near its course, having scouts stationed unseen, but watchful of its movements, upon all the heights around, and when it has reached the ambuscade, they dart upon it with a force and rapidity that defies resistance or escape, bear down all opposition, and bind as prisoners all whom they lay hands upon; then begins the work of plunder and often of blood; the old, and unfit for work are massacred, the cattle unlikely to be of use in their retreat, or unable to keep up with them, are disabled, or cut to pieces: such goods as may be thought worth the carriage are laden upon the rest, and they commence a rapid return to their fastnesses. The prisoners, with their arms tied behind their backs, are fastened by ropes to the horses of the Toorkomans who have them in charge, and who, if they do not willingly move fast enough, drive them on, with blows of their heavy whips, to increase their speed. Whatever may be the state of the weather, they are stript to the drawers; even shoes are seldom left them; they are never accommodated with a horse unless pursuit renders it necessary for their captors to quicken their rate of travelling beyond what it may be possible for those on foot to keep up with; then every man whose horse can bear it takes up a captive behind him, and away they scour. If there are any whom they cannot thus assist, or if they doubt the power of their cattle to proceed sufficiently fast with the double burthen, they put the prisoners to death on the spot, and continue their flight unencumbered.

When they reach a spot, however, where they consider themselves in safety from pursuit, this severity relaxes; indeed, it appears to be assumed more from the necessity of the case, and to discourage any attempt at escaping, than from malevolence, or wanton cruelty, to beings whose lives are of too much value to them to be lightly thrown away. They then move more slowly and pay more attention to the necessities of their captives, whom they carry to some recess far beyond the haunts of civilized man, where the existence of a little water enables the Toorkomans to have a sort of depôt, and there they are kept on very spare food until they can be sent at once to Khyvah for sale; or they are taken to one of the regular camps, and put to do duty, until the owner may have business there, or at Bockhara; or that merchants who trade in slaves come round to purchase captives: in either case, one or other of these places is the ultimate destination of most of the prisoners taken by the Toorkomans. Long established custom has made the trade in captives a regular branch of commerce in these parts; and there are many merchants, both at Khyvah and Bockhara, who do little else than travel twice a-year through the country of the Toorkomans, to purchase up such of their unfortunate prisoners as they believe are likely to pay for their ransom, and even those from which no such hope is entertained; the former they carry to such places as they themselves indicate, as their home, and where they agree to pay the stipulated ransom; or leaving the captives themselves at Bockhara or Khyvah, they take letters from them to their friends, and on being satisfied regarding the money, they send and order their release. The latter are purchased merely on speculation, to resell at the slave markets of these towns.

From *Narrative of a Journey into Khorasan in the Years 1821 and 1822* by James B. Fraser

A Qajar Governor

One of the most powerful provincial governors in the first half of the nineteenth century was not a Qajar prince, but a Georgian eunuch by the name of Manuchihr Khan, who bore the title of Mutamad al-Daula or Trust of the State. He helped to secure the throne for Muhammad Shah in 1835 by ending a rival bid by one of the new Shah's uncles in Shiraz and four years later he took back Isfahan from an alliance of Shiite clerics and local toughs who had seized control of the city. By this time Manuchihr Khan was governing much of central and south-western Iran. Shortly afterwards, in 1840, the intrepid British traveller and archaeologist, Sir Henry Layard (1817–1894), met him at a public audience he was holding in one of the former Safavid palaces in Isfahan. Layard paints an unforgettable picture of the scene and the man he calls the Matamet in reference to his title.

After entering, through a narrow dark passage opening into the street, a spacious yard with the usual fountains running water, and flowers, we passed into the inner court, where the governor gave audience. The palace, which at one time must have been of great magnificence, was in a neglected and ruined condition, but had been splendidly and profusely decorated with paintings, glass, and inlaid work. The building was thronged with miserably clad soldiers, ferrashes (servants), men and women having complaints to make or petitions to present, and the usual retinue and hangers-on of a Persian nobleman in authority.

The Matamet himself sat on a chair, at a large open window, in a beautifully ornamented room at the upper end of the court. Those who had business with him, or whom he summoned, advanced with repeated bows, and then stood humbly before him as if awestruck by his presence, the sleeves of their robes, usually loose and open, closely buttoned up, and their hands joined in front – an immemorial attitude of respect in the East. In the *hauz* or pond of fresh water in the centre of the court were bundles of long switches from the pomegranate tree, soaking to be ready for use for the bastinado, which the Matamet was in the habit of administering freely and indifferently to high and low. In a corner was the pole with two loops of cord to raise the feet of the victim, who writhes on the ground and screams for mercy. This barbarous punishment was then employed in Persia for all manner of offences and crimes; the number of strokes administered varying according to the guilt of the culprit. It was also constantly resorted to as a form of torture to extract confessions. The pomegranate switches, which when soaked for some time become lithe and flexible, were generally employed. The pain and injury which they inflicted were very great, and were sometimes even followed by death. Under ordinary circumstances the sufferer was unable to use his feet for some time, and frequently lost the nails of his toes. This punishment was inflicted upon men of the highest rank – governors of provinces, and even prime ministers – who had, justly or unjustly, incurred the displeasure of the Shah.

Manuchar Khan, the Matamet, was a eunuch. He was a Georgian, born of Christian parents, and had been purchased in his childhood as a slave, had been brought up as a Musulman, and reduced to his unhappy condition. Like many of his kind, he was employed when young in the public service, and had by his remarkable abilities risen to the highest posts. He had for many years enjoyed the confidence and the favour of the Shah. Considered the best administrator in the kingdom, he had been

sent to govern the great province of Isfahan, which included within
its limits the wild and lawless tribes of the Lurs and the Bakhtiyari,
generally in rebellion, and the semi-independent Arab population
of the plains between the Luristan mountains and the Euphrates.
He was hated and feared for his cruelty, but it was generally
admitted that he ruled justly, that he protected the weak from
oppression by the strong, and that where he was able to enforce his
authority life and property were secure. He was known for the
ingenuity with which he had invented new forms of punishments
and torture to strike terror into evil-doers, and to make examples of
those who dared to resist his authority or that of his master the
Shah, thus justifying the reproach addressed to beings of his class,
of insensibility to human suffering. One of his modes of dealing
with criminals was what he termed 'planting vines'. A hole having
been dug in the ground, men were thrust headlong into it and then
covered with earth, their legs being allowed to protrude to represent
what he facetiously called 'the vines'. I was told that he had ordered
a horse-stealer to have all his teeth drawn, which were then driven
into the soles of his feet as if he were being shod. His head was then
put into a nose-bag filled with hay, and he was thus left to die. A
tower still existed near Shiraz which he had built of three hundred
living men belonging to the Mamesenni, a tribe inhabiting the
mountains to the north of Shiraz, which had rebelled against the
Shah. They were laid in layers of ten, mortar being spread between
each layer, the heads of the unhappy victims being left free. Some of
them were said to have been kept alive for several days by being fed
by their friends, a life of torture being thus prolonged by a false
compassion. At that time few nations, however barbarous, equalled
– none probably exceeded – the Persian in the shocking cruelty,
ingenuity, and indifference with which death or torture was
inflicted.

The Matamet had the usual characteristics of the eunuch. He
was beardless, had a smooth colourless face, with hanging cheeks
and a weak, shrill, feminine voice. He was short, stout, and flabby,
and his limbs were ungainly and slow of movement. His features,
which were of the Georgian type, had a wearied and listless
appearance, and were without expression or animation. He was

dressed in the usual Persian costume - his tunic being of the finest Cashmere – and he carried a jewel-handled curved dagger in the shawl folded round his waist. He received us courteously, said a few civil things about the English nation, which he distinguished from the English government, and invited us to come into the room in which he was seated and to take our places on a carpet spread near him.

From *Early Adventures in Persia, Susiana, and Babylonia*
by Sir Henry Layard

At Home with the Queen Mother

Lady Mary Sheil, the wife of the British minister in Tehran, Sir Justin Sheil (1803–1871), was one of the first British women to write about her experiences in Persia. She went there in 1849, after marrying Sir Justin, and remained in the country until the end of his term of office in 1853. Being a woman, she had access to the royal harem, where she was invited to meet the Shah's mother, referred to here as the Khanum.

The *Khanum*, or lady, having fixed the day, a large retinue of servants with a gaudy *takhterewan*[5] were sent by her to convey me to the palace, which, joined to my own servants, made an inconvenient procession through the narrow bazars. After much shouting and turning of people's faces to the wall, we arrived at a small door. Here our cavalcade stopped, and I alighted from the *takhterewan*. The men servants were forbidden to advance, and, accompanied by my maid, I was conducted along a damp passage into a fine court with a large tank full of water in the centre; from various apartments round this court women hastened out, curious to see the *Khanum e Inglees*, the English lady. I passed on, ascended

[5] James Morier gives this description of a *takhterewan*, which was generally used for conveying women and children: 'It consists of a cage of lattice work, covered over with cloth, borne by two mules, one before, the other behind; and conducted by two men, one of whom rides on a third mule in front, and the other generally walks by the side.'

a flight of steps, and reached a nice room hung round with looking-glasses, where a chair had been placed for me. Here I was joined by a Frenchwoman, who, when very young, had married a Persian she met in Paris, and whose faith she has since adopted. She is interpreter to the Shah's mother, and is a very clever, agreeable person. In a few minutes a negress entered the room, and informed us that the *Khanum* waited, and that I was to 'take my brightness into her presence'.

We were then ushered into the adjoining chamber, and found her seated on a chair at a table which was covered with coarse white unhemmed calico. On each side of her, on a chair likewise, sat a pretty young lady covered with jewels. The *Khanum* said a great many amiable things to me, and went through all the usual Persian compliments, hoping my heart had not grown narrow, that my nose was fat, etc, etc. She then introduced the two young ladies as the Shah's two principal wives and cousins. Neither of them uttered a word, but sat like statues during my interview, which lasted two hours. The Shah's mother is handsome, and does not look more than thirty, yet her real age must be at least forty. She is very clever, and is supposed to take a large share in the affairs of the government. She has also the whole management of the Shah's *anderoon*;[6] so that I should think she must have a good deal to occupy her mind, as the Shah has three principal wives, and eight or nine inferior ones. These ladies have each a separate little establishment, and some a separate court from the rest, but all the courts have a communication with one another.

I do not admire the costume of the Persian women. The Shah's mother was dressed with great magnificence. She wore a pair of trousers made of gold brocade. These Persian trousers are always very wide, each leg being, when the means of the wearer allow it, wider than the skirt of a gown, so that they have the effect of an exceedingly ample petticoat; and as crinolines are unknown, the *elegantes* wear ten and eleven pairs of trousers, one over the other in order to make up for the want of the above important invention.

[6] The private quarters of the palace, also called the harem, where the women reside.

But to return to the Shah's mother: her trousers were edged with a border of pearls embroidered on braid; she had a thin blue crepe chemisette, also trimmed with pearls; this chemisette hung down a little below the waist, nearly meeting the top of the trousers, which are fastened by a running string. As there was nothing under the thin gauze, the result of course was more display than is usual in Europe. A small jacket of velvet was over the chemisette, reaching to the waist, but not made to close in front, and on the head a small shawl, pinned under the chin. On the shawl were fastened strings of large pearls and diamond sprigs; her arms were covered with handsome bracelets, and her neck with a variety of costly necklaces. Her hair was in bands, and hung down under the shawl in a multitude of small plaits. She wore no shoes, her feet being covered with fine Cashmere stockings. The palms of her hands and tips of her fingers were dyed red, with a herb called henna, and the edges of the inner part of the eyelids were coloured with antimony.

All the Kajars have naturally large arched eyebrows, but, not satisfied with this, the women enlarge them by doubling their real size with great streaks of antimony: her cheeks were well rouged, as is the invariable custom among Persian women of all classes. She asked me many questions about the Queen;[7] how she dressed, how many sons she had, and said she could not imagine a happier person than her Majesty, with her fine family, her devoted husband, and the power she possessed. She made me describe the ceremonial of a drawing-room. I much regretted I had no picture of the Queen to show her. She was also curious to have an account of a theatre.

My maid had been taken to another room, where, surrounded by the servants and slaves of the *anderoon*, she was surfeited with sugarplums, and where her dress excited much curiosity. These attendants had the same costume as the Shah's mother, only English printed calico of bright flowered patterns took the place of brocade and velvet. Some of them had their hair cut short in front, and combed straight down to the eyebrows, with two stiff curls at each cheek, peeping out from under the shawl. Tea, coffee, and pipes were brought in repeatedly, and after some time a nice collation of

[7] Queen Victoria.

fruit. Various kinds of sherbets, ices, and cakes were spread on the table, and on the ground. We were surrounded by ladies, who attended as if they had been servants. No one was seated, excepting the Shah's mother, his wives, and myself. Some of the former were wives of the late Shah and his predecessor, Fetteh Ali Shah. None of them were young, excepting one, who was very handsome as well as youthful. Her name was Miriam Khanum, wife of a brother of the Shah's mother. She was much flattered at my telling her she was like a European. The women in Persia have only one name, sometimes a fanciful one; such as *Beebee Asr*, 'the Lady of the Era'; *Mehrban Khanum*, 'the Lady of Courtesy'; *Sheereen Khanum*, "Lady of Sweetness', etc, etc. At length I departed, and regained my *takhterewan*, highly pleased with the novelty of the scene. When I had acquired a sufficient knowledge of their language to be able to form an opinion, I found the few Persian women I was acquainted with in general lively and clever; they are restless and intriguing, and may be said to manage their husband's and son's affairs. Persian men are made to yield to their wishes by force of incessant talking and teasing.

From *Glimpses of Life and Manners in Persia*
by Lady Sheil

The Bricklayers' Song

Among Lady Sheil's many engaging 'glimpses', as she puts it, of Persian life is this delightful account of the way the bricklayers sang to one another as they worked. This was clearly a long-standing custom, as it was already remarked on by travellers to Persia in the seventeenth century. Lady Sheil's account is especially interesting because she was able to record the peculiarly Shiite nature of the song.

In passing through the streets of Tehran, one would be disposed to consider the Persians a very musical race. From all sides melodious sounds, somewhat monotonous, it is true, constantly strike the ear. And yet they cannot be called a musical people; far from it. The combination of second tenor and bass is unknown to them, and unison is all they aim at, no matter what number of voices, or of fiddles, guitars, harps, and dulcimers, form the concert. A lad warbling in his throat, at his highest and loudest scream, in imitation of a nightingale, is the perfection of vocal music, which they will listen to with pleasure for hours, and beguile the longest day's journey with the same dulcet strains. But the street music I allude to is a different thing: it proceeds from the bricklayers. In bricklaying in Persia the brick is thrown from hand to hand until at length it is pitched to the *oostad*, the master mason. To relieve his monotonous labour the *oostad* has recourse to a chant, full as monotonous as his work, but sweet in tone. In general he combines a little polemical casuistry and devotion with his psalmody, by directing a vast quantity of abuse against Omar, the second caliph after Mahommed, whom the Persians regard with bitter enmity, as being the leader in the exclusion of Ali from the Caliphate. He sings to words in this style:

> *Khishtee bideh mara janum*
> *Laanat illaheee ber Oma-a-ar.*
> (Give me a brick then my life,
> And the curse of God light on Omar.)
> *Yekee deeger bideh bimun azeezum*
> *Inshaallah kheir neh beened Oma-a-r.*
> (Give me another, now, my darling,
> Please God, Omar will not have any luck.)

On the day on which Omar was assassinated, the powers of the bricklayers in poetical and melodious imprecations wax stronger. It is a strange circumstance that a man should daily suffer malediction twelve hundred years after his death. Judas Iscariot is better off. The women distinguish themselves by their devotion on this anniversary, though their mode of evincing their piety is both inconvenient and whimsical. Perched on the flat roof of their houses overlooking the street, they lie in wait for the passers by, and the heedless passenger is soused with the water, while a triumphant scream proclaims '*Omar, laanehoo Allah* (Omar, God curse him!).'

From *Glimpses of Life and Manners in Persia*
by Lady Shiel

An Attempt on the Shah's Life

Early on the morning of August 15th, 1852, a group of Babis attacked Nasir al-Din Shah as he was leaving his summer residence of Niyavaran on the northern outskirts of Tehran to go on a hunting expedition. The news quickly reached Sir Justin and Lady Sheil, who were at the British Legation's summer quarters in the village of Gulhak, which in those days was about eleven kilometres (seven miles) to the north of Tehran, in the foothills of the Elburz mountains.

A few days after our return, when seated in the coolest chamber of a house in the village, the heat having driven us from our tents, Meerza Hoossein Koolee, the first Persian secretary of the mission, entered the room ghastly and gasping, 'The Shah has been killed!' faltered the Meerza, who used himself frequently to assert that he was the most timid man in Persia. 'We shall all be murdered,' I immediately exclaimed.

We were quite alone in this moment of deep anxiety, all the members of the mission having happened to go to town that day, though in a few minutes two or three princes came to our camp, thinking it the safest place in such a crisis. We had, it is true, a guard of Persian soldiers, but on them no dependence could be placed; perhaps they would be the first to plunder us. No time was lost in despatching three messengers: one to the Shah's camp, two miles distant, to learn the state of affairs; another to Tehran, to purchase ammunition and bring some fifty carbines and pistols from the mission stores; and a third was despatched to an Afghan friend, a pensioner of the Indian Government, to send us some of his countrymen to resist the marauders, who would certainly soon make their appearance. In three hours thirty or forty trusty horsemen were in our camp, and we were promised one hundred and fifty before night.

I know not if I ever experienced greater relief than when a note arrived from the prime minister, saying that the Shah had been only slightly hurt, and that all was well. His Majesty, just after mounting his horse to proceed on a hunting-excursion, had been attacked in the midst of his guards by four Babees, who had approached him under the pretence of delivering a petition. The King had been thrown from his horse, and slightly wounded by a pistol-shot, and was on the point of being despatched, when some of his guards, recovering from their stupor, seized the assassins, one only of whom was killed in the scuffle. The two missions, English and Russian, immediately proceeded to wait on the Shah, to offer their congratulations, which were assuredly most sincere. Notwithstanding his wound, they found his Majesty seated as usual. He was pale, but looked more angry than alarmed. The Shah said that such a thing had never been heard of as the attack he had suffered. In condoling on the event, it was easy, though scarcely appropriate, to allude to Nadir, and to the founder of his own dynasty; so his Majesty was reminded that occurrences like this were not uncommon in Petersburg, and that our own gracious sovereign had not been free from such attempts. The Shah did not, however, seem to derive any consolation from companionship in his danger.

It appeared a party of Babees in town had organised a conspiracy and had held nightly meetings to mature their schemes. These were simple enough. Their plan was to murder the Shah, sally out, sword in hand, in the midst of the confusion and commotion, seize the government, and then commence the reign of terror and the reign of the saints on earth. Four of the conspirators were chosen to execute the behest of the plotters. What a fearful state of things had we providentially escaped from!

The panic at Shemeroon[8] became general; no one thought himself safe unless within the walls of Tehran. Every bush was a Babee, or concealed one. Shah, ministers, *meerzas*, soldiers, priests,

[8] Shemeroon (modern spelling: Shemiran) is the district in which the Legation's summer quarters at Gulhak was situated. Gulhak is still used by the British embassy, though it has long since been swallowed up by Tehran.

merchants, all went pell-mell into Tehran although a month of the country season still remained. The Russian mission fled too, so that not a being was left in Shemeroon excepting ourselves, nor a tent excepting those of our camp. Colonel Sheil declared that he did not think it creditable to take flight, and that he would remain the usual time in his summer-quarters; moreover, if there were any danger, the English mission would be the last to suffer injury. Indeed the measures adopted to repress Babeeism removed all danger for the moment, whatever retaliation may hereafter inflict should their faith ever acquire the ascendancy.

About thirty persons were put to death, and, as is customary in that sect, or, perhaps, in all new sects, they met their doom without shrinking. Suleiman Khan, the chief of the conspirators, and two others suffered torture previously to execution. The two last were either cut to pieces, or shot or blown from mortars. Holes were pierced in various parts of Suleiman Khan's body, into which lighted candles were placed, and allowed to burn down to the flesh, and, while still alive, he was divided into two parts with a hatchet. During these horrible tortures he is said to have preserved his fortitude to the last, and to have danced to the place of execution in defiance of his tormentors, and of the agony caused by the burning candles. Among the conspirators was a moolla of some reputation. After the attack on the Shah had failed, he had persisted in urging on the accomplishment of the plot. He told the disciples the work must not be left incomplete, and that he was resolved to bare his arm, and, sword in hand, to attack the Shah on his entrance into Tehran; that if they saw him lying as if dead, they were not to believe it; they were to fight, and he would rise and be among them.

Strange was the device adopted by the prime minister to elude the danger personal to himself of slaying so many fanatical Babees. Their vengeance was to be apprehended, as about this time many persons were unaccountably murdered in Tehran, who, it was supposed, had been too explicit in the expression of their feelings against Babeeism. His Excellency resolved to divide the execution of the victims among the different departments of the state; the only person he exempted was himself. First came the Shah, who was entitled to *khissas*, or legal retaliation for his wound. To save the dignity of the crown, the steward of the household, as the Shah's representative, fired the first shot at the conspirator selected as his victim, and his deputies, the *ferashes*, completed the work. The prime minister's son headed the home office, and slew another Babee. Then came the foreign office. The secretary of state for foreign affairs, a pious, silly man, who spent his time in conning over the traditions of Mahommed, with averted face made the first sword-cut, and then the under-secretary of state and clerks of the foreign office hewed their victim into pieces. The priesthood, the merchants, the artillery, the infantry, had each their allotted Babee. Even the Shah's admirable French physician, the late lamented Dr Cloquet, was invited to show his loyalty by following the example of the rest of the court. He excused himself, and pleasantly said he killed too many men professionally to permit him to increase their number by any voluntary homicide on his part. The *sedr* (*sedr azem* or prime minister) was reminded that these barbarous and unheard-of proceedings were not only revolting in themselves, but would produce the utmost horror and disgust in Europe. Upon this he became very much excited, and asked angrily, 'Do you wish the venegeance of all the Babees to be concentrated upon me alone?'

No people love jesting and bantering more than the Persians. In Tehran, when any one is installed in office, it is usual for his friends and those under his authority to send him *sheereenee*, sweatmeats, as a token of congratulation. When these executions were over, it was said that the Shah's *meerghazabs* (executioners) had presented *sheereenee* to all the ministers of state, as a mark of their admission into the brotherhood. The chief executioner at the Shah's court is a very important personage. Hateful as he is to every one, it is curious, I hear, to observe the deference with which he is treated. As the highest of the courtiers may one day fall into his fangs, and his eyes or feet be in jeopardy, they do the utmost to propitiate him beforehand by flattering civilities, something on the principle of the Indians' worship of his infernal majesty.

There was still another victim. This was a young woman, the daughter of a moolla in Mazanderan, who, as well as her father, had adopted the tenets of the Bab. The Babees venerated her as a prophetess; and she was styled the *khooret-ool-eyn*, which Arabic words are said to mean, pupil of the eye. After the Babee insurrection had been subdued in the above province, she was brought to Tehran and imprisoned, but was well treated. When these executions took place she was strangled. This was a cruel and useless deed.

It was said that the general impression produced on the people by all this bloodshed was not favourable. Indignation at the attempt on the Shah's life was lost in sympathy for the fate of so many sufferers. The common opinion was, that the poor misguided conspirators of mean condition, whose poverty more than any sentiment of disloyalty or irreligion had enrolled them in the ranks of Babeeism, might have been spared. It thus appears that, even in Persia, a vague undefined feeling of liberality in religion is taking root.

From *Glimpses of Life and Manners in Persia*
by Lady Sheil

A Winter Journey though Persian Kurdistan

Just how severe the winter can be in the higher altitudes of the Iranian plateau was experienced by a Victorian travel writer, Isabella Bird (1831–1904), who was a woman of quite extraordinary courage and grit. She was nearly sixty years old when, in the winter of 1890, she rode on a mule from Baghdad up into the mountains of Persian Kurdistan at the start of a journey through western Persia. She was accompanied by servants hired in Baghdad and an Indian army major, Herbert Sawyer, who was twenty years younger than her and had been sent to survey and gather intelligence in the Bakhtiyari tribal lands further to the south-east in the Zagros Mountains. He is referred to simply as 'M' or the 'sahib'. Isabella Bird is a fine writer with wonderful descriptive powers. Here she tells of a night spent in a Kurdish home while the snow lay deep outside.

The small and ruinous caravanserai was really full of caravans detained by the snowstorm, and we lodged in a Kurdish house, typical of the style of architecture common among the settled tribes. Within a wide doorway without a door, high enough for a loaded mule to enter, is a very large room, with a low, flat mud roof, supported on three rows of misshapen trunks of trees, with their branches cut off about a foot from the stem, all black and shiny with smoke. Mud and rubble platforms, two feet high, run along one side and one end, and on the end there is a clay, beehive-shaped fireplace, but no chimney. Under this platform the many fowls are shut in at night by a stone at the hole by which they enter. Within this room is a perfectly dark stable of great size. Certainly forty mules, besides asses and oxen, were lodged in it, and the overflow shared the living-room with a number of Kurds, *katirgis* (muleteers), servants, dogs, soldiers, and Europeans. The furniture consisted of guns and swords hanging on the walls.

The owner is an old Kurd with some handsome sons with ruddy complexions and auburn hair. The big house is the patriarchal roof, where the patriarch, his sons, their wives and children, and their animals, dwell together. The women, however, had all been got rid of somehow. The old Kurd made a great fire on the dais, wood being plentiful, and crouched over it. My bed was pitched near it, and enclosed by some reed screens. With chairs and a table, with routes, maps, writing materials, and a good lantern upon it, an excellent dinner of soup and a leg of mutton, cooked at a bonfire in the middle of the floor, and the sight of all the servants and *katirgis* lying round it, warm and comfortable, and the knowledge that we were above the mud, the clouds of blinding smoke which were the only drawback scarcely affected the comfort of the blazing, unstinted fire. The doorway gave not only ample ventilation but a brilliant view of snow, and of myriads of frosty stars.

It was infinitely picturesque, with the fitful firelight falling on the uncouth avenues of blackened tree-stumps, on big dogs, on mild-eyed ox faces and long ass ears, on turbaned Indian heads, and on a confused crowd of Turks, Kurds, and Persians, some cooking, some sleeping, some smoking while from the black depth beyond a startling bray of an ass or the abortive shriek of a mule occasionally proceeded, or a stray mule created a commotion by rushing in from the snow outside.

Isabella Bird covered six hundred miles by mule from Baghdad to Tehran, much of it in freezing cold and deep snow, as here on the road from Kermanshah to Hamadan.

To write that we all survived the march of that day is strange, when the same pitiless blast or 'demon wind', blowing from 'the roof of the world' – the Pamir desert, made corpses of five men who started with a caravan ahead of us that morning. We had to climb a long ascending plateau for 1,500 feet, to surmount a pass. The snow was at times three feet deep, and the tracks even of a heavy caravan which crossed before us were effaced by the drift in a few minutes.

A sun without heat glared and scintillated like an electric light, white and unsympathetic, out of a pitiless sky without a cloud. As soon as we emerged from Sannah the 'demon wind' seized on us – a steady, blighting, searching, merciless blast, no rise or fall, no lull, no hope. Steadily and strongly it swept at a temperature of 9 degrees (fahrenheit), across the glittering ascent – swept mountain-sides bare; enveloped us at times in glittering swirls of powdery snow, which after biting and stinging careered over the slopes in twisted columns; screeched down gorges and whistled like the demon it was, as it drifted the light frozen snow in layers, in ripples, in waves, a cruel, benumbing, blinding, withering invisibility!

The six woollen layers of my mask, my three pairs of gloves, my sheepskin coat, fur cloak and mackintosh piled on over a swaddling mass of woollen clothing, were as nothing before that awful blast. It was not a question of comfort or discomfort, or of suffering more or less severe, but of life or death, as the corpses a few miles ahead of us show. I am certain that if it had lasted another half-hour I too should have perished. The torture of my limbs down to my feet, of my temples and cheekbones, the anguish and uselessness of my hands, from which the reins had dropped, were of small consequence compared with a chill which crept round my heart, threatening a cessation of work.

There were groans behind me; the cook and *Hadji*[9] had rolled off into the snow, where *Hadji* was calling on Him 'who is not far from every one of us'. M was on foot. His mask was frozen hard. He was using a scientific instrument, and told his orderly, an Afghan, a

[9] A Gulf Arab employed by Isabella Bird to assist her on her travels through Iran. He was called *Hadji* because he had made the *Hadj* or pilgrimage to Mecca ten times. She describes him as 'a big, wild-looking Arab in a rough *abba* (cloak) and a big turban, with a long knife and a revolver in his girdle.'

smart little duffadar of a crack Indian corps, to fasten a strap. The man replied sadly, 'I can't, Sahib.' His arms and hands were useless. My mask was frozen to my lips. The tears extorted from my eyes were frozen. I was so helpless and in such torture, that I would gladly have lain down to die in the snow. The mercury fell to four degrees (fahrenheit).

After fighting the elements for three hours and a half, we crossed the crest of the pass at an altitude of 7,000 feet, to look down upon a snow world stretched out everywhere, pure, glistering, awful; mountains rolling in snowy ranges, valleys without a trace of man, a world of horror, glittering under a mocking sun.

Hadji, with many pious ejaculations, gasped out that he was dying (in fact, for some time all speech had been reduced to a gasp); but when we got over the crest there was no more wind, and all the benumbed limbs resumed sensation, through an experience of anguish.

From *Journeys into Persia and Kurdistan*
by Isabella L. Bird

In Tribal Country

In May 1890 Isabella and the Major arrived at the summer grazing grounds of the Bakhtiyari, on a plain two thousand, three hundred and forty-three metres (seven thousand, five hundred feet) up in the Zagros mountains. Here, at a place called Chigakhor, was the residence of the two heads of the Bakhtiyari tribes; the ilkhani, *who was the paramount chief, and the* ilbegi, *who was his lieutenant. Isabella and the Major arrived there shortly after a period of feuding between the* ilkhani, *Imam Quli Khan, and the* ilbegi, *Isfandiyar Khan, who was his nephew.*

I have heard so much of Chigakhor that I am disappointed with the reality. There are no trees, most of the snow has melted, the mountains are not very bold in their features, the plain has a sort of lowland look about it, and though its altitude is 7,500 feet, the days

267

and even nights are very hot. The interest of it lies in it being the summer resort of the *ilkhani* and *ilbegi*, which makes it the great centre of Bakhtiari life. As many as 400 tents are pitched here in the height of the season and the coming and going of khans and headmen with tribute and on other business is ceaseless.

The plain, which is about seven miles long by three broad, is quite level. Near the southeast end is a shallow reedy mere, fringed by a fertile swampiness, which produces extraordinary crops of grass far out into the middle of the level.

Near the same end is a rocky eminence or island, on which is the fortress castle of the *ilkhani*. The 'season' begins in early June, when the tribes come up from the warm pastures of Dizful and Shuster, to which they return with their pastoral wealth in the autumn, after which the plain is flooded and frozen for the winter. At the north end are the villages of Dastgird and Aurugun, and a great deal of irrigated land producing wheat. Except at that end the plain is surrounded by mountains; on its southern side, where a part of the Sukhta range rises into the lofty peak of Challeh Kuh, with its snow-slashes and snow-fields, they attain an altitude of 12,000 or 13,000 feet.

It is not easy, perhaps not possible, to pass through the part of the Bakhtiari country for which we are bound, without some sort of assistance from its feudal lords, a responsible man, for instance, who can obtain supplies from the people. Therefore we have been detained here for many days, waiting for the expected arrival of the *ilkhani*. A few days ago a rumour arrived, since unhappily confirmed, that things were in confusion below, owing to the discovery of a plot on the part of the *ilkhani* to murder the *ilbegi*. Stories are current of the number of persons 'put out of the way' before he attained his present rank for the second time, and it is not 'Bakhtiari custom' to be over-scrupulous about human life. No doubt his nephew, the *ilbegi*, is a very dangerous rival, and that his retainers are bent on seeing him in a yet higher position than he now occupies.

A truce has been patched up, however, and yesterday the *ilkhani* and Isfandyar Khan arrived together, with their great trains of armed horsemen, their harams, their splendid studs, their crowd of unmounted retainers, their string of baggage, mules and asses laden with firewood, and all the 'rag, tag, and bobtail' in attendance on Oriental rulers. Following them in endless nocturnal procession come up the tribes, and day breaks on an ever-increasing number of brown flocks and herds of mares, asses, dogs, black tents, and household goods. When we arrived there were only three tents, now the green bases of the mountains and all the platforms and ravines where there are springs are spotted with them, in rows or semi-circles, and at night the camp fires of the multitude look like the lights of a city. Each clan has a prescriptive right to its camping-ground and pasture (though both are a fruitful source of quarrels), and arrives with its *ketchuda*[10] and complete social organisation, taking up its position like a division of an army.

When in the early morning or afternoon the tribe reaches the camping-ground, everything is done in the most orderly way. The infants are put into their cradles, the men clear the ground if necessary, drive the pegs and put up the poles, and if there be wood – of which there is not a stick here – they make a fence of loose branches to contain the camp, but the women do the really hard work. Their lords, easily satisfied with their modicum of labour, soon retire to enjoy their pipes and the endless gossip of Bakhtiari life.

After the ground has been arranged the tents occupy invariably the same relative position, whether the camp is in a row, a semi-circle, a circle, or streets, so that the cattle and flocks may easily find their owners' abodes without being driven. The tents, which are of black goats' hair cloth, are laid out and beaten, and the women spread them over the poles and arrange the rest, after which the inside is brushed to remove the soot. In a good tent, reed screens are put up to divide the space into two or more portions, and some of the tribes fence round the whole camp with these screens, leaving one opening, and use the interior for a sheepfold. The small bushes are grubbed up for fuel. The women also draw the water, and the boys attend to the flocks. Many of the camps, however, have neither fences nor environing screens, and their inmates dwell without any attempt at privacy, and rely for the safety of their flocks on big and trustworthy dogs, of which every camp has a number.

[10] Head of a Bakhtiyari clan or sub-tribe.

When they move the bulk of the labour again falls on the women. They first make the baggage into neat small packages suited for the backs of oxen; then they take up the tent pegs, throw down the tents and roll them up in the reed screens, all that the men undertake being to help in loading the oxen. It is only when a division halts for at least some days that this process is gone through. In fine weather, if a tribe is marching daily to its summer or winter camping-grounds, the families frequently sleep in the open.

The chief's tent is always recognisable by its size, and is occasion-ally white. I have seen a tent of a wealthy khan fully sixty feet long. A row of poles not more than ten feet high supported the roof, which was of brown haircloth, the widths united by a coarse open stitch. On the windward side the roof was pinned down nearly to the top of a loosely-laid wall of stones about three feet high. If the tent was sixty feet long, it was made by this arrangement twenty feet broad. At the lower end was a great fire-hole in the earth, and the floor of the upper end was covered with rugs, quilts, and pillows, the household stuff being arranged chiefly on and against the rude stone wall.

The process of encamping for a camp of seventy tents takes about two hours, and many interruptions occur, especially the clamorous demands of unweaned infants of mature years. De-camping the same number of tents takes about an hour. A free, wild life these nomads lead, full of frays and plots, but probably happier than the average lot.

Below the castle is the great encampment of the chiefs, brown tents and white bell tents, among which the tall white pavilion of the *ilkhani* towers conspicuously. The *ilkhani* and *ilbegi* called on me, and as they sat outside my tent it was odd to look back two years to the time when they were fighting each other, and barely two weeks to the discovery of the plot of the dark-browed *ilkhani* to murder his nephew. The *ilkhani*'s face had a very uncomfortable expression. Intrigues against him at Tihran (Tehran) and nearer home, the rumoured enmity of the prime minister, the turbulence of some of the tribes, the growing power of the adherents of Isfandyar Khan and his own baffled plot to destroy him must make things unpleasant.

In the evening I visited the ladies who are in the castle leading the usual dull life of the *haram*, high above the bustle which centres round the *ilkhani*'s pavilion, with its crowds of tribesmen, mares and foals feeding, tethered saddle horses neighing, cows being milked, horsemen galloping here and there, firing at a mark, asses bearing wood and flour from Ardal being unloaded – bustle masculine solely.

Isfandyar Khan, with whose look of capacity I am more and more impressed, and Lutf received us and led us to the great pavilion, which is decorated very handsomely throughout with red and blue *appliqué* arabesques, and much resembles an Indian *durbar* tent. A brown felt carpet occupied the centre. The *ilkhani*, who rose and shook hands, sat on one side and the *ilbegi* on the other, and sons, khans, and attendants to the number of two hundred, I daresay, stood around. We made some fine speeches, rendered finer, doubtless, by Mirza; repeated an offer to send a doctor to itinerate in the country for some months in 1891, took the inevitable tea, and while the escorts were being arranged for I went to the fort.

It is the fortress of the Haft Lang, one great division of the Bakhtiari Lurs, which supplies the ruling dynasty. The building is a parallelogram, flanked by four round towers, with large casemates and a keep on its southern side. It has two courtyards, surrounded by stables and barracks, but there is no water within the gates, and earthquakes and neglect have reduced much of it to a semi-ruinous condition. Over the gateway and along the front is a handsome suite of well-arranged balconied rooms, richly decorated in Persian style, the front and doors of the large reception-room being of fretwork filled in with amber and pale blue glass, and the roof and walls are covered with small mirrors set so as to resemble facets, with medallion pictures of beauties and of the chase let in at intervals. The effect of the mirrors is striking, and even beautiful. There were very handsome rugs on the floor, and divans covered with Kashan velvet; but rugs, divans, and squabs were heaped to the depth of some inches with rose petals which were being prepared for rose-water, and the principal wife rose out of a perfect bed of them.

These ladies have no conversation, and relapse into apathy after asking a few personal questions. Again they said they wished to see the *agha*,[11] of whose height and prowess many rumours had reached

[11] 'The gentleman', in this case Major Sawyer.

them, but when I suggested that they might see him from the roof or balcony they said they were afraid. Again they said they had such dull lives, and regretted my departure, as they thought they might come and see my tent. I felt sorry for them, sorrier than I can say, as I realised more fully the unspeakable degradation and dullness of their lives. A perfect rabble of dirty women and children filled the passages and staircase.

From *Journeys into Persia and Kurdistan* by Isabella L. Bird

A Pilgrim Caravan

Caravans of pilgrims regularly made their way to Mashhad and the shrine of the Imam Reza, the Eighth Shiite Imam. There is no more evocative description of the sight of one of these caravans than that given by Lord Curzon (1859–1925) in his fascinating and magisterial work, Persia and the Persian Question. *This was the outcome of immense research and a three-month journey through Persia which began when he crossed from Russian territory into the north-eastern province of Khurasan in September 1889. He encountered the caravans as he was riding on horseback from Mashhad, the provincial capital of Khurasan, to Tehran.*

Sometimes for miles in the distance could be seen the *kafilah*, or caravan, slowly crawling at a foot-pace across the vast expanse. Then, as it came nearer, would be heard the melancholy monotone of some devout or musical member of the band, droning out in quavering tones a verse from the Koran; sometimes, in less solemn companies, a more jovial wayfarer trolling some distich from the Persian classics. As the long cavalcade approached, it would be seen to consist of every kind of animal and of every species of man. Horses would carry the more affluent, who would be smoking their *kalians* as they paced along; some would affect camels; mules were very common, and would frequently support *kajavehs*, a sort of wooden pannier, with an arched framework for a hood, in which men as often as women were curled up beneath mountains of quilts. The donkey, however, was the favourite beast of burden. Tiny animals would bear the most stupendous loads, with pots and pans, guns, and water-bottles hanging on either side, and with the entire furniture of a household on their backs; the poultry of the owner perched with ludicrous gravity upon the top of all. It is a common thing for the poorer pilgrims to take shares in a donkey and to vary riding with walking. In the early morning the equestrians would often be seen fast asleep upon their asses, lying forward upon their necks, and occasionally falling with a thump to the ground. Each *kafilah* would have a *caravan-bashi,* or leader, who not infrequently bore a red pennon fluttering from a lance. It was often difficult to discern the men's faces as they rode by shrouded in huge woollen blanket-coats, pulled up over their heads, while the stiff, empty arm-holes stood out on either side like monstrous ears. But, if it was not easy to discern the males, still less could be distinguished of the shapeless bundles of blue cotton that were huddled upon the donkeys' backs, and which chivalry almost forbade me to accept for the fairer sex.

Perhaps the weirdest and most impressive of the many unwonted memories that the traveller carries away with him from such-like travel in the East is the recollection of the camel caravans which he has encountered at night. Out of the black darkness is heard the distant boom of a heavy bell. Mournfully, and with perfect regularity of iteration, it sounds, gradually swelling nearer and louder, and perhaps mingling with the tones of smaller bells, signalling the rearguard of the same caravan. The big bell is the insignia and alarum of the leading camel alone. But nearer and louder as the sound becomes, not another sound, and not a visible object, appear to accompany it. Suddenly, and without the slightest warning, there looms out of the darkness, like the apparition of a phantom ship, the form of the captain of the caravan. His spongy tread sounds softly on the smooth sand, and, like a great string of linked ghouls, the silent procession stalks by and is swallowed up in the night.

From *Persia and the Persian Question*
by George N. Curzon

The Development of Tehran

Tehran was a relatively minor city when the first of the Qajar shahs, Aqa Muhammad, made it his new capital at the end of the eighteenth century. Although its population inevitably grew thereafter, it did not really begin to take on the aspect of a capital city until the late 1860s, when Nasir al-Din Shah (ruled 1848–1896) began a serious programme of reconstruction and development. Curzon gives a wonderfully rich and detailed description of the city as he found it towards the end of 1889. By that time its population, which had been around fifty thousand at the beginning of the nineteenth century, had topped one hundred thousand. Today it is well over seven million.

Nasr-ed-Din Shah, among other titles to distinction, may claim to have made his city a capital in something more than the name. After being twenty years upon the throne, it appears to have occurred to him that the 'Point of Adoration (*Kibleh*) of the Universe'[12] was framed in a somewhat inadequate setting. Accordingly, Teheran was suddenly bidden to burst its bonds and enlarge its quarters. The old walls and towers were for the most part pulled down, the ditch was filled up, a large slice of surrounding plain was taken in, and, at the distance of a full mile from the old enclosure, a new rampart was constructed upon Vauban's system, copied from the fortifications of Paris before the German war. A good deal of the money sent out from England by the Persian Famine Relief Fund in 1871 was spent in the hire of labour for the excavation of the new ditch, which has a very steep outer profile, and for the erection of the lofty sloping rampart beyond. There is no masonry work upon these new fortifications; they are not defended by a single gun; they describe an octagonal figure about eleven miles in circuit; and, I imagine, from the point of view of the military engineer, are wholly useless for defence. Their main practical service consists in facilitating the collection of the town *octroi*.[13] Nevertheless, Teheran can now boast that it is eleven

[12] One of the Shah's titles.
[13] Duty levied on goods entering Tehran.

miles round, that it has European fortifications, and twelve gates; while its interior features have developed in a corresponding ratio.

That the city has yet much to do before it realises the full aspirations of its royal Haussman is evident, as soon as we enter the gates. These consist of lofty archways, adorned with pinnacles and towers, and presenting from a distance a showy appearance, which has caused to some incoming travellers paroxysms of delight. A closer inspection shows that they are faced with modern glazed tiles, in glittering and frequently vulgar patterns, depicting the phenomenal combats of Rustam,[14] or the less heroic features and uniform of the modern Persian soldier. After entering the gates, where a guard is stationed, we are again in the open country, for on most sides the city has not yet grown up to its new borders, which embrace a large extent of bare, unoccupied desert. This passed, a ride through squalid suburbs brings us to the more central and pretentious quarters of the town. At every turn we meet in juxtaposition, sometimes in audacious harmony, at others in comical contrast, the influence and features of the East and West. A sign-board with *Usine à Gaz* inscribed upon it will suddenly obtrude itself in a row of mud hovels, ostentatiously Asiatic. Tram-lines are observed running down some of the principal thoroughfares. Mingled with the turbans and *kolahs* (traditional lambskin hat) of the Oriental crowd are the wide-awakes and helmets of Europeans. Through the jostling throng of cavaliers and pedestrians, camels, donkeys, and mules, comes rolling the two-horse brougham of some minister or grandee. Shops are seen with glass windows and European titles. Street lamp-posts built for gas, but accommodating dubious oil-lamps, reflect an air of questioning civilisation. Avenues, bordered with footpaths and planted with trees, recall faint memories of Europe. A metalled and watered roadway comes almost as a shock after weeks of mule track and rutty lane. Strange to say, it does not appear to be mistaken by the inhabitants for the town sewer. We ride along broad, straight streets that conduct into immense squares and are fringed by the porticoes of considerable mansions. In a word, we are in a city which was born and nurtured in

[14] The hero of the Persian epic poem by Firdausi, the *Shahnama* or *Book of Kings*.

the East, but is beginning to clothe itself at a West-End tailor's. European Teheran has certainly become, or is becoming; but yet, if the distinction can be made intelligible, it is being Europeanised upon Asiatic lines. No one could possibly mistake it for anything but an Eastern capital. Not even in the European quarter has it taken on the insufferable and debauched disguise with which we are familiar in the hideous streets of Galata and Pera.[15] Its most distinctive features retain an individuality of their own, differing from what I have noticed anywhere else in Central Asia. Jeypore (Jaipur) is sometimes extolled as the finest specimen of a native city, European in design, but Oriental in structure and form, that is to be seen in the East. The 'rose-red city' over which Sir Edwin Arnold has poured the copious cataract of a truly Telegraphese vocabulary struck me, when I was in India, as a pretentious plaster fraud. No such impression is produced by the Persian capital. Though often showy, it is something more than gilt gingerbread; and, while surrendering to an influence which the most stolid cannot resist, it has not bartered away an originality of which the most modern world would not wish to deprive it.

The street scenes in Teheran are not to be compared from the artistic point of view, with those that may be witnessed either in the great Indian cities or in the old capitals of Central Asia. With the Kajar (Qajar) dynasty, a hundred years ago, came in a new and soberer fashion in dress as well as a change of rulers. The turban has gradually disappeared and is worn only by merchants, *hajis*, *seyids*, and mullahs. The flowing robes and daring colours of the East, such as one may see alike in Benares and Bokhara, have been exchanged for tight-fitting garments of European or semi-European cut, and for neutral tints such as dark blues, browns, greens and greys, with a very plentiful admixture of uncompromising black. There is manifold jostling in the streets and bazaars, and everywhere are the contrast and variety so inseparable from Asiatic life, and from a crowd where three out of four men are mounted; but there are not the kaleidoscopic change and glitter that bespeak the true and unredeemed Orient. A good deal of colour, however, as well as of noise, is lent to the street life of the capital

---

[15] Two districts of Istanbul which were reshaped in the second half of the nineteenth century to resemble a European city.

by the number of soldiers, in every variety of uniform, who are seen lounging about the streets, and by the military bands, which play in the public squares, their favourite tune being the so-called 'Royal Air', which has considerable merits, and was, I believe, composed by the French bandmaster, M. Lemaire. Soldiers in Prussian helmets, soldiers in sheepskin *shakoes*, soldiers in cloth busbies, soldiers with sartorial reminiscences of nearly every army in Europe, are encountered on all sides. Very apparent too are the city police, about three hundred strong, organised and commanded by an Italian, Count Monteforte, who, after being an officer in Bomba's army at Naples, retired to Austria, and was passed on either by the Emperor of that country, or, more probably, by himself, to the service of the Shah. They are constantly to be seen hanging about the guardhouses which are scattered through the town, and their black uniform, with violet velvet facings, is decidedly smart and picturesque. Queerest, however, and most parti-coloured of the street figures of Teheran are the *shatirs*, or royal runners, who precede the Shah whenever he goes out, running in front of his horse or carriage. They strike a stranger, unacquainted with the court history of Persia, with amused astonishment, their costume being an apparent cross between that of a liveried servant and a harlequin at a pantomime. They wear white stockings, green knee-breeches, a red coat with large skirts and green breast-facings, and a tall erection upon the head, surmounted by a sort of coloured crest like a cock's comb. In their hand they carry a staff or wand. Some writers have too hastily attributed this amazing uniform to the fanciful taste of His reigning Majesty: therein at once exaggerating the fancy and ignoring the conservative instincts of that monarch. As a matter of fact, this dress is a faithful reproduction of that which was worn by the *shatirs* of the Sefavi (Safavid) kings in the halcyon days at Isfahan, two and three centuries ago; and what is apt to look ridiculous in a semi-modernised court and capital was, no doubt, in thorough keeping with an age and a ceremonial of almost barbaric splendour.

From *Persia and the Persian Question*
by George N. Curzon

The Court Levée of Nasir al-Din Shah

While he was in Tehran, Curzon witnessed the royal levée of Nasir al-Din Shah. This was not, as he explains, an occasion for the Shah to receive people, but an opportunity to emphasise his majesty and how high he stood above his subjects by making a brief ceremonial appearance before assembled princes, courtiers, officers and officials. Curzon, who was to demonstrate his own fondness for ceremony when he later became Viceroy of India, was left unimpressed.

The theory of the court *levée* in Persia is not that the subjects attend upon, or are introduced to, the sovereign, but that the sovereign displays himself to his awestruck and admiring subjects. Accordingly, the two central and essential attributes of the scene are the monarch being gazed at on the one side, and the audience gazing on the other. Very little else transpires, and not more than half-a-dozen persons play any other part than that of statues during the ceremony. I will describe, however, exactly what takes place.

Upon entering the palace I was conducted to a chamber where the regulation coffee and *kalians* were served. Soldiers and officials were pouring pell-mell into the palace on every side. Bands were aimlessly tuning up or playing in different corners. Officers in every variety of uniform were marshalling troops in every variety of disorder. *Mirzas* (i.e government clerks) and accountants were hurrying to the scene of action. The royal executioner, clothed in red, was stalking about, while some attendants carried the *fellek*, a red pole about eight feet in length with a double loop or noose of cord attached to the middle, into which are fixed the upturned soles of the culprit condemned to the bastinado. He was the Persian counterpart of the Roman lictor with his axe and rods. The members of the royal or Kajar tribe were all congregated together, and wore the old court costume, which was obligatory on all alike at the beginning of the century, and which consists of a lofty and voluminous Kashmir (more probably Kerman) turban, big, flowing, Kashmir cloaks, and the well-known red leggings, or *chakshurs*, which the English ministers and plenipotentiaries were obliged to pull on over their breeches when attending the audiences of Fath Ali Shah, but of wearing which they were ultimately relieved by treaty. Here I was met by the Lord Chamberlain, or master of the ceremonies, known as the *zahir-ed-dowleh* (supporter of the government), a young man of magnificent stature and singularly handsome countenance, who belongs to the Kajar house, and is married to a favourite daughter of the Shah. This gorgeous individual was clothed in a resplendent white frock coat and trousers beneath his Kashmir robe of state; a jewelled sword hung by his side; a portrait of the Shah set in diamonds depended from his neck; and he carried a silver wand or staff of office.

I was conducted to a room next to that in which the Shah was to appear, the uplifted sashes of both apartments opening on to the garden, where, on the broad, paved pathway running in front and down the central alleys between the tanks and flower beds, were disposed in order the various participators in the ceremonial. A little to the right of the middle spot stood the Naib-es-Sultaneh the third son of the Shah and commander-in-chief of the army, standing at the head of a long line of field-marshals and generals. His bosom blazed with decorations, and was crowned by a light-blue ribbon that might have been mistaken for that of St Patrick. Next to him, also in field-marshal's uniform and with a tiny sword, stood the diminutive favourite of the Shah, whose features had become so familiar in Europe during the royal journey of the preceding summer. Next in order, and accentuating the ludicrous contrast, came a tottering veteran, the oldest field-marshal in the Persian army; then a row of full-blown generals; finally, the officers of the so-called Cossack regiments, including two Russians. In front and in the middle stood alone the former *ilkhani* of the Kajar tribe, a white-bearded elder, once out of favour with his sovereign but long since reconciled. Behind stood the solid and forbidding figure of the *kawam-ed-dowleh*, minister of foreign affairs; and beyond again the various functionaries, each in his due rank and position. The whole of the assemblage was now arranged, every man stood shoulder to shoulder with eyes fixed in front, and absolute silence prevailed.

Suddenly a cry was raised. The Shah appeared in the room adjoining that in which I was placed and took his seat upon a gilded chair in the window. His principal ministers accompanied him and stood in the background. As the King appeared every head was bowed low, the hands outspread and resting upon the knees. Bands struck up the royal air in different parts of the garden and guns banged away at a slight distance. The *ilkhani* of the Kajars now, acting as spokesman of the entire assembly, exchanged formal compliments with the King, who spoke in short, brusque sentences in reply. Then a mullah, standing behind, recited in a loud voice the *khutbah*, or prayer for the sovereign This done the poet laureate advanced, and, pulling out a sheet of paper, read a complimentary ode. Meanwhile the bands went on playing different tunes in different parts, and the guns boomed noisily outside. When the ode was at an end, the Shah rose from his chair, and slowly stalked from the chamber; the troops, with very little attempt at precision, slouched past the windows; and a waving mass of helmets, plumes, and turbans was seen disappearing through the garden entrance. Such is a *levée* as held by H.I.M Nasr-ed-Din Shah at Teheran.

From *Persia and the Persian Question*
by George N. Curzon

The Problem of Corruption

Almost all Europeans who had some involvement with Persia under the Qajars were struck by the widespread corruption that was present at all levels of government – although some of them aided and abetted it. Europeans and reform-minded Persians alike saw it as the main obstacle to administrative and economic progress. There is no better description of its roots and ramifications than that given by Curzon.

Government, nay, life itself, in that country (Persia) may be said to consist for the most part of an interchange of presents. Under its social aspects, this practice may be supposed to illustrate the generous sentiments of an amiable people; though even here it has a grimly unemotional side, as, for instance, when, congratulating yourself upon being the recipient of a gift, you find that not only must you make a return of equivalent cost to the donor, but must also liberally remunerate the bearer of the gift (to whom your return is very likely the sole recognised means of subsistence) in a ratio proportionate to its pecuniary value. Under its political aspects, the practice of gift-making, though consecrated in the adamantine traditions of the East, is synonymous with the system elsewhere described by less agreeable names. This is the system on which the government of Persia has been conducted for centuries, and the maintenance of which opposes a solid barrier to any real reform. From the Shah downwards, there is scarcely an official who is not open to gifts, scarcely a post which is not conferred in return for gifts, scarcely an income which has not been amassed by the receipt of gifts. Every individual, with hardly an exception, in the official hierarchy has only purchased his post by a money present either to the Shah, or to a minister, or to the superior governor by whom he has been appointed. If there are several candidates for a post, in all probability the one who makes the best offer will win.

Along with, and perhaps even more than, the bribe or gift required to secure or retain office of any description, is a cherished national institution in Persia, viz. the *mudakhil*, i.e. consideration, recompense, or profit which is required to balance the personal account, and the exaction of which, in a myriad different forms, whose ingenuity is only equalled by their multiplicity, is the crowning interest and delight of a Persian's existence. This remarkable word may be variously translated as commission, perquisite, *douceur*, consideration, pickings and stealings, profit, according to the immediate context in which it is employed. Roughly speaking, it signifies the balance of personal advantage, usually expressed in money form, which can be squeezed out of any and every transaction. A negotiation, in which two parties are involved as donor and recipient, as superior and subordinate, or even as equal contracting agents, cannot take place in Persia without the party which can be represented as the author of the favour or service claiming and receiving a definite cash return for what he has done or given. It may of course be said that human nature is much the same the world over; that a similar system exists under a different name in our own or other countries, and that the philosophic critic will welcome in the Persian a man and a brother. To some extent this is true. But in no country that I have ever seen or heard of in the world, is the system so open, so shameless, or so universal as in Persia. So far from being limited to the sphere of domestic economy or to commercial transactions, it permeates every walk and inspires most of the actions of life. By its operation, generosity or gratuitous service may be said to have been erased in Persia from the category of social virtues, and cupidity has been elevated into the guiding principle of human conduct.

If we examine this system in the light in which it affects the pockets and the interests of the governed, it is obvious that it must result in wholesale and illicit extortion. Take the case of the tenant or farmer of any office who has had to pay a substantial price for his nomination. He requires, in the first place, to recoup himself for this outlay. Next he has to collect the stipulated annual revenue for the royal or ministerial exchequer. Thirdly, he must be ready to purchase a continuance of the ever-precarious favour of his superiors; and lastly, not knowing when he may fall, he must provide for himself against a rainy day. Hereby is instituted an arithmetical progression of plunder from the sovereign to the subject, each unit in the descending scale remunerating himself from the unit next in rank below him, and the hapless peasant being the ultimate victim.

It is not surprising, under these circumstances, that office is the common avenue to wealth, and that cases are frequent of men who, having started from nothing, are found residing in magnificent houses, surrounded by crowds of retainers and living in princely style. 'Make what you can while you can' is the rule that most men set before themselves in entering public life. Nor does popular spirit resent the act; the estimation of anyone who, enjoying the opportunity, has failed to line his own pockets, being the reverse of complimentary to his sense. No one turns a thought to the sufferers from whom, in the last resort, the material for these successive *mudakhils* has been derived, and from the sweat of whose uncomplaining brow has been wrung the wealth that is dissipated in luxurious country houses, European curiosities, and enormous retinues.

It may be wondered why a system that seems to press so hardly upon the taxpayers, who are in a numerical majority, and which is attended with such obvious injustice, should be mildly acquiesced in by a people who have never been slow at rebellion. I conceive the reason in part to lie in the fact that, from one point of view, Persia is the most democratic country in the world. Lowness of birth or station is positively not the slightest bar to promotion or office of the most exalted nature. Nor must it necessarily, as in European countries, be compensated or supplemented by distinguished abilities. Interest or the capacity to pay is sufficient to procure a post for anyone, even of menial origin. Many a Persian governor has started by filling a subordinate post in the household or retinue of some great man, and has passed through every grade of society before arriving at the top. The present grand vizier was himself of humble descent, while his father was an attendant in the royal household. The prime minister who accompanied the Shah on his first visit to Europe was the grandson of a barber, and the great Amir-i-Nizam, Mirza Taki Khan, was the son of a cook. Consequently, every man sees a chance of some day profiting by the system of which he may for the moment be the victim, and as the present hardship or exaction is not to be compared in ratio with the pecuniary advantage which he may ultimately expect to reap, he is willing to bide his time, and to trust to the fall of the dice in the future.

A second fact which may variously be regarded as a reason for the continuance, and as a product of the existence, of this system is the low and inadequate figure of official salaries in Persia. In most cases, the government allowance is sufficient for little more than household expenses, and takes no thought of the personal remuneration of the official. What a grudging treasury declines to give, *mudakhil*, it is well understood, is intended to supply, and were it conceivable that by some miraculous transformation of the Persian character, or by a decree from some iconoclastic sovereign this most sacred of institutions should perish without a corresponding rise at the same time of fifty per cent in official salaries, the machine of government would be brought to a standstill. Quite apart, therefore, from the inherent popularity of a system by which all aspire to profit, so long as a miserly sovereign sits upon the throne, and the treasury is administered in the present niggardly fashion, *mudakhil* remains an essential feature of public life in Persia, and no reform is to be anticipated.

From *Persia and the Persian Question*
by George N. Curzon

The Garden of the King of Merchants

An English writer who captured some of the magic of Persia was Gertrude Bell (1868–1926) who spent six months there in 1892, staying with her uncle, Sir Frank Lascelles, who was British Minister in Tehran. She was later to become one of the leading British political figures in the Arab Middle East. Much of her time in Persia was spent in the company of one of the secretaries of the British Legation, Henry Cadogan, with whom she fell deeply in love. Her parents, however, forbade her to marry him and nine months after she left Persia he died of pneumonia. In a book published shortly afterwards, she recalled many of their excursions together, among them this one to the enchanting garden near Tehran owned by the King of Merchants – a title bestowed by the Shah on the head of the local merchant community.

Quite early in the morning we rode out to his garden. We had left Tehran, and moved up to one of the villages lying eight miles nearer the mountains on the edge of the belt of fertile country which stretches along their lower slopes. Our road that morning led us still further upwards through a green land full of wild-flowers, which seemed to us inexpressibly lovely after the bare and arid deserts about the town. The air was still fresh with the delicious freshness of the dawn; dew there was none, but a light, brisk wind, the sun's fore-runner, had shaken the leaves and grass by the roadside and swept the dust from them, and dying, it had left some of its cool fragrance to linger till mid-day in shadowy places. We rode along dark winding paths, under sweet-smelling walnut-trees, between the high mud walls of gardens, splashing through the tiny precious streams which came down to water fields, where, although it was only June, the high corn was already mellowing amidst the glory of purple vetch. The world was awake – it wakes early in the East. Laden donkeys passed us on their way to the town, veiled women riding astride on gaily-caparisoned mules, white-turbaned priests, and cantering horsemen sitting loosely in their padded saddles. Ragged beggars and half-naked dervishes were encamped by the roadside, and as we passed implored alms or hurled imprecations, as their necessity or their fanaticism indicated.

At the foot of the mountains we stopped before a long wall, less ruinous than most – a bare mud wall, straight and uncompromising, with an arched doorway in the midst of it. At our knock the double panels of the door were flung open, disclosing a flight of steps. Up these we climbed, and stood at the top amazed by the unexpected beauty which greeted us. The garden ran straight up the hillside; so steep it was that the parallel lines of paths were little but flights of high narrow stairs - short flights broken by terraces on which flower-beds were laid out, gay with roses and nasturtiums and petunias. Between the two staircases, from the top of the hill to the bottom, ran a slope of smooth blue tiles, over which flowed cascades, broadening out on the terraces into tiny tanks and fountains where the water rose and fell all day long with a cool, refreshing sound, and a soft splashing of spray. We toiled up the stairs till we came to the topmost terrace, wider than the rest. Here the many-coloured carpet of flowers gave place to a noble grove of white lilies, which stood in full bloom under the hot sunlight, and the more the sun blazed the cooler and whiter shone the lilies, the sweeter and heavier grew their fragrance. Those gardens round Tehran to which we were accustomed had been so thickly planted with trees that no ray of light had reached the flower-beds, but here in the hills, where the heat was tempered by cool winds, there was light and air in abundance. On the farther side of this radiant bodyguard was a pleasure-house – not a house of walls, but of windows and of shutters, which were all flung open, a house through which all the winds of heaven might pass unchallenged. There was a splashing fountain in the midst of it, and on all four sides deep recesses arched away to the wide window-frames. We entered, and flinging ourselves down on the cushions of one of these recesses, gazed out on the scene below us. First in the landscape came the glitter of the little garden; lower down the hillside the clustered walnuts and poplars which shaded the villages through which we had ridden; then the brown, vacant plain with no atmosphere but the mist of dust, with no features but the serpentining lines of mounds which marked the underground course of a stream, bounded far away by a barren line of hills, verdureless and torrent-scored, and beyond them more brown plains, fainter lines of barren hills to the edge of the far horizon. Midway across the first desert lay a wide patch of trees sheltering the gardens of Tehran. Down there in the town how the sun blazed! The air was a haze of heat and dust, and a perspiring humanity toiled, hurrying hither and thither, under the dark arches of the bazaar; but in the garden of the king of merchants all day long cool winds blew from the gate of the hills, all day long the refreshing water rippled and sparkled, all day long the white lilies at our feet lay like a reflection of the snow-capped mountains above us.

We sat idly gazing while we sipped our glasses of milkless tea much sugared, nibbled sweetmeats from the heaped-up dishes on the ground beside us, handed round the gurgling *kalyans*, and held out our hands to be filled with stalkless jessamine blossoms deliciously scented. At noon we rose, and were conducted yet deeper into the domains of the royally hospitable merchant – up more flights of steps, past a big tank at the further side of which stood the *andarun*, the women's lodging, where thinly-clad and shrouded forms stepped silently behind the shutters at our approach, down long shady paths till we came to another guest-house standing at the top of another series of cascades and fountains. Here an excellent repast was served to us – piles of variously flavoured rice mixed with meat and fruits and sauces, roasted kabobs, minces wrapped in vine-leaves, ices, fruits, and the fragrant wine of Shiraz.

Towards the cool of the evening the king of merchants appeared on the threshold of his breeze-swept dwelling, a man somewhat past the prime of life, with a tall and powerful figure wrapped in the long brown cloak, opening over the coloured under-robe and spotless linen, which is the dress of rich and poor alike. He was of pleasing countenance, straight-browed, red-lipped, with a black beard and an olive complexion, and his merry dark eyes had a somewhat unexpected twinkle under his high, white-turbaned forehead. A hospitable friend and a cheerful host is he, the ready quip, the apt story, the appreciative laugh, for ever on his lips; a man on whom the world has smiled, and who smiles back at that Persian world of his which he has made so pleasant for himself, strewing it with soft cushions and glowing carpets, and planting it round with flowers. Every evening the hot summer through, he is to be found in his airy garden at the foot of the mountains; every evening strings of guests knock at his hospitable gates, nor do they knock in vain. At the top of his many staircases he greets them, smiling, prosperous – those stairs of his need never be wearisome for alien feet to climb. He takes the newcomers by the hand, and leads them into one of his guest-houses; there, by the edge of a fountain, he spreads carpets on which they may repose themselves; there, as the night draws on, a banquet of rice and roasted meats and fruits is laid before them, tall pitchers of water, curiously flavoured sherbets, silver *kalyans*; and while they eat the king of merchants sits with them and entertains them with stories garnished with many a cheerful jest, many a seasonable quotation from the poets. At length he leaves them to sleep till dawn, when they arise, and, having drunk a parting glass of weak golden tea, repair to the nearest bath, and so away from the cool mountain valley and back to the heat and labour of the day. He himself spends the night in his *andarun*, or lying wrapped in a blanket on the roof of his gatehouse, from whence he can watch the day break over the wide plain below.

We took our share in his welcome, listened to his anecdotes, and played backgammon with him, nor did we bid him farewell until the ring of lighted lamps on the mosque close at hand warned us that unless we intended to spend the night on his house-top it was time to be gone.

From *Safar-Nameh: Persian Pictures*
by Gertrude Bell

6

The Modernizing Dictatorship of the Pahlavis

*T*HIS PERIOD *(1925–1979) was one of rapid modernisation and Westernisation, driven and enforced by the two Pahlavi monarchs, Reza Shah and his son, Muhammad Reza Shah. It was interrupted by the Second World War, the deposition of the pro-German Reza Shah in favour of his son, and the temporary Allied occupation of the country, which became a vital supply route to Russia. After the war the United States supplanted Britain as the major Western power involved in Iran, which was on the front line of the Cold War. The importance of oil in the world economy made British ownership of Iran's large oil reserves an increasingly contentious issue and lead to the nationalisation of the oil industry by the Iranian Prime Minister, Musaddiq, in 1951. The overthrow of Musaddiq in a military coup aided and abetted by the CIA heralded a strengthening of American influence in Iran.*

Encouraged by the Americans, the Shah pushed ahead with a progressive reform programme, which included the redistribution of land to the peasant farmers and the extension of the vote to women. Both issues inflamed the already strained relations between the Pahlavi monarchy and the Shiite clergy and lead to violent protests. These were crushed and the Shah's main clerical opponent, Ayatollah Khomeini, was sent into exile, first to Turkey and then to Iraq. The Shah's rule became more dictatorial and leant ever more heavily on his notorious secret police, SAVAK. Rapid economic development financed by huge oil revenues came to a halt in a climate of inflation. There was growing criticism in the West of the Shah's authoritarian ways which emboldened the widespread opposition within the country. The Ayatollah Khomeini emerged as the leader of a popular revolution which succeeded in driving the Shah into exile early in 1979 and putting an end to the monarchy.

Although the commander of the Persian Cossack Brigade, Reza Khan, was the moving force behind the coup that was carried out in Tehran on February 20th 1921, he did not immediately seek to seize power for himself. Instead he advanced towards this goal by careful stages. He assumed the post of army commander while his civilian associate, Sayyid Ziya al-Din Tabatabai, was appointed prime minister by Ahmad Shah.

Sayyid Ziya's premiership lasted a mere three months. One of his first acts was to annul the Anglo-Persian Agreement devised by British foreign secretary, Lord Curzon, which would have effectively left Britain running the country. He also signed a treaty with the Soviet Union which cancelled almost all the concessions granted to Tsarist Russia and opened the way for the withdrawal of Soviet troops from the Caspian province of Gilan. But Sayyid Ziya made influential enemies by arresting around one hundred and thirty prominent notables and demanding, as a condition for their release, that they disgorge the corrupt fortunes he accused them of having amassed. He desperately needed funds to pay for his ambitious reform programme, at the heart of which was the creation of a strong army. He also antagonised Ahmad Shah by treating him with scant ceremony and cutting the civil list, while at the same time he forfeited popular support by imposing taxes on basic necessities. All this left him in a weak position when Reza Khan turned against him. The army commander demanded control of the war ministry and the gendarmerie, which was conceded, opposed Sayyid Ziya's wish to use British military advisers, and finally, towards the end of May, forced him to resign and go into exile.

For the best part of the next eighteen months Reza Khan continued to serve as minister of war and commander of the army under various grandees. During this time he concentrated on building up a modern European-style army, merging the Cossack

Brigade and the gendarmerie into the regular army. He made the army the basis of his power and the instrument for realising his goal of a strong, centralised state. He crushed the various insurrections in northern Persia and planned to bring to heel the tribal chiefs in southern Persia who had become clients of the British, protecting British commercial, strategic and oil interests in the region. He also supported the government in avoiding dependence on Britain by turning to the United States for financial and other assistance. The services were secured of another American financial mission, led this time by Arthur C. Millspaugh, a former adviser on foreign trade to the US State Department, who managed to restore Persia to solvency and to lay the foundations of an effective financial administration.

The improved order and security brought about by Reza Khan with the help of his new army won him increased popular support. To further strengthen his hand, he deliberately courted Persian politicians, the British and other foreign envoys and the different sections of the community, including the clergy. Where the press was concerned, he freely resorted to bribery and intimidation. Ahmad Shah disliked and feared him, but was left with no choice but to appoint him prime minister on October 28th 1923, having run out of alternative candidates. The Shah then left on yet another trip to Europe, which he much preferred to his own country. He was never to return.

Reza Shah's aim now was to remove the Qajar dynasty and establish a republic with himself as president. He instigated a press campaign to promote republicanism and manipulated the parliamentary elections to achieve a working majority in favour of a republic. But the conservative opposition made skilful use of delaying tactics and by the time the bill came to be discussed a number of deputies otherwise favourable to Reza Khan had gone over to the opposition. Among other things, they feared that a republican government would lack authority with the tribes. There was also growing hostility to the idea of a republic on the streets of Tehran, and when Reza Khan made his way to parliament in his carriage through an angry crowd, he made the mistake of ordering troops to disperse the demonstrators, which they did with some violence. Rebuked for this by the president of the parliament, he then went to the holy city of Qom where he consulted with religious leaders who advised him to abandon republicanism. After making an announcement to this effect he resigned as prime minister, but was soon reinstated by parliament which was inundated with somewhat threatening telegrams from military officers across the country.

Realising that the Persian people remained committed to the institution of monarchy, Reza Khan decided to wrest the throne from the Qajars and found a new dynasty. He stepped up his efforts to broaden the basis of his support by paying particular attention to the clergy and his conservative opponents. He also took further steps towards unifying the country and restoring the authority of the central government by defeating an insurgency among the Lur tribes of the central Zagros Mountains and by occupying the far south-western province of Arabistan – subsequently renamed Khuzistan – which had become a virtually autonomous British protectorate. This last move was not opposed by Britain and did more than anything to restore Reza Khan's prestige after the republican debacle. On his return to Tehran, he oversaw the suppression of tribal revolts among the Kurds in the north-west and the Turkomans in the north-east.

In the spring and summer of 1925 a pliant parliament adopted a series of laws put forward by Reza Khan and his government. In a nationalist move, the Arabic lunar year was replaced by the Persian solar year, and the Arabic and Turkish names of the months were replaced by their Persian equivalents. A Persian bank was set up for the first time. Honorary titles, which had proliferated under the Qajars, were abolished and all Persians were required to adopt a family name. Reza Khan chose the name Pahlavi, which had associations with ancient Persia and was also suggestive of heroic qualities. Two of the most widely consumed commodities, tea and sugar, were made a state monopoly to finance the construction of a trans-Iranian railway. Finally, a national military service of two years was introduced, despite opposition from landowners and clergy.

At the beginning of October, supporters of Reza Khan organised a fresh propaganda campaign against Ahmad Shah, after the monarch, who was in France, had announced his intention of returning. There were mass demonstrations in a number of cities and on October 31st 1925 the parliament adopted a resolution abolishing the Qajar monarchy and appointing Reza Khan as the country's interim ruler, pending the convening of a constituent assembly. Only four deputies opposed the resolution. One of them was Dr Muhammad Musaddiq, who was to achieve prominence in 1951 when he nationalised the British-owned oil industry.

The government carefully controlled the elections to the constituent assembly, which approved the bestowal of the throne on Reza Khan and his male descendants with only three abstentions – all of them Socialist party deputies who supported the policies of the new ruler, but opposed the institution of monarchy. The coronation of Reza Shah, as he now was, took place on April 25th 1926 in the ceremonial hall of the Golestan Palace of the Qajars in Tehran. It represented a remarkable rise to power for a man of humble background and scant education who had joined the Persian Cossack Brigade as an ordinary trooper more than thirty years earlier. The only parallel was Nadir Shah, who also rescued the country from chaos, ousted the existing dynasty, and founded an equally ephemeral one of his own.

Reza Shah ruled Persia for the next fifteen years. In this short period he imposed fundamental changes on the country. His aim was to create a strong, secular nation state, united and homogeneous in a way that Persia had not been before, free of foreign interference, with a modern economy, modern institutions and a modern way of life, following the example of the industrialised countries of the West.

One of first things he did was to abolish the hated capitulations. These had been conceded to Western countries by the Qajars and exempted their subjects from the due process of Persian law, on the grounds that this was mainly Islamic law, which treated non-Muslims less favourably than Muslims. Reza Shah overcame this objection by having a new civil code drawn up, based on that of France. During his reign, the whole justice system was largely secularised and taken out of the hands of the clergy.

Other measures were taken to reduce foreign influence. The

right to issue paper currency was taken away from the British-owned Imperial Bank of Persia and given to a new National Bank. Foreign-run schools were closed and all sorts of restrictions were placed on official contacts with foreigners and on what foreigners could do in Persia. The national identity was further asserted by an attempt to purge the language of foreign – mainly Arabic – words and by a decree of 1935 insisting that the country be known internationally as Iran, meaning 'the land of the Aryans', and not as Persia, the name used in the West since the time of the Achaemenids. This was done at the suggestion of Persian diplomats in Berlin, where the Nazis were now in power and promoting their 'Aryan' racist ideology.

His main disappointment was his failure to reduce the influence of the British-owned Anglo-Iranian Oil Company, as it was now known. He cancelled its concession in 1932, but signed a new agreement a year later, which left the company in as strong a position as ever with the term of its concession extended until 1993. The world economic recession and the production of oil in Iraq weakened his negotiating hand.

While Reza Shah had been obliged to cultivate the Shiite clergy during his rise to power, he was now determined to reduce their influence, convinced that they were largely responsible for Persia's backwardness. Just as he diminished their judicial role, so he ended their virtual monopoly of education through a massive expansion of state schools and institutions of higher learning, which followed a modern, secular curriculum and were open to men and women alike. Secularisation was further promoted by the two years military service. This was opposed by the clergy as were the laws imposing European clothing and headgear for both sexes, the encouragement given to women to take their place alongside men in the workplace and the public arena, and the ban on women wearing the veil. Protest demonstrations led by the clergy against these moves in July 1935 in the shrine city of Mashhad were suppressed by the security forces with considerable loss of life.

In his drive to unify the country, Reza Shah made a determined effort to eliminate regional and ethnic differences. He banned the wearing of traditional ethnic costumes and closed schools teaching local languages other than Persian, such as the Azeri Turkish language of Azerbaijan or the Arabic widely spoken in Khuzistan. Above all, he waged a relentless campaign against the nomadic tribes, which were used to enjoying considerable autonomy, and in the case of the large Bakhtiyari tribal confederation in the south had close ties with Britain by providing protection for the oil industry. Once again, Britain did not attempt to oppose him, as it now saw its interests better served by a strong central government than by supporting tribal autonomy. But not content with bringing the tribes under his control, he tried to put an end to their nomadic way of life altogether by forcibly settling them in new villages. This policy was brutally implemented and many of the tribespeople died as a consequence.

Reza Shah also brought the different parts of a vast country closer together through a network of new roads and the first extensive railway-building programme – something that had been blocked in the past by Anglo-Russian rivalry. His pet project was the Trans-Iranian railway which ran from the south-east corner of the Caspian Sea, through Tehran, to the top of the Persian Gulf, and was built between 1927 and 1938 by an assortment of American and European companies. Covering one thousand, three hundred kilometres (eight hundred and forty miles) of mainly rugged, mountainous terrain, it is regarded as a miracle of engineering. More importantly for Reza Shah, its huge cost was met entirely out of taxation, with no recourse to foreign loans. But as the taxes were levied on basic commodities, they fell unduly heavily on the less well off.

The improved communications benefited commerce and industrial development. Reza Shah used protective tariffs and state monopolies to promote a manufacturing industry that had only existed in a very embryonic state when he came to the throne. Very little was done, however, to develop agriculture, although the majority of the population lived on the land. Rural poverty encouraged a flight to the cities, which created new social and political problems and ultimately became one of the factors behind the Islamic Revolution of 1978–1979.

Reza Shah was obsessed with ensuring the survival of his new dynasty. To make it seem less parvenu he took two Qajar princesses as wives and married the crown prince, Muhammad Reza Pahlavi, to Princess Fawzieh, a daughter of King Fuad of Egypt. But through some of the controversial measures he introduced and through his increasingly arbitrary rule, he gradually forfeited most of the support he had enjoyed at the outset of his reign. The press was muzzled, parliament emasculated and anyone suspected of opposing him was liable to be arrested, imprisoned, banished, or murdered. Persia became a modern police state, with spies everywhere. Suspected Communists were the main targets of the repression, but even government ministers and senior army officers fell victim to the Shah's growing paranoia. He also lost popular support through the aura of corruption that came to surround Pahlavi rule, as it had his Qajar predecessors. Reza Shah himself accumulated vast wealth and extensive landed estates by the most dubious means, although he continued to live the rather frugal life of a simple soldier.

In the end it was the British and the Russians, whose controlling hands Reza Shah had hoped to remove from Persia, who brought about his downfall, and not an internal conspiracy. Always seeking a counter-weight to these two powers, he developed intensive commercial and political relations with Nazi Germany. When the Second World War broke out, he declared Persia's neutrality, and after Germany invaded the Soviet Union in June 1941 he refused successive Anglo-Soviet demands for the expulsion of German nationals. He considered a German victory likely and discounted the possibility of a Russian attack on Persia while it was heavily engaged in resisting the German advance.

He was wrong. Russia desperately needed to be able to receive supplies of military equipment through Persia from the Gulf, while Britain was anxious to prevent the Persian oil fields from falling into German hands.

On the evening of August 24th and during the early hours of August 25th 1941, British and Indian troops invaded Persia from the south and west, while Russian troops attacked from the north. Reza Shah's much-vaunted army proved wholly inadequate and on August 28th the Persian government ordered its forces to cease resistance. On September 10th the government agreed to break off diplomatic relations with Germany and its allies, to close their legations and expel their nationals. It also agreed to the occupation of most of the country by Britain and Russia and to facilitate the transport of Allied war materials. But the Allies were no longer willing to work with Reza Shah and the British government made this clear by getting the BBC Persian-language service to broadcast attacks on his repressive rule and alleged corruption – an action that compromised the independence of the BBC. On September 16th Reza Shah abdicated in favour of the crown prince and was taken by the British with the rest of his family into exile in South Africa, in Johannesburg, where he died of a heart attack on July 26th 1944.

For most of the first twelve years of his reign, Muhammad Reza Shah, the second and last of the Pahlavis, was in too weak a position to assert himself and was compelled to rule as a constitutional monarch. During this period, Iranians probably enjoyed a greater degree of freedom than at any time before or since. Political parties and trade unions were active and there were few constraints on the freedom of the press.

The country was under Allied occupation from 1941 to 1945, with once again a Russian zone in the north and a British zone in the south. American troops also arrived in Iran after the United States entered the war and helped with the transport of military supplies to Russia on the Trans-Iranian railway.

The war marked the beginning of a growing American influence, which at this stage was not in any way resented, but regarded instead as a way of escaping from Anglo-Russian influence. American advisers were attached to the Iranian army and gendarmerie and another Millspaugh mission returned in 1943 to take charge of Iran's finances, although Millspaugh resigned two years later after running into opposition to his efforts.

During its occupation of northern Iran, the Soviet Union did all it could to promote the Iranian communist party, known as the *Tudeh* or 'Masses' party, which became a major political force in the country. It also refused to follow the example of Britain and America and withdraw its troops when the war ended, as it had undertaken to do. Instead, it used the presence of these troops to prevent the Iranian government from suppressing Soviet-backed separatist movements which took control of Azerbaijan and Kurdistan towards the end of 1945. After some complex political and diplomatic manoeuvring the Iranian prime minister, Qavam al-Saltana, eventually succeeded in getting the Soviet troops to leave in exchange for the promise of an oil concession in the north. He then sent in the army, which rapidly took control of the rebel provinces, with the Shah personally leading the troops into the Azerbaijan capital, Tabriz. The proposed oil concession was subsequently vetoed by the Iranian parliament.

Muhammad Reza Shah, like his father, cultivated the army and made it the basis of is power. His role in restoring the unity of the country gave him a new prestige, while an attempt on his life in February 1949 by a young man linked to both communist and religious circles gained him public sympathy as well. He took advantage of this to try to increase his power at the expense of parliament, but lost the initiative in 1950 to Musaddiq who rallied public opinion behind him as he persuaded parliament to nationalise the British-owned Anglo-Iranian Oil Company.

Musaddiq, who became prime minister in May 1951, headed a disparate coalition of religious and secular forces called the National Front. He ultimately failed in his confrontation with the Anglo-Iranian Oil Company because he lost the support of the United States and antagonised too many of his allies at home. The Americans were frustrated by his refusal to compromise and alarmed by his association with the *Tudeh* party. As a result they joined the British embargo on Iranian oil sales, which dealt a heavy blow to the economy. He forced a confrontation with the Shah, undermined the authority of the parliament he had so long championed, and alienated his clerical allies by leaning towards the left. He was finally overthrown in August 1953 in a coup carried out by royalist army officers with the active support of the CIA, who in turn had been working with British intelligence. But the manner of his overthrow made him a heroic figure in the eyes of most Iranians, while it bred a new hostility to the United States.

The Shah was now determined to concentrate power in his own

hands. Political repression became the order of the day and was particularly directed at the *Tudeh* party. A new internal security organisation known by its acronym as SAVAK (*Sazman-e Itillaat va Amniyat-e Keshvar*, the State Intelligence and Security Organization) was set up in 1957, with the help of the CIA and the Israeli Mossad. It soon became notorious for its brutality and its all-pervasive influence. The Shah's friendly relations with Israel, which he supplied with oil, became as unpopular as his close ties with the United States.

For the next ten years, however, he did his best to keep the Shiite clergy on his side. He made frequent pilgrimages with the queen and maintained personal contact with the most senior cleric, Ayatollah Borujerdi, who was firmly opposed to the clergy playing a political role. In 1955 he even pandered to the intense Muslim hostility towards the Bahais, by tolerating a nation-wide campaign of persecution.

The Shah's marriage to the Egyptian princess, Fawzieh, was dissolved in 1948 and in 1951 he married Soraya Isfandiyar, the daughter of a Bakhtiyari tribal chief. But she failed to give him an heir and he divorced her in 1958. The following year he married an Iranian of more modest background, Farah Dibah, who bore him two sons and two daughters. Her gentle manner and interest in social welfare and the arts helped to give the monarchy a softer and more appealing aspect.

A new agreement on the oil industry was reached in 1954, enabling exports to resume. This provided for an equal sharing of profits between Iran and a consortium of oil companies, in which the former Anglo-Iranian Oil Company, renamed British Petroleum, had a forty percent share, with another forty percent going to American companies. The agreement acknowledged Iranian sovereignty over the oilfields, but left the important operations in the hands of the consortium.

With the oil revenue and fresh loans from the United States, the Shah was able to press ahead with the economic development and modernisation of the country. But corruption, the failure to control imports and credits, and heavy military spending led to a financial crisis by 1960, with sharply rising inflation and a deteriorating balance of payments. This provoked discontent, strikes and open criticism of the government, which increased after fraudulent elections in 1960 and 1961. American pressure on the Shah to liberalise and to introduce progressive reforms, resulted in the creation of a wholly artificial two-party system but was followed up more importantly in 1961 with the appointment of a liberal prime minister, Dr Ali Amini, who was charged with introducing a land reform. This had long been opposed, not only by the landlords but also by most of the clergy, who derived much of their income from landed estates held in religious endowments. Amini made the Shah dissolve the parliament, where the landlords were strongly represented, and rule by decree, enabling him to put through the first stage of a land reform. This finally broke the economic and political power of the landlords, and created a new class of independent farmers. Amini also began seriously to tackle corruption and pursued austerity policies to stabilise the economy. But he came into conflict with the Shah when he demanded cuts in the military budget and resigned in July 1962.

The Shah now assumed the mantle of reformer himself. In January 1963 he announced a six-point programme, soon to be officially labelled the 'White Revolution', which was to be voted on in a national plebiscite. This promised a continuation of land reform, the sale of state factories, profit sharing for industrial workers, voting rights for women, the nationalisation of forests, and the creation of a literacy corps to bring basic education to the most remote villages.

This brought the Shah into serious conflict with the clergy, who were no longer restrained by Ayatollah Borujerdi, who had died the previous year. Led by a sixty-year-old Ayatollah, Ruhollah Khomeini, the majority came out in open opposition to the plans to give women the vote and to continue the land reform. They organised protest demonstrations and called for a boycott of the referendum (according to the government, this resulted in almost one hundred percent approval), while the Shah hit back with attacks on what he called the 'black reaction' of the clergy. The agitation reached a climax in June 1963 when Khomeini was arrested after an outspoken attack on the Shah and there were violent demonstrations in Tehran and other cities, in which hundreds of people were killed or wounded. After being freed, rearrested and freed again, Khomeini delivered a blistering attack in October 1964 on the granting of diplomatic immunity to American military personnel and was deported to Turkey. A year later he was allowed to move to the Shiite holy city of Najaf in Iraq, where he evolved his theory of theocratic government and continued his attacks on the Shah, which were smuggled into Iran on cassettes and widely circulated.

Over the next twelve years the Shah pressed ahead with his modernising and Westernising policies. There was a huge expansion right across the board in almost all fields, from industry through to education. This was made possible by big increases in the oil revenue, especially after the leap in world oil prices in 1973, for which the Shah was largely responsible. Representatives of foreign companies descended on Iran like locusts, keen to mop up some of the oil wealth.

There were no Western-style political reforms, however. The Shah even dispensed with his two existing political parties – one a governing party and the other a token opposition party – and turned the country instead into a one-party state. Western governments turned a blind eye to the political repression and fed the Shah's growing megolomania. Regarding him as the best defence against Communism and any potential Soviet threat, the United States and Britain were happy to sell him a limitless supply of the latest weaponry and to entrust him with policing the oil-rich Gulf region after Britain withdrew in 1971. That year he held lavish celebrations at the Achaemenid palace of Persepolis to mark what he claimed was two-and-a-half thousand years of Persian monarchy – ignoring the fact that for much of this time there was no Persian monarchy. By now, he was following his father in identifying firmly with pre-Islamic Iran. In a foolish move that was deeply offensive to Muslim sentiment, he changed the starting date of the calendar from the Prophet Muhammad's migration from Mecca to Medina to the founding of the Achaemenid Empire by Cyrus the Great. He also gave himself the title of *Aryamehr*, meaning the 'Light of the Aryans'.

The Shah's march towards what he called 'the Great Civilisation' began to falter in 1976–1977. The Western media and human rights organisations suddenly began to highlight the political repression in Iran, but more importantly, the Shah's closest ally, the United States, elected a new president, Jimmy Carter, who was committed to promoting human rights. To protect his image, the Shah decided to relax controls, believing firmly in his own propaganda that opposition was limited to a handful of anarchists and communists. He was taken aback by the scale of the resulting protests and street demonstrations against his rule. Rampant inflation, meanwhile, forced the government to impose austerity policies, which increased discontent by throwing people out of work and depressing wages.

The Shah, who was suffering from cancer, vacillated, as did the Carter administration, between repressive and conciliatory approaches. The repression invariably resulted in bloodshed which only fuelled the street protests and made them more radical. Urged on by Khomeini, the protestors stopped merely calling for a return to constitutional government and began to demand instead an end to the monarchy and the establishment of an Islamic Republic.

In October 1978 Khomeini moved to Paris where he was able to put across his message though the international media. In his pronouncements he was careful to avoid alienating other opposition forces that did not share his vision of an Islamic theocracy. By the end of the year, the Shah had effectively lost control. On January 16th 1979, after appointing a leader of the secular opposition, Shahpour Bakhtiyar, to head a new government, he flew out of the country with his family into an exile from which, like his father, he was never to return. Khomeini flew into Tehran on February the 1st to a tumultuous welcome from a crowd of some three million. Bakhtiyar hung on for another ten days, until a successful uprising against what was left of the army and the security forces in Tehran compelled him to surrender power. He went into hiding and eventually into exile in Paris. That marked the final end of the Pahlavi monarchy. A new era began on February 12th 1979, when a prime minister appointed by Khomeini took over at the head of a Provisional Revolutionary Government.

The Pahlavi period produced some of the most stylish writing on Persia by such authors as Vita Sackville-West, Freya Stark and Robert Byron. It also introduced two new kinds of writers: Persians living abroad and writing in English about their experiences in their homeland, and journalists. The former are wonderfully represented by Sattareh Farman Farmaian and Shusha Guppy, the latter in their very different styles by the Pole, Ryszard Kapuscinski, and the Englishman, John Simpson. At the same time, the long-standing tradition of diplomats writing on Persia is maintained by Harold Nicolson and Anthony Parsons in their memorable accounts of the first and second Pahlavi shahs respectively.

A Qajar Nobleman's Home

The modernising rule of Reza Shah did not immediately end the way of life of the old Qajar nobility. One of the greatest Qajar nobles who survived until almost the end of the reign of Reza Shah was Abdul Husayn Mirza Farmanfarma (1857–1939), a great-grandson of Fath Ali Shah and son-in-law of Muzaffar al-Din Shah. He had been a prominent political figure during the first two decades of the twentieth century and had briefly held the office of prime minister during the First World War. His daughter, Sattareh Farman Farmaian (1920–), grew up in his house and compound in Tehran during the reign of Reza Shah. In her autobiography, Daughter of Persia, *she gives a wonderfully evocative description of the domestic establishment of a great Qajar nobleman.*

I can never forget this marvellous home of my childhood, whose like has surely vanished from Iran forever. In it my father watched over the welfare of more than a thousand people whose very survival depended entirely on him: wives, children, countless paid servants, secretaries, craftsmen, and labourers, as well as many faithful elderly retainers and old soldiers who had served him in the past. For the shelter and protection of all these people, as well as of their families, he alone was responsible.

This had become a heavy burden for him to bear. Under Reza Khan's regime his eldest sons had once again become men of distinction. But the new ruler was confiscating for his own use the property of numerous Qajar noblemen, and no one could predict his future plans for my father or any of his male children.

All Qajar families knew that Reza's secret police were everywhere. 'When you pray', my mother would instruct us, 'always ask God to let Shahzdeh[1] live one hundred and ten years.' This was her way of saying, 'Pray that your father lives for ever, for when he dies, we and all these people will be nothing.' Being nothing meant having no father, brother, husband, or son to protect you. In our country, if you were not yourself strong, wealthy or powerful, or if you did not have somebody strong to protect you, you were nobody, and you did not survive.

Yet my father's compound was also a place of enchanting tranquillity and beauty. Its centre was a great oval park or garden bordered by poplar trees, and the entire compound, which was about half a mile long, was surrounded by a ten-foot wall whose iron-studded wooden gate on Sepah Avenue was guarded by liveried watchmen. Inside, circling the gravel carriage road around the central garden, like stones on a giant's necklace, were my father's home and the walled sub-compounds of his younger wives, along with storehouses, a carpentry shop, and even a garage, for my father's dark blue Essex sedan was one of the country's few motorcars. There were a smithy, a dairy, a bathhouse, a greenhouse, and a big kitchen where food was prepared each day for my father, his staff, and his servants, and where his Persian chef supervised the daily concoction of pastries and French delicacies for my father and his Persian and foreign luncheon guests.

The sub-compounds where we and our mothers lived were known collectively as the *andarun*, the 'inner' quarter, or harem; everything else, including the central garden and the other buildings surrounding it, was the *biruni*. This was the 'outer', or public, quarter where my father lived, and was the realm of men. It reflected the greater world beyond, which was also a realm of men.

At the northernmost end of the great garden of the *biruni* stood

---

[1] 'The Prince'. He was a grandson, on his father's side, of Fath Ali Shah's Crown Prince, Abbas Mirza.

a sparkling blue reflecting pool in which a fountain murmured throughout the long hot season. Bright tiles of Persian blue surrounded the pool, and from its sides stretched ornamental flower beds of roses and narcissus among which my father in his enforced retirement might stroll, chat with old political and diplomatic friends and military comrades, or sip tea under the shade of pines and cypresses, poplars and old sycamores.

Only four of the eight wives my father married in the course of his long life lived in our compound: my mother; two other ladies, Batul and Fatimeh, whom my father had married at about the same time as my mother and who lived across the park from us; and, after about 1928, another lady, Hamdam, whom we did not often see because she lived at the opposite end of the park. His second wife, a Kurdish chieftain's daughter, had long since died, but his first wife, the Qajar princess Ezzatdoleh, who was much older than the rest, had an establishment of her own next door to our compound, as did their four adult sons, while two more ladies whom my father married late in life had houses elsewhere in the city. All the wives in the compound looked upon each others' children as their own, and Batul and Fatimeh were my mother's best friends. We also regarded the princess Ezzatdoleh and her sons as part of our family. She was extremely fond of my mother, who was an exceptionally kind and compassionate person, and they saw each other often, for the princess and my father, though on good terms, had long been separated, and Ezzatdoleh, who was lonely, frequently needed my mother's soothing company.

My father did not allow our mothers to leave home often, but they did not often need to. Both the *biruni* and the *andarun* were places of ceaseless activity. *Droshkies* (horse-drawn carriages) constantly rattled up the gravel road carrying visitors to our mothers' homes, as well as the Persian and foreign guests of my father or men who had come to see him on business. Male servants travelled continually back and forth, bearing messages from my father to his wives' homes or from one wife to another, or lugging baskets of charcoal and firewood for them, or prodding donkeys laden with bricks to repair their houses and courtyards, or carrying bolts of cloth for them to sew our clothing and their servants' on the

Singer sewing machines my father had given each of them for this purpose. In their walled-off sub-compounds, which were closely guarded and where no men other than near relatives were permitted entry, women servants in snug embroidered bodices, narrow trousers, full swinging skirts, and flowing head scarves or gaily coloured *chadors* (a chador is simply any veil covering the whole body) brought bedding or preserved foods to and from storage, prepared meals in courtyard kitchens, washed clothes in outdoor brick pools, and laid out branches of turmeric and other herbs and spices to dry in the patios.

So it is engraved on my heart, a bustling, almost completely self-contained world inside the encircling wall. Everyone there was linked with everyone else, for 'family' in our small universe meant not only our father and mothers and brothers and sisters and other relatives who lived in and around the compound, but all the other people inside our walls: our nannies, our *lalehs* or male caretakers, the cooks, guards, porters, stewards, secretaries, artisans, old male pensioners, and everyone else my father supported. They and we all belonged to him, and were fed, protected, and cared for by him. This supreme bond with our benefactor, which Iranians call 'the bond of bread and salt', gave us all an indissoluble connection. No one in the compound, from the most decrepit ex-sergeant to the youngest schoolchild, ever forgot this allegiance for a single moment. I seemed myself to remember it almost hourly.

From *Daughter of Persia*
by Sattareh Farman Farmaian with Dona Munker

A Meeting with the New Shah, Reza Khan

Sir Harold Nicolson (1886–1968) diplomat, writer and politician, was born at the British legation in Tehran, where his father, Arthur Nicolson, one of the foremost British diplomats of his day, was secretary. Following in his father's footsteps, Harold Nicolson was counsellor of legation in Tehran from 1925–1927, under the ambassador, Sir Percy Loraine. In this letter to his parents, he gives a vivid description of his impressions

*on meeting Reza Khan, shortly after a constituent assembly in Tehran
had deposed the Qajars and made him shah in their place.*

I went with Percy Loraine to meet the Shah, Reza Khan. He received
us in a little pavilion in the garden of the house he built for himself.
It is quite unpretentious: very clean; lots of new paint and ghastly
new chairs of terrible shapes. A roaring fire. They went to tell him
that we had arrived, and shortly a step of huge weight was heard on
the pavement of the colonnade and two of the windows were
successively darkened by a huge form walking past them. By the
third window he entered. He must be six foot three, inclined to
corpulence, simple khaki uniform with no decorations, high
uncomfortable collar in which he evidently feels ill-at-ease, high-
peaked cap like a Greek general which adds to his height. Coarse red
hands. Rather coarse nose. Fine chin. Clipped moustache turning up
at the ends. Unshaven. Bushy eyebrows. Fine but rather bulging eyes.
He looked tired and in ill health. At first his face seemed sullen and
rather too much jowl. But after I had paid him some compliments
he cheered up, laughed in a way that was half-shy and half-sly, I can't
be sure which – pats his fat fingers over his unshaven chin and began
to talk quietly and sensibly about the situation and his own
prospects. I was frankly puzzled by him. At one moment he took off
his hat, disclosing a tiny round skull (much better shaved than his
chin) and making him look exactly like a Cossack. That, of course, is
the dominant impression at first – a non-commissioned officer in
the Cossack brigade: coarse humour, ungainly manner, latent
brutality. But then his voice is so gentle, and at certain angles his face
suddenly becomes fine and distinguished, and his simplicity is
attractive. He teased me about looking so young, said he did not
believe I was more than 28 and added that I must have had no
trouble in love or politics. After a bit his sudden animation left him,
and he talked listlessly and without much point. When we said goodbye, he suddenly burst out into real cordiality. He begged Loraine
not to let him become pompous when he becomes Shah and
thanked him for all he had done to help him in a very simple and
absolutely convincing way. In fact I am puzzled. There is certainly
great force in him somewhere, but I am not sure whether it will

survive the luxury of the throne, or whether it might not become mere brutality. I don't like that sly look.

From *a letter from Harold Nicolson to his parents, 1925*

The Coronation of Reza Shah

In another letter to his parents the following year, Harold Nicolson described the coronation of Reza Shah, which both he and his wife, Vita Sackville-West, witnessed.

Yesterday was the coronation of the Shah. We drove there in State – a thing I particularly abominate. I never did like amateur theatricals, and I loathe bumping along a street surrounded by escorts. My friendly profile does not lend itself to such pro-consular antics and the collar of my uniform cuts cruelly into my chubby neck. Then we arrived. But Loraine, who has a weakness for the processional, insisted on our continuing through the gardens of the palace. First stalk six guards in solemn idiocy, then the Loraines in equal solemnity, and then I come with Vita. At the main court of the palace there is a band. There is an awful moment as Loraine springs rigidly to attention while they play God Save the King. Lady Loraine bares her head as do the devout after receiving Holy Communion and I get hot and uncomfortable, longing with a home-sick passion for my pipe. Finally, with much bowing on the part of court officials, we climb the steep staircase. Under Vita's orders this vast railway station had been painted a simple apricot. It looked very well. So did Vita. She wore in the centre of her black toque the emeralds which Nasir-id-Din-Shah had presented to mummy, feeling that it would be pleasant for them to revisit the scene of their youth. We were then ranged to the left of the throne. The rest of the palace was filled with mullahs. Half an hour after it was supposed to have begun, there were a series of cries from the entrance signifying the approach of the *valiahd* (crown prince, then aged eight). This infant thereupon entered dressed as a general and surrounded by members of the cabinet carrying the regalia on red velvet pads.

Another pause and then another shrill cry at the entrance. Slowly the Shah, dressed in a blue mantle embroidered with pearls, slouched up the aisle and climbed onto the throne. The latter is not what you know as the Peacock Throne. The new throne was really magnificent. He sat on it – rigid, theocratic, rather superb – this Cossack trooper, the ruler of the world, the king of kings. When they had ceased intoning, the minister approached with the regalia. Taking the vast diamond crown in both his red hands he clapped it firmly upon that Cossack pate, becoming instantly rigid again like an idol, the diamonds shooting points of fire. A vast and bulbous sceptre was then placed in his right hand, and in his left the carbon copy of the speech. Still rigid and motionless he read the speech in a toneless voice. The guns boomed distantly, and in a few minutes, bowing to right and left, the king of kings slouched from the room followed by his little mosquito son.

Next night the Shah gave a party in the gardens of the palace. They were beautifully illuminated and there was much champagne and many excellent fireworks. But for Vita and me God lay in wait preparing unfortunate incidents. Mine came first. We were dining with the opium commission and on climbing into the car my uniform trousers split across the seat. A trail of white shirt emerged from the aperture. I found safety pins at the commission and the tails of my coat hid what might otherwise have seemed ungainly. Vita's incident occurred at the end of the party. She was wearing her big emerald chain and the central drop fell off during the evening. It seemed hopeless to find it as she had been walking all over the garden. But on proceeding to the throne room to break the news to one of the palace officials, I found the prime minister and the minister of public works anxiously going round the Peacock Throne trying to fit into it an emerald which had been found lying at its feet. So I reclaimed the emerald and put it in my pocket.

Vita leaves on Tuesday. I don't like to think about it.

From *a letter from Harold Nicolson to his parents, 1926*

The Peculiar Beauty of a Persian Garden

Persia has always been famous for its gardens, yet Europeans have sometimes felt a touch of disappointment on seeing one for the first time. As the writer and gardener, Vita Sackville-West (1892–1962), acknowledges, it is not what they have come to expect from a garden. Vita Sackville-West went out to Persia in 1925 when her husband, Harold Nicolson, was posted to the British embassy in Tehran. In her book, Passenger to Tehran, *which was the product of her time there, she explains most movingly just what it is that makes a Persian garden so special.*

Ever since I have been in Persia I have been looking for a garden and have not yet found one. Yet Persian gardens enjoy a great reputation. Hafiz and Sa-adi sang frequently, even wearisomely, of roses. Yet there is no word for rose in the Persian language; the best they can manage is 'red flower'. It looks as though a misconception had arisen somewhere. Indeed I think the misconception is ours, sprung from that national characteristic by which the English exact that everything should be the same, even in Central Asia as it is in England, and grumble when it is not. 'Garden?' we say; and think of lawns and herbaceous borders, which is manifestly absurd. There is no turf in this parched country; and as for herbaceous borders, they postulate a lush shapeliness unimaginable to the Persian mind. Here, everything is dry and untidy, crumbling and decayed; a dusty poverty, exposed for eight months of the year to a cruel sun. For all that, there are gardens in Persia.

But they are gardens of trees, not of flowers; green wildernesses. Imagine that you have ridden in summer for four days across a plain; that you have then come to a barrier of snow-mountains and ridden up the pass; that from the top of the pass you have seen a second plain, with a second barrier of mountains in the distance, a hundred miles away; that you know that beyond these mountains lies yet another plain, and another, and another; and that for days, even weeks, you must ride, with no shade, and the sun overhead, and nothing but the bleached bones of dead animals strewing the track. Then when you come to trees and running water, you will call it a garden. It will not be flowers and their garishness that your eyes crave for, but a green cavern full of shadow, and pools where goldfish dart, and the sound of little streams. That is the meaning of a garden in Persia, a country where the long slow caravan is an everyday fact, and not a romantic name.

Such gardens there are; many of them abandoned, and these one may share with the cricket and the tortoise, undisturbed through the hours of the long afternoon. In such a one I write. It lies on a southward slope, at the foot of the snowy Elburz, looking over the plain. It is a tangle of briars and grey sage, and here and there a judas tree in full flower stains the whiteness of the tall planes with its incredible magenta. A cloud of pink, down in a dip, betrays the peach trees in blossom. Water flows everywhere, either in little wild runnels, or guided into a straight channel paved with blue tiles, which pours down the slope into a broken fountain between four cypresses. There, too, is the little pavilion, ruined, like everything else; the tiles of the facade have fallen out and lie smashed upon the terrace; people have built, but, seemingly, never repaired; they have built, and gone away, leaving nature to turn their handiwork into this melancholy beauty. Nor is it so sad as it might be, for in this spacious, ancient country it is not of man that one thinks; he has made no impression on the soil, even his villages of brown mud remain invisible until one comes close up to them, and, once ruined, might have been ruined for five or five hundred years, indifferently; no, one thinks only of the haven that this tangled enclosure affords, after the great spaces. One is no longer that small insect creeping across the pitiless distances.

There is something satisfying in this contrast between the garden and the enormous geographical simplicity that lies beyond. The mud walls that surround the garden are crumbling, and through the breaches appears the great brown plain, crossed by the three pale roads: to the east, the road to Meshed and Samarcand; to the west, the road to Bagdad; to the south, the road to Isfahan. The eye may travel, or, alternately, return to dwell upon the little grape-hyacinth growing close at hand. These Asian plains are of exceeding beauty, but their company is severe, and the mind turns gratefully for a change to something of a more manageable size. The garden is a place of spiritual reprieve, as well as a place of shadows. The plains are lonely, the garden is inhabited; not by men, but by birds and beasts and lowly flowers; by hoopoes, crying 'Who? Who?' among the branches; by lizards rustling like dry leaves; by the tiny sea-green iris. A garden in England seems an unnecessary luxury, where the whole countryside is so circumscribed, easy and secure; but here, one begins to understand why the garden drew such notes from Sa-adi and Hafiz. As a breeze at evening after a hot day, as a well in the desert, so is the garden to the Persian.

The sense of property, too, is blessedly absent; I suppose that this garden has an owner somewhere, but I do not know who he is, nor can any one tell me. No one will come up and say that I am trespassing; I may have the garden to myself; I may share it with a beggar; I may see a shepherd drive in his brown and black flock, and, sitting down to watch them browse, sing a snatch of the song that all Persians sing at the turn of the year, for the first three weeks of spring. All are equally free to come and enjoy. Indeed there is nothing to steal, except the blossom from the peach trees, and no damage to do that has not already been done by time and nature. The same is true of the whole country. There are no evidences of law anywhere, no sign-posts or milestones to show the way; the caravanserais stand open for any one to go in and rest his beasts; you may travel along any of those three roads for hundreds of miles in any direction, without meeting any one or anything to control you; even the rule of the road is nominal, and you pass by as best you can. If you prefer to leave the track and take to the open, then you are free to do so. One remembers – sometimes with irritation, sometimes with longing, according to the fortunes of the journey – the close organisation of European countries.

The shadows lengthen, and the intense light of sunset begins to spread over the plain. The brown earth darkens to the rich velvet of burnt umber. The light creeps like a tide up the foothills, staining the red rock to the colour of porphyry. High up, above the range of the Elburz, towers the white cone of Demavend,[2] white no longer now, but glowing like a coal; that white loneliness, for ten minutes of every day, suddenly comes to life. It is time to leave the garden, where the little owls are beginning to hoot, answering one another, and to go down into the plain, where the blue smoke of the evening fires is already rising, and a single star hangs prophetic in the west.

From *Passenger to Teheran*
by Vita Sackville-West

Village Weddings

Until not very long ago, much of the population of Persia lived in villages, many of them remote from urban centres and often difficult of access. Such was the village of Garmrud situated in a valley in the Elburz Mountains between Tehran and the Caspian Sea, which Freya Stark (1893–1993) visited in the summer of 1931. The purpose of her arduous journey through the mountains on a mule was to seek out the castles of the Assassins – that extremist Shiite order which Marco Polo wrote about. She managed to identify some of the more important castles and to map part of this remote region for the first time. But she also had a lively curiosity for the lives of the people who lived there, as in this thoroughly engaging account of a triple wedding in Garmrud - the home of her muleteer Aziz, who was also one of the bridegrooms. It is taken from her book, The Valleys of the Assassins and other Persian Travels, *which established her reputation as one of the great travel writers of the twentieth century.*

In the dusk we came to Garmrud, which leans against the cliffs that close the valley. Aziz's wife was out to meet us with many of the village women, dressed in reds and yellows, a pretty sight among the poplar trees and boulders of the stream. She ran out to hold the bridle

[2] Situated in the centre of the Elburz range and about forty miles northeast of Tehran, Demavend is the highest mountain in Iran, rising to 18,955 feet. W. Taylor Thomson in 1837 is believed to have been the first European to climb the summit, which is not difficult.

rein, and led me in triumph, while the people on the roofs of their houses bade me welcome. There was a general air of holiday, for three weddings were to be celebrated on the morrow, one being, so to say, an international affair between our village and that of Pichiban on the way to the pass.

Under these circumstances, the Throne of Solomon (a high mountain) must again wait, for nothing would drag Aziz away before the festivities.

Aziz's wife was as pretty as ever, but disunion now rent the little household. Aziz had married again, and spent most of his time with the new bride, who lived across the stream. I will say in his defence that things were not made too pleasant for him when he did come to his old home. The eagle-faced old lady, his mother, stood up for him staunchly, but the offended wife would not hear of compromise. Like Medea, and many lesser ladies, she held up to him with tactless reiteration the mirror of the past with all his faults recorded, ever since their wedding sixteen years before, when she was fourteen and he sixteen. Even the best of men could not be expected to enjoy this, but the poor woman's grief was so deep that it was useless to point out how much worse she made the matter by railing. Love, like broken porcelain, should be wept over and buried, for nothing but a miracle will resuscitate it: but who in this world has not for some wild moments thought to recall the irrecoverable with words?

Aziz enjoyed the situation in a shamefaced sort of way, being teased for a gay dog by his friends, and being no little in love with the new lady, a determined sort of beauty with black hair and iron muscles who could crush the little man to powder with one hand, and will no doubt be doing so one of these days.

'What do *you* feel about it?' he asked me in confidence, and looked rather glum when I remarked that, in my opinion, a man's days of peace are over when he has married two wives simultaneously.

Everyone joined in bearing with my pretty friend in the old house, listening to her outbursts with compassion, as to a regrettable but natural disease – a sad episode to be expected in woman's life of sorrow in this world. But when she became too violent in her remarks, her father, a mild old man who sat in a corner over his long pipe, would pull her up, reminding her that she had nothing out of the way to complain about, for the general opinion naturally gave Aziz a perfect right to a second wife if he wanted one. At such times, the only comfort one could think of was a mention of the little son, Muhammad, whom she embraced with passionate sobs, to which he submitted with an air of bored masculine condescension, remarkable and alarming in one so young.

Muhammad, at the age of eight, was just engaged to a little playmate of five, a red-haired, blue-eyed minx whom everyone spoiled, and who made the most of her short years of sovereignty as if she knew how transitory they were. Little Muhammad enjoyed the mention of his *namzadeh* (his bethrothed) and took great pride in her, and it was pretty to see the two children playing together, growing up in the village freedom which Persian townswomen might envy.

The next day was that of the triple wedding, and the village was already buzzing with it by the time I got up.

A visit to the bride was the first ceremony. My hostess arranged a tray for me, with nuts, raisins, *nuhud* (dried peas), and a cone of sugar in the middle, to be borne ahead of us as an offering when we went to call. We followed, in our best: my hostess in a very starched chintz ballet skirt over black trousers, a yellow damask shirt, striped velvet waistcoat, and white lace coif fastened under the chin with a dangling ornament of cowrie shells. She had four bracelets and an amber necklace with silver coins, turquoises, and many little odds and ends attached to it: an amulet was fastened on her right arm. Her mother-in-law was even gayer, with a yellow silk shirt, green waistcoat with gold buttons, and one white kerchief with a red one above it tied into a point over the forehead.

We climbed up among houses till we came into a room crowded with women, in a confused twilight lighted from the middle of the ceiling by a small round hole. The dower chest was being filled: an affair of gilt and coloured tin with three locks, and all the ladies were helping with the packing. The whole female part of the village was passing in and out, bearing gifts, looking over the bride's trousseau, rushing into an inner room to give a hand with the *pilau*, and talking in high excited voices.

In one corner, apart from it all and completely hidden under a pale blue *chadur*, or veil, stood the bride. She stands motionless for hour after hour, while the stream of guests goes by, unable to sit down unless the chief guest asks her to do so, and taking no part in the general gaiety. I went up and lifted the veil to greet her, and was horrified to see large tears rolling down her painted cheeks. The palms of her hands and her finger-nails were dyed with henna; her hair was crimped with cheep green celluloid combs stuck into it: she wore a pink machine-embroidered shirt in atrocious taste, and a green velvet waistcoat brought specially from Qazvin; and all this splendour, covered away under the blue *chadur*, was weeping with fright and fatigue, thinking who knows what thoughts while it stood there like a veiled image at the feast. She was not to appear in public again for twenty-one days after the wedding, they told me.

The male relatives of the bride sat round the guest room floor in a quieter and more dignified manner. They were being provided with food, and I was soon taken in to join them and given bowls of soup covered with saffron, with pieces of chicken floating about in it. When this was cleared away, and when the women had also eaten in their noisier part of the establishment, we began to enjoy ourselves. Two copper trays were brought to use as drums; the bride's aunt, a lady with as many chains and bangles as an Indian idol, sat cross-legged to beat the time, and one after another the women danced to the clapping of hands. They held up a handkerchief which, at intervals, they threw to one or another of the company, who would wrap it round a piece of silver and toss it back. They danced with remarkable abandon, cracking their finger-joints and leaping into the air with both feet close together.

In the corner the bride still stood, her face completely hidden. But it was soon time for her to start: already various messengers had come to say that the young men were on their way. The friends of the bridegroom would come to fetch her: they would be repulsed three or four times, to show that there was no indecent eagerness about the affair: but finally they would succeed and escort her to the new home.

When we stepped out into the village, the young men were already galloping wildly up and down. Their mules, delighted to have no packs on their backs, and very gay under household carpets that covered them, were kicking their heels and tearing up and down the narrow beehive streets.

Two weddings were now in progress. The bride from Pichiban was expected at any moment. She had a three hours' ride down the precipitous track from Salambar to negotiate under her *chadur*. She was coming: a beating of wooden sticks and drums announced her; '*Chub chini ham Iaria. Chub chini ham Iaria[3],*' the boys cried, dancing round her. A vague and helpless look of discomfort made itself felt from under the *chadur* which hid the lady on her mule, all except her elastic-sided boots. Two uncles, one on each side, kept her steady on the extremely bumpy path. So, in complete blindness, the modest female is expected to venture into matrimony. The village seethed around, waiting. The lady approached, riding her mule like a galleon in a labouring sea. At a few yards from the door she was lifted down: a lighted candle was put into either hand: in front of her on trays they carried her mirror, her Quran (Koran) and corn and coloured rice in little saucers, with lighted candles: these were all borne into her new home, but she herself paused on the threshold with her two lights held up in white cotton-gloved hands; and her bridegroom from the roof above took small coins and corn and coloured rice, and flung it all over her as she stood. The little boys of Garmrud were on the look out: a great scrum ensued for the pennies: the bride, unable to see what was going on and with the responsibility of the candles, which must not blow out, in her hands, swayed about, pushed hither and thither, and only sustained by the buttressing uncles: it is as well to have relatives at such moments.

With a great heave the threshold was transcended: in the shelter of her new home the lady unveiled, while the bridegroom, paying her not the slightest attention now he had got her, devoted himself to our reception.

The bridegroom also has to stand at the end of the room till one

[3] The meaning of this is not clear.

of the guests takes pity on him, and asks him to sit down. The young man, however - he was just fifteen – bore it with more cheerfulness than his fiancée. His new boots and orange tie – for he was dressed up as a *ferangi* in honour of the occasion – were sufficiently glorious in themselves to make up for any other discomforts of matrimony. We had more dancing and a village idiot to come and tie himself into knots on the floor for our amusement; a revolting spectacle. And then, leaving the Pichiban bride to settle into her new house, we returned to our own show, which was just now reaching the dramatic moment of the meeting between bride and groom at the outskirts of the village.

After three or four attempts, and as many gallops up and down the open space by the torrent, the young men of her family had induced the bride to leave the shelter of the paternal home. Accompanied by seven female friends the little procession encircled the village and was now coming back to it across the cornfields on the west. The bridegroom, climbing his roof, saw his bride in the distance, flung himself on to his mule, and with his friends behind him dashed to meet her. The two little cavalcades came together just where the valley slopes down into a peaceful distance of trees and river and figures threshing their harvests far away: against this background, the gay dresses of the little crowd, the coloured rugs on the mules' backs, the blue veiled figure of the bride on her steed, looked right and significant, an old ceremonial that expressed the meaning of life here where it is still so simply lived.

The bride and groom now parted again after the meeting, and came to his house by separate ways. The dower chest was brought staggering after, and various treasures such as lamps and *samovars* carried separately on peoples' heads. From the flat roofs under the cliff wall that closes in Garmrud from north and east, the bride's new neighbours gathered to welcome her, and joined in the *Hymen io-Hymenee*,[4] or its Persian equivalent. Here she came to live her new life – to be a part of the village in a sense which we who make so much to do over the community and our share in it – but can leave it whenever we wish – may hardly conceive.

[4] A marriage song of the Ancient Greeks.

The village in these remote mountains is the one unit by which all else is measured, the censor from whom no one who belongs to it will ever escape. It is the focus for all loyalty, the standard for all judgement. You are happy or unhappy, according to what the village thinks of you: and even your virtue is practised chiefly because the village expects it. A week or two later I came to one of these little communities and enquired for some potatoes; the man I asked shrugged his shoulders.

'We do not grow potatoes,' said he. He pointed to the next group of houses, scarce a mile away. 'They grow them there,' he added: 'but our village has never grown them. It is not our custom.'

In face of this innate conservative instinct of the human animal, the force that yet makes us do new things in spite of all is very amazing, an energy for exploration whose power must truly be incalculable when we consider what a mass of inertia it is always attacking. And let us not think too strangely of the village where potatoes were not grown. Any civilized British community would provide half a dozen things and more that are either 'done' or 'not done' with just so small a show of reason.

From *The Valleys of the Assassins and Other Persian Travels*
by Freya Stark

Architectural Glories of Isfahan

Nobody has written about Persian architecture with such passion and insight as the art historian and travel writer, Robert Byron (1905–1941), who made a journey through Persia and Afghanistan in 1933 and 1934, in the company of another writer, Christopher Sykes. The book he wrote as a result, The Road to Oxiana, *has become one of the great classics of travel literature. What initially excited him most in Persia was the medieval Islamic architecture, and he tended to be scornful of the colourful Safavid architecture of the seventeenth century, so beloved of those he dismissively referred to as 'the Omar Khayam fiends.' That is, until he saw the Safavid capital of Isfahan, and found himself overwhelmed by the beauty of two contrasting buildings - the medieval Friday Mosque and the Safavid Mosque of Sheikh Lutfullah.*

Isfahan, March 18th. – The beauty of Isfahan steals on the mind unawares. You drive about, under avenues of white tree-trunks and canopies of shining twigs; past domes of turquoise and spring yellow in a sky of liquid violet-blue; along the river patched with twisting shoals, catching that blue in its muddy silver, and lined with feathery groves where the sap calls; across bridges of pale toffee brick, tier on tier of arches breaking into piled pavilions; overlooked by lilac mountains, by the Kuh-i-Sufi (the Sufi Mountain) shaped like Punch's hump and by other ranges receding to a line of snowy surf; and before you know how, Isfahan has become indelible, has insinuated its image into that gallery of places which everyone privately treasures.

I gave it no help in doing so. The monuments have kept me too busy.

One could explore for months without coming to the end of them. From the eleventh century, architects and craftsmen have recorded the fortunes of the town, its changes of taste, government, and belief. The buildings reflect these local circumstances; it is their charm, the charm of most old towns. But a few illustrate the heights of art independently, and rank Isfahan among those rarer places, like Athens or Rome, which are the common refreshment of humanity.

The two dome-chambers of the Friday Mosque point this distinction by their difference. Both were built about the same time, at the end of the eleventh century. In the larger, which is the main sanctuary of the mosque, twelve massive piers engage in a Promethean struggle with the weight of the dome. The struggle in fact obscures the victory: to perceive the latter demands a previous interest in mediaeval engineering or the character of the Seljuks. Contrast this with the smaller chamber, which is really a tomb-tower incorporated in the mosque. The inside is roughly thirty feet square and sixty high; its volume is perhaps one-third of the other's. But while the larger lacked the experience necessary to its scale, the smaller embodies that precious moment between too little experience and too much, when the elements of construction have been refined of superfluous bulk, yet still withstand the allurements of superfluous grace; so that each element, like the muscles of a trained athlete, performs its function with winged precision, not concealing its effort, as over-refinement will do, but adjusting it to the highest degree of intellectual meaning. This is the perfection of architecture, attained not so much by the form of the elements – for this is a matter of convention – but by their chivalry of balance and proportion. And this small interior comes nearer to that perfection than I would have thought possible outside classical Europe.

The very material is a signal of economy: hard small bricks of mousy grey, which swallow up the ornament of Kufic[5] texts and stucco inlay in their puritan singleness of purpose. In skeleton, the chamber is a system of arches, one broad in the middle of each wall, two narrow beside each corner, four miniatures in each squinch, eight in the squinch zone, and sixteen above the squinches to receive the dome. The invention of Firuzabad[6] has expanded; and will expand much further before Persian architecture dies in the seventeenth century. Here we catch it in the prime of youth and vigour. Even at this stage, the system is repeated or varied in many other buildings: the tomb-tower at Maragha[7] for instance. But I doubt if there is another building in Persia, or in the whole of Islam, which offers so tense, so immediate an apparition of pure cubic form.

According to the inscription around the dome, the tomb-tower was built by Abul Ghanaim Marzuban, the minister of Malek Shah,[8] in 1088. One wonders what circumstance at that moment induced such a flight of genius. Was it the action of a new mind from Central Asia on the old civilization of the plateau, a procreation by nomadic energy out of Persian aestheticism? The Seljuks were not the only conquerors of Persia to have this effect. The Ghaznavid dynasty before them, the Mongol and Timurid dynasties after them, all came from

[5] The oldest form of Arabic calligraphy, characterised by the use of straight lines and angles. It is named after the city of Kufa in Iraq.
[6] The site of a Sasanid palace, 110 kilometres south of Shiraz. It has the earliest known example of the squinch, a specially constructed support which made it possible to place a round dome on a square or rectangular base.
[7] In north-west Persia, near the south-east corner of Lake Orumiyeh.
[8] Saljuq Sultan (reigned 1072-1092).

north of the Oxus, and each produced a new Renaissance on Persian soil. Even the Safavids, who inspired the last and most languid phase of Persian art, were Turks[9] originally.

It was this last phase which gave Isfahan the character it has today, and which produced, curiously enough, its other great masterpiece. In 1612, Shah Abbas was occupied with the Royal Mosque at the southwest end of the Maidan, whose huge blue bulk and huge acreage of coarse floral tilework form just that kind of 'oriental scenery' so dear to Omar Khayam fiends – pretty, if you like, even magnificent, but not important in the general scale of things. In 1618, however, he built another mosque on the southeast side of the Maidan, which was called after his father-in-law Sheikh Lutfullah.

This building stands at the opposite pole of architectural virtue to the small dome-chamber in the Friday Mosque. The latter is remarkable because, apart from its unique merit, that merit is of a kind which most people have regarded as the exclusive property of the European mind. The Mosque of Sheikh Lutfullah is Persian in the fabulous sense: the Omar Khayam brigade, to whom rational form is as much anathema as rational action, can wallow in it to their hearts' content. For while the dome-chamber is form only, has no colour, and obliterates its ornament by the intentness of its construction, the Mosque of Sheikh Lutfullah hides any symptom of construction or dynamic form beneath a mirage of shallow curved surfaces, the multitudinous offspring of the original squinch. Form there is and must be; but how it is created, and what supports it, are questions of which the casual eye is unconscious, as it is meant to be, lest its attention should wander from the pageant of colour and pattern. Colour and pattern are a commonplace in Persian architecture. But here they have a quality which must astonish the European, not because they infringe what he thought was his monopoly, but because he can previously have had no idea that abstract pattern was capable of so profound a splendour.

As though to announce these principles as soon as possible, the outside of the mosque is careless of symmetry to a grotesque degree.

---

[9] Although the main supporters of the Safavids were Turkoman tribesmen, they themselves were almost certainly of Kurdish origin.

Only the dome and portal are seen from the front. But owing to the discrepancy between the axis of the mosque and that of the Ali Gapu[10] opposite, the portal, instead of being immediately under the dome, is set slightly to one side of it. Yet such is the character of the dome, so unlike is it to any other dome in Persia or elsewhere, that this deformity is hardly noticeable. Round a flattened hemisphere made of tiny bricks and covered with prawn-coloured wash runs a bold branching rose-tree inlaid in black and white. Seen from close to, the design has a hint of William Morris, particularly in its thorns; but as a whole it is more formal than pre-Raphaelite, more comparable to the design of a Genoese brocade immensely magnified. Here and there, at the junction of the branches or in the depths of the foliage, ornaments of ochre and dark blue mitigate the harshness of the black and white tracery, and bring it into harmony with the soft golden pink of the background: a process which is continued by a pervading under-foliage of faint light blue. But the genius of the effect is in the play of surfaces. The inlay is glazed. The stucco wash is not. Thus the sun strikes the dome with a broken highlight, whose intermittent flash, moving with the time of day, adds a third texture to the pattern, mobile and unforeseen.

If the outside is lyric, the inside is Augustan. Here a still shallower dome, about seventy feet in diameter, swims above a ring of sixteen windows. From the floor to the base of the windows rise eight main arches, four enclosing right-angles, four flat wall-space, so that the boundaries of the floor form a square. The space between the tops of the arches is occupied by eight pendentives divided into planes like a bat's wing.

The dome is inset with a network of lemon-shaped compartments, which increase in size as they descend from a formalised peacock at the apex and are surrounded by plain bricks; each is filled with a foliage pattern inlaid on plain stucco. The walls, bordered by broad white inscriptions on dark blue, are similarly inlaid with twirling arabesques or baroque squares on deep ochre stucco. The colours of all this inlay are dark blue, light greenish blue, and a tint of indefinite wealth like wine. Each arch is framed in turquoise corkscrews. The

[10] This is the Ali Qapu palace described by Herbert in Chapter 3.

mihrab[11] in the west wall is enamelled with tiny flowers on a deep blue meadow.

Each part of the design, each plane, each repetition, each separate branch or blossom has its own sombre beauty. But the beauty of the whole comes as you move. Again, the highlights are broken by the play of glazed and unglazed surfaces; so that with every step they rearrange themselves in countless shining patterns; while even the pattern of light through the thick window traceries is inconstant, owing to outer traceries which are several feet away and double the variety of each varying silhouette.

I have never encountered splendour of this kind before. Other interiors came into my mind as I stood there, to compare it with: Versailles, or the porcelain rooms at Schönbrunn, or the Doge's Palace, or St Peter's. All are rich; but none so rich. Their richness is three-dimensional; it is attended by all the effort of shadow. In the mosque of Sheikh Lutfullah, it is a richness of light and surface, of pattern and colour only. The architectural form is unimportant. It is not smothered, as in rococo; it is simply the instrument of a spectacle, as earth is the instrument of a garden. And then I suddenly thought of that unfortunate species, modern interior decorators, who imagine they can make a restaurant, or a cinema, or a plutocrat's drawing-room look rich if giving money enough for gold leaf and looking-glass. They little know what amateurs they are. Nor, alas, do their clients.

From *The Road to Oxiana*
by Robert Byron

A Tehran Childhood

Fifty years ago Tehran was a much smaller and more intimate city than it is today. The social and cultural atmosphere of that time is recalled in an enchanting memoir by Shusha Guppy, who has gone on to achieve distinction as a singer, a songwriter and an author. In this

[11] An ornamented niche in the wall of a mosque which shows worshippers the direction of Mecca for prayers.

excerpt from her memoir of those early years, The Blindfold Horse,
*she describes the neighbourhood where she grew up as well as some of
her neighbours, one or two of whom had become addicted to opium.
She brings them all wonderfully to life.*

Our neighbourhood was a typical Persian town in miniature. It
had a high street and a *bazaarcheh* – a tiny covered bazaar lined
with shops – a bakery, a butcher's, a grocery and greengrocery,
and a cooked-food shop which sold hot beetroots and porridge in
winter, ice-cream and soft drinks in summer, and kebabs all year
round. There was a little mosque at the entrance of the
bazaarcheh and a *hammam* a few yards further in. It even had a
caravanserai – a large courtyard surrounded with rooms which
provided temporary accommodation for country people who
came to town in search of work; for the rush to the city had
already begun, long before the petrol boom of the 1960s and
1970s, when it gathered catastrophic speed and dimensions. The
caravanserai was a kind of job centre for navvies and unskilled
workers of all sorts, male and female. Many of its lodgers moved
on after a short period for better, permanent homes near steady
employments, others stayed for years and years, hoping that
something would soon turn up.

The population of our district ranged over the whole social
spectrum: shopkeepers lived above or behind their shops,
workmen in the caravanserai or in shared homes, civil servants
and teachers in small modern houses, and patrician families in
large old houses with expansive gardens. But although people's
social positions varied, there was a sense of community and of
everyone performing his or her function within a structure that
transcended class stratification. It was much later that the oil
boom and new industries created a wealthy bourgeoisie and a
new ruling class, whose members began to build themselves
grand villas in new residential suburbs in the foothills north of
the city: ghettoes of the rich and powerful, out of contact with the
lives of ordinary people and without any community feeling,
which became the first scenes of looting and carnage in 1979.

Among our immediate neighbours were some friends of my

parents: a couple of Qajar princes, a university professor or two, a cabinet minister, some high-ranking civil servants and diplomats, an army general, etc. In the following decades, every one of these moved away, until in the end there were three old houses left, of which ours was one. It was a corner house at the junction of two streets. On the opposite corner lived Professor Bahram and his wife, in a large house with a very long garden. The Bahrams came from Kerman, a city in southeast Persia famous for its rugs of which many fine specimens adorned their home, and spoke with a delicious regional accent. Like many of the university's dons, Professor Bahram had started life as a mullah. He had studied in a traditional *madrasah*, where he had specialised in Arabic grammar and literature, and had worn the traditional cloak-and-turban clerical costume. But, in 1930 when Reza Shah decreed that Western clothes – suit, tie, and trilby – were *de rigeur* for all government employees including university staff, Professor Bahram had changed and defrocked himself like everyone else. My father was the only professor to be allowed, by a special dispensation from the Shah, to keep his costume.

Every morning, at eight o'clock punctually you heard the front door of Professor Bahram's house open and shut, and if you looked out of the window you saw him leave for the university: a tiny, trim figure in a dark suit, with a trilby, and in winter a black overcoat. He wore horn-rimmed glasses and carried an elegant ivory-topped walking-stick on his arm. He walked briskly, with short rapid steps, and never lifted his eyes from the ground in front of him. Occasionally he would touch his hat and bow slightly to acknowledge a passer-by's greetings.

The Bahrams had three sons, all of whom were studying in France at the time and were to return home several years later. Mrs Bahram missed them terribly and talked about them constantly - how clever and handsome they were, how well they were doing, what greatness they would surely achieve:

'Well this is a modern world and one has to bring up one's children accordingly,' she would sigh, 'Nowadays if you don't have a degree from a foreign university you have no hope of advancing in the world.'

When their sons were about to return to Persia, the Bahram's cut some trees at the end of their garden and had a modern bungalow built for their eldest to live in. They would have done better to keep the trees, for the ambitious young men married heiresses and moved up town as soon as they could. Mrs Bahram wanted one of them to marry my sister, but when she discovered that, contrary to appearances, my sister had no 'settlement', she gave up the idea and managed to find other brides who had.

I liked old Mrs Bahram who made delicious Kermani cakes and pastries and always gave me some when I visited her. On school holidays, I would sometimes knock on the door and go in to see her and listen to her tales about her sons in Europe. She described Paris in detail, as if she had been there, exaggerating its magnificent amenities to magical proportions. Her tales fired my own imagination and I dreamed about Paris as if it were the promised land. I could see myself sitting on a bench in the Jardin du Luxembourg, like Cosette in *Les Misérables*, or going for walks by the Seine in the company of a beautiful young man. I was about 10 or 11 then, and the likelihood of my going to Paris was as remote as my flying to the moon, yet I dreamed on.

One day, Mrs Bahram acquired a dog, Snowy, a pretty fluffy little white puppy which looked like a snowball as it ran around the garden yapping furiously as if pursued by a pack of wolves.

The acquisition of a dog was an unusual event, for although the Bahrams had adopted modern ways and sent their sons to Europe, they were still devout Muslims, and dogs are considered *najis* (impure) in Islam, allowed only as guards and sheepdogs, never as pets. The notion of keeping a dog purely for pleasure was a Western one, which over the years became a symbol of freedom from old-fashioned prohibitions.

In Persian folk-songs and tales, 'man's best friend' is not his dog but his horse, whose loyalty and affection is expressed in stories about great warrior heroes and saints, and sometimes contradicted:

They say that a man's best friend is his horse,
But I say it's his gun,
For where would a horseman be without a gun?

I had a silver-barrelled gun which I sold
To buy a gown of golden brocade for my Beloved
 But she refused it, and now I have lost my gun
And I have lost my heart...

So goes a folk-song from the tribal South.

Snowy had a wicked bite and tried it on the postman and the dustman, who had to be silenced with hefty tips, and thereafter she had to be chained to her kennel and let loose only at night, and when no visitors were expected. Mrs Bahram 'put a religious hat' on her dog-keeping by saying that Snowy was indeed a guardian, and a good one at that – you could ask the postman and the dustman if you didn't believe her! The religious interdict was based on health grounds – fear of rabies and other germ-induced diseases – but it was not a licence for cruelty. Yet in practice it was sometimes used as such. There were plenty of stray dogs roaming in the streets looking for food, or scavenging on garbage tips. They attacked wayward cats and fought with each other – more from hunger than malice – and were often found dead in wastelands, their putrefying mutilated corpses covered with flies and insects. Sometimes they would follow passers-by at a respectful distance to their doorsteps, hoping for food and shelter, only to be disappointed when doors were slammed shut. They were tormented and teased by street urchins who outnumbered them and were not that much better off themselves. People chased away stray dogs with stones which occasionally hit a spindly leg and cracked it. A howl of anguish would ensue, followed by pitiful yapping, and the poor animal would limp away on three legs for days, holding up the injured limb like a finger pointed at human cruelty. Things changed gradually over the years. Stray dogs disappeared or were collected by the municipality when the city became more affluent – at least in residential areas – and quite a few people adopted mongrels as pets.

Snowy was highly pampered, regularly washed and combed, and adorned with a red ribbon. It provoked one of Aunt Ashraf's philosophical extrapolations:

'Even animals are divided into two categories – the lucky and the unlucky. Look at Snowy, eating the best meat, living in a clean

327

house, with his custom-made kennel; and look at a stray dog, born on a rubbish dump, hungry and kicked all its miserable life, paying for each morsel of food with humiliation and misery... Yes, even for animals, it's all written here...' And she ran her index finger over her forehead to show the exact location of fate's inexorable inscription.

Opposite the Bahrams lived the family of a well-known poet and landowner, Mr Javadi. He had three daughters, all clever and pretty, especially the eldest, Jaleh, who was a couple of years older than me but went to the same school and became my friend. Soon after the Javadis moved to our neighbourhood, Jaleh invited me to their house for tea, to meet her parents. Her mother was a tall, handsome woman, with reddish-brown wavy hair and beautiful sad eyes. But her father seemed prematurely aged: he was unusually thin and stooping; his skin was very dark, his cheeks sunken, and his eyes surrounded with a bluish shadow. Above all, his lips were black, and when he smiled his teeth were stained and unhealthy looking. Altogether, a gaunt, sickly man, but elegantly dressed and courteous. When he spoke, his voice was tremulous and had a nasal twang.

There was a peculiar smell in the house – a mixture of honey, charcoal and burnt flesh, sweet and sickly at once. Soon after tea, Mr Javadi disappeared, and presently the funny odour intensified.

'Let's go and play in your house now', Jaleh suggested and, before I could say anything, ushered me out of the house. I felt something was amiss but did not know what it was.

Eventually it transpired that the peculiar smell of the house was that of opium, and that Mr Javadi's appearance and nasal speech were tell-tale signs of his 'habit'. Mrs Javadi had hoped to keep it a secret in the neighbourhood, but soon everyone knew. One day, she called on my mother to make friends and after a while told us the story: her husband had inherited a vast estate in the north, with rice-fields, orange groves and woodlands. He was a young poet, handsome and rich, and much sought after by young girls - or rather their parents - but had chosen her:

'I was 17, and he 21. At first, all went well, but then he kept going out in the evenings and coming back looking tired and sleepy. One day I found a box of opium in his pocket and confronted him with it – he had to confess that he was an addict. But by then I was pregnant and there was nothing I could do.'

She had cried and made scenes and threatened suicide; she had even fled to her family for a while, but he had persuaded her to go back to him, promising to kick the habit. He never had. In the end, she had said to him:

'Alright, you needn't go out, you can smoke at home.'

I later discovered that this was the usual scenario: secret smoking followed by discovery and resignation on the part of relatives. Lower-class addicts ended up in dingy opium dens; the wealthy ones abdicated their responsibilities to other members of their families and lived to smoke. By the time they moved to our neighbourhood, Mr Javadi was on nearly one 'stick' a day, which is a great deal of opium, considering that each pipe used only a tiny piece, the size of half a finger-nail. He went out in the morning and occasionally in the early evenings, but the rest of the time he was reclining on a mattress, propped up against pillows, smoking. His visitors sat around him and his children went in and out of the room without taking any notice of what he was doing.

He would cut a little piece from the cigarette-shaped opium stick and press it to the round china bowl of his pipe beneath a little hole, then take an ember from the brazier with a pair of brass tongs, hold it over the opium and blow. The ember would glow red and the opium sizzle, and he would inhale the smoke in long, hissing draughts. When the piece of opium had burnt out he would rub the ember on the bowl to clean away the debris, poke the hole with a brass pin, and repeat the motions. After a few times he would lie back, close his eyes and enjoy the 'high'. If there were other smokers among his guests, he would pass the pipe round to them. When they were all 'high', they recited their poetry and drank wine accompanied by Mrs Javadi's delicious mezes.

For years now, Mr Javadi had done nothing but smoke and write poetry. His wife ran his estate, or what was left of it, and they lived off the proceeds. One day, I told my mother that Mr Javadi had guests and how several of them smoked opium and drank wine. She was horrified that I had witnessed such a scene and forbade me ever to go there again. But Jaleh and I walked home from school and she sometimes came and played with me, or we did our homework together, while Mrs Javadi visited my mother regularly 'to open her chest and empty her heart'.

Mr Javadi lived to a ripe old age, as smoked as a kipper. He left a couple of volumes of good lyrical poetry in classical style. Jaleh became a poet and lady of letters, and married another literary figure. I lost touch with them after a while, but that early experience of addiction produced a lasting horror of any form of dependence, indeed of anything that curtails human freedom and sovereignty, that is with me to this day. I saw how opium had destroyed Mr Javadi's will-power and made him a slave to his pipe. He was a good poet, a decent man and a fond father, but he had lost control over his life. I thought it a calamity and resolved that I would not allow anything like that ever to happen to me.

From *The Blindfold Horse: Memories*
of a Persian Childhood by Shusha Guppy

A Legend of the Qanats

Anthony Smith was an Oxford University undergraduate when he went out to Persia during the summer vacation of 1950 to investigate the report that there were blind white fish in the underground water channels, known as qanats, *which brought water from the foothills of the mountains to villages on the parched plains. Accompanied by three other Oxford undergraduates – Philip Beckett, Eric Gordon and Louis Armstrong – he spent two months exploring the* qanats *in villages near the town of Kirman in south central Persia. His companions meanwhile investigated the local flora and the village economy. The book Anthony Smith wrote of their experiences,* Blind White Fish in Persia *focuses on the* qanats, *but also provides a fascinating picture of the way of life and the attitudes of the villagers and others they lived among or came into contact with. Here he describes being shown the* qanat *system in the first village they spent time in – the village of Jupar, thirty miles south of Kirman.*

On the evening of the first day we were taken on a tour of inspection of Jupar. About fifty people decided to be our guides; any wish of ours was immediately granted and the more wishes we uttered the greater was the satisfaction of our hosts. A motley procession wandered around the village. It drifted into the mosque and then down below the ground to see the grinding of the corn. I was shown the fishes in the *qanat* and told that one day a year the largest fish wore a golden crown which it borrows from the treasure that lies at the head of every *qanat*. I was told that for five days in every twenty-one the outflow of water is less and that this is caused by the breathing of the mountains. They said that hedgehogs lived on sunlight and that crocodiles lived in the desert, that the porcupine was immortal and that fish only live on their eggs. It was obviously a night for credulity; I looked up at the stars and they all winked back at me. Finally, the whole gathering climbed up a little hill that appears suddenly on one side of Jupar. Although it is only one hundred foot high, it dominates the village and the surrounding desert. There we all sat upon the ground with the two of us in a place where everyone could see us. The sun had set and all the earth was blue. Lamps were beginning to appear in the village and people were sitting outside enjoying the warmth of the evening. The dome of the mosque was black against the sky. The trees waved silently. A car was being driven along the India road.

An interpreter had been found and an old man told us of the history of Jupar. 'Many years ago there was no Jupar in the whole world,' he began; and my eyes looked over the land. 'One of the soldiers guarding the road to India, in that fort, thought that there would be water near this place. Many people believed this, because at one time there was a small stream in the summer time. They used to call it *Ja-i-parsal*, 'the place of last year'; but they changed the name to Jupar. The soldier, who was a poor man, managed to persuade a rich man to build a *qanat*. That *qanat* is still flowing and still gives water; but the fort fell down many years ago.' I looked at the ruins of the fort which only just stood out on the horizon; so much time had passed since that fort had guarded the trade route from India, the route of Alexander, and the way witnessed at

Kirman by Marco Polo. 'This rich man called it the *Gauhariz qanat*, the *qanat* of flowing jewels.' He pointed towards it and we all turned to look in that direction although, being dark, there was nothing to be seen except the peaks of Kuh-i-Jupar. By this time all the light had gone from the sky and it was the hour for everybody to eat; the assembly stumbled down to the village. Then Louis and I bade good night to our guides: it is a slow business shaking hands with fifty people.

I wished to be shown around the *qanat* system of Jupar. If I was to do any work in the *qanats*, it was primarily necessary to find out just what their internal aspect was like. The bailiff presented me with a *muqanni*.[12] I collected Abu Ali, a boy of twelve or so with a great character and a few words of English. He brought with him his brother-in-law, a medical student called Mahmud, who talked incessantly and someone else whose name I never learnt. Leaving our shoes at the entrance, we stepped into the water and into the *qanat*. At the beginning it was about six feet wide and six feet high, with the water reaching up to our knees. Abu Ali began chanting eerily and got great satisfaction from the echoes. Mahmud continued to talk; he said that he knew English only from text-books but, which was true, knew nothing of its pronunciation. He constantly asked for medical sentences so that he could puzzle out what they meant: he was apparently oblivious of his environment. I, very definitely, was not. Sometimes the roof was less than four feet high, in other places it was many yards above. Occasionally there were great caverns where many roof falls had occurred and also, as a relief, would come the light from one of the shafts to the surface. There are many reasons for the irregularities: a blockage may have necessitated a new detour, the thin portions might have been an attempt at economy; the deep parts are proof of the everlasting search for more water when its level in the channel begins to drop. So, sometimes scraping our shoulders, sometimes bumping our heads and always stubbing our toes, this small party waded on towards the source. Abu Ali continued to chant, Mahmud to talk;

[12] A *muqanni* is someone whose job it is to go down into the *qanats* to clear any blockages or carry out any necessary repairs.

and only by their efforts were we not enveloped by the silence which threatened all the while to close in on us.

A *muqanni* leads a risky life and may meet his death in one of many ways: he may slip when climbing down the well, he may be concussed by a stone that is dislodged above him or be crushed by an ordinary roof collapse. He is likely to be asphyxiated in the deeper wells, as there is little circulation of air; he may be poisoned by gases that occasionally seep into a *qanat* or be bitten by one of the snakes which has fallen into the water and has not been able to climb out again. Also, many cases of drowning occur in a *qanat*: a blockage may have occurred below a *muqanni*, in which case the water will accumulate on his side; or, if he is clearing such a blockage from the lower side, then the sudden onrush of liberated water is quite capable of drowning him. This all results in making him a very superstitious man: a bad dream or a sneeze occurring within his family is considered sufficient warning of danger and he will not go down any *qanat* that day. No *qanat* owner will force him to or deny him his wage: there is reason why the *qanats* are often called 'the murderers'.

Gauhariz qanat has many branches flowing down to its single exit. Every now and then we would come to a junction; sometimes one of the channels would be dry but more often they contained water. Whichever it was Abu Ali would shout up it and listen to the tubular noise which it produced: Mahmud would take this opportunity to demand another sentence from me. I started writing down which route we had taken but the *muqanni* saw my map and protested. '*Lazim nist*,' he said, 'it is not necessary.' And then followed one of the most confident assertions that I have ever heard. It seems that if you are lost and on dry land, then you should walk until you find water; if you have a lamp, then see which way the water is flowing and follow it; if you have no lamp (and are not suffering from paroxysms of fear) walk in the water until the light from a well shaft appears; even if it is night there will be stars at the top of the shaft. He finished the formula at that point with the presumption that a well shaft many metres deep presented no difficulty: I continued with my map, but surreptitiously.

As no branch of *Gauhariz* stretched for more than three miles it was after a couple of hours that we reached the end. There was no well from this point to the surface; only 150 ft. of desert. The channel was far narrower than it had been all the way along; we crouched on our haunches and got in each other's way: it was not a pleasant spot down there. I flicked my torch about but the beam rested either on solid wall and roof or the muddy water and ourselves. Abu Ali had stopped singing, Mahmud had stooped asking questions, the other friend and the *muqanni* were even quieter; I think we were all subdued by the place; it was not a situation for arrogance of any sort. I asked Mahmud what claustrophobia meant and crawled away backwards the way we had come.

For most of that day we plunged about in those *qanats*: always it was exhausting and usually it was cold; but certain channels felt quite warm. It was possible to float down them, either face downwards or upwards; you would then push yourself along from the bottom or the roof. It was possible if an occasional submerged and jagged rock was not a deterrent: the fish would bump into you whichever way up you were; the bumpings and their numbers increased as we neared the exit. It was good to get out into the open again, to lie in the heat of the sun, and to see nothing but the sky above you. Some goats were regarding with disdain the foully muddy water which was now exuding from the *qanat*; we looked sympathetic, collected our shoes and went off to eat some food.

I had now discovered that fish did live in the *qanats* and in large numbers, but they were neither white nor blind. The Persians still said that they got there automatically; this view did not seem particularly tenable in the modern scientific world. I was told that they lived on water, they ate air or simply that they ate all their eggs, leaving only a few to propagate the race; they said that there was no food problem for not one of the fish ever died. Everybody denied that anybody had put them there and all agreed that there was no point in doing a thing if nothing was to be gained from it. It is true that no one ever ate them, yet there they were in all but the saltiest *qanats*. The only natural and stream-like parts of the *qanat* occurred at the exit; here, with *Gauhariz*, the water ran for a short distance before being divided according to the ownership laws and flowing into the highest gardens of the village. The laws are complex for the *qanat* owners but the complexity does ensure that today's owner receives the money due to him, either because an ancestor of his built the *qanat*, or because some other relative of his had craftily arranged a marriage so that neither he, nor his descendants, should ever be short of water and money. The water flows into the first and highest garden. The owner of a garden pays for water according to the size of his garden; for it is assumed that he will take all the water necessary to irrigate every square inch of that garden. However, so far as the fish are concerned the stream is too polluted a dwelling place just as soon as it flows through the hole in the wall: no fish were seen to penetrate very far into a Persian garden. Therefore the fish, and there were many hundreds of them in *Gauhariz*, have only a short natural stretch which is bounded on one side by darkness and on the other by pollution.

The stream flows on through the village, sometimes dividing and occasionally being joined again. A division may be made to flow over one of its previous branches or out into the street to serve as a public washing place. These deviations are all resultant of deaths and marriages in the past and all culminate in producing the simplest distribution of infection known to man; down they flow with the streams becoming smaller, dirtier and more insanitary; down to the poor part of the town, until finally the streams are no more: the clear stream of the *qanat* of the flowing jewels is then not even a muddy trickle. That part of the village is poor and squalid, for the flow of water cannot be relied upon; perhaps at one time the *qanat* output was bigger, perhaps optimism about its future was larger or faith in the merciful bounty of Allah greater; whichever it was that caused those houses and gardens to be built they are always there and always crumbling away. Somewhere before the end of the village, and long before the decrepit area, a reservoir for water is made; into this the water flows at night, for little irrigation goes on during that time. This practice ensures that no water flows right out of the village; it damps whatever hopes there may still be in the hearts of the decrepit ones and provides a breeding place for mosquitoes, the like of which they could never find elsewhere.

This stream is the life of the village; without it the village would be as dust. Although mainly used for irrigation it also provides all the drinking water; and the first duty of a Persian's day is to go and collect this water from the mouth of the *qanat* before too many other Persians have paddled in it or the animals have come down to drink from it. Drinking water is free; not because of any benevolence on the part of the owners but because of the impossibility of charging for it. As it is, there is much disregard for the private ownership of the *qanat*; a second duty of the Persian's day is to cover up the traces of any robbing of water he may have made during the night; for a man who has no money, who has a stream flowing near his garden and who has an unscrupulous bent, in short a Persian peasant, the gurgling of that stream provides too great a temptation. So when the *kadkhoda*, the bailiff of the village, blows out his lamp and retires to bed a good many shovels are grabbed by a good many unseen hands: it may be necessary to remove a large chunk from the bottom of your own or your neighbour's wall, but it does not take long for it has been removed so many, so very many times before: whatever has to be done is done quickly and efficiency comes with practice. There is never any question of the water not flowing correctly; with the passage of time the unlawful channel has become too deep.

Once, when I was returning late at night from a walk into the mountains along a route that I knew quite well, I suddenly found myself wading through a small stream that had never been there before; the odd thing was that it flowed straight under a garden door. I couldn't think up the Persian for 'There is a stream flowing under your garden door' and anyway, it was late; so I strode on. I was soon splashing down a path which had previously, as I remembered it, been a dry and dusty way; many streams had dried up but more had been born in the night. It chanced that I should pass that way again the next morning and there was the dust I knew, the dust of ageless time, the dust as old as the desert itself. Sometimes, of course, the diverter is so fatigued by the night's work that he falls asleep when the warmth of the day begins to seep into his system ; then it is that the stream continues on its unnatural course. Its owner will hastily put things right, but the tell-tale dampness will be there for the *kadkhoda* to see, even if the owner hadn't gone bounding off to find him. All three then argue until the heat of the day becomes too oppressive: the argument swells to a climax and finally all is forgotten under the beneficence of sleep.

From *Blind White Fish in Persia*
by Anthony Smith

The Stench of Corruption

Many factors contributed to the downfall of Muhammad Reza Shah and the overthrow of the monarchy in the Revolution of 1978–1979. Not the least of these was the perception of an all-pervading corruption presided over by members of the royal family. This is tellingly described by the Polish journalist, Ryszard Kapuscinski (1932–2007) in the following 'snapshot,' as he calls it, from his book on the Iranian Revolution, Shah of Shahs. *Kapuscinski won international fame with this and other books he wrote on wars and revolutions around the world.*

Photograph 11. A Lufthansa airliner at Mehrabad airport in Teheran. It looks like an ad, but in this case no advertising is needed because all the seats are sold. This plane flies out of Teheran every day and lands at Munich at noon. Waiting limousines carry the passengers to elegant restaurants for lunch. After lunch they all fly back to Teheran in the same airplane and eat their suppers at home. Hardly an expensive entertainment, the jaunt costs only two thousand dollars a head. For people in the Shah's favour, such a sum is nothing. In fact, it is the palace plebeians who only go to Munich for lunch. Those in somewhat higher positions don't always feel like enduring the travails of such long journeys. For them an Air France plane brings lunch, complete with cooks and waiters, from Maxim's of Paris. Even such fancies have nothing extraordinary about them. They cost hardly a penny when compared to a fairy-tale fortune like the one that Mohammed Reza and his people are amassing. In the eyes of the average Iranian the Great Civilization, the Shah's Revolution, was above all a Great Pillage at which the elite busied itself. Everyone in authority stole. Whoever held office and did not steal created a desert around himself; he made everybody suspicious. Other people regarded him as a spy sent to report on who was stealing how much, because their enemies needed such information. Whenever possible they got rid of someone like that in short order - he spoiled the game. All values thus came to have a reverse meaning. Whoever tried to be honest looked like a paid stoolie. If someone had clean hands, he had to keep them deeply hidden because there was something shameful and ambivalent about purity. The higher up, the fuller the pockets. Anyone who wanted to build a factory, open a business, or grow cotton had to give a piece of the action as a present to the Shah's family or one of the dignitaries. And they gave willingly, because you could get a business going only with the backing of the court. With money and influence you could overcome every obstacle. You could buy influence and use it afterward to multiply your fortune further. It is hard to imagine the river of money that flowed into the till of the Shah, his family, and the whole court elite. Bribes to the Shah's family generally ran to a hundred million dollars and more. Prime ministers and generals took bribes of from thirty to fifty million dollars. Lower down, the bribe was smaller, but it was always there! As prices rose, the bribes got bigger and ordinary people complained that more and more of their earnings went to feed the moloch of corruption. In earlier times Iran had known a custom of auctioning off positions. The Shah would announce a floor price for the office of governor and whoever bid highest became governor. Later, in office, the governor would plunder his subjects to recover (with interest) the money that had gone to the monarch. Now this custom was revived in a new form: The ruler would buy people by sending them to negotiate contracts, usually military ones.

The Shah's big money enabled him to breathe life into a new class, previously unknown to historians and sociologists: the petro-bourgeoisie. An unusual social phenomenon, the petro-bourgeoisie produces nothing, and unbridled consumption makes up its whole occupation. Promotion to this class depends on neither social conflict (as in feudalism) nor on competition (as in industry and trade), but only on conflict and competition for the Shah's grace and favour. This promotion can occur in the course of a single day, or even in a few minutes: The Shah's word or signature suffices. Whatever most pleases the ruler, whoever can best and most ardently flatter him, whoever can convince him of his loyalty and submission, receives promotion to the petro-bourgeoisie. This class of freeloaders quickly makes a significant part of the oil revenues its own and becomes proprietor of the country. At their elegant villas its members entertain visitors to Iran and shape their guests' opinions of the country (though the hosts themselves often have scant familiarity with their own culture). They have international manners and speak European languages – what better reasons for the Europeans to depend on them? But how misleading these encounters can be, how far these villas are from from the local realities that will soon find a voice to shock the world! This class we are speaking about, guided by the instinct of self-preservation, has premonitions that its own career will be as short-lived as it is glittering. Thus, it sits on its suitcases from the start, exporting money and buying property in Europe and America. But since it has such big money, it can earmark a part of its fortunes for a comfortable life at home. Super-luxurious neighbourhoods, with enough conveniences and ostentation to stupefy any sightseer, begin to spring up in Teheran. Many of the houses cost more than a million dollars. These neighbourhoods take root only a few streets away from districts where whole families huddle in narrow, crowded hovels without electricity or running water. This privileged consumption, this great hogging, should go on quietly and discreetly – take it, hide it, and leave nothing showing. Have a feast, but draw the curtains first. Build for yourself, but deep in the forest so as not to provoke others. So it should be - but not here. Here, custom ordains that you dazzle, light all the lights, stun them, bring them to their knees, devastate them, pulverize them! Why have it at all, if it's to be on the sly, some alleged thing that somebody has seen or heard about? No! To have it like that is not to have it at all! To really have it is to blow your horn, shout it, let others come and gawk at it until their eyes pop out. And so, in plain sight of a silent and increasingly hostile people, the new class mounts an exhibition of the Iranian *dolce vita*, knowing no measure in its dissoluteness, rapacity, and cynicism. This provokes a fire in which the class itself, along with its creator and protector, will perish.

When I want to cheer myself up, I head for Ferdousi Street, where Mr Ferdousi sells Persian carpets. Mr Ferdousi, who has passed all his life in the familiar intercourse of art and beauty, looks upon the surrounding reality as if it were a B-film in a cheap, unswept cinema. It is all a question of taste, he tells me: The most important thing, sir, is to have taste. The world would look far different if a few more people had a drop more taste. In all horrors (for he does call them horrors), like lying, treachery, theft, and informing, he distinguishes a common denominator – such things are done by people with no taste. He believes that the nation will survive everything and that beauty is indestructible. You must remember, he tells me as he unfolds another carpet (he knows I am not going to buy it, but he would like me to enjoy the sight of it), that what has made it possible for the Persians to remain themselves over two and a half millennia, what has made it possible for us to remain ourselves in spite of so many wars, invasions and occupations, is our spiritual, not our material strength - our poetry, and not our technology; our religion, and not our factories. What have we given the world? We have given poetry, the miniature, and carpets. As you can see, these are all useless things from the productive viewpoint. But it is through such things that we have expressed our true selves. We have given the world this miraculous, unique uselessness. What we have given the world has not made life any easier, only adorned it – if such a distinction makes any sense. To us a carpet, for example, is a vital necessity. You spread a carpet on a wretched, parched desert, lie down on it, and feel you are lying in a green meadow. Yes, our carpets remind us of meadows in flower. You see before you flowers, you see a garden, a pool, a fountain. Peacocks are sauntering among the shrubs. And carpets are things that last – a good carpet will retain its colour for centuries. In this way, living in a bare, monotonous desert, you seem to be living in an eternal garden from which neither colour nor freshness ever fades. Then you can continue imagining the fragrance of the garden, you can listen to the murmur of the stream and the song of the birds. And then you feel whole, you feel eminent, you are near paradise, you are a poet.

From *Shah of Shahs*
by Ryszard Kapuscinski

Farewell to a Broken Shah

Sir Anthony Parsons (1922–1996) was the last British ambassador to Iran under Muhammad Reza Shah. In his book The Pride and the Fall, *he recounts his experience of the Iranian Revolution and the events leading up to it. Although conscious of the Shah's failings, Parsons saw him as a tragic figure as the edifice he had constructed collapsed around him. He gives a moving account of his final audience with the Shah, just eight days before the Shah left the country for good.*

I called on the Shah to say goodbye on January 8th. I found him calm and detached, talking about events as though they no longer had relevance to him as a person. It was for me a profoundly emotional experience. I had come to know the Shah well over the previous five years and we had become intimate through the many long discussions which we had had over the four months of his ultimate travail. I started by saying that I had never imagined myself saying goodbye to him in such tragic circumstances and that I was finding it difficult to speak. I suggested that we should part without further ceremony or discussion: I would find another long session unbearable. The Shah smiled and put his hand on my arm as I dried up, literally with tears in my eyes. 'Never mind, I know how you feel. But we must have one last talk.' He told me that he was still receiving three conflicting sets of advice. Some people were telling him that he must stay and 'tough it out'. Others were saying that he should withdraw to Bandarabbas[13] and let the army do the job in his absence. Others were advising him to leave the country. What did I think? I replied that I would prefer not to answer. Whatever I said would be construed by him as a British plot, and I had no comfort to offer. The Shah insisted. I said that I would only reply if he gave me his word of honour that he would accept what I said as my personal view, the opinion of someone who wished him and his country well, and that I was not speaking in any sense to a brief from London. The Shah accepted these conditions.

[13] Bandar-e Abbas, the port at the entrance to the Persian Gulf.

I told him that I saw him in what the Americans would describe as a 'no-win' situation. To borrow one of his metaphors, Bakhtiar[14] was melting like snow in water every day that the Shah stayed in the country. But if he left I could see little or no possibility of his ever returning; I had no faith in Bakhtiar's ability to restore the situation. As regards the other choices, he knew what I felt about military crack-downs. I did not believe that such action was possible, and after all, it was really the strikes which had brought the regime to its knees: could the military 'crack down' on every house in the country and oblige its occupants to return to work? The Bandarabbas idea I dismissed out of hand. If the revolutionaries forced him to withdraw that far, would they not redouble their efforts to force him the whole way?

With a strange gesture the Shah looked at his watch. 'If it was up to me, I would leave in ten minutes.' He went on to say that he could not leave before Bakhtiar was confirmed by parliament. If he left before that process was complete, parliament might collapse and there would be no quorum. I told him that Iran was in the middle of a cataclysmic revolution – no one cared about the parliament and its procedures. The Shah shook his head and we then discussed where he should go when he left the country. He did not appear to have made up his mind and said something to the effect that he might go to 'one of those Arab kingdoms'. No mention of Egypt but he did say that he could not come to Britain: the security problem would be too acute with tens of thousands of Iranian students in the country.

We turned to the past. Why, the Shah asked, had the people turned against him after all that he had done for them? I said that we had discussed this many times before. I thought that the basic reason was that he had tried to turn the people of Iran into something which they were not, and they had at last rebelled under the leadership of their traditional authorities, the religious classes. It was interesting that the same forces which had humbled Nasruddin Shah in 1892 when he had awarded a tobacco concession

[14] Shapur Bakhtiar (or Bakhtiyar), the Shah's last prime minister, assassinated in Paris in 1991.

342

to a foreign firm, and had prevailed over Muzafferiddin Shah in 1906 over the constitution, had combined to bring down Mohammed Reza Shah – the mullahs, the bazaar and the intelligentsia. I had never admired the Iranian people so much as I had done in the past few months. Their courage, discipline and devotion to the cause of overthrowing the monarchy had been amazing; if only he had been able to mobilise these qualities in his pursuit of the Great Civilisation...The Shah agreed about the performance of his people but rejected my analogies with his Qajar predecessors. 'I have done more for Iran than any Shah for 2,000 years; you cannot compare me to those people.'

He saw me to the door with his usual courtesy and I wished him luck whatever happened. He smiled and said nothing. I never saw him again.

From *The Pride and the Fall, Iran 1974–1979*
by Anthony Parsons

The Triumph of Khomeini

When the Ayatollah Khomeini ended his long exile in Iraq and moved to France in October 1978, he immediately became the focus of attention of the world's media as the effective leader of the revolution in Iran. The doyen of BBC Television's foreign correspondents, John Simpson (1944–), who had reported on Iran for many years, was among those who went to see the Ayatollah at his new residence in the village of Neauphle-le-Château, just outside Paris. In the following passages from his book, Strange Places, Questionable People, *John Simpson recalls with journalistic verve his first meeting with Khomeini, how he accompanied him on his triumphant return to Iran after long years of exile, and the dramatic scenes he witnessed in Tehran in the following days. Bill Handford and Dave Johnson, whom he mentions, were his cameraman and his recordist respectively.*

Soon after he had settled in the village of Neauphle-le-Château outside Paris, I went to interview him. He had taken over two houses on opposite sides of a small street. We filmed him crossing from one side to the other, and I had my first glimpse of the man whose revolution was to be an important part of my professional life for years to come. I had seen his features on posters and stencils and banners back in Iran, but now, looking at those beetling brows and that ferocious frown, I though he looked like vengeance personified.

We set up our lights in the main sitting-room of the house where he lived, and settled down to wait while he prepared himself for the interview. All the Western furniture had been taken out, and the floor was thick with Persian carpets. Around the walls were the large, comfortable cushions which Iranians like to lounge against. I practised kneeling down. Then the door opened and he entered. You could feel the man's personality emanating from him: he was small, but he seemed to fill the room. He also looked extraordinarily clean: his robes were white and starched, and beautifully pressed. I wasn't quite sure what to do, so I said, 'Welcome' and put my hand out to shake his, forgetting that some of the most particular Muslims feel they have to wash after touching a non-believer.

It was potentially awkward, but he dealt with it well. Looking down, he busied himself with the folds of his robe in such a way that it seemed he hadn't noticed my outstretched hand. Yet he showed no real interest in me at all: I was merely the loud-hailer through which he was about to address a message to the Iranian people.

Transcript of interview recorded 3.11.78 in Paris.
Speakers: *Ayatollah Khomeini (non-staff), John Simpson (staff)*

JS: Is it your intention to lead a revolution against the Shah, or do you simply wish to force him to change his policies?
AK: The Shah has ruled Iran as though it were his private estate, his property, to do with as he chooses. He has created a dictatorship, and he has neglected his duties. The forces of Islam will bring this situation to an end. The monarchy will be eradicated.
JS: What kind of government do you wish to see in Iran, and what form would an Islamic Republic take?
AK: The Islamic Republic will be based on the will of the people,

as expressed by universal suffrage. They will decide on the precise form it takes...But there are aspects of life under the present corrupt form of government in Iran which will have to be changed: we cannot allow our youth to be corrupted and our Islamic culture to be destroyed, and drugs such as alcoholic beverages will be prohibited.

Around us as we sat on the carpet were three of his aides, whose fates would shortly be determined by the experience of working with him. One, Abolhassan Bani-Sadr, became president and then escaped into exile; the second, Ibrahim Yazdi, was hounded out of government and spent his life as a dissident, in and out of gaol; and the third, Sadeq Qotbzadeh, became foreign minister and was then executed for treason.

Now they were all enthusiastic about the prospect that Khomeini's interview would be broadcast on the BBC, knowing it would be heard all over Iran. Of course I understood that this kind of thing often had a profound effect on the politics of the country in question, but a decision not to interview Khomeini would have been as much of a political move as the decision to interview him. In such cases I was happy to leave it to the set of principles Waldo Maguire, my former editor, had given me before I went to South Africa: if it was of interest, if it was newsworthy, then we should report it and not bother our heads with the possible consequences.

Two hours later we... boarded Khomeini's chartered Air France jet. An amusing gay steward explained to us that by special request there was no alcohol on board. A curtain blocked our view of the first-class section, where Khomeini and his advisers were sitting. We were back in steerage, and the students who wanted to shed their life's blood for the revolution were praying around us.

'This is a gloomy start,' Bill said as the heads went down. He was a small, wiry, bearded yachtsman in his late forties, and I had always enjoyed working with him.

There was a colleague of ours on board, a radio reporter who was usually good company. Now, though, he was badly scared by the prospect of the flight and was gloomy and depressed. He went to sleep quickly. I found it harder to sleep, partly because

Khomeini's supporters were so excited. For one thing, they were going home, and for another they thought there was a good chance the plane would be shot down by the Shah's air force; which meant they would go straight to Paradise as martyrs. This was precisely the possibility that made the correspondent so miserable.

It was light outside the plane by now, and people were starting to stir. The curtains dividing us from the first-class section parted without warning. Sadeq Qotbzadeh came through and stood on an empty seat in the front row of the tourist class section.

'I have a serious announcement to make,' he said. There was a rustle of excitement. 'We have just received a warning over the aircraft radio that the Iranian air force has orders to shoot us down directly we enter Iranian airspace.'

More rustling: it was depressingly clear that many of our fellow passengers thought this would be the best outcome imaginable. As for me, I shrugged my shoulders and drank some coffee.

> Of all the wonders that I have yet heard,
> It seems to me most strange that men should fear,
> Seeing that death, a necessary end,
> Will come when it will come.

It wasn't that I didn't care whether I lived or died: I was thirty-four, and I had a wife and two daughters, and I wanted to live very badly indeed. But it wasn't going to be up to me. It would be up to a general with a lot of gold braid somewhere down below, and a pilot with his finger on the button of a missile.

I suppose it was like being back in the Rhodesian farmer's car on the Mozambique border: if we weren't shot down, if we survived, I didn't want everybody to remember that I'd behaved embarrassingly badly. I looked across at Bill. He was sitting calmly in his seat, checking his equipment. He didn't understand Qotbzadeh's French, but he knew exactly what was going on. Nearby sat the radio man, complaining and moaning to himself. I knew which one I wanted to be like; or perhaps, to be a little more honest, I knew which one I wanted other people to think I was like.

By now, anyway, there was something to do: which always seems to chase away the fear and introspection. Qotbzadeh beckoned us forward, and we went through the curtains and saw Khomeini sitting in the front row of first class, next to his son Ahmad. For a man who was returning from fifteen years of exile in order to start a revolution, he looked remarkably calm. I asked him that dreary, unimaginative broadcaster's question, how he felt. Deservedly, I was ignored. The grim head turned away from me and looked down. It was a few minutes later that a rather better-phrased question from a French journalist received the reply that went around the world.

'We are now over Iranian territory. What are your emotions after so many years of exile?'

'*Hichi,*' said Khomeini: nothing.

It was no good trying to explain that as a Muslim cleric he had striven to banish every emotion within himself except the love of God; that he believed the love of one's country, or hope for the future, or even the desire for revenge, were all emotions which, divorced from the worship of God, had no value or meaning. For people everywhere, even in Iran, it seemed as though this personification of vengeance had no feelings whatever for the nation he had convulsed.

Our plane wasn't shot down, of course; it merely flew round and round for a very long time, waiting for permission to land, until we were all thoroughly airsick. Down below us the greatest crowd in human history was waiting for him, and as we made our final approach I could see the vast gathering around the aiport buildings and along the route Khomeini would take into Tehran. On the tarmac I recorded a long piece to camera about what had happened and what the situation was now and we all waited for Khomeini to appear at the top of the aircraft steps. It took a long time; but when he did, a roar came from the onlookers and was taken up by the enormous, expectant crowd outside the airport buildings.

By now, though, Bill and I had ceased to play any further part in things. Having come there against instructions, our job was to hand over to the correspondent and camera crew who were already in Tehran. It was deeply anti-climactic, but we were exhausted after working hard for nearly thirty hours. And although we could hear the noise as Khomeini met and addressed a crowd of thousands of mullahs in the main part of the airport, we left that to our colleagues and slumped down exhausted on the seats in the arrivals hall. Half an hour or so later we were awakened when the doors opened and Khomeini appeared, being half-carried by a group of very worried acolytes.

No one stopped us as we followed them into a side-room. Nobody even seemed to notice we were filming as Khomeini lay down, apparently unconscious. Bill turned and looked at me, with a look on his face that seemed to say 'This could be one of the world's great exclusives.' But of course it wasn't. After a while Khomeini opened his eyes and asked for water. He had merely fainted from the heat and from nervous exhaustion; and if he ever showed such weakness again, there was no one present to see it.

The next twelve days were some of the most intense and exciting I have ever lived through. The Shah had left Iran before Khomeini arrived, but his power-structure was still more or less in place and the prime minister he left behind him, the charming and brave Shahpour Bakhtiar, was still in office. (Years later Bakhtiar would be murdered in Paris by agents sent by the government in Tehran.) But now that Khomeini was setting up his rival government it was only a matter of time before the empty structures left over from the Shah's rule collapsed and the new regime seized power.

The moment came twelve days later, on 12 February. I had been up much of the night, watching and filming at a road block outside our hotel. At 6.30 I was awakened by a loud grinding noise in the street outside. A column of twenty or more tanks was heading for a confrontation with the pro-Islamic militants: the Imperial Guard was on the move.

It was an utterly bewildering day. We drove round Tehran in the direction of gun-fire, always managing to get there a little too late. Once, as we walked along a flyover we were buzzed by a pro-government helicopter which seemed about to attack us; yet we didn't even get good pictures of that. But our luck had already started to change. We found a crowd attacking the SAVAK building...and filmed them.

By this time our driver, a man called Mahmoudi, whom I was to get to know very well indeed in the years that followed, had found out for us where the main action was going on and drove us there. There was no shortage of action any more. Dave Johnson, the enormous piano-playing sound recordist, had joined us by this stage. And although he did not relish the action he stayed connected up to Bill Handford's camera as we walked along a street towards the fighting with bullets striking the walls a few feet above our heads. I was nervous enough: Dave, with his great bulk must have felt that he offered an unfairly large target.

At the end of the street we at last understood what was going on: the crowds, and soldiers who had gone over to them, were attacking a barracks. The resistance had been strong at first, but was wearing down as we arrived. Soon a breach was made in the outer wall, and the soldiers inside began surrendering in their hundreds. For me, it was like watching the storming of the Winter Palace. I had reached the stage where filming the action was more important to me than my own safety, and I could see Bill had too. The fact that Dave stayed with us seemed to me admirable in itself. It was a dangerous time, and we were pinned down by gunfire in place after place. An American correspondent had been killed that morning, merely looking out of a window.

In north Tehran, in the foothills of the Elburz mountains, we found a crowd gathering outside the Niavaran Palace, where the Shah and his family had lived. These were really just local people, scarcely revolutionaries at all, and their motive seemed to be a kind of militant curiosity and a desire to loot, rather than hatred for the old imperial order. Their eyes flashed with excitement as they stormed into the grounds and saw the grand style in which the Shah had lived. He seemed to have left everything behind him there. But the crowd was disappointed: the real revolutionary movement had sent some volunteers to make sure there was no theft or destruction, and the crowd obediently halted near the entrance to the palace, still avid to see the wealth of the monarch who had been overthrown. Looking through the windows, I felt a certain guilt, as though I were a looter myself. The Shah had been no friend to the BBC, and as the originator of the plan to raise the price of oil in 1973 he was the cause of a good deal of economic pain in the Western world. I detested his record in human rights. But here at Niavaran he wasn't a monarch but a man who had been forced out of his country forever; and there was something poignant even in the showiness and poor taste which was evident as I peered through the windows of his palace.

By the entrance stood a sheepish group of several dozen men wearing nothing but their underpants. These were the Imperial Guards, 'the Immortals', each of whom had taken a personal oath to defend the Shah with the last drop of blood in his veins. Instead the Shah had left them, and they had only defended him as far as their underwear. There was nothing grand about this revolution, any more than there was about the Russian Revolution. It was mostly absurdity and confusion.

We satellited our material from the television station at around midnight. While we were waiting for the satellite bookings to start there was a wild outbreak of shooting outside. Soon hundreds of rounds were hitting the building and coming in through the windows.

'The counter-revolutionaries are getting in! They'll kill us all!' someone shouted in rather good English from the passage-way outside. From where I lay on the floor I looked around for somewhere to hide, and the only place I could see was a locker against one of the walls. I got into it for a moment or two, but felt distinctly foolish. The floor seemed a better place. In the end it turned out that there were no counter-revolutionaries anyway; it was just one group of excitable volunteers with guns shooting at one another. But a lot of people were killed or injured all the same.

As we were leaving a man with a scarf tied round his head, revolution-chic style, stuck his gun into my stomach and asked me who I was and what I was doing.

'Stop play-acting, you silly wanker,' I answered in English. I had been through a lot that day, and this seemed like the final straw. I pushed the gun-barrel away.

'I speak English', he said grimly. 'I went to university in Manchester.'

Bad call, I thought. Then it seemed so ludicrous I grinned, and after a moment he grinned back at me. I could sense Bill Handford physically relax as he stood beside me.

'Perhaps you ought to be a bit more careful, John', he said gently as we walked away. I agreed. My instant's irritability could have got us both killed.

In the empty streets we and a group of other television people were given a lift back to our hotel in an ambulance reeking of blood. The sides and beds were covered with it.

A few days later we left Tehran. The blood-letting was beginning to frighten as well as sicken me.

From *Strange Places, Questionable People*
by John Simpson

7

Iran becomes a Theocracy: The Islamic Republic

*A*FTER THE OVERTHROW *of the Shah, clerical rule was established under the leadership of the Imam Khomeini and enshrined in a new constitution. The American embassy in Tehran was seized by Islamic radicals and more than fifty diplomats held hostage for over a year. The first president, Bani Sadr, opposed the clerical hardliners and was dismissed by Khomeini. Islamic Marxist fighters of the People's Mujahedin then launched a campaign of violence to overthrow the regime, which responded with a reign of terror in which many thousands were arbitrarily executed. In the meantime the Iraqi leader, Saddam Hussein, invaded Iran, starting a war that cost hundreds of thousands of lives. A UN call for a ceasefire was reluctantly accepted by Khomeini in 1988. Early the following year he issued a fatwa imposing a death sentence on the writer, Salman Rushdie, for his novel,* The Satanic Verses. *Khomeini died a few months later. The country's new leadership pursued a more pragmatic economic and foreign policy. Muhammad Khatami, elected president in 1997 and again in 2001 attempted but failed to liberalise the political system. He was succeeded in 2005 by a hardliner, President Ahmadinejad.*

The undisputed leader of the revolution that overthrew the Pahlavi monarchy was the Ayatollah Khomeini, who was seventy-six when he returned to his homeland in triumph. He was soon accorded the title of Imam, which inevitably associated him in the minds of ordinary, pious Iranians with the Imams of Shiism, the semi-divine guides of mankind.

Khomeini had clearly set out his belief in a theocratic state in a series of lectures he gave in 1969 during his exile in the Shiite holy city of Najaf, in Iraq. In the lectures, later published as a book entitled *The Vice-regency of the Jurist*, Khomeini argued that government must be in the hands of religious scholars well versed in the laws of Islam contained in the Sharia, since only by implementing these laws could the just society ordained by God be realised. The idea that Muslim clerics should govern was highly controversial. It was rejected by other Shiite religious leaders at the time and has continued to have its opponents within the Shiite community ever since. Khomeini himself made no further reference to it in the years that followed leading up to the revolution. He insisted that once the monarchy was overthrown Iran should become an Islamic republic, but in order to rally behind him all the various forces of opposition to the Shah, both religious and secular, he was deliberately vague about the sort of Islamic republic he envisaged. He even explicitly disavowed any intention to impose clerical rule and indicated that once the revolution had succeeded he would withdraw from political involvement.

This seemed borne out by his appointment of a layman, Mehdi Bazargan, to head the Provisional Revolutionary Government which took office on February 12th 1979. Although a devout Muslim, Bazargan was a former member of Musaddiq's National Front, who had spent several years in prison for his opposition to the Shah. Now seventy-two, he was a firm believer in democracy and the rule of law. He had studied engineering in Paris and the ministers he chose were mainly Western-educated technocrats.

The appointment was, however, a tactical move to avert a premature conflict over the nature of the post-revolutionary state. The opposition that had overthrown the monarchy under the charismatic leadership of Khomeini contained widely differing ideological positions. There were hard line Islamists like Khomeini himself, liberal Islamists, Marxist Islamists, secular liberals and secular Marxists – to name only the main groupings. The Shiite clergy themselves were split. Khomeini needed time to overcome the other factions. So while Bazargan was attempting to normalise the situation in the country, Khomeini and his ideological supporters set about reinforcing their position. Khomeini tightened his grip on the Revolutionary Council he had established in January as the supreme decision-making body and turned it increasingly into a governing body issuing a stream of regulations and decrees which undermined the authority of Bazargan's provisional government. He backed the creation of a Khomeinist party, the Islamic Republican Party, which quickly acquired the means to intimidate its opponents through a shadowy organisation known as Hezbollah which disposed of a small army of club-wielding vigilantes and through a new paramilitary corps, the Revolutionary Guard, set up by Khomeini in May. Khomeini was also able to influence public opinion by appointing the prayer leaders who delivered the sermons in the mosques on Friday.

During and after the revolution large numbers fled the country. They were overwhelmingly from the better-off classes and included many highly skilled and professional people. This emigration was still going on a quarter of a century later, impeding economic development and creating a huge Iranian diaspora in Europe and the United States. The new revolutionary regime contributed to this exodus with its purges, which left no area untouched, but mainly affected the army, the security services, the administration, and education. Without consulting the government, Khomeini set up revolutionary courts which handed out summary justice to those closely identified with the Shah's regime. Several hundred people were executed in a matter of months, among them the Shah's longest-serving prime minister, Amir Abbas Hoveyda. Bazargan and a senior liberal cleric, Ayatollah Shariatmadari, protested at these secret trials without defence lawyers, which damaged the image of the revolution abroad, but Khomeini replied that open trials were a symptom of the 'Western sickness' and that criminals deserved to be killed without a trial of any kind.

Khomeini was now realising his conception of an Islamic society. One aspect of this was to root out all manifestations of Western influence. Early in March 1979 he suspended a law passed under the Shah which gave women divorce rights and imposed restrictions on polygamy. In a national referendum at the end of the month on the future nature of the state, Khomeini refused to include the word 'democratic' because of its Western origin and merely asked the electorate whether or not they wanted an Islamic republic. Although some political movements abstained, strong pressure from Khomeini and the clergy across the country enabled the government to announce over ninety-eight percent approval.

The next task before the provisional government was to draft a constitution. The document it came up with was based on the Iranian constitution of 1906 and gave no special role to the clergy, beyond providing for a Guardian Council of Muslim jurists with the power to veto any legislation that was contrary to the Sharia. Khomeini, however, was determined to set up an Islamic theocracy with ultimate power in the hands of the religious jurist, as envisaged in his lectures in Najaf twenty years earlier. He rejected the government's plan to have the draft reviewed by a large Constituent Assembly and announced instead that it would be put to a much smaller elected Assembly of Experts. Vote-rigging and intimidation secured the return in elections in August of an Assembly of Experts dominated by clerics and laymen who supported Khomeini's aims. The constitution they produced in November made 'the just and pious jurist' the leader of the nation and granted him extensive powers, including control of the armed forces and the judiciary. He would also appoint, directly or indirectly, the twelve jurists on the Guardian Council who would vet all legislation to see that it conformed to the Sharia. The executive power was to be headed by a president elected for a four-year-term, who had to be a Shia Muslim and whose candidature had to be approved by the jurist-leader. The president would nominate a prime minister for approval by parliament. The constitution guaranteed a number of rights and freedoms, but only so far as these conformed to Islamic norms. Khomeini was appointed the jurist-leader for life and announced a referendum on the constitution for the beginning of December, to be followed by presidential and parliamentary elections.

But on the November 6th Bazargan resigned over Khomeini's support for the occupation two days earlier of the American embassy in Tehran by radical students, an action which destroyed his efforts to normalise relations with the United States. Khomeini used the occupation, in which fifty-two American diplomats were held hostage, to deflect opposition to his theocratic constitution on the part of powerful left wing movements like the People's Mujahedin by temporarily rallying them behind him in a confrontation with the United States. This helped him secure popular approval of the constitution in the referendum. It also left him free to deal with his main clerical critic, Ayatollah Shariatmadari, who opposed the dominant role of the jurist as theologically wrong and undemocratic. As Khomeini began to orchestrate a campaign against him, there were violent clashes between supporters of the two clerics both in Qom and in Tabriz, the capital of Shariatmadari's home province of Azerbaijan, where he enjoyed strong popular support. But by the latter part of January 1980 the movement in support of Shariatmadari had been crushed and he himself placed under virtual house arrest.

The presidential election on January 25th was won by Abolhassan Bani Sadr (1933–), the middle-class son of an ayatollah, who had spent many years studying in Paris, where he wrote a number of books and essays expounding an idealistic vision of an Islamic society. It was a society in which no individual, group or class exercised power over others – a very different vision to Khomeini's concept of clerical rule. Nonetheless a shared determination to see the Shah overthrown had brought the two men together. Bani Sadr became a close aide to Khomeini in Paris and remained close to him after the revolution. He was elected president somewhat by accident after the candidate from the Islamic Republican Party, initially favoured by Khomeini, was found to be ineligible because he had an Afghan father. Bani Sadr, who ran as an independent, had little difficulty seeing off his two opponents, a new but unknown candidate from the IRP and a secularist.

Bani Sadr's aim, after his election, was similar to Bazargan's – to bring about a return to normality. But unlike Bazargan he had a popular mandate and believed this would enable him to assert his authority over all the branches of government and rescue the revolution from what he called 'a fistful of fascist clerics'. This ambition suffered a serious setback in the two-round parliamentary elections in March and May in which clerical hardliners of the Islamic Republican Party and its allies won an overwhelming majority. An immediate consequence was that Bani Sadr was unable to obtain parliamentary approval for any of his chosen candidates for prime minister. In the end he was forced to accept a hardliner, Muhammad Rajai, who was close to the IRP and with whom he had poisonous relations from the start. Despite his best efforts to withhold agreement to Rajai's ministerial nominations, he also had to live with a cabinet that was little to his liking. Bani Sadr argued that the main qualification for a minister should be professional expertise, while Rajai put Islamic zeal and piety first.

With a hostile parliament and government, an Islamic Republican Party that was extending its influence everywhere, and a jurist leader whose natural sympathies lay with the hardliners, Bani Sadr found himself virtually powerless. After his election, he worked hard to reach an agreement with the United States that would lead to the freeing of the hostages, but was blocked in the end by Khomeini. The abortive attempt by President Carter in April to rescue the hostages with an airborne mission, followed by the uncovering of two military plots against the government, resulted in the execution of over a hundred officers and a purge of thousands more which continued, despite objections from Bani Sadr, until the Iraqi invasion of Iran in September. Bani Sadr also had to stand by while Khomeini launched a major purge of the bureaucracy which deprived the president of valuable supporters within the administration. Earlier, in April, Bani Sadr put himself at the head of a 'cultural revolution' instigated by Khomeini to Islamise the universities and end the influence of leftist activists. But his hope of thereby controlling and moderating the action proved vain. Students at universities across the country were subject to violent attacks by Hezbollah thugs, often incited by preachers, after which the universities were closed, not to reopen for two years.

On September 22nd the Iraqi leader, Saddam Hussein, launched his attack on Iran, hoping to take advantage of the country's perceived weakness to win territorial concessions and perhaps even overthrow the Shiite regime which was arousing the interest of

Iraq's oppressed Shiite majority. After an initial success in capturing the Iranian oil terminal of Khorramshahr, the Iraqi advance was halted, but the war dragged on for nearly eight years at the cost of hundreds of thousands of lives. However, it hastened the conclusion of an agreement with the United States, which led to the hostages being freed at the end of January 1981. The agreement was negotiated by an aide to Khomeini and its financial terms were criticised by Bani Sadr, who said better ones could have been obtained earlier.

The war gave Bani Sadr an opportunity to assert himself. Khomeini had already devolved the office of commander-in-chief to him, and he now made him chairman of the Supreme Defence Council. Bani Sadr took charge of the campaign, spending much of the time at the front and identifying closely with the army. But he was increasingly opposed by the prime minister, Rajai, who criticised his conduct of the war and his reliance on the professional skills of the army rather than the religious commitment of the Revolutionary Guards and the volunteer organisation, the Basij, most of whose fighters were under sixteen, from poor families and signed up by clerics in their local mosque. Rajai also did his best to ignore or usurp the president's constitutional role. He had the full backing of the clerical hardliners of the IRP with their dominant position in parliament, their influence over the revolutionary institutions and their control of radio and television. Before long this escalated into a bitter propaganda war, with Bani Sadr accusing the IRP of trying to impose a dictatorship, and the IRP seeking to portray Bani Sadr as an enemy of the Islamic Republic.

In this power struggle, Bani Sadr drew support from a wide range of groups including secular liberals, the Islamic Marxists of the People's Mujahedin, prominent bazaar merchants, moderate clerics who opposed not only the excesses of the revolution but clerical rule itself, the professional middle class, students and the intelligentsia. The IRP had on their side the great majority of the clergy across the country, some left-wing groups like the communist Tudeh party, and the urban masses who looked to the new order to better their condition. They were well funded through revolutionary foundations which had taken over much of the economy and they disposed of such persuasive forces as the broadcast media, the revolutionary guards, tribunals and local committees, and the club-wielding thugs of the Hezbollah. The conflict turned increasingly violent with Hezbollahis regularly breaking up public rallies in support of the president. Both sides appealed to Khomeini, who eventually came to see Bani Sadr as a threat to the clerical regime and turned against him. Bani Sadr went into hiding and on June 21st 1981 the parliament voted overwhelmingly to declare him incompetent, which paved the way for his dismissal.

Continuing demonstrations by the Mujahedin in support of Bani Sadr were met with on-the-spot executions. Then, on June 28th, a bomb exploded at the Tehran headquarters of the IRP, killing seventy-four people, among them the secretary-general of the party and chief justice of the Supreme Court, Ayatollah Beheshti, four cabinet ministers, six ministerial undersecretaries and twenty-seven members of parliament. This marked the start of a period of extreme violence in which the Mujahedin, which had thousands of armed supporters in Tehran and other cities, sought to destabilise and overthrow the regime through bomb attacks and assassinations, to which the authorities responded with waves of arrests and mass executions, often quite indiscriminate. Rajai was elected president in July in place of Bani Sadr and the new secretary-general of the IRP, Hojjat al-Islam Muhammad Javad Bahonar, became prime minister. Both, however, were killed in a bomb attack on August 30th. By this time Bani Sadr and the leader of the Mujahedin, Masud Rajavi, had managed to escape to Paris where they set up a National Council of Resistance. Two other opposition movements joined shortly after – the Kurdish Democratic Party, which was fighting for an autonomous Kurdistan, and the National Democratic Front, a leftist liberal movement which had absorbed Musaddiq's old National Front.

The presidential election in October 1981 was won by a cleric, Hojjat al-Islam Ali Khamenei. Forty-two years old, he was much trusted by Khomeini, who had appointed him to the influential post of leader of the Friday prayer in Tehran. The foreign minister, Mir Husayn Musavi, a religious hardliner, became prime minister.

The cycle of violence between the regime and the Mujahedin continued through 1982. There was also an alleged plot to overthrow the regime involving the former foreign minister and close aide to Khomeini in France, Sadeq Qotbzadeh, who was executed in September along with about seventy army officers. Under interrogation, Qotbzadeh implicated Ayatollah Shariatmadari in the plot, as a result of which Shariatmadari was not only kept under house arrest until his death four years later but was deprived of his special religious position – an unprecedented step of very questionable validity. Both were forced to make humiliating confessions on television – something that became a common practice of the regime.

In the meantime, the process of Islamising the state and society was carried very much further. Clerics came to dominate almost all areas of public life. Particular attention was paid to the judiciary, where judges were required to be senior clerics, the Sharia replaced legal codes of Western inspiration, and the traditional Islamic punishments were introduced, including the amputation of hands for theft and stoning for adultery. Women were now compelled to veil themselves in public and Islamic morality was strictly enforced by teams of zealots who were liable to raid private houses to combat illicit drinking. Homosexuals risked severe whippings and executions.

In the autumn of 1981 Iran counter-attacked with great success in the war with Iraq, recovering much of the territory it had lost and recapturing Khorramshahr in May 1982. The Iranian leadership then decided to carry the war into Iraq and advanced to within seven miles of Basra. The United Nations Security Council issued calls for a ceasefire and a mutual withdrawal to international frontiers. These were accepted by Iraq but rejected by Iran, which demanded the overthrow and punishment of Saddam Husayn (Hussein) as a pre-condition for ending the war. Buoyed up by their victories, the Iranians entertained hopes of capturing Baghdad and even of marching on to Jerusalem. Over the following years they launched a succession of major offensives, but the Iraqis managed to hold them off with the aid of chemical weapons and growing support from the Soviet Union, the United States and Arab countries. The teenage volunteers of the Basij corps took the lead in the human wave tactics adopted by the Iranians. In Paris, meanwhile, Bani Sadr broke with the Mujahedin leader, Masud Rajavi over the latter's support for Iraq. Subsequently the Mujahedin based themselves in Iraq, from where they launched attacks into Iran.

By the second half of 1982 the reign of terror instituted by the regime, in which several thousand people were executed, was taking its toll on the Mujahedin. In December Khomeini considered the situation stable enough to call a halt to the worst excesses of the repression. The universities were gradually reopened after the curricula had been suitably Islamicised. But there was no loosening of clerical control. In 1983 the authorities moved against the last independent political party of any significance. This was the pro-Moscow communist party, the Tudeh, which had consistently supported the regime, even against other leftist parties, but was now suspect in the light of Soviet support for Iraq. The party was accused of spying for the Soviet Union, its leaders paraded on television and forced to make confessions, and hundreds of its members arrested. Clerics were even more dominant in the new parliament elected in 1984 when only candidates who subscribed to clerical rule were allowed to stand. The following year Khamenei was re-elected as president. An elected Assembly of Experts also chose a former student of Khomeini's, Ayatollah Husayn Montazeri (1922–), to be Khomeini's successor as the religious leader of the country after his death.

There were growing divisions within the clerical leadership over such matters as the economy, which had deteriorated sharply since the revolution, and relations with the outside world, which were not helped by Khomeini's attempts to export the revolution. Pragmatists headed by the speaker of parliament, Hashemi Rafsanjani, were ready to do a deal with the United States in 1986 whereby American hostages held by Iranian surrogates in Lebanon would be freed in exchange for badly needed military supplies. However, the negotiations in what became known as the Irangate or Iran-Contra affair had to be abandoned after their secret was leaked to a Beirut newspaper. The following year Rafsanjani was instrumental in persuading a reluctant Khomeini to accept a UN resolution calling for a ceasefire between Iran and Iraq. Khomeini likened it to drinking a 'chalice of poison'.

A breach was opened up between Khomeini and his appointed successor, Ayatollah Montazeri, in 1988 when a Mujahedin force made a brief foray into Iran from Iraq and Khomeini retaliated by instigating the execution of several thousand political prisoners, many of whom did not belong to the Mujahedin. Montazeri wrote to Khomeini to protest and accused him publicly of compromising the values of the revolution. Khomeini hit back in such strong terms that Montazeri offered his resignation, which was immediately accepted. Khomeini then summoned an Assembly of Experts to modify the constitution so as to make Khamenei eligible to be his successor, although he lacked the religious standing. The assembly also made other changes to the constitution by eliminating the office of prime minister and introducing an Expediency Council set up by Khomeini to resolve differences between parliament and the Council of Guardians. Khomeini, meanwhile, placed a serious obstacle in the way of improved relations with the West by issuing a fatwa condemning the Indian-born British writer, Salman Rushdie, to death for his novel, *The Satanic Verses*, which had stirred protests by Muslims in a number of countries. He died a few months later, on June 3rd 1989, and the following day the Assembly of Experts named President Ali Khamenei as his successor. A vast crowd of mourners accompanied Khomeini's coffin to the martyrs' cemetery in Tehran, the Behesht-e Zahra.

The former hard-liner turned pragmatist, Hashemi Rafsanjani, was elected president in August 1989 and held office for two terms until 1997. He had some success in reviving the economy by introducing a degree of free market reform and reducing the huge government subsidies and the dominant role of the state. But corruption, inflation, high unemployment and lower living standards than under the monarchy remained serious problems. Sporadic outbreaks of labour unrest were violently suppressed. Rafsanjani also achieved some improvement in foreign relations, especially with the Arab world, through a less confrontational approach, but relations with the West were damaged by Iran's opposition to an Arab-Israeli peace settlement, its support for armed factions in Lebanon, the assassination of prominent opposition leaders abroad and the continuing death sentence on Salman Rushdie. The United States imposed economic sanctions which deprived Iran of badly needed foreign investment, especially for its oil industry on which the government continued to depend for much of its revenue. Rafsanjani made no attempt to introduce political liberalisation. Parliamentary and other elections were marred by the large number of candidates barred from standing by the Guardian Council on ideological grounds.

An Islamic liberal democracy was what Rafsanjani's successor, Muhammad Khatami, tried to achieve. An intellectual cleric with a record as a progressive minister of culture, Khatami campaigned in the 1997 presidential election on a platform of greater freedom. He won a surprise landslide victory over his conservative opponent, the speaker of parliament, Ali Akbar Nateq Nuri, taking nearly seventy percent of the vote. Press restrictions were relaxed and many reformist newspapers appeared in which controversial political and social issues were openly discussed. People were also allowed greater personal freedom and the Islamic dress code for women was less strictly enforced.

But Khatami was hampered by the limited power of his office, a conservative parliament, and lack of support from the religious leader, Khamenei. He could do nothing when the judiciary closed down reformist newspapers, when vigilante groups raided newspaper offices and attacked demonstrators, or when dissident writers were murdered and the intelligence ministry was implicated. In July 1998 he was forced to condemn student protestors who fought for days with police and vigilante groups in Tehran and Tabriz after parliament approved a bill restricting press freedom. Although Khatami had a reformist parliament after elections in 2000 and was re-elected the following year, conservatives on the Guardian Council vetoed any legislation that would have allowed for real reforms. His failure to realise his vision of a liberal Islamic state caused widespread disillusionment among his supporters.

Khatami did much to improve Iran's relations with the West,

visiting a number of European countries, calling for a 'Dialogue of Civilisations', and repairing relations with Britain by removing any threat to Salman Rushdie on the part of the Iranian government. He was not, however, able to do much to tackle the country's economic problems.

A conservative parliament was elected in February 2004 after the Guardian Council prevented most reformist candidates from standing. This was followed by the election of a lay religious hard-liner, Mahmud Ahmadinejad, as president in 2005. A former Revolutionary Guard, he had been mayor of Tehran since 2003. Presenting himself as a simple man of the people and promising a better life for the poor and an end to corruption and cronyism, Ahmadinejad defeated the veteran politician, Rafsanjani, who was widely perceived as tainted by corruption. Since then, Ahmadinejad has presided over a return to the aggressive imposition of narrowly conceived Islamic norms. He has also adopted a more confrontational stance in relations with the West over Israel and over Iran's development of nuclear energy. But there has been growing unrest over his failure to deliver on his promise to 'put oil wealth on the people's tables'. The poor state of the economy remains the Achilles heel of the Islamic Republic.

The balance sheet of the Islamic Republic to date is certainly not without positive elements. It is generally recognised that there have been major advances in the provision of health care and education. Iran also remains a highly creative country, as the achievements of the Iranian cinema make clear. The Iranians themselves are as individualist and outspoken as ever, and always ready to exploit any opportunity for expanding the boundaries of political, artistic and personal freedoms – as their rulers repeatedly discover to their discomfort.

The role of journalists in providing first-hand accounts of Iran has increased under the Islamic Republic. The best of them have risen to the challenge of explaining a country that has once again become 'different' and that has played a key role in the wider Islamic revival. Iranians who have left Iran and who have written of their experiences there in English have also provided unique insights into the nature of the Islamic Republic.

The Imam in Valedictory Mood

Most great revolutionary leaders have been somewhat stern figures, but none more so, at least to Western observers, than the Imam Khomeini. There seemed little about him that could be described as touching or moving. Yet such sentiments are aroused in this description by the BBC foreign correspondent, John Simpson (1944–), of one of the audiences he gave for the faithful towards the end of his life.

Half a mile from the Niavaran Palace, where the Shah once lived in splendour, lies the village of Jamaran. For the inhabitants of north Tehran, Jamaran has never had a good name: literally, since it means 'the abode of snakes'. A roadblock manned by Revolutionary Guards prevents you from turning left onto the Jamaran Road as you drive along the Hojat-ol-Eslam Doctor Bahonar Highway (formerly the Niavaran Road). The reason is not snakes, but security: virtually the entire village of Jamaran has been turned into a headquarters for the Imam Khomeini.

Farther along the road, set into the hillside, is an anti-aircraft battery which has seen action several times. The Iraqi air force has made several determined but unsuccessful attempts to bomb Jamaran, and a number of supposed plots have been uncovered to capture or assassinate Khomeini. None of them, however, seems to have gone farther than the planning stage, though my old acquaintance from Neauphle-le-Château, Khomeini's spokesman and later foreign minister, Sadeq Qotbzadeh, was executed for his alleged involvement in one of them. A passing Western visitor, if he arrives without an invitation and an official escort, will be told politely that he cannot turn into the Jamaran Road and his bullet-headed driver will laugh sympathetically as their white Paykan continues along the Bahonar Highway.

Almost every day small groups of people are, however, allowed past the roadblock and up to the group of houses where the Imam lives. The layout is curiously reminiscent of the Alawi Girls' School which formed his headquarters during the Revolution: the surrounding buildings have been subsumed into the complex, and the area where Khomeini and his family live and pray lies in the very centre of it, protected not just by the large contingent of Revolutionary Guards but also by an expensive electronic security system, with cameras set on the angles of the buildings and corridors and alarm-bells high on the walls. Within the living-quarters Khomeini and his wife Batoul share a few simple rooms, unadorned with pictures and empty of furniture except for cushions on the thick carpets. Batoul, who is twenty-three years younger than her husband (she was born in 1925, the daughter of an ayatollah), prepares each of his meals with her own hands: small portions of vegetarian dishes, together with a little milk and yoghurt. She ministers also to his heart condition, which has troubled him since his late fifties, although his personal physician lives in the complex. Batoul was herself injured in July 1987 when she led the women's section of Iranian pilgrims to the Grand Mosque in Mecca. Shortly before the Saudi Arabian police opened fire on the Iranian group, and several hundred people were killed either by bullets or in the stampede which followed, Batoul Khomeini was struck on the forehead by a stone thrown from an overpass across the road. A group of Saudis had gathered on the overpass, and were angered by the anti-Saudi chanting from the Iranians below.

Visitors are ushered into a bare, open yard, at the very heart of the complex. Some of the windows which look out onto the yard are those of Khomeini's living quarters. On a fixed platform at the end of the yard is a large outside broadcast camera of the national television: the Islamic Republic of Iran Broadcasting Authority, IRIB. Another camera was installed at the rear of the yard. Almost every audience with the Imam is televised and shown at length on the evening news. On this particular day the favoured group was military, from the regular army, and about a hundred senior officers accompanied by their sons, some of them mere children, settled themselves down on the ground to wait for the Imam to appear. They had to wait about half-an-hour before the french windows of the ugly bungalow slid open, and a small group of clerics processed slowly out, followed by Khomeini himself.

His appearance was a considerable shock to me. Somehow the icon had seemed unchanging, because it had been reproduced so many millions of times around the globe and had become so familiar, and because he had always exuded a granite-like determination which it seemed could not be deflected by anything: not even the passage of time itself. But the figure which presented itself to us now was that of a very old and frail man. The black turban, denoting his status as a descendant of the Prophet, had been replaced by a black skull-cap. He was shrunken and bent, in a way that would have been unimaginable when I had seen him last, at his press conference in the Alawi School in Tehran. His beard and moustache had taken on a soft whiteness, and the angry, disapproving blackness had gone from the fierce eyebrows. He was now faint-voiced, and gentler and more vulnerable than anyone could have thought.

And yet the voice had not lost its effectiveness, only volume. His words were still clearly enunciated, and he spoke without notes, never raising his eyes from the microphone in front of him. He was teaching his audience a history lesson about the system they were fighting to protect, and to extend to other countries: 'This Revolution is completely different from any other that has taken place in the world. What usually happens after a Revolution is that people take power from one oppressive régime and give it to another régime, which becomes oppressive in its turn. The French Revolution, the Russian Revolution – you should study them. Nothing happened as a result of them. Before and after, they were the same; they didn't do anything for the nation. In Iran, the greatest change imaginable took place – a change in the attitude of the people.'

He paused for breath, and perhaps for effect as well: and the crowd, seizing their cue, chanted obediently, 'O God, keep Khomeini until the Coming of the Messiah.' He lectured them further, and although his words were elusive and gnomic, he seemed to be rebuking them for the rivalry they had shown towards the Revolutionary Guards, who had been doing most of the really successful fighting in the war with Iraq, and had obtained a far larger share of the credit than the regular army; not least because the régime had never entirely trusted the army.

Nowadays his light grey robes made the Imam seem more like a wraith than the personification of revenge, as he had once seemed to me, seven years before: on this occasion he was so fragile he looked almost transparent, and he talked more and more about death and the afterlife:

'Everything in this world lasts for a short time only. All that remains is the soul. I am old now, too old. I am already a dead man. You have to take over now, and I know that I have not done enough for you.'

People in his audience were crying unaffectedly and saying, 'No, no.' But soon they broke into another chant.

'You are our soul, you are the breaker of idols, you can do anything. We are ready to give you our blood, for as long as it runs in our veins. Khomeini is our leader.'

One of his acolytes took his hand, reverently, and placed it like some inanimate, holy relic on the rail that separated him from them; and the military leaders, some still with tears of emotion running down their faces, lined up to kiss the shrunken, veined, tendonous object that was presented to them. He seemed scarcely aware of it, as if feeling that his physical hand had nothing to do with either him or them; and he was sunk in his own thoughts, a frail figure who had smashed images and seemed now to be fading away, very slowly, in the presence of people who worshipped him. And over all there hung the memory of his voice, no less compelling than it had always been, telling them that his Revolution had changed the nature of things in Iran, but that now they must prepare themselves to continue without him.

From *Behind Iranian Lines* by John Simpson

A Work of the Great Satan Stands Trial

From the start, the Islamic Republic set itself against many of the values and even the symbols (like neckties) of the Western way of life. The anti-Western mindset of the more hardline Islamic elements has been well captured by an Iranian scholar of English-language literature, Azar Nafisi (1955–) in her remarkable book, Reading

Lolita in Tehran. *The book describes, among other things, her experiences as a lecturer at various universities in Tehran during the first two decades of the Islamic Republic, including the pressures to conform to the Islamic norms of the régime, which finally led her to give up her university post in 1995 and two years later to move to the United States. One of the most memorable episodes in the book is the 'trial' which she organised at the University of Tehran, towards the end of 1979, of Scott Fitzgerald's novel,* The Great Gatsby. *She decided to do this after one of her more religious students, a Mr Nyazi, told her she ought not to be teaching* The Great Gatsby *as it was an immoral novel. Mr Nyazi assumed the role of prosecutor, while the lawyer for the defence was a female student called Zarrin.*

All through the week before the trial, whatever I did, whether talking to friends and family or preparing for classes, part of my mind was constantly occupied on shaping my arguments for the trial. This after all was not merely a defence of *Gatsby* but of a whole way of looking at and appraising literature – and reality, for that matter. Bijan,[1] who seemed quite amused by all of this, told me one day that I was studying *Gatsby* with the same intensity as a lawyer scrutinizing a textbook on law. I turned to him and said, 'You don't take this seriously, do you?' He said, 'Of course I take it seriously. You have put yourself in a vulnerable position in relation to your students. You have allowed them – no, not just that; you have forced them into questioning your judgement as a teacher. So you have to win this case. This is very important for a junior member of the faculty in her first semester of teaching. But if you are asking for sympathy, you won't get it from me. You're loving it, admit it – you love this sort of drama and anxiety. Next thing you know, you'll be trying to convince me that the whole revolution depends on this.'

'But it does – don't you see?' I implored. He shrugged and said, 'Don't tell me. I suggest you put your ideas to Ayatollah Khomeini.'

On the day of the trial, I left for school early and roamed the leafy avenues before heading to class. As I entered the Faculty of

[1] Azar Nafisi's husband.

Persian and Foreign Languages and Literature, I saw Mahtab[2] standing by the door with another girl. She wore a peculiar grin that day, like a lazy kid who has just gotten an A. She said, 'Professor, I wondered if you would mind if Nassrin sits in on the class today.' I looked from her to her young companion; she couldn't have been more than thirteen or fourteen years old. She was very pretty, despite her own best efforts to hide it. Her looks clashed with her solemn expression, which was neutral and adamantly impenetrable. Only her body seemed to express something: she kept leaning on one leg and then the other as her right hand gripped and released the thick strap of her heavy shoulder bag.

Mahtab, with more animation than usual, told me that Nassrin's English was better than most college kids', and when she'd told her about *Gatsby*'s trial, she was so curious that she'd read the whole book. I turned to Nassrin and asked, 'What did you think of *Gatsby*?' She paused and then said quietly, 'I can't tell'. I said, 'Do you mean you don't know or you can't tell me?' She said, 'I don't know, but maybe I just can't tell you.'

That was the beginning of it all. Nassrin asked permission to continue attending my classes whenever she could. Mahtab told me that Nassrin was her neighbour. She belonged to a Muslim organization but was a very interesting kid, and Mahtab was working on her – an expression the leftists used to describe someone they were trying to recruit.

I told Nassrin she could come to my class on one condition: at the end of term, she would have to write a fifteen-page paper on *Gatsby*. She paused as she always did, as if she didn't quite have sufficient words at her command. Her responses were always reluctant and forced; one felt almost guilty for making her talk. Nassrin demurred at first, and then she said: 'I'm not that good.' 'You don't need to be good,' I said. 'And I'm sure you are – after all, you're spending your free time here. Tell me in your own words what *Gatsby* means to you.' She was looking at the tip of her shoes, and she muttered that she would try.

[2] One of Azar Nafisi's students.

From then on, every time I came to class I would look for Nassrin, who usually followed Mahtab and sat beside her. She would be busy taking notes all through the session, and she even came a few times when Mahtab didn't show up. Then suddenly she stopped coming, until the last class, when I saw her sitting in a corner, busying herself with the notes she scribbled.

Once I had agreed to accept my young intruder, I left them both and continued. I needed to stop by the department office before class to pick up a book Dr. A[3] had left for me. When I entered the classroom that afternoon, I felt a charged silence follow me in. The room was full; only one or two students were absent – and Mr. Bahri,[4] whose activities, or disapproval, had kept him away. Zarrin was laughing and swapping notes with Vida, and Mr Nyazi stood in a corner talking to two other Muslim students, who repaired to their seats when they caught sight of me. Mahtab was sitting beside her new recruit, whispering to her conspiratorially.

I spoke briefly about the next week's assignment and proceeded to set the trial in motion. First I called forth Mr Farzan,[5] the judge, and asked him to take his seat in my usual chair, behind the desk. He sauntered up to the front of the class with an ill-disguised air of self-satisfaction. A chair was placed near the judge for the witnesses. I sat beside Zarrin on the left side of the room, by the large window, and Mr Niyazi sat with some of his friends on the other side, by the wall. The judge called the session to order. And so began the case of the Islamic Republic of Iran versus *The Great Gatsby*.

Mr Nyazi was called to state his case against the defendant. Instead of standing, he moved his chair to the centre of the room and started to read in a monotonous voice from his paper. The judge sat uncomfortably behind my desk and appeared to be mesmerized by Mr Nyazi. Every once in a while he blinked rather violently.

A few months ago, I was finally cleaning up my old files and I came across Mr Nyazi's paper, written in immaculate handwriting. It began with 'In the Name of God', words that later became

[3] The Head of the English Department at Tehran University.
[4] A very religious student.
[5] Another of Azer Nafisi's students, chosen to act as judge.

mandatory on all official letterheads and in all public talks. Mr. Nyazi picked up the pages of his paper one by one, gripping rather than holding them, as if afraid they might try to escape his hold. 'Islam is the only religion in the world that has assigned a special sacred role to literature in guiding men to a godly life,' he intoned, 'This becomes clear when we consider that the Koran, God's own word, is the Prophet's miracle. Through the Word you can heal or you can destroy. You can guide or you can corrupt. That is why the Word can belong to Satan or to God.'

'Imam Khomeini has relegated a great task to our poets and writers,' he droned on triumphantly, laying down one page and picking up another. 'He has given them a sacred mission, *much more exalted* than that of the materialistic writers in the West. If our Imam is the shepherd who guides the flock to its pasture, then the writers are the faithful watchdogs who must lead according to the shepherd's dictates.'

A giggle could be heard from the back of the class. I glanced around behind me and caught Zarrin and Vida whispering. Nassrin was staring intently at Mr Nyazi and absentmindedly chewing her pencil. Mr Farzan seemed to be preoccupied with an invisible fly, and blinked exaggeratedly at intervals. When I turned my attention back to Mr Nyazi, he was saying, 'Ask yourself which you would prefer: the guardianship of a sacred and holy task or the materialistic reward of money and position that has corrupted –' and here he paused, without taking his eyes off his paper, seeming to drag the sapless words to the surface – 'that has *corrupted*,' he repeated, 'the Western writers and deprived their work of spirituality and purpose. *That* is why our Imam says that the pen is mightier than the sword.'

The whispers and titters in the back rows had become more audible. Mr Farzan was too inept a judge to pay attention, but one of Mr Nyazi's friends cried out: 'Your Honour, could you please instruct the gentlemen and ladies in the back to respect the court and the prosecutor?'

'So be it,' said Mr Farzan, irrelevantly.

'Our poets and writers in this battle against the Great Satan,' Nyazi continued, 'play the same role as our faithful soldiers, and they will be accorded the same reward in heaven. We students, as the future guardians of culture, have a heavy task ahead of us. Today we have planted Islam's flag of victory inside the nest of spies on our own soil.[6] Our task, as our Imam has stated, is to purge the country of the decadent Western culture and...'

At this point Zarrin stood up. 'Objection, Your Honour!' she cried out.

Mr Farzan looked at her in some surprise. 'What do you object to?'

'This is supposed to be about *The Great Gatsby*,' said Zarrin. 'The prosecutor has taken up fifteen minutes of our time without saying a single word about the defendant. Where is all this going?'

For a few seconds both Mr Farzan and Mr Nyazi looked at her in wonder. Then Mr Nyazi said, without looking at Zarrin, 'This is an Islamic court, not *Perry Mason*. I can present my case the way I want to, and I am setting the context. I want to say that as a Muslim I cannot accept *Gatsby*.'

Mr Farzan, attempting to rise up to his role, said, 'Well, please move on then.'

Zarrin's interruptions had upset Mr Nyazi, who after a short pause lifted his head from his paper, and said with some excitement, 'You are right, it is not worth it...'

We were left to wonder what was not worth it for a few seconds, until he continued. 'I don't have to read from a paper, and I don't need to talk about Islam. I have enough evidence – every page, *every* single page,' he cried out, 'of this book is its own condemnation.' He turned to Zarrin and one look at her indifferent expression was enough to transform him. 'All through this revolution we have talked about the fact that the West is our enemy, it is the Great Satan, not because of its military might, not because of its economic power, but because of, because of–' another pause, 'because of its sinister assault on the very roots of our culture. What our Imam calls cultural aggression. This I would call a rape of our culture,' Mr Nyazi stated, using a term that later became the hallmark of the Islamic Republic's critique of the West. 'And if you want to see cultural rape, you need

[6] The American Embassy.

go no further than this very book.' He picked his *Gatsby* up from beneath the pile of papers and started waving it in our direction.

Zarrin rose again to her feet. 'Your Honour,' she said with barely disguised contempt, 'these are all baseless allegations, falsehoods.'

Mr Nyazi did not allow his honour to respond. He half rose from his seat and cried out: 'Will you let me finish? You will get your turn! I will tell you why, I will tell you why.' And then he turned to me and in a softer voice said, 'Ma'am, no offence meant to you.'

I, who had by now begun to enjoy the game, said, 'Go ahead, please, and remember I am here in the role of the book. I will have my say in the end.'

'Maybe during the reign of the corrupt Pahlavi regime,' Nyazi continued, 'adultery was the accepted norm.'

Zarrin was not one to let go. 'I object!' she cried out. 'There is no factual basis to this statement.'

'Okay,' he conceded, 'but the values were such that adultery went unpunished. This book preaches illicit relations between a man and a woman. First we have Tom and his mistress, the scene in her apartment – even the narrator, Nick, is implicated. He doesn't like their lies, but he has no objection to their fornicating and sitting on each other's laps, and, and, those parties at Gatsby's … remember, ladies and gentlemen, this Gatsby is the hero of the book – and who is he? He is a charlatan, he is an adulterer, he is a liar … this is the man Nick celebrates and feels sorry for, this man, this destroyer of homes!' Mr. Nyazi was clearly agitated as he conjured up the fornicators, liars and adulterers roaming freely in Fitzgerald's luminous world, immune from his wrath and from prosecution. 'The only sympathetic person here is the cuckolded husband, Mr Wilson,' Mr Nyazi boomed. 'When he kills Gatsby, it is the hand of God. He is the only victim. He is the genuine symbol of the oppressed, in the land of, of, of the Great Satan!'

The trouble with Mr Nyazi was that even when he became excited and did not read from his paper, his delivery was monotonous. Now he mainly shouted and cried out from his semi-stationary position.

'The one good thing about this book,' he said, waving the culprit in one hand, 'is that it exposes the immorality and decadence of American society, but we have fought to rid ourselves of this trash and it is high time that such books be banned.' He kept calling Gatsby 'this Mr Gatsby' and could not bring himself to name Daisy, whom he referred to as 'that woman'. According to Nyazi, there was not a single virtuous woman in the whole novel. 'What kind of model are we setting for our innocent and modest sisters,' he asked his captive audience, 'by giving them such a book to read?'

As he continued, he became increasingly animated, yet he refused throughout to budge from his chair. 'Gatsby is dishonest,' he cried out, his voice now shrill. 'He earns his money by illegal means and tries to buy the love of a married woman. This book is supposed to be about the American dream, but what sort of a dream is this? Does the author mean to suggest that we should all be adulterers and bandits? Americans are decadent and in decline because this is their dream. They are going down! This is the last hiccup of a dead culture!' he concluded triumphantly, proving that Zarrin was not the only one to have watched Perry Mason.

'Perhaps our honourable prosecutor should not be so harsh,' Vida said once it was clear that Nyazi had at last exhausted his argument. 'Gatsby dies, after all, so one could say that he gets his just deserts.'

But Mr Nyazi was not convinced. 'Is it just Gatsby who deserves to die?' he said with evident scorn. 'No! The whole of American society deserves the same fate. What kind of a dream is it to steal a man's wife, to preach sex, to cheat and swindle and to … and then that guy, the narrator, Nick, he claims to be moral!'

Mr Nyazi proceeded in this vein at some length, until he came to a sudden halt, as if he had choked on his own words. Even then he did not budge. Somehow it did not occur to any of us to suggest that he return to his original seat as the trial proceeded.

(*Zarrin went on to conduct a spirited defence of* The Great Gatsby. *There was no formal verdict, but Azar Nafisi says she discovered later that most students supported Zarrin.*)

From *Reading Lolita in Tehran* by Azar Nafisi

The Iconography of Martyrdom

Many, if not most of the estimated three hundred thousand Iranians who were killed in the Iran-Iraq war were volunteers who were encouraged to embrace death in the Shiite tradition of martyrdom. In Tehran, their memory is kept alive at the great Behesht-e Zahra martyrs' cemetery, where fountains flow with water the colour of blood, and on huge billboards across the city depicting some of those who died. It was these giant portraits of the dead that caught the attention of Jason Elliot on his arrival in Tehran and led him to reflect on the messages they convey in his book on Iran, Mirrors of the Unseen *— a book full of intriguing reflections on the country's history and culture.*

All over Tehran, from billboards, vast hoardings, and windowless facades, the eyes of the nation's war dead look onto the world of the living. At first I had thought these giant paintings, some of them thirty feet high, to be of present-day military leaders. But by degrees they became more articulate and I began to realise they were nothing of the sort. They were impossible to miss, though no one had pointed them out to me; to the local inhabitants they had perhaps acquired, like the clamour of the streets they overlooked, the invisibility of the familiar.

The portraits depict faces among the hundreds of thousands of Iranian soldiers who died in the decade-long war with Iraq. They are heroic, as they are intended to be: giant in scale, ubiquitous, and powerful, as statements with political dimension are meant to be. But no medals glint on their chests; there are no jaws clenched in martial fervour. Aggression is the last emotion to cross their brows and the youngest are, on the contrary, almost meek, their features suggesting an untempered idealism more fitting to a gallery of poets than of soldiers.

They are family members, whose ordinariness evokes their untimely departure from home. In the faces of the older men, there is an avuncular quality, and their gentle smiles suggest the inner resolve born of great suffering. Such faces do not speak in the conventional language of heroism; the very concept of their portrayal reaches for a different place in the scale of the pathetic. The note is struck by their eyes, which look on to a distant world with a gaze that expresses the singular knowledge of men who have already glimpsed their fate: they are doomed, and know they are doomed.

Sometimes these portraits lie against a sun-coloured, eight-pointed star, bearing in an upper corner the insignia of a military unit. More often it is the imagery in the surrounding field which tells the victim's story. There is little technical merit to these background elements; but their coarseness, executed at times with almost childlike strokes, renders them more articulate. Above the faces of a four-man aircrew, the bulky silhouette of a bomber, its wings streaked by moonlight, tells of an ill-fated night-time mission. In another, behind a pair of youthful faces, stretches a field of blood-red tulips, and from the nearest, a shimmering drop hangs from a rim of petals: dew or tear? Another man's reckoning is told, beneath the martyr's otherworldly gaze, by a pair of dog tags draped over a landmine. Elsewhere, an amphibious assault unfolds amid plumes of watery detonations, or a ragged line of men return at dusk from an operation along a muddy embankment lined with palm trees. Behind them, rid now of the enemy, lies a ruined village, from whose charred and fractured walls a plume of black smoke ascends into the sky.

Often the symbolism borders on the evangelical: a troop of infantrymen cross an open field on patrol, and through gaps in the clouds above them, the sun's rays stream over them in broadening shafts of gold benediction. Everywhere the message is driven home with calligraphic sayings of the Imam: 'The greatest sin is to forget the heroism of the martyrs'; 'The smiles of the martyrs shine like stars from Paradise'; 'The martyred are like the *suras* (chapters) of the Holy Qur'an'. This alliance of religion and slaughter strikes a sinister note, until one remembers that the walls of every other English church are draped with regimental flags, and chiselled with countless elegies to our own glorious dead. But stripped of their political connotation, the iconography of these visual memorials, against which our own seem mute, betrays a predisposition to both nuance and suggestion; an acute sensitivity to suffering, a susceptibility to tragedy. They allude, also, to a different geography of time. The dead are not merely dead: they have been resurrected into the present, where they subvert the usual continuum by carrying with them the knowledge of their impending extinction. Their gaze is purgatorial: it is a strange and haunting manipulation.

I had stopped beneath one such giant portrait and was copying the script into my notebook ('martyrdom is the courageous art of the men of God') when a teenage girl stopped on the pavement next to me, waiting to cross. She wore sunglasses, violet lipstick, and a light coloured scarf. A phone was clutched to her ear; her nail varnish was a lurid pink, and her chador was no more than a baggy shirt. On the far side of the road a brand new Peugeot had pulled up, and a pair of young men, phones clipped like pistols to their belts, stepped out to wait. She waved to them, mid-conversation, then skipped across.

This sudden glimpse of youthful purpose, decked with the brash trappings of modernity, had woken me as if out of a day-dream. Suddenly I regretted I had not stopped her to ask what she thought of the looming face above. She would have been an infant when the war had ended, nearly fifteen years earlier, and tasted nothing of the immediate horrors of revolution and conflict; she would have little time for the doleful sayings of the kind I had just been writing down. For a moment I wondered what her answer might have been, but it wasn't difficult to guess.

From *Mirrors of the Unseen: Journeys in Iran*
by Jason Elliot

Elites and Masses

In his book Persian Pilgrimages *the Iranian-American journalist and writer, Afshin Molavi, draws on his knowledge of the cultural and political history of Iran for a thoughtful exploration of contemporary Iranian attitudes. Here he highlights a division within the Islamic Republic that has deep historical roots.*

Among Shi'a Muslim clerics, there is a distinction between *khawass* (elites) and *awwam* (masses). The *khawass* are religious scholars and clerics. Certain things may be said in front of the elites but not the masses. These things usually involve complex religious discourse, the sort of talk that might confuse 'the simple believer'. There are also some things that elites might have license to say in public, but the masses do not. For example, a cleric can question the mysteries of God, but a 'simple believer' cannot.

Taken to a government level, it means this: President Rafsanjani can stand up in front of a crowd of reporters and say openly, 'Ninety percent of what we do in the Islamic Republic is un-Islamic,' and get away with it, as he did during his presidency. If someone else, not considered an elite, said the same words in front of reporters, there could be serious repercussions.

The Islamic Republic, true to this tradition, distinguishes between insiders and outsiders. The insider is a revolutionary who sided with Khomeini and other religious revolutionaries, not the leftists or democrats or Marxists. President Khatami is an insider. That's why the other insiders allowed him to run for office in the first place. His conservative foes are also insiders. The current struggle between reformists and conservatives remains, thus far, an insider-only struggle. Few outsiders – secular nationalists or liberal democrats or opponents of the Islamic Republic – have a public voice in the debate. A conservative election supervisory body stymies outsider attempts to run for parliament by denying them insiderness.

But President Khatami and other insider reformists have found a breach in the line, or so their conservative opponents often complain. Khatami talks too directly to the people, 'the simple believers'. He 'confuses' them with these ideas of democracy and civil society. Some conservatives whisper that Khatami may not even be a true insider, that his ideas on democracy seem to go too far. Several former insiders, like the revolutionary turned investigative journalist Akbar Ganji, have been booted out of the circle. Ganji is currently in jail[7] on charges of 'insulting Islamic sanctities' and 'defaming public officials' for his book and articles criticizing what he deems as the 'religious fascism' of conservatives. In today's Iran the circle of insiders shrinks as opposition grows. As more reformists speak out vigorously and boldly, conservatives cry 'betrayal', and yet another insider becomes

[7] He has since been released.

an outsider. As the circle shrinks, it will become increasingly untenable for the insiders to silence the outsider voices crying for change.

The ultimate public proponent of this *awwam/khawass* idea is the hardline and powerful cleric Ayatollah Mesbah Yazdi. He once said: 'It doesn't matter what the people think. The people are ignorant sheep.' This viewpoint was reflected in the young hardliner's assertion that he does not need a poll to guage people's opinions. The hardliner did not care about people's opinions. Vice should be stopped. That is the way it should be. The opinions of 'simple believers' do not matter. They are sheep.

This *awwam/khawass* distinction, on a more subtle level, refracts the complex lines between private and public space in Iranian society. High walls separate traditional Iranian homes. Some of what goes on inside the home should not occur outside. Across social classes, Iranians constantly assert, in effect, 'Not in front of the guests.' Of course, most traditional societies erect these walls of secrecy around their private lives. They are necessary. The Islamic Republic, however, sought to disrupt this age-old system. By knocking on people's doors, to check for dancing couples or alchoholic drinks, the new system knocked down private walls fortified by centuries of use.

I wondered what Omar Khayyam, the eleventh-century poet, might think of today's Iran. He might have seen some familiarity to his own era. In Neishapour (in north-eastern Iran), where Khayyam was born in 1044, the Turkish Seljuks ruled. A powerful and alien tribe from Central Asia, they needed legitimacy to bolster their rule in newly conquered Iran. They sought this legitimacy in traditional Sunni Muslim orthodoxy, which had risen as a counter to Shi'a victories across the Muslim world in the tenth century. The orthodox Sunni cleric became a court fixture. Sunni clerics derided and often killed philosophers. The Seljuk era vexed speculative men like Khayyam, who reached beyond the simple truths provided by rulers or orthodox clerics.

Still, Khayyam was a member of the *khawass*, an elite. He garnered great respect as a court astronomer and mathematician. His calendar, based on the sun's movement and his interpretation of the weather through the movement of the stars, demanded attention. What's more, he could engage with other members of the religious *khawass* on deep issues concerning the faith. Thanks to such exploits, the ruling elites granted Khayyam his private space to philosophize, criticize, and even display skepticism toward religion. The Persian literature expert Ahmad Karimi Hakkak puts it this way: 'Khayyam was allowed to say things a normal man could be hanged for. He had a certain license that most men do not. He was told, however, to keep his poetry and philosophizing to himself and close associates. It should not invade the public space.'

For nearly eight centuries, Khayyam's poetry remained in the world's private space until a minor Victorian poet, Edward FitzGerald, translated in free verse the Khayyam quatrains, winning for himself – and Khayyam – a place in the pantheon of world literary masterpieces. FitzGerald's translations also renewed interest in Khayyam among Iranians. Today intellectuals and free spirits flock to Khayyam's tomb, largely ignored just a century ago.

From *Persian Pilgrimages: Journeys across Iran*
by Afshin Molavi

The Politics of Personal Appearance

Afshin Molavi observes that how men and women choose to appear in public has become a political statement in today's Iran. All Muslim women have to wear the veil in public, but Afshin Molavi discovered that there are three ways of doing this, each of which represents a different political statement.

Women are on the front line of this politics of personal appearance because of the hijab, the mandatory Islamic covering placed upon them. As a result, the woman draped in a black chador, the most severe form of *hijab*, has become the most visible symbol of the Islamic Republic to the outside world. After President Khatami's first election in 1997, when the veils started to slip and the makeup became more pronounced and colorful, diplomats and political observers saw it as defiance of the revolution. There seems to be an undefined 'veil-o-meter' that gauges the mood of the country and its leaders by looking at the relative adherence to the veil. Bright toenail polish in open-toed sandals has also become part of the 'veil-o-meter' gauge. In fact, I heard a mullah in a Tehran mosque rail for more than fifteen minutes against the temptations of brightly polished toenails. It was sad to me to hear this man of the cloth, one who represented an old and noble faith, reduced to worries about toenail polish.

Ayatollah Khomeini was a proud advocate of the *hijab*. He once remarked that if nothing else, the veiling of women was a great victory for the revolution. The issue of *hijab* is complicated. Some Iranian women adhere to it voluntarily and would do so even if it were not the law of the land. There are others, a significant number, who see forced *hijab* as a blatant violation of their most basic civil rights. The Quran, Islam's holy book, is ambiguous on the matter. It recommends only that women dress modestly, without clear specifications on what that means. The veil, some Islamic scholars point out, is an accretion from pre-Islamic Byzantine Rome or Sassanian Persia, societies that veiled their noblewomen. Others point out that the patriarchy of traditional societies has as much to do with veiling as does religion. Whatever the case may be, female veiling has come to be seen as an integral element of the faith, and early Islamic jurists, acting after the death of the Prophet Muhammad, wrote it into law. Women dressed in *hijab* are the most visible reminder that the Islamic Republic is still in power.

As a result of this politics of personal appearance, Iranians have come to refer to three types of woman, defining their politics by the clothes they wear: the *chadory*, the *manteauy*, and the *maghna'eh-poosh*. The *chadory* woman wears the most severe covering in layers of black that require a hand to hold the cloth from the inside, thus preventing the *chadory* woman from working. The *chadory* tends to be socially conservative and less inclined to support social reforms. The widespread Iranian view in the politics of personal appearance lumps *chadory* women with Iran's ruling conservatives, though I found several exceptions to this rule. Rarely, however, did I find a *chadory* who agitated for meaningful social reform.

In contrast, the *manteauy* woman wears the loose-fitting *manteau*, often fashionably with a colorful, loosely tied head scarf. She generally supports both political and social reform. The *manteauy* woman might speak foreign languages, is usually educated, and tends to hail from Iran's modern middle and upper classes. In Iran's politics of personal appearance, the *manteauy* woman is believed to be either opposed outright to the Islamic Republic or favoring the reform movement.

The *maghna'eh-poosh* lies somewhere between the two. She wears a loose-fitting *manteau* that frees her arms for work but a tight-fitting scarf that covers all her hair. She tends to be more liberal than the *chadory* but less than the *manteauy*. Often she hails from the more socially conservative traditional middle classes. She is an active participant in the workplace and generally favors the reforms of President Khatami.

Interestingly, the religious-minded *manteauy* woman (and there are many; one must not confuse opposition to the government with irreligion) often dons the *chador* when she visits the shrines of Shi'a saints. Iran's younger *manteauy* woman must wear the *maghna'eh*, the tighter head scarf, in the workplace and on the university campus. Many *manteauy* young women carry the *maghna'ehs* with them, in their bags, and reluctantly place them on their heads as they enter university grounds.

Regardless of whether a woman chooses to be a *chadory*, *manteauy*, or *maghna'eh-poosh*, she has no right to discard some form of veil altogether. Many Western scholars of Iran say the veil is not the issue. It is the laws that do not grant women equal rights or that do not grant them even the same protections they had before the revolution. The scholars have a point, but what more basic human right is there in the twenty-first century than choosing how you want to dress? If the law on *hijab* were lifted, who knows how many Iranian women would unveil entirely, but it seems to me they deserve the same right as women in other Muslim countries, excluding Saudi Arabia, who have the legal option to choose (of course, patriarchal societies and family pressures in many Islamic countries make that legal right meaningless).

By making the *hijab* such a critical part of the Islamic Republic's propaganda, however, there appears to me little way that it could be discarded entirely. The republic has boxed itself in. Lifting the *hijab* would signal a severe defeat for it, a repudiation of Ayatollah Khomeini. While the conservative ruling clergy has made room for talks of limited democracy, it is certainly not ready to give up its 'God-given' right to veil women.

From *Persian Pilgrimages: Journeys across Iran*
by Afshin Molavi

The Tehran Bazaar

The bazaar, with its concentration of merchants, shopkeepers and artisans, is a focal point of every Iranian town and city. It has also long been an important political as well as economic institution because of its traditional ties with the Shiite clergy. It supported the overthrow of the monarchy and remains a pillar of the Islamic Republic. The Tehran bazaar is the biggest and most important of all. The American journalist, Elaine Sciolino, describes its workings and its conservative influence on the economy in her book Persian Mirrors *– one of the most interesting and wide-ranging accounts of the Islamic Republic.*

I have gone looking for clues to Iran's economic predicament in Tehran's Grand Bazaar. What I have found is a hive of tradition, immensely captivating in its colour and cultural roots, impressive in the spirit of its private enterprise, that is nevertheless playing a big part in stifling the country's economy. It also provides a power base for a class of politically conservative merchants.

There is permanence to the bazaar. What the British writer, traveller, and diplomat Gertrude Bell wrote in 1894 about the vast marketplace in Tehran holds true today. 'The whole bazaar resounds with talk, with the cries of the mule-drivers, the tinkling bells of the caravans, and the blows of the smiths' hammers,' she said. 'The air is permeated with the curious smell, half musty, half aromatic, of fruits and frying meats, merchandise and crowded humanity.'

The bazaar in Tehran covers a vast area in the city's oldest sector and is built on an angle to the street grid so that it can face Mecca. The six hundred shops and stalls spill out into neighbouring streets lined by crumbling buildings with wrought iron balconies dating back to the early part of the century.

Except for the carpet sellers, most of the Tehran bazaar is not geared to outsiders and especially not to tourists. Rather it is a vast shopping warehouse for wholesalers and the lower classes. I once tried to buy a few sheets of gift-wrapping paper. I was told I had to buy a hundred. It really isn't necessary for most shoppers to go to the bazaar anymore, especially since Mayor Karbaschi[8] built twenty-four hour chain stores throughout Tehran.

The Tehran bazaar is divided according to trade. There are streets named after the gold sellers, the shoe sellers, the fabric sellers. The narrow passageways are choked with people, not only shoppers but wizened porters pushing wide wooden carts piled high with goods, boys carrying scalding pots of tea and trays of glasses, other boys pretending to sell tea who are really selling pirated CDs and cassette tapes, men driving their motorcycles through the bazaar oblivious to the no-driving rule.

The bazaar is also a densely built community centre – a maze of mosques, public baths, religious schools, teahouses, unlit alleys, and back rooms that serve as meeting places and centres of discovery. I turn one corner and come upon *Timche Hajebol-doleh*, an open space lit from a hole in the beautifully tiled ceiling. I turn another and find a headquarters of the Revolutionary Guards. I turn yet another and find myself at a mosque at midday where some men pray while others carry food, mend clothes, sell cigarettes. A lone leper begs; a dervish negotiates a deal.

I went to the bazaar one day with Peyman, a charming young man who owns a small clothing manufacturing company. He knows his way around because he goes there to buy his fabric. He told me that Mayor Karbaschi had wanted to make changes in the bazaar, but the merchants don't much like change. Peyman pointed out a nearby park – not much of a park, with mangy grass and scraggly flowers. 'Karbaschi tried to build a ten-storey parking lot,' Peyman told me. 'The project started and the cement was laid. But there were

[8] A prominent reformist and mayor of Tehran from 1989 to 1998, when he was imprisoned on what he alleged were trumped-up charges of embezzlement. He was amnestied in January 2000.

objections. The *bazaari* said, 'The bazaar has been like this for a hundred years. We want to keep it that way.' Karbaschi was an outsider and they didn't want him to get a foot in here. They took their objections to their supporters in parliament who also objected. It went all the way up to the leader. The parking lot was stopped.'

There are invisible boundaries here – of smell, of sound. And there are closed places where only the invited enter. On my trip with Peyman, I peered into small rooms behind glass doors where a group of six to eight men sat, talking. The Azeris[9] dominate the bazaar, and much of its business is conducted in Turkish, not Persian. Instead of secret handshakes and passwords, the *bazaari* call each other *haj agha*, an honorific that combines 'Mr' with the title *haji*, an assumption that the addressee has made the pilgrimage to Mecca at least once.

There are no computers in sight but plenty of abacuses and adding machines. There are no female merchants either. In Tehran's bazaar, women have only one role. 'It's tradition,' Peyman said. 'Women can shop but they cannot sell.'

We stopped at the stall of a young fabric merchant named Shahin, who asked us to sit and served us tea. His grandfather had been a bazaar merchant, and his father's stall was nearby. Shahin called himself a 'new *bazaari*'.

He didn't pray; he didn't believe in the superstitions that governed the *bazaari* world. 'Don't misplace anything on Wednesdays or Sundays,' Shahin said mockingly. 'Otherwise you will not sell them. Always cut fabric on Mondays.'

I asked Shahin why there were no computers in any of the stalls. Superstition, it turned out, had nothing to do with it.

'*Bazaari* are afraid of tax collectors,' he said. '*Bazaari* will do anything to avoid taxes. Sometimes people have big offices upstairs. That's where they hide their computers. They don't want the tax collectors to see them. We want to have everything as simple and as old as possible. People with mobile phones hide them in a drawer.'

'We have an expression in the bazaar. You have five fingers, but you

[9] Persians from the north-western province of Azerbaijan who speak a Turkish dialect called Azeri.

have to hide one of them. Show only four fingers. We always say that business is bad. There's always a recession. If people don't think your business is bad, they may give you the evil eye and make your business bad. There's always the fear that if one businessman is too successful the others will unite against him.'

In a taxi on the way home, Peyman asked me what I thought of the *bazaari*. Then he answered his own question. 'I hate the *bazaari*. They have very cushy jobs. I'm a producer. I make things. I have to buy the buttons, the zippers, the cloth, the thread. I have to employ seamstresses. I create jobs for others. In my workshop I support at least ten people and their families. Under the law, I can't fire them if they don't perform. All the *bazaari* do is buy and sell. They don't put things in the ground to grow. They don't pay taxes. Every time the rial loses its value, *bazaari* hoard their goods. But they make a lot of money. If they invested their money in production, things would change. It would build strong pillars for the economy. But they're just middlemen. Buy and sell. Sell and buy. That's all they do.'

Peyman had put his finger on one of the reasons why Iran's economy doesn't grow. The *bazaari* aren't investors looking to build the country over the long haul. They are cash-and-carry merchants looking for quick deals. They finance most private industry at interest rates of seven percent per month. The government allows them to import goods at special exchange rates. Traditional in their business habits, they don't computerise or trade on the Internet, or they hide the fact that they do so. Religious, the *bazaari* have had a close alliance with the clerics since the nineteenth century. The money that many *bazaari* gave to the mosques and their decision to shut down in the months before the revolution were critical for Ayatollah Khomeini's success. They continue to support some of the country's key clerics, and in turn those clerics protect the interests of the bazaar.

From *Persian Mirrors: The Elusive Face of Iran*
by Elaine Sciolino

A Taxi Drive in Isfahan

One of the most penetrating books written about the Iran of the Islamic Republic is Christopher de Bellaigue's (1971–) In the Rose Garden of the Martyrs. De Bellaigue, an English journalist and writer who is fluent in Persian, manages to get under the skin of the Islamic Republic through his ability to engage with Iranians on a personal level. He has an instinctive feel and sympathy for the country and its people. This is well illustrated in this entertaining account of a shared taxi journey in Isfahan. De Bellaigue captures perfectly the attitudes and conversational tone of his Iranian fellow passengers.

One afternoon in the spring I set out from the Armenian quarter in the lovely city of Isfahan, towards the seminary of the Four Gardens. The following day was the anniversary of the investiture of the Imam Ali as the Prophet's successor. The people were in a good mood. They revered Ali for being modest and just, and looked forward to celebrating these qualities by visiting family members, stuffing themselves with *beryan* – a dish that features minced sheep's lungs – and passing judgement on their hosts' new daughter-in-law. They strolled in the mild afternoon sun, mothers and daughters arm in arm (and fathers in their wake), buying tulips to put in iced water to keep overnight, and sweetmeats to take as gifts.

I reached one of the main roads that head north towards the river, and hailed an old shared taxi. The back seat had its compliment of three. The occupant of the front passenger seat stepped out so that I could sit between him and the driver; I was suspended over the gap between their seats. The driver sat hunched over the steering wheel, leaning slightly against the door. We moved off. The driver changed gears like a surgeon replacing dislocated bones.

We were soon stuck in traffic outside one of the big banks, in front of which was a shiny blue car mounted on a gantry. The car – new, French-made – was an incentive: every account holder stood a chance of winning it in a prize draw. It was caparisoned with bunting and flashing light bulbs. It had metallic paint that had been devised by a computer. The bank had put it on the gantry to publicise it – and to make it hard to steal.

I looked in the rear-view mirror and my eye was taken by a fat woman sitting in the middle of the back seat. She was staring longingly out of the window at the zippy French car. She caught me looking at her and pretended to be scandalised, tucking her fringe under her headscarf. 'What's happening up there, Mr Driver?' she demanded. 'Why aren't we moving?'

A car, a Buick from the 1970s, was stuck at the intersection, having carried out half a U-turn. Another car, an Iranian-made Paykan, had grazed one of the Buick's tailfins. The drivers had got out of their cars. The wife of the Buick driver was leaning out of the window, yelling.

'Look at the wife, egging him on!' said our driver. 'What difference does it make? That poor Buick's been wounded more times than I have.' The side of the Buick was discoloured from dents that had been amateurishly smoothed out. The engine was still running. It emitted black smoke.

The taxi driver reached under his seat, pulled out a thermos and unscrewed the cap. He poured a little tea into a dirty glass that rested on the dashboard, swilled it around and poured it out of the window. He filled the glass with tea and, putting it back on the dashboard, closed the thermos and put it back under his seat. Then he held up the glass and said, 'Please go ahead.'

He was offering us tea. In such instances, you don't accept. It would be bad form. It's his tea, but he has to offer it. It would be bad form not to. But he'd be put out if someone said, 'Yes, I'd like some of your tea.' No one does. The driver gets to drink his tea and appear courteous at the same time. Both ways he wins.

There was polite murmuring around the taxi: 'Thanks, but no' ... 'You go ahead and have some' ... 'I don't feel like tea' ... 'I've just had some tea.'

Lies. We'd all enjoy a glass of tea.

The driver took out a packet of cigarettes and went through the same rigmarole. We felt our breast pockets for imaginary packets of cigarettes. Eventually, the driver withdrew a cigarette from his packet, lit it and settled down to watch. A policeman had arrived at the intersection. He was trying to broker a reconciliation. The driver of the Paykan was a cocky brute, well-built, young enough to be the Buick driver's son. He danced from one foot to another. Soon, the policeman seemed to make a breakthrough. The youth hugged the Buick driver.

During the argument, the traffic lights at the intersection had turned green several times, at which cars had surged forward from all directions. Lots of them wanted to turn, this way or that, but the Buick and the Paykan were blocking their way. The cars were revving, edging forward, kissing bumpers. Someone would have to reverse. Iranian drivers don't like reversing. It's a form of defeat. I felt sorry for the policeman.

He did a good job. He positioned himself in the middle – whistling, gesturing, occasionally giving a winning smile. He was a professional. In a little while, at his prompting, a car edged forward from the middle, and away. Another followed. The knot was untied.

'Well done!' the taxi driver murmured, and we moved forward. The protagonists stayed where they had been. They would wait for more policemen, who would take statements and measure angles to determine who was at fault. As we went past, the Buick driver's wife, a woman in a red scarf, leaned out of the window and shouted at her husband, 'I should have known you wouldn't have the balls to stand up for yourself! You, who took the full brunt of the Iraqi attacks! Why don't you stand firm, instead of letting some beardless chick trample your pride?'

The woman's husband turned around. His face was full of anguish. His wife wasn't much older than the Paykan driver.

The taxi driver sighed as we drove off. 'You've got to show them who's boss from day one. I mean, now it's too late. He's let her get out of control, challenge his authority. Nothing he can do now.'

A little further down the road, a man who was sitting next to the woman in the back seat got out. He was replaced by a thin woman who recognised the succulent woman: they were distant relatives. They didn't seem pleased to see one another. They passed on regards to each other's families, and extended invitations for tea and lunch.

The thin woman said, 'Did you get much rain in Tehran?'

'More than dear Isfahan, I can tell you! You know, what with struggling to combat the illness of my late husband – may God show him mercy – and the demands it's made on my time and health, this is the first time I've been to Isfahan for five years. Oh! My heart burned when I saw the river – dried up like a burned courgette, with the wretched boatmen standing about in the mud, with nothing else to do but pray for rain. I mean, is it possible for a river to have no water? Our river? In this day and age?'

'They sold our water to Yazd,'[10] the driver said. 'They sent it off in a pipeline. Cost a fortune to build. The fathers of bitches.'

We were in a long queue of cars. The driver leaned out, far enough to see past the cars in front. He swung the wheel and pressed down hard on the accelerator. We emerged from the queue of cars, into the oncoming traffic. There weren't many cars coming: the lights ahead were red. By the time the oncoming traffic started to move, we were elbowing our way into a gap between two cars, now much nearer the traffic lights. One of the other drivers raised his hand, but was too lazy to clench it.

'I don't know why everyone drives so fast,' the fat woman said to her relative. 'All they do when they get to their destination is drink tea.'

The driver grinned. 'God forbid, madam, you were offended by my efforts to expedite you to your destination! Or perhaps it was what I said? Do you have Yazdi blood, by any chance?'

'Lord no! My parents – may God show them mercy – were from Isfahan, and proud of it. But the president[11] is from Yazd, isn't he?, she said slyly. 'That might explain why they're allowed to drink our water. The Yazdis have always had it in for Isfahan. I should know; my son married a Yazdi. She won't even iron his

[10] A city about 320 kilometres south-east of Isfahan.
[11] President Muhammad Khatami.

shirts. She says he gets through too many. He gives them to me, my poor darling. Too proud to iron an Isfahani's white shirt, the Yazdis are!'

'At least they opened the dam again, in time for the holidays,' said the third passenger in the back seat. 'There's water in the river now, thanks be to God.'

'Exactly!' said the fat woman, 'They were scared the Isfahanis would flay them if they didn't open the sluices. But they'll shut the dam again after the holidays and say there's no more water. They'll send it to Yazd instead.'

'And our poor Isfahani kids will carry on topping themselves,' the man said. 'Everyone knows the suicide rate goes up when the river's dry. It's bad for the soul.'

The man next to me stirred in his seat. 'Pardon me, but you're wrong. The problem is not Yazd, but the farmers in Isfahan province. They're planting rice along the river banks, even though rice needs more water than almost any other crop. Only an idiot would plant rice when there's a drought.'

'And what would you have us eat if there's no rice?' the fat woman demanded. 'You want us to get thin and weak?'

'We should buy our rice from elsewhere.'

'Sir, you'd prefer that we eat Pakistani rice that has no perfume? Or that sticky revolting stuff the Turks call rice? You can't make a respectable *polov* with that.'

The man sitting next to her said, 'She's right; our rice is the best in the world. Everyone says so.'

'And there's another thing,' said the woman, 'our dear motherland has been dependent on foreigners for hundreds of years. Now you want to put our bellies at the mercy of Pakistan! Everyone knows who's behind Pakistan: the English! It wouldn't surprise me if the English had something to do with our water shortage. They always stir up trouble in countries they fear. That's why they're the best politicians, and we've never been any good.'

'The English are indeed very devious,' said the man next to me, 'but I haven't heard of them altering the climate.'

The woman snorted. 'I wouldn't put anything past them.' Then she said, 'With your permission, Mr Driver, I'll get out here.'

The thin woman said, 'I thought your brother lived further on.'

'He does,' the fat woman replied. 'But I like to exercise before a holiday. I'll walk the last half-kilometre.' The taxi stopped. The thin woman got out to allow the fat woman to do so. The fat woman put out both her arms to try and lever herself from the hollow she had created in the back seat. For a moment, one of her hot hands gripped my shoulder. She stood at the window and looked in.

The fat woman said: 'How much, sir?'

'Be my guest,' said the driver.

The fat woman said: 'I beg you.'

'Whatever you like,' he grinned. 'Really, it's not important.'

'How much? I beg of you.' The woman was getting out her purse.

'I'm serious; be my guest.'

'How much?'

The driver surrendered. 'Seventy-five *tomans*, if you'd be so kind.'

'Seventy-five *tomans*? I only got in at Hakim Street. It's fifty *tomans* from there.'

The driver frowned. 'Seventy-five. It's been seventy-five *tomans* for three weeks now.'

'I gave fifty tomans two days ago. I'm not giving more than fifty.' She looked sharply at her relative who was examining her nails.

'It's seventy-five *tomans*,' said the driver. His smile had disappeared.

Suddenly, the woman was angry. 'Is this the correct treatment, the day before we celebrate the investiture of the Imam Ali, *salaam* to him and his family?' She looked accusingly at me. 'Is this the right impression to give foreigners, that Iran's a country of unprincipled hat-lifters? I'm not giving a penny more than fifty.' She threw the note in the window.

The driver picked it off my knee. As he put the car into gear, he said, 'She eats my head with her worthless prattle. She's too stingy to stay in as far as her destination. Then, she rips me off.'

393

'Were only related by marriage,' said the thin woman.

I said: 'I may as well get out here, Mr Driver. I want to cross the bridge.'

'Where are you from?' said the driver, as I gave him the fare.

'France,' I said.

He patted my shoulder. 'Whatever you do, don't marry an Iranian.'

From *In the Rose Garden of the Martyrs*
by Christopher de Bellaigue

Dynasties of Persia

Ancient Persia

The Achaemenids

Cyrus II the Great	c.558–530BC
Cambyses	530–522
Gaumata/Bardiya	522
Darius I	522–486
Xerxes I	486–465
Artaxerxes I	465–424
Xerxes II	424–423
Darius II	423–404
Artaxerxes II	404–359
Artaxerxes III	359–338
Arses	338–336
Darius III	336–330

The Seleucids

Seleucus I Nicator	305–281BC
Antiochus I Soter	281–261
Antiochus II Theos	261–246
Seleucus II Callinicus	246–225
Seleucus III Soter	225–223
Antiochus III the Great	223–187
Seleucus IV Philopator	187–175
Antiochus IV Epiphanes	175–164
Antiochus V Eupator	164–162
Demetrius I Soter	162–150

Alexander Balas	150–145
Demetrius II Nicator	145–141
Antiochus VI Epiphanes	145–142
Antiochus VII Sidetes	138–129
Demetrius II Nicator	129–125

The Arsacids (Parthians)

Arsaces I	c.247/238–217BC
Arsaces II	c.217–191
Phriapatius	c.191–176
Phraates I	176–171
Mithridates I	171–139/38
Phraates II	139/38–128
Artabanus I	128–124/23
Mithridates II	124/23–88/87
Gotarzes I	91/90–81/80
Orodes I	81/80–76/75
Sinatruces	c.78/77–71/70
Phraates III	71/70–58/57
Mithridates III	58/57
Orodes II	58/57–38
Phraates IV	38–3/2
Phraates V	2BC–AD2
Orodes III	4–6
Vonones I	8/9
Artabanus II	10/11–38
Vardanes	38–45
Gotarzes II	43/44–51
Vonones II	51
Vologeses I	51–76
Pacorus	77/78–108/109
Vologeses II	77/78
Artabanus III	79–81
Osroes	108/109–127/128
Vologeses III	111/112–147/148
Vologeses IV	147/148–191/192
Vologeses V	191/192–207/208

Muslim Persia

Samanids (Khurasan and Transoxania)

Ahmad I ibn Asad ibn Saman	819–864
Nasr I	864–892
Ismail I	892–907
Ahmad II	907–914
Nasr II	914–943
Nuh I	943–954
Abd al-Malik I	954–961
Mansur I	961–976
Nuh II	976–997
Mansur II	997–999
Abdul Malik II	999–1000
Ismail II al-Muntasir	1000–1005

Ghaznavids (Khurasan, Afghanistan and Northern India)

Sebüktigin	971–977
Ismail	977–998
Mahmud	998–1030
Muhammad	1030–1031
Masud	1031–1041

The Great Saljuqs

Toghril Beg	1037–1063
Alp Arslan	1063–1072
Malikshah	1072–1092
Mahmud	1092–1094
Berk-yaruq	1094–1105
Muhammad	1105–1118
Sanjar	1118–1157

The Ilkhans

Hülegü	1256–1265
Abaqa	1265–1282
Tegüder Ahmad	1282–1284
Arghun	1284–1291
Geikhatu	1291–1295

Baidu	1295
Ghazan	1295–1304
Öljeitü	1304–1316
Abu Said	1316–1335

Timurids

Timur (Tamerlane)	1370–1405
Shah Rukh	1405–1447
Ulugh Beg	1447–1449
Abd al-Latif	1449–1450
Abu Said	1451–1469
Husayn Bayqara	1470–1506

The Safavids

Ismail I	1501–1524
Tahmasp I	1524–1576
Ismail II	1576–1577
Muhammad Khudabanda	1578–1587
Abbas I the Great	1587–1629
Safi I	1629–1642
Abbas II	1642–1666
Sulayman	1666–1694
Sultan Husayn	1694–1722

Afsharids

Nadir Shah	1736–1747
Adil Shah	1747–1748
Ibrahim	1748
Shah Rukh (in Khurasan)	1748–1796

Zands

Muhammad Karim Khan	1750–1779
Abul Fath and Muhammad Ali	1779
Sadiq (in Shiraz)	1779–1781
Ali Murad (in Isfahan)	1779–1785
Jafar	1785
Lutf Ali Khan	1789–1794

Qajars

Aqa Muhammad Khan	1779–1797
Fath Ali Shah	1797–1834
Muhammed Shah	1834–1848
Nasir al-Din Shah	1848–1896
Muzaffar al-Din Shah	1896–1907
Muhammad Ali Shah	1907–1909
Ahmad Shah	1909–1924

Pahlavis

Reza Shah	1925–1941
Muhammad Reza Shah	1941–1979

The Islamic Republic

Supreme Leaders

Imam Khomeini	1979–1989
Ayatollah Ali Khamenei	1989–

Presidents

Abolhasan Bani Sadr	1980–1981
Muhammad Ali Rajai	1981
Hojjatoleslam Ali Khamenei	1981–1989
Ali Akbar Hashemi Rafsanjani	1989–1997
Muhammad Khatami	1997–2005
Mahmud Ahmadinejad	2005–

Bibliography

General Books
The Cambridge History of Iran. 7 Volumes, CUP, 1968-1991.
The Persians, Gene R. Garthwaite, Blackwell, 2005
The Persians, Alessandro Bausani, Elek, 1971
Zoroastrians, Mary Boyce, Routledge 1979
An Introduction to Shi'i Islam: The History and Doctrines of Twelver Shi'ism, Moojan Momen, Yale, 1985
Medieval Persia 1040-1797, David Morgan, Longman, 1988
Modern Iran, Nikki R.Keddie, Yale, 2006
Classical Persian Literature, A.J.Arberry, Allen and Unwin, 1958

Pre-Islamic Persia
Ancient Persia, Josef Wieshöfer, I.B.Tauris 1996
Iran from the Earliest Times to the Arab Conquest, R.Ghirshman, Penguin Books, 1954.
Persian Fire, Tom Holland, Little Brown, 2005

Safavid Persia
Safavid Iran: Rebirth of a Persian Empire, Andrew J.Newman, I.B.Tauris, 2006
Isfahan, Pearl of Persia, Wilfred Blunt, Elek Books, 1966

Nader Shah
The Sword of Persia: Nader Shah, from Tribal Warrior to Conquering Tyrant, Michael Axworthy, I.B.Tauris, 2006

Qajar Persia

Qajar Persia: Eleven Studies, Ann K.S.Lambton
Pivot of the Universe, Nasir al-Din Shah Qajar and the Iranian Monarchy, 1851-1896., Abbas Amanat, I.B.Tauris, 1997.
Russia and Britain in Persia: A Study in Imperialism, Firuz Kazemzadeh, Yale, 1968.
Persia in the Great Game: Sir Percy Sykes, Explorer, Consul, Soldier, Spy, Antony Wynn, John Murray, 2004.
Islam and Modernism: The Iranian Revolution of 1906, Venessa Martin, Syracuse, 1989.
The English amongst the Persians, Denis Wright, Heinemann, 1977.
The Persians amongst the English, Denis Wright, I.B.Tauris, 1985

The Pahlavis and the Islamic Republic

Iran Between Two Revolutions, Ervand Abrahamian
The Mantle of the Prophet: Learning and Power in Modern Iran, Roy Mottahedeh, Chatto and Windus, 1986.
Mission for my Country, Mohammed Reza Shah Pahlavi, Hutchinson, 1961.
Iran: Dictatorship and Development, Fred Halliday, Penguin Books, 1979.
The Persian Sphinx: Amir Abbas Hoveyda and the Riddle of the Iranian Revolution, Abbas Milani, Mage Books, 200-2001.
Khomeini, Life of the Ayatollah, Baqer Moin, I.B.Tauris, 1999
The Reign of the Ayatollahs: Iran and the Islamic Revolution, Shaul Bakhash, I.B.Tauris, 1985.

About the author

David Blow studied History at Cambridge and Persian at SOAS, was Assistant Director of the British Institute of Persian Studies in Tehran 1968-69 and worked for the BBC Persian Service 1969-1971, broadcasting in Persian. He went on to work in publishing and for the BBC World Service, where he was correspondent in Berlin and Vienna.

ELAND

61 Exmouth Market, London EC1R 4QL
Tel: 020 7833 0762   Fax: 020 7833 4434
Email: info@travelbooks.co.uk

Eland was started in 1982 to revive great travel books
that had fallen out of print. Although the list has diversified
into biography and fiction, it is united by a quest to define the
spirit of place. These are books for travellers, and for readers who aspire
to explore the world but who are also content to travel in their own
minds. Eland books open out our understanding of other
cultures, interpret the unknown and reveal different environments
as well as celebrating the humour and occasional horrors of travel. We
take immense trouble to select only the most readable
books and therefore many readers collect the entire series.

All our books are printed on fine, pliable, cream-coloured paper. Most
are still gathered in sections by our printer and sewn as well as glued,
almost unheard of for a paperback book these days.
This gives larger margins in the gutter, as well as
making the books stronger.

Extracts from each and every one of our books can be read
on our website, at www.travelbooks.co.uk. If you would like a free copy
of our catalogue, please contact us by phone,
email or in writing.